Linux® Administration
A Beginner's Guide

Third Edition

Linux® Administration
A Beginner's Guide

Third Edition

Steven Graham and Steve Shah

McGraw-Hill/Osborne

New York   Chicago   San Francisco
Lisbon   London   Madrid   Mexico City
Milan   New Delhi   San Juan
Seoul   Singapore   Sydney   Toronto

The McGraw·Hill Companies

McGraw-Hill/Osborne
2600 Tenth Street
Berkeley, California 94710
U.S.A.

To arrange bulk purchase discounts for sales promotions, premiums, or fund-raisers, please
contact **McGraw-Hill**/Osborne at the above address. For information on translations or
book distributors outside the U.S.A., please see the International Contact Information page
immediately following the index of this book.

Linux® Administration: A Beginner's Guide, Third Edition

1234567890 FGR FGR 0198765432

ISBN 0-07-222562-9

Publisher   Brandon A. Nordin
Vice President & Associate Publisher   Scott Rogers
Acquisitions Editor   Francis Kelly
Project Editors   Jody McKenzie, Janet Walden
Acquisitions Coordinator   Martin Przybyla
Technical Editor   Steve Shah
Copy Editor   Lunaea Weatherstone
Proofreaders   Claire Splan, Susie Elkind
Indexer   Jack Lewis
Computer Designers   Tara A. Davis, George Toma Charbak
Illustrators   Melinda Moore Lytle, Michael Mueller, Lyssa Wald
Series Design   Jean Butterfield
Cover Series Design   Sarah F. Hinks

This book was composed with Corel VENTURA™ Publisher.

In memory of Jack Sunderland, who among many other things taught me that "Things have a way of working out."

—Steven Graham

About the Authors

Steven Graham is the manager of Software Quality Assurance at Array Networks. He previously managed a large Red Hat Linux server farm at an ISP, and was Manager of Technical Operations of the Computer Science Department at the University of California, Riverside.

Steve Shah is the Director of Product Management at Array Networks (www.arraynetworks.net) where he is responsible for the technical direction of traffic management and security products. His other author credits include contributions to *Unix Unleashed*, *Red Hat Linux Unleashed*, *Using Linux*, and *Content Delivery Networks*. Prior to Array Networks, Steve was a developer and systems administrator for several companies, including Alteon Web Systems and the Center for Environmental Research and Technology. Besides Linux, Steve has been responsible for a variety of operating systems including Solaris, Irix, FreeBSD, SunOS, HPUX, and the many flavors of Microsoft Windows.

Contents at a Glance

Contents

PART II
Single-Host Administration

PART IV
Intranet Services

PART V
Appendixes

Acknowledgments

After signing up to write this book, I remember sitting outside at work with my two good friends Steve and Michael. As Steve tells Michael, "Mr. Graham here is going to know the hell that it is to write a book," I simply laughed, and as naïve as I was about being a writer, I relished the thought of writing the book.

My wonderful wife, Jacki, has supported me from the beginning. Without her help and patience I wouldn't have been able to accomplish the writing of this book. Also, my two-year-old daughter, Elizabeth, who asks the question "Daddy work?" every time she sees me on the computer. Both of them provide me with a daily dose of happiness and joy.

I would also like to thank my family, who has supported every aspiration I have had. In particular I would like to thank my parents, Linda and Kevin Lemon, and Rickey Graham.

Franny Kelly, Jody McKenzie, Lunaea Weatherstone, and Martin Przybyla from McGraw-Hill/Osborne who all did a wonderful job making the third edition of this book happen. Thank you all for the awesome experience of writing this book.

Lastly, I would like to thank Steve Shah, my co-author and technical editor, and Michael Mann, who have provided advice as writers and friends. I can now proudly say, "I know the hell that it is to write a book." That is not to say that I regret the experience—indeed, it has been a pleasure and I look forward to the next book.

—*Steven Graham*

Introduction

System administrators are a unique bunch. As a group, we are probably the most significant consumers of reference and training books, and we probably demand the most from them (at least, all of my peers do). And, of course, we get really annoyed with books that waste our time.

We're also a curious bunch. Most of my IT friends are gadget freaks. We love to live on the edge of new technologies and find out what all the buzz is about before our users do. We like to do this for two very simple reasons: because it's fun and because we need to understand the technology before the CEO reads about it in *BusinessWeek* and demands to know why we aren't running it.

And Linux is one of those buzzes.

My first exposure to Linux came in 1996 when I took a systems administration class at college. Little did I know that Linux would become as powerful as it is now in both the server and desktop market. Installing Linux in 1996 was a fight to get it going, and it is good to see the strides in ease of use that distributions like Red Hat and Mandrake have made in the past years. And with Red Hat 8.0, Linux looks poised to take hold in the desktop market. This book will provide you with the necessary toolset to administer a variety of Linux systems, in a variety of applications.

Who Should Read this Book

The title of this book says it's a beginners guide, and that's mostly true. What the title should really say is that it's a beginners-to-Linux guide, because we do make a few assumptions about you, the reader.

First, we assume you are already familiar with the Windows environment. At the very least, you should be a strong user in Windows and know something about the networked Windows environment. Although you needn't be an NT or 2000 expert, some exposure to NT/2000 will help your understanding of the hairier concepts we discuss. We started with this assumption because we didn't want to waste time repeating what most folks from a Windows background already know, and instead focused on the new stuff that Linux brings to the table.

In addition to your Windows background, we assume that you're interested in having more information about the topics introduced here. After all, we're spending 30 or 40 pages on topics that have entire books devoted to them! So several chapters include references to other texts. We urge you to take advantage of these references no matter how advanced you think you're becoming. There is always more to learn.

What's in this Book

Linux Administration: A Beginner's Guide is organized into several modules covering several aspects of Linux administration.

Part I: Installing Linux as a Server

The first part is targeted at users with no experience in Linux who want a hand installing it and getting rolling.

Module 1 focuses on the architectural differences between NT/2000 and Linux, and will help you understand why some things in the Linux environment are the way they are. Module 2 puts a unique spin on an installation chapter: instead of just regurgitating installation notes from the product, we help you specifically configure your Linux system as a server. Module 3 expands on the installation process by showing you how to set up the two most popular graphical environments for Linux, Gnome and KDE. Module 4 documents the process of installing software under Linux. We cover the two most popular methods (at least for system administrators): using RPMs and compiling the package yourself.

Part II: Single Host Administration

The second part is geared toward the administration of features common to all Linux systems, not just servers.

Module 5 covers the administration of users on a Linux system. Module 6 explains how to use the Linux CLI or shell. Module 7 starts getting into the nitty-gritty of startup and shutdown, as well as setting up Linux's boot managers, LILO and GRUB. Module 8 takes a turn toward the disk and discusses the process of managing disks, creating partitions, and configuring quotas. Module 9 visits some of the lowest levels of the system that you'll work with as a system administrator: core system services. Module 10 covers the somewhat tricky task of compiling a Linux kernel. Module 11 covers the aspects of securing your Linux server.

Part III: Internet Services

In the third part, you'll study all the services needed to run an Internet site.

Module 12 explains how to set up and use the Domain Name System. Module 13 covers the FTP daemon ProFTPD. Module 14 shows how to set up a Web server using Apache. Module 15 explains the use of SMTP and how to set up the Postfix mail server. Module 16 covers POP, a popular method of e-mail retrieval. Module 17 covers the Secure Shell (SSH).

Part IV: Intranet Services

The fourth part goes in the opposite direction of Part III. Rather than studying services for everyone on the internet, we examine services offered only to people on your internal network.

Module 18 explains the NFS protocol and how to set up file sharing under Linux. Module 19 covers the Network Information Servers (NIS) and how to distribute system information. Module 20 shows how to make your Linux server act like a Windows server through the use of Samba. Module 21 explains the printing process under Linux using CUPS. Module 22 shows how to set up a DHCP server to allow dynamic configuration of IP addresses. Module 23 covers the set up of networking under Linux.

Part V: Appendixes

Appendix A contains the answers to the Mastery Checks at the end of each module. Appendix B documents the programming languages that come with Red Hat Linux. Appendix C lists the many tools available for Linux that make it possible to use Linux as your primary desktop operating system.

Updates and Feedback

To get updates on errata issues regarding this book, visit http://www.planetoid.org/linux/ for more information. This is especially important if you find that some URLs I refer to have changed since I wrote a chapter.

Also, you can find extra material related to this book on the publisher's Web site. Go to http://www.osborne.com/ to find information about backups, advanced Linux networking, and the **/proc** file system.

I would also like to hear your feedback. Feel free to e-mail me at linuxadmin@planetoid.org. Unfortunately, due to the volume of e-mail I currently deal with (along with silly things like my day job), I may not have time to individually respond. If you have questions about Linux, I highly recommend you visit one of the many Linux-oriented Web sites that host piles of experts who are ready to help. A good place to start is the Linux home page at http://www.linux.org/.

Part I

Installing Linux as a Server

Module 1

Technical Summary
of Linux Distributions
and Windows 2000

L inux has hit the mainstream. Recently I walked through my local Best Buy store and noticed that the signs for software included the word Linux. Even Wal-Mart now carries the Mandrake Linux distribution in its stores. What was only a hacker's toy a couple of years ago has grown up tremendously and is known for its stable and fast server performance. With the KDE and GNOME environments, Linux is also making inroads into the Windows 2000 desktop market. In this module, we will take a look at the technical differences between Linux and Windows 2000 (likely the platform for which you are considering Linux as a replacement). This module also explains the GNU (GNU's Not UNIX) license, which may help you understand why much of Linux is the way it is.

CRITICAL SKILL

1.1 Learn About the Linux Operating System

Usually people understand Linux to be an entire package of developer tools, editors, GUIs, networking tools, and so forth. More formally, such packages are called *distributions*. You've most likely heard of the Linux distributions named Red Hat, Mandrake, Caldera, and SuSE, which have received a great deal of press and have been purchased for thousands of installations. Noncommercial distributions of Linux such as Debian are less well known and haven't reached the same scale of popularity.

What's interesting about all Linux distributions is that almost all of the tools with which they ship were not written by the companies themselves. Rather, other people have released their programs with licenses, allowing their redistribution with source code. By and large, these tools are also available on other variants of UNIX, and some of them are becoming available under Windows as well. The makers of the distribution simply bundle them up into one convenient package that's easy to install. (Some distribution makers also develop value-added tools that make their distribution easier to administer or compatible with more hardware, but the software that they ship is generally written by others.)

So if we consider a distribution everything you need for Linux, what then *is* Linux exactly? Linux itself is the core of the operating system: the *kernel*. The kernel is the program acting as Chief of Operations. It is responsible for starting and stopping other programs (such as editors), handling requests for memory, accessing disks, and managing network connections. The complete list of kernel activities could easily be a chapter in itself, and in fact, several books documenting the kernel's internal functions have been written.

The kernel is known as a nontrivial program. It is also what puts the Linux into all those Linux distributions. All distributions use the exact same kernel, and thus the fundamental behavior of all Linux distributions is the same.

What separates one distribution from the next is the value-added tools that come with each one. For example, Red Hat includes a very useful tool called Xconfigurator that makes configuring the graphical interface a very straightforward task. Asking "Which distribution is better?" is much like asking "Which is better, Coke or Pepsi?" Almost all colas have the same

Technical Summary of Linux Distributions and Windows 2000

1

basic ingredients—carbonated water, caffeine, and high fructose corn syrup—thereby giving the similar effect of quenching thirst and bringing on a small caffeine-and-sugar buzz. In the end, it's a question of personal preference.

CRITICAL SKILL
1.2 # Discover What Free Software and GNU Are All About

In the early 1980s, Richard Stallman began a movement within the software industry. He preached (and still does) that software should be free. Note that by free, he doesn't mean in terms of price, but rather free in the same sense as freedom. This meant shipping not just a product, but the entire source code as well.

Stallman's policy was obviously a wild departure from the early Eighties mentality of selling prepackaged software, but his concept of free software was in line with the initial distributions of UNIX from Bell Labs. Early UNIX systems did contain full source code. Yet by the late 1970s, source code was typically removed from UNIX distributions and could be acquired only by paying large sums of money to AT&T. The Berkeley Software Distribution (BSD) maintained a free version but had to deal with many lawsuits from AT&T until it could be proven that nothing in the BSD was from AT&T.

The idea of giving away source code is a simple one: users of the software should never be forced to deal with a developer who might or might not support that user's intentions for the software. The user should never have to wait for bug fixes to be published. More important, code developed under the scrutiny of other programmers is typically of higher quality than code written behind locked doors. The greatest benefit of free software, however, comes from the users themselves: should they need a new feature, they can add it to the program and then contribute it back to the source, so that everyone else can benefit from it.

From this line of thinking has sprung a desire to release a complete UNIX-like system to the public, free of license restrictions. Of course, before you can build any operating system, you need to build tools. And this is how the GNU project was born.

NOTE

GNU stands for GNU's Not UNIX—recursive acronyms are part of hacker humor. If you don't understand why it's funny, don't worry. You're still in the majority.

What Is the GNU Public License?

The most important thing to emerge from the GNU project has been the *GNU Public License (GPL)*. This license explicitly states that the software being released is free, and no one can ever take away these freedoms. It is acceptable to take the software and resell it, even for a profit; however, in this resale, the seller must release the full source code, including any changes. Because the resold package remains under the GPL, the package can be distributed for free and resold yet again by anyone else for a profit. Of primary importance is the liability clause: the programmers are not liable for any damages caused by their software.

It should be noted that the GPL is not the only license used by free software developers (although it is arguably the most popular). Other licenses, such as BSD and Apache, have similar liability clauses but differ in terms of their redistribution. For instance, the BSD license allows people to make changes to the code and ship those changes without having to disclose the added code. (The GPL would require that the added code be shipped.) For more information about other open-source licenses, check out http://www.opensource.org/.

The Advantages of Free Software

If the GPL seems a bad idea from the standpoint of commercialism, consider the recent surge of successful freeware packages—they are indicative of a system that does indeed work. This success has evolved for two reasons. First, as mentioned earlier, errors in the code itself are far more likely to be caught and quickly fixed under the watchful eyes of peers. Second, under the GPL system, programmers can release code without the fear of being sued. Without that protection, no one would ever release his or her code.

This concept of course begs the question of why anyone would release his or her work for free. Most projects don't start out as full-featured, polished pieces of work. They may begin life as a quick hack to solve a specific problem bothering the programmer. As a quick-and-dirty hack, the code has no sales value. But when this code is shared with others who have similar problems and needs, it becomes a useful tool. Other program users begin to enhance it with features they need, and these additions travel back to the original program. The project thus evolves as the result of a group effort and eventually reaches full refinement. This polished program contains contributions from possibly hundreds, if not thousands, of programmers who have added little pieces here and there. In fact, the original author's code is likely to be little in evidence.

There's another reason for the success of generally licensed software. Any project manager who has worked on commercial software knows that the *real* cost of development software isn't in the development phase. It's really in the cost of selling, marketing, supporting, documenting, packaging, and shipping that software. A programmer carrying out a weekend lark to fix a problem with a tiny, kluged program lacks the interest, time, and backing money to turn that hack into a profitable product.

When Linus Torvalds released Linux in 1991, he released it under the GPL. As a result of its open charter, Linux has had a notable number of contributors and analyzers. This participation has made Linux very strong and rich in features. Torvalds himself estimates that since the v.2.2.0 kernel, his contributions represent only 5% of the total code base.

Since anyone can take the Linux kernel (and other supporting programs), repackage them, and resell them, some people have made money with Linux. As long as these individuals release the kernel's full source code along with their individual packages, and as long as the packages are protected under the GPL, everything is legal. Of course, this means that packages released under the GPL can be resold by other people under other names for a profit.

In the end, what makes a package from one person more valuable than a package from another person are the value-added features, support channels, and documentation. Even IBM can agree to this; it's how they made a bulk of their money between the 1930s and 1970s. The money isn't in the product, it's in the services that go with it.

Progress Check

1. What does the acronym GNU stand for?

2. If you sell GPL software, do you have to release source code?

CRITICAL SKILL
1.3 Understand the Differences Between Windows and Linux

As you might imagine, the differences between Microsoft Windows 2000 and the Linux operating systems cannot be completely discussed in the confines of this section. Throughout these modules, topic by topic, we'll examine the specific contrasts between the two systems. In some modules, you'll find that we don't derive any comparisons because a major difference doesn't really exist.

But before we attack the details, let's take a moment to discuss the primary architectural differences between the two operating systems.

Single Users vs. Multiusers vs. Network Users

Windows 2000 Professional was designed according to the "one computer, one desk, one user" vision of Microsoft's cofounder Bill Gates. For the sake of discussion, we'll call this philosophy *single-user*. In this arrangement, two people cannot work in parallel running (for example)

---

1. The acronym GNU stands for GNU's Not Unix.

2. Yes, part of the agreement is that you have to provide the source code to your work.

Microsoft Word on the same machine at the same time. (On the other hand, one might question the wisdom of doing this with an overwhelmingly weighty program like Word!) You can buy Windows 2000 Advanced Server and run what is known as Terminal Server, but this requires huge computing power and lots of money in licensing. Of course, with Linux you don't run into the cost problem, and Linux will run fairly well on just about any hardware.

Linux borrows its philosophy from UNIX. When UNIX was originally developed at Bell Labs in the early 1970s, it existed on a PDP-7 computer that needed to be shared by an entire department. It required a design that allowed for *multiple users* to log in to the central machine at the same time. Various people could be editing documents, compiling programs, and doing other work at the exact same time. The operating system on the central machine took care of the "sharing" details, so that each user seemed to have an individual system. This multiuser tradition continued through today, on other versions of UNIX as well. And since Linux's birth in the early 1990s, it has supported the multiuser arrangement.

NOTE

Most people believe that with the advent of Windows 95 the term "multitasking" was invented. UNIX has had this capability since 1969! You can rest assured that the concepts put into Linux have had many years to develop and prove themselves.

Today, the most common implementation of a multiuser setup is to support *servers*—systems dedicated to running large programs for use by many clients. Each member of a department can have a smaller workstation on the desktop, with enough power for day-to-day work. When they need to do something requiring significantly more CPU power or memory, they can run the operation on the server.

"But hey! Windows 2000 can allow people to offload computationally intensive work to a single machine!" you may argue. "Just look at SQL Server!" Well, that position is only half correct. Both Linux and Windows 2000 are indeed capable of providing services such as databases over the network. We can call users of this arrangement *network users,* since they are never actually logged into the server, but rather, send requests to the server. The server does the work and then sends the results back to the user via the network. The catch in this case is that an application must be specifically written to perform such server/client duties. Under Linux, a user can run any program allowed by the system administrator on the server without having to redesign that program. Most users find the ability to run arbitrary programs on other machines to be of significant benefit.

The Monolithic Kernel and the Micro Kernel

In operating systems, there are two forms of kernels. You have a monolithic kernel that provides all the services the user applications need. And then you have the micro kernel, a small core set of services and other modules that perform other functions.

Linux for the most part adopts the monolithic kernel architecture; it handles everything dealing with the hardware and system calls. Windows 2000 works off a micro-kernel design. The kernel provides a small set of services and then interfaces with other executive services that provide process management, I/O management, and other services. It has yet to be proven which methodology is truly the best way.

Separation of the GUI and the Kernel

Taking a cue from the Macintosh design concept, Windows 2000 developers integrated the graphical user interface (GUI) with the core operating system. One simply does not exist without the other. The benefit to this tight coupling of the operating system and user interface is consistency in the appearance of the system. Although Microsoft does not impose rules as strict as Apple's, with respect to the appearance of applications, most developers tend to stick with a basic look and feel among applications. One reason this is dangerous is that the video card driver is now allowed to run at what is known as "Ring 0" on a typical *x*86 architecture. Ring 0 is a protection mechanism—only privileged processes can run at this level, and typically user processes run at Ring 3. Since the video card is allowed to run at Ring 0, the video card could misbehave (and it does!), which can bring down the whole system.

On the other hand, Linux (and UNIX in general) has kept the two elements—user interface and operating system—separate. The X Window System interface is run as a user-level application, which makes it more stable. If the GUI (which is very complex for both 2000 and Linux) fails, Linux's core does not go down with it. The process simply crashes and you get a terminal window. The X Window System also differs from the Windows 2000 GUI in that it isn't a complete user interface. It only defines how basic objects should be drawn and manipulated on the screen.

The most significant feature of the X Window System is its ability to display windows across a network and onto another workstation's screen. This allows a user sitting on host A to log in to host B, run an application on host B, and have all of the output routed back to host A. It is possible for two people to be logged in to the same machine, running a Linux equivalent of Microsoft Word (such as ApplixWare, WordPerfect, or StarOffice) at the same time.

In addition to the X Window System core, a window manager is needed to create a useful environment. Linux distributions come with several window managers and include support for GNOME and KDE, both of which are available on other variants of UNIX as well. If you're concerned with speed, you can look into the WindowMaker and FVWM window managers. They might not have all the glitz of KDE or GNOME, but they are really fast. When set as default, both GNOME and KDE offer an environment that is friendly even to the casual Windows user.

So which is better—Windows 2000 or Linux—and why? That depends on what you are trying to do. The integrated environment provided by Windows 2000 is convenient and less complex than Linux, but it lacks the X Window System feature that allows applications to display their windows across the network on another workstation. Windows 2000's GUI is consistent, but cannot be turned off, whereas the X Window System doesn't have to be running (and consuming valuable memory) on a server.

Progress Check

1. Is the X Window System integrated into the core of the operating system?

2. Can you "shut off" the Windows 2000 GUI?

The Network Neighborhood

The native mechanism for Windows folk to share disks on servers or with each other is through the Network Neighborhood. In a typical scenario, users *attach* to a share and have the system assign it a drive letter. As a result, the separation between client and server is clear. The only problem with this method of sharing data is more people-oriented than technology-oriented— people have to know which servers contain which data.

With Windows 2000, a new feature borrowed from UNIX has also appeared: *mounting*. In Windows terminology, it is called *reparse points*. This is the ability to mount a CD-ROM drive into a directory on your C drive. This may seem a little strange, but as you get used to Linux you'll understand this is the *only* way mounting works. The amazing thing is that on Windows you cannot mount network shares this way. You have to map a network share to a drive letter.

Linux, using the Network File System (NFS), has supported the concept of mounting since its inception. Unlike Windows 2000, mounting under Linux does not require a reboot. In fact, the Linux Automounter dynamically mounts and unmounts partitions on an as-needed basis.

A common example of mounting partitions under Linux is with mounted home directories. The user's home directories reside on a server, and the client mounts the directories at boot time (automatically). So **/home** exists on the client, but **/home/username** exists on the server.

Under Linux NFS, the user never has to know server names or directory paths, and their ignorance is your bliss. No more questions about which server to connect to. Even better, users need not know when the need arises to change the server configuration. Under Linux, you can change the names of servers and adjust this information on client-side systems without making any announcements or having to reeducate users. Anyone who has ever had to reorient users to new server arrangements is aware of the repercussions that can occur.

---

1. No, the X Window System runs as a separate user process.

2. No, you cannot turn off the Windows 2000 GUI.

Printing works much in the same way. Under Linux, printers receive names that are independent of the printer's actual host name. (This is especially important if the printer doesn't speak TCP/IP.) Clients point to a print server whose name cannot be changed without administrative authorization. Settings don't get changed without your knowing it. The print server can then redirect all print requests as needed. The Linux uniform interface will go a long way toward improving what may be a chaotic printer arrangement in your installation. It also means you don't have to install print drivers in several locations.

NOTE

If you intend to use Linux to serve Windows 2000/NT/98 clients via the Samba package, you'll still have to deal with notifying users about server shares and printer assignments. You can read more about Samba in Module 20.

The Registry vs. Text Files

I think of the Windows 2000 Registry as the ultimate configuration database—thousands upon thousands of entries, very few of which are completely documented, some located on servers and some located on clients.

"What? Did you say your registry *got corrupted?*" <maniacal laughter> "Well, yes, we can try to restore it from last night's backups, but then Excel starts acting funny and the technician (who charges $50 just to answer the phone) said to re-install . . ."

If you're not getting my message, I'm saying that the Windows 2000 Registry system is, at best, very difficult to manage. Although it's a good idea in theory, I've never emerged without injury from a battle with the registry.

Linux does not have a registry. This is both a blessing and a curse. The blessing is that configuration files are most often kept as a series of text files (think of the Windows .INI files before the days of the registry). This setup means you're able to edit configuration files using the text editor of your choice rather than tools like **regedit**. In many cases, it also means you can liberally comment those configuration files so that six months from now you won't forget why you set something up in a particular way. With most tools that come with Linux, configuration files exist in the **/etc** directory or one of its subdirectories.

The curse of a no-registry arrangement is that there is no standard way of writing configuration files. Each application or server can have its own format. Many applications are now coming bundled with GUI-based configuration tools to alleviate some of these problems. So you can do a basic setup easily, and then manually edit the configuration file when you need to do more complex adjustments.

In reality, having text files hold configuration information usually turns out to be an efficient method. Once set, they rarely need to be changed; even so, they are straight text files and thus easy to view when needed. Even more helpful is that it's easy to write scripts to read the same configuration files and modify their behavior accordingly. This is especially helpful when automating server maintenance operations, which is crucial in a large site with many servers.

NOTE

An interesting side effect of having configuration files exist as a series of text files is that configuration of these files can be automated. This is very useful in situations where a large number of workstations needs to be deployed or new workstations are added frequently. You can easily set up Linux on a floppy disk that simply mounts an NFS share and begins an installation. While you can do this on Windows, the supported way involves using binary differences called sys-diffs and automated install scripts (ini files). The other way is to use clone tools like Norton Ghost and duplicate the install. The problem with this is that each Windows 2000 box has a Security Identifier (SID) associated with it and this is stored all throughout the registry. Automated installs of Windows 2000 can be done, it just takes a lot more effort.

Domains

For a group of Windows NT systems to work well together, they should exist in a domain. This requires a dedicated NT Server system configured as a primary domain controller (PDC). Domains are the basis of the Windows NT security model.

The basis of Linux's network security model is NIS, Network Information Service. NIS is a simple database (based on text files) that is shared with client workstations. Each primary NIS server (which, by the way, does not require a complete dedicated system as a PDC usually does) establishes a domain. Any client workstation wanting to join this domain is allowed to do so, as long as it can set its domain name. To set the domain name, you must use the **root** user—Linux's equivalent to an Administrator user. Being part of the domain does not, however, immediately grant you rights that you would otherwise not have. The domain administrator must still add your login to the master NIS password list so that the rest of the systems in the network recognize your presence.

The key difference between NIS and NT domains is that the NIS server by itself does not perform authentication the way a PDC does. Instead, each host looks up the login and password information from the server and compares it to the user's entered information. It's up to the individual application to properly authenticate a user. Thankfully, the code necessary to authenticate a user is very trivial.

Another important difference is that NIS can be used as a general purpose database and thus hold any kind of information that needs to be shared with the rest of the network. (This usually includes mount tables for NFS and e-mail aliases.) The only limitation is that each NIS map can only have one key, and the database mechanism doesn't scale well beyond about 20,000 entries. Of course, a site with 20,000 users shouldn't keep them all in a single NIS domain, anyway!

A final note about NT domains and NIS: neither is required for the base operating system to work. Nevertheless, they are key if you need to maintain a multiuser site with a reasonable level of security.

Active Directory

So how does NIS stack up to Active Directory? Good question. The answer is, "It doesn't." Active Directory was designed to be much more than what NIS was designed for. This really places the two into different classes of applications.

Active Directory (AD) is designed to be a generic solution to the problem of large sites that need to have their different departments share administrative control—something that NT's Domain model did very poorly. Setting up interdomain trusts under NT often required a great deal of patience and a willingness to fix "broken" trusts on a regular basis. AD is also an opportunity for Microsoft to fix many of its broken naming schemes and move toward an Internet-centric scheme based on DNS. The result is quite beastly and requires a lot of time to master. Mark Minasi's book, *Mastering Windows 2000 Server, Second Edition* (Sybex, 2000), dedicates well over 100 pages to the subject. However, in a smaller network, most folks will find that it looks and feels mostly like NT-style domains with some new whiz-bang features thrown in for good measure.

Don't get me wrong, though—AD is a strong step in the right direction for Windows 2000 and presents solid competition for the Linux camp to think about how directory services can be better integrated into their designs. But despite what Microsoft tells you, AD will not solve all the world's problems, let alone all of yours, in one easy step.

So does Linux have anything that compares to AD? Yes, actually, it does. Several implementations of LDAP (Lightweight Directory Access Protocol) now exist for Linux, and work is actively being done to allow NIS to tie into LDAP servers. The radius authentication protocol is also becoming more common. What makes LDAP interesting is that it is the same underlying technology that Active Directory uses in Windows 2000. This means that, in theory, it is possible to share LDAP databases between your UNIX and Windows systems and possibly unify authentication between them. In theory, anyway . . .

Project 1-1   Finding Linux Resources

Another major difference between Windows and Linux is how information is obtained. If you want low-level information and HOWTOs for Microsoft products, you can either buy the resource kit or buy a yearly MSDN subscription. The Linux documentation project is completely free and a worthwhile source of information. This project will introduce you to the Linux documentation project and provide some direction when you're looking for information.

(continued)

Step by Step

1. Go to the Web site http://www.tldp.org/.

2. Click the HOWTOs link.

3. Click the HTML Alphabetical Index link.

4. Click the Laptop-HOWTO link to read about laptop Linux installations.

Project Summary

This project was a quick and light introduction to the Linux documentation project. As you become familiar with Linux and start asking questions, this is a good place to start looking for information. Although the Laptop-HOWTO is a little outdated (by two and a half years, as of this writing), it still might provide some insight if you are installing on a laptop. The most recent versions of Red Hat now include a special "laptop" installation. Some distributions also install the LDP files directly on your system. If not, you can download the whole package from the LDP Web site.

Other References

If you are interested in getting under the hood of the technology revolution (and it's always helpful to know how things work), I recommend the following texts:

- *Computer: A History of the Information Machine,* by Martin Campbell-Kelly and William Aspray (Harper Collins, 1997)

- *A Quarter Century of Unix,* by Peter Salus (Addison-Wesley, 1994)

Neither of these texts discusses Linux specifically. *A Quarter Century of Unix* does tell the Linux history up to the point where the system was just becoming a serious player. Peter Salus writes an interesting discussion of why Linus Torvalds saw a need to create Linux in the first place.

To get the scoop on Linux itself, start with the Linux home page at http://www.linux.org/.

Module 1 Mastery Check

1. What is a Linux distribution?

2. What is the kernel?

3. Name three methods of authentication for a Linux system.

4. What are some advantages of not having a registry like Windows 2000 has?

5. What are some advantages of having a centralized registry?

6. Do Linux users have to search the network for network shares?

7. Why is it a good thing that the X Window System runs as a user process?

8. What does the acronym GNU stand for?

9. What does the acronym GPL stand for?

10. What benefits are there to releasing code under the GPL?

Module 2

Installing Linux in a
Server Configuration

A key attribute in Linux's recent success is the remarkable improvement in installation tools. What once was a mildly frightening process many years back has now become almost trivial. Even better, there are many ways to install the software; CD-ROMs are no longer the only choice (although they are still the most common). Network installations are part of the default list of options as well, and they can be a wonderful help when installing a large number of hosts.

Most default configurations where Linux is installed are already capable of becoming servers. This is due to an unfortunate, slightly naive design decision: being designated a server means that the machine serves everything! From disk services to printers to mail to news to . . . it's all turned on from the start. As we all know, the reality is that most servers are dedicated to performing one or two tasks, and any other installed services simply take up memory and drag on performance.

In this module, we discuss the installation process as it pertains to servers. This requires us to do two things: differentiate between a server and client workstation and streamline a server's operation based on its dedicated functions.

CRITICAL SKILL
2.1 Find the Right Distribution

There are many distributions of the GNU/Linux system. This section will cover some of the more popular distributions and pointers to get more information on each one. Remember that there are several ways of obtaining a Linux distribution. One way is to go to your local computer store and see what they have—a surprising number of stores are starting to carry Linux. The other way is to download the distribution off of the Internet. I typically download the Linux ISOs and burn them to a CD, then use the CD to install. Table 2-1 lists some popular Linux distributions and their associated Web sites.

NOTE

Downloading a Linux ISO can take hours, even on a DSL line. If you have problems downloading from the following sites, try http://www.linuxiso.org/. This site mirrors several distributions of Linux (and FreeBSD).

Ask the Expert

Q: **What distribution should I pick?**

A: I would suggest either Red Hat or Mandrake Linux. The choice is up to you. If you have a fast Internet connection and plenty of spare CD-Rs laying around, I would suggest installing a couple of distributions and see which one suits you best.

Linux Distribution	Description
Red Hat Linux http://www.redhat.com/	Red Hat Linux is one of the more popular distributions for servers and workstations. It has become even more popular since they have certification programs, and it is gaining corporate attention. As of this writing, 8.0 is the latest release.
Mandrake Linux http://www.mandrake.com/	I was a die-hard Red Hat user until a friend of mine showed me Mandrake. The installation program rivals the ease of installing Windows, and the distribution comes with lots of goodies, like reiserfs, xfs, and many other file systems' support right out of the box. As of this writing, the current version is 8.2; 9.0 is in beta and should be out soon. You can go to your local Wal-Mart to pick up a copy!
Debian http://www.debian.org/	Debian is like most GNU/Linux distributions, but they chose to use their own package management system instead of RPM. As of this writing, their current distribution sits at version 3.0.
SuSE Linux http://www.suse.com/	SuSE is another distribution that I have been seeing a lot of. Its current version is 8.0.
Slackware http://www.slackware.com/	Slackware was one of the first distributions I ever installed. Unfortunately, I haven't installed a recent version, but as of this writing they have just released 8.1 with KDE 3.0 and the latest Linux kernel.
Yellow Dog Linux http://www.yellowdog.com/	If you are a Mac head, this is the distribution for you. Their current version is 2.3, and it runs on most of the old and new Apple hardware. It is a lot of fun to convert a Macintosh to a Linux box and then compile netatalk (a version of AppleTalk for Linux) and share file systems to other Macs.

Table 2-1 Popular Linux Distributions

CRITICAL SKILL
2.2 Prepare for the Installation

Before getting into the actual installation phase, it is important that we take a moment and evaluate two things:

- The hardware the system is going to run on

- The server's ideal configuration to provide the services you need

  Let's start by examining hardware issues.

Hardware

As with any operating system, before getting started with the installation process, you should determine what hardware configurations would work. Each commercial vendor publishes a hardware compatibility list (HCL) and makes it available on its Web site. (Red Hat's HCL is at http://www.redhat.com/support/hardware/.) Be sure you obtain the latest version of the list so that you are confident in the hardware selected. In general, most popular Intel-based configurations work without difficulty.

A general suggestion that applies to all operating systems is to avoid cutting-edge hardware and software configurations. While they appear to be really impressive, they haven't had the maturing process some of the slightly older hardware has gone through. For servers, this usually isn't an issue since there is no need for a server to have the latest and greatest toys, such as fancy video cards. After all, your main goal is to provide a stable and available server for your users, not to play Doom. (Although it should be noted that this author, during his less responsible days as a junior-level administrator, found that Linux is wonderfully stable even while running Doom and being a file server.)

Server Design

When a system becomes a server, its stability, availability, and performance become a significant issue. These three factors are usually improved through the purchase of more hardware, which is unfortunate. It's a shame to pay thousands of dollars extra to get a system capable of achieving in all three areas when you could have extracted the desired level of performance out of existing hardware with a little tuning. With Linux, this is not hard. Even better, the gains are outstanding.

The most significant design decision you must make when managing a server configuration is not technical but administrative. You must design a server to be *un*friendly to casual users. This means no cute multimedia tools, no sound card support, and no fancy Web browsers (when at all possible). In fact, it should be a rule that casual usage of a server is strictly prohibited— not only to site users but site administrators as well.

Another important aspect of designing a server is making sure that it has a good environment. As a system administrator, you must ensure the physical safety of your servers by keeping them in a separate room under lock and key (or the equivalent). The only access to the servers for nonadministrative personnel should be through the network. The server room itself should be well ventilated and kept cool. The wrong environment is an accident waiting to happen. Systems that overheat and nosy users who think they know how to fix problems can be as great a danger to server stability as bad software (arguably even more so).

Once the system is in a safe place, installing battery backup is also crucial. Backup power serves two key purposes:

- To keep the system running during a power failure so that it may gracefully shut down, thereby avoiding file damage or loss

- To ensure that voltage spikes, drops, and other noises don't interfere with the health of your system

Here are some specific things you can do to improve your server situation:

- Take advantage of the fact that the graphical user interface is uncoupled from the core operating system, and avoid starting the X Window System (Linux's GUI) unless someone needs to sit on a console and run an application. After all, like any other application, the X Window System requires memory and CPU time to work, both of which are better off going to the server processes instead.

- Determine what functions the server is to perform, and disable all other functions. Not only are unused functions a waste of memory and CPU time, but they are just another issue you need to deal with on the security front.

- Unlike some other operating systems, Linux allows you to pick and choose the features you want in the kernel. (You'll learn about this process in Module 10.) The default kernel will already be reasonably well tuned, so you won't have to worry about it. But if you do need to change a feature or upgrade the kernel, be picky about what you add and what you don't. Make sure you really need a feature before adding it.

NOTE

You may hear an old recommendation that you recompile your kernel to make the most effective use of your system resources. This is no longer true—the only reason to recompile your kernel is to upgrade or add support for a new device.

Uptime

All of this chatter about taking care of servers and making sure silly things don't cause them to crash stems from a long-time UNIX philosophy: *Uptime is good. More uptime is better.*

The UNIX (Linux) **uptime** command tells the user how long the system has been running since its last boot, how many users are currently logged in, and how much load the system is experiencing. The last two are useful measures that are necessary for day-to-day system health and long-term planning. (For example, the server load has been staying high lately, so maybe it's time to buy a faster/bigger/better server.)

But the all-important number is how long the server has been running since its last reboot. Long uptimes are a sign of proper care, maintenance, and, from a practical standpoint, system stability. You'll often find UNIX administrators boasting about their server's uptimes the way you hear car buffs boast about horsepower. This is also why you'll hear UNIX administrators cursing at system changes (regardless of operating system) that require a reboot to take effect. You may deny caring about it now, but in six months you'll probably scream at anyone who reboots the system unnecessarily. Don't bother trying to explain this phenomenon to a nonadmin, because they'll just look at you oddly. You'll just know in your heart that your uptime is better than theirs.

Dual-Booting Issues

If you are new to Linux, you may not be ready to commit to a complete system when you just want a test drive. All distributions of Linux can be installed on only certain partitions of your hard disk while leaving others alone. Typically, this means allowing Microsoft Windows to coexist with Linux.

Because we are focusing on server installations, we will not cover the details of building a dual-booting system; however, anyone with a little experience in creating partitions on a disk should be able to figure this out. If you are having difficulty, you may want to refer to the installation guide that comes with your distribution or another of the many available beginner's guides to Linux.

Some quick hints: if a Windows 95/98 partition currently consumes an entire hard disk as drive C, you can use the **fips** tool to repartition the disk. Simply defragment and then run **fips.exe**. If you are using Windows NT/2000 with NTFS and have already allocated all the disk with data on each partition, you may have to move data around a bit by hand to free up a partition. Don't bother trying to shrink an NTFS partition, though; because of its complexity, it doesn't like being resized, and doing so will lead to corruption.

NOTE

From the perspective of flexibility, NTFS doesn't sound like a good thing, but in reality it is. If you have to run NT or 2000, use NTFS.

You may find using a commercial tool such as Partition Magic to be especially helpful, because it offers support for NTFS, FAT32, and regular FAT, as well as a large number of other file system types. Its user interface is also significantly nicer than **fips**.

Methods of Installation

With the improved connectivity and speed of both local area networks and Internet connections, it is becoming an increasingly popular option to perform installations over the network rather than using a local CD-ROM.

In general, you'll find that network installations become important once you've decided to deploy Linux over many machines and therefore require a fast installation procedure in which many systems can install at the same time.

Typically, server installations aren't well suited to automation, because each server usually has a unique task; thus, each server will have a slightly different configuration. For example, a server dedicated to handling logging information sent to it over the network is going to have especially large partitions set up for the appropriate logging directories, compared to a file server that performs no logging of its own. (The obvious exception is for server farms where you have large numbers of replicated servers. But even those installations have their nuances that require attention to detail specific to the installation.)

Because of this, we will focus exclusively on the technique for installing a system from a CD-ROM. Of course, once you have gone through the process from a CD-ROM, you will find performing the network-based installations to be very straightforward.

If It Just Won't Work Right

You've gone through the installation procedure—twice. This book said it should work. The installation manual said it should work. The Linux guru you spoke with last week said it should work. But it's just not working.

In the immortal words of Douglas Adams, *don't panic*. No operating system installs smoothly 100% of the time. (Yes, not even the MacOS!) Hardware doesn't always work as advertised, combinations of hardware conflict with each other, that CD-ROM your friend burned for you has CRC errors on it (remember: it is legal for your buddy to burn you a copy of Linux), or the software has a bug.

With Linux, you have several paths you can follow for help. If you have purchased your copy from Caldera or Red Hat, you can always call tech support and reach a knowledgeable person who is dedicated to working through the problem with you. If you didn't purchase a box set, you can try contacting companies such as LinuxCare (http://www.linuxcare.com/), which is a commercial company dedicated to providing help. Last, but certainly not least, is the option of going online for help. An incredible number of Web sites are available to help you get started. They contain not only useful tips and tricks but also documentation and discussion forums where you can post your questions. Obviously, you'll want to start with the site dedicated to your distribution: http://www.redhat.com/ for Red Hat Linux, and http://www.caldera.com/ for Caldera Linux. Other distributions have their own sites. Check your distribution for its appropriate Web site information.

Here are some recommended sites for installation help:

- **comp.os.linux.admin**   This is a newsgroup, not a Web site. You can read it on the Web at http://groups.google.com/.

- **http://www.tldp.org/LDP/lame/LAME/linux-admin-made-easy/**   This site contains a book titled *Linux Administration Made Easy*. The book is geared toward cookbook administration tasks and contains some useful tips for installing Red Hat Linux. Unfortunately, the book lacks in more advanced areas of Linux administration—but then again, that's why you bought this book!

- **http://www.linuxdoc.org/**   This site is a collection of wonderful information about all sorts of Linux-related topics, including installation guides. Just a warning, though: not all documents are up-to-date. Be sure to check the date of any document's last update before following the directions. There is a mix of cookbook-style help guides as well as guides that give more complete explanations of what is going on.

Progress Check

1. Name two methods of installing Linux.

2. Where can you go for installation help?

2.3 Install Red Hat Linux

In this section, we will document the steps necessary to install Red Hat Linux 7.3 on a standalone system. We will take a liberal approach to the process, installing all of the tools possibly relevant to server operations. Later modules explain each subsystem's purpose and help you determine which ones you really need to keep.

NOTE

Don't worry if you chose to install a distribution other than Red Hat; luckily, most distributions follow the same steps when installing. Some are just prettier than others.

Project 2-1   Installing Red Hat Linux

You have two ways to start the boot process: you can use a boot floppy disk or the CD-ROM. This installation guide assumes you will boot off the CD-ROM to start the Red Hat installation procedure. If you have an older machine not capable of booting off the CD-ROM, you will need to use a boot disk and start the procedure from there.

NOTE

Using the boot disk alters the order of some of the installation steps, such as which language to use and whether to use a hard disk or CD-ROM for installation. Once past the initial differences, you will find that the graphical steps are the same.

 If your system supports bootable CD-ROMs, this is obviously the faster approach. If your distribution did not come with a boot disk and you cannot boot from the CD-ROM, you will need to create the boot disk. We will assume you have a working installation of Windows to create the boot disk.

---

1. CD-ROM or network installation.

2. You can go to several places on the Net. You can visit your distribution's Web site, search the Web through a search engine such as Google, or find your local Linux guru.

NOTE

Users of other UNIX operating systems can use the **dd** command to create the boot image on a floppy disk. Follow the instructions that came with your distribution on using the **dd** command with your floppy device.

Step by Step

1. Create a boot disk.

   Once Windows has started and the CD-ROM is in the appropriate drive, open an MS-DOS Prompt window (Start | Program Menu | MS-DOS Prompt), which will give you a command shell prompt. Change over to the CD-ROM drive letter and go into the **dosutils** directory. There you will find the **rawrite.exe** program. Simply run the executable; you will be prompted for the source file and destination floppy disk. The source file will be on the same drive and is called **/images/boot.img**.

NOTE

If you are installing on a laptop, it has been my experience that using a boot disk rather than booting off of the CD-ROM has a much better success rate. In general, you will want to check out the Internet for any tips on installing Linux on laptops. Most of the time you won't have any problems, but since laptops typically have customized hardware, you are bound to run into something.

2. Start the installation.

   To begin the installation process, boot off the CD-ROM. This will present you with a splash screen introducing you to Red Hat 7.3. At the bottom of the screen will be a prompt that reads

   ```
   boot:
   ```

   If you do not press any key, the prompt will automatically time out and begin the installation process. You can press ENTER to start the process immediately.

   If you have had some experience with Red Hat installations in the past and do not want the system to automatically probe your hardware, you can type **expert** at the **boot:** prompt. For most installations, though, you will want to stick with the default.

   If you don't have a mouse, or if the installer cannot find yours, you will be presented with a screen that asks whether you want to use the text mode installation or if you want to help the installer figure out what kind of mouse you have. Use the TAB key to select which choice you want, and press ENTER to continue. If you proceed with the text mode, you will find that the basic steps to the installation are similar to those of the graphical interface, and you should be able to follow along with this installation guide.

   (continued)

Project
2-1

Installing Red Hat Linux

NOTE

As the initial part of the operating system loads and autodetects hardware, do not be surprised if it does not detect your SCSI subsystem. SCSI support is activated later on in the process.

3. Choose the language for the installation.
   The first menu will ask which language you want to use to continue the installation process. The interface works much like any other Windows-style interface. Simply point to your selection and click. When you are ready, click the Next button in the lower-right portion of the screen.

   On the left side of the screen is context-sensitive help. If you don't want to see it, you can click the Hide Help button at the lower-left part of the screen.

   The Back button in the lower right of the screen is grayed out at this point, because there have been no prior options to select.

4. Select your keyboard type.
   This next menu allows you to select what kind of keyboard you have. The options are broken into three dialog boxes. The first lists the types of keyboards supported, the second lists available layouts the keyboard can have, and the third box allows you to enable *dead keys*, which let you type special characters with multiple keystrokes (such as Ñ and Ô). The bottom dialog box is meant for you to type in, thereby allowing you to test whether your keyboard works. You do not have to type anything there if you don't want to.

   For most of us, the keyboard model will be one of the Generic options and the layout will be U.S. English (see Figure 2-1).

TIP

If you ever want to change your keyboard layout or type, you can run the program `/usr/sbin/kbdconfig`.

When you are done, click Next to continue, or click Back to go back to the language selection menu.

5. Select your mouse type.
   You now can select the type of mouse you want to use with the X Window System environment. More than likely, the autoprobe will have been able to identify what kind of mouse you have.

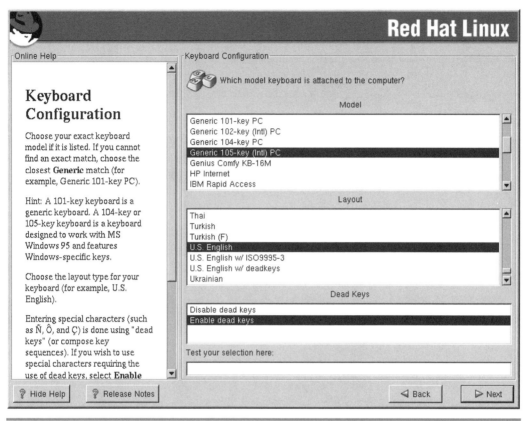

Figure 2-1 Selecting the keyboard configuration

If you need to help Linux, simply pick your mouse type from the top menu box (see Figure 2-2). If you see the name brand of the mouse with a plus sign (+) to the left of it, clicking the plus sign will open a new level of choices for that particular brand.

If you have a serial mouse, you will also need to select the serial port it is using, which you can do in the lower box of the screen.

If you have a two-button mouse, click Emulate 3 Buttons at the bottom of the screen, because some features of the X Window System environment work with a three-button mouse only. The emulation allows you to click both buttons of a two-button mouse to simulate the third (middle) button.

(continued)

2

Installing Linux in a Server Configuration

Project
2-1

Installing Red Hat Linux

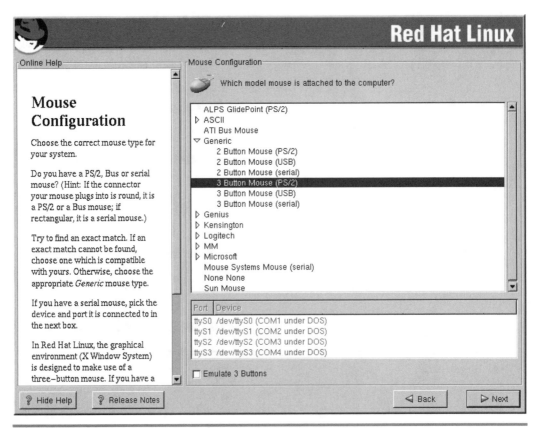

Figure 2-2 Selecting the mouse configuration

TIP

If you change the type of mouse you have later, you can run
/usr/sbin/mouseconfig to reconfigure your mouse.

With the language and input devices selected, you are now ready to begin the actual installation phase of Red Hat Linux. This starts with a splash screen whose corresponding help bar tells you how to register Red Hat Linux if you purchased the boxed version.

6. Choose the ugrade or installation path.
   Now you will see a screen that lets you pick how you want to install Red Hat Linux. If you are on an upgrade path, this selection is easy—simply click Upgrade and then click Next. You'll see some screens informing you of what is being currently upgraded.

For this module, we're assuming that you're doing a clean installation. This will wipe all the existing contents of the disk before freshly installing Linux.

Note that under the Install button is an option to install Linux in a Server configuration (see Figure 2-3). This method has all of the packages selected for you, as well as a disk-partitioning scheme. For this module, you want to choose Custom so that you can fine-tune what you install and how you configure it.

7. Create the partitions for linux.
Since you selected the custom installation, you will need to create partitions for Linux to install on. If you are used to the Windows installation process, you will find that this process is a little different from how you partition Windows into separate drives.

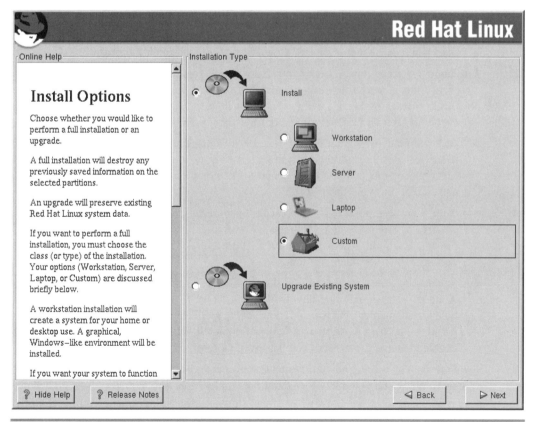

Figure 2-3 Choosing an installation method

(continued)

In short, each partition is *mounted* at boot time. The mount process makes the contents of that partition available as if it were just another directory on the system. For example, the root directory (/) will be on the first (*root*) partition. A subdirectory called **/usr** will exist on the root directory, but it will have nothing in it. A separate partition can then be mounted such that going into the **/usr** directory will allow you to see the contents of the newly mounted partition Since all of the partitions, when mounted, appear as a unified directory tree rather than as separate drives, the installation software does not differentiate one partition from another. All it cares about is which directory each file goes into. As a result, the installation process automatically distributes its files across all the mounted partitions, as long as the mounted partitions represent different parts of the directory tree where files are usually placed. Under Linux, the most significant grouping of files is in the **/usr** directory where all of the actual programs reside. (In Windows terms, this is similar to **C:\Program Files.**)

Because you are configuring a server, you need to be aware of the additional large grouping of files that will exist over the life of the server. They are

- **/usr**, where all of the program files will reside (similar to **C:\Program Files**).
- **/home**, where everyone's home directory will be (assuming this server will house them). This is useful for keeping users from consuming an entire disk and leaving other critical components without space (such as log files). This directory is synonymous with **C:\Documents and Settings** in Windows 2000.
- **/var**, the final destination for log files. Because log files can be affected by outside users (for instance, individuals visiting a Web site), it is important to partition them off so that no one can perform a denial-of-service attack by generating so many log entries that the entire disk fills up.
- **/tmp**, where temporary files are placed. Because this directory is designed so that it is writable by any user (similar to the **C:\Temp** directory under Windows), you need to make sure arbitrary users don't abuse it and fill up the entire disk. You ensure this by keeping it on a separate partition.
- **Swap**, where the virtual memory file is stored. This isn't a user accessible file system. Although Linux (and other flavors of UNIX, as well) can use a normal disk file to hold virtual memory the way Windows does, you'll find that having it on its own partition improves performance. You will typically want to configure your swap to be double the physical memory that is in your system.

Now you see why it is a good idea to create multiple partitions on a disk rather than a single large partition, which you may be used to doing under Microsoft Windows. As you become more familiar with the hows and whys of partitioning disks under Linux, you may choose to go back to a single large partition. At that point, of course, you will have enough knowledge of both systems to understand why one may work better for you than the other.

Now that you have some background on partitioning under Linux, let's go back to the installation process itself.

The installation screen gives you three options: automatically partition the disk, manually partition the disk with Disk Druid, or manually partition the disk with fdisk. You don't want the first, because you want tight control over how the disk gets allocated in a server environment. And while the method of using fdisk is extremely powerful, it can also be a bit daunting at first. (Don't worry: we go over it in Module 8.) So this leaves you with Disk Druid. Simply select Disk Druid and click Next. This will take you to the screen shown in Figure 2-4.

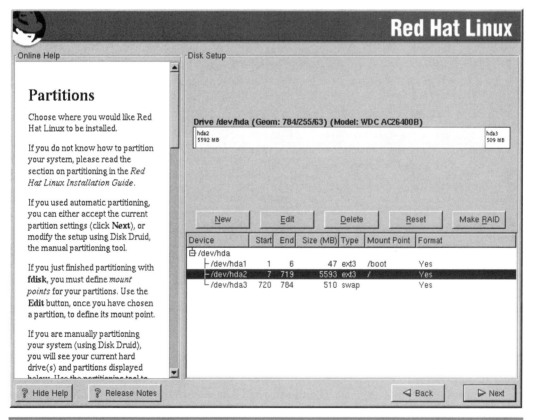

Figure 2-4 The Disk Druid partitioning tool

(continued)

2

Installing Linux in a Server Configuration

Project 2-1

Installing Red Hat Linux

The Disk Druid partitioning tool was developed by Red Hat as an easy way to create partitions and associate them to the directories they will be mounted as. When starting Disk Druid, you will see all of the existing partitions on your disk. Each partition entry will show the following information:

- **Mount point**   The location where the partition is mounted. Initially, this should not contain any entries.

- **Device**   Linux associates each partition with a separate *device*. For the purpose of installation, you need to know only that under IDE disks, each device begins with /**dev/hd**XY, where X is either:
  a for IDE master on the first chain
  b for IDE slave on the first chain
  c for IDE master on the second chain
  d for IDE slave on the second chain
  and Y is the partition number of the disk. For example, /**dev/hda1** is the first partition on the primary chain, primary disk. SCSI follows the same basic idea, except instead of starting with /**dev/hd**, each partition starts with /**dev/sd** and follows the format /**dev/sd**XY, where X is a letter representing a unique physical drive (**a** is for SCSI ID 1, **b** is for SCSI ID 2, and so on). The Y represents the partition number. Thus, /**dev/sdb4** is the fourth partition on the SCSI disk with ID 2. The system is a little more complex than Windows, but each partition's location is explicit—no more guessing, "What physical device does E: correspond to?"

- **Requested**   The minimum size that was requested when the partition was defined.

- **Actual**   The actual amount of space allocated for that partition.

- **Type**   The partition's type. Linux's default type is Linux native, but Disk Druid also understands many others, including FAT, FAT32, and NTFS.

The second half of the screen shows the drive summaries. Each line represents a single drive and its characteristics. The information presented includes:

- The drive name (without the preceding /**dev/**)
- The disk geometry in *Cylinders/Heads/Sectors* format
- Total size of the disk
- Amount of disk that has been allocated (partitioned)
- Amount of available disk that can still be partitioned

In the middle of the screen are the menu choices for what you can do with Disk Druid. These buttons are

- **Add**   Create a new partition.
- **Edit**   Change the parameters on the highlighted partition.
- **Delete**   Delete the highlighted partition.

- **Reset** Restore all of the changes you've made to the partition table but have not committed to.

- **Make RAID Device** This button will only appear if you have multiple disks that are identical in size and configuration. This installation guide does not cover RAID installations.

- **Next** Commit changes to disk.

- **Back** Abort all changes made using Disk Druid and exit the program.

NOTE

The changes made within Disk Druid are not committed to disk until you click the Next button.

8. Add new partitions.

To create a new partition, click the Add button. This will bring up a dialog box that should resemble the one shown in Figure 2-5. Its elements include the following:

- **Mount Point** The directory where you want this partition to be automatically mounted at boot time.

- **Size (MB)** The size of the partition in megabytes.

```
Mount Point:          [                    ▼]
Filesystem Type:      [ ext3            ▲▼]
Allowable Drives:     ┌──────────────────────┐
                      │ hda: WDC AC26400B - 6150 │
                      │                      │
                      │                      │
                      │ ◄ [    ]          ► │
                      └──────────────────────┘
Size (MB):            [ 1               ▲▼]
┌─Additional Size Options──────────────────┐
│ ⦿ Fixed size                             │
│ ○ Fill all space up to (MB):  [ 1   ▲▼] │
│ ○ Fill to maximum allowable size         │
└──────────────────────────────────────────┘
☐ Force to be a primary partition
☐ Check for bad blocks

              [   OK   ]   [  Cancel  ]
```

Figure 2-5 Adding a partition

(continued)

2

Installing Linux in a Server Configuration

Project
2-1

Installing Red Hat Linux

- **Filesystem Type** The type of partition that will reside on that disk. By default, you will want to select Linux Native except for the swap partition, which should be Linux Swap.

- **Allowable Drives** Specifies on which drives the partition should be created.

Once you are done entering all of the information, click OK to continue.

At a minimum, you need to have two partitions: one for holding all of the files and the other for swap space. Swap space is usually sized to be double the available RAM if there is less than 128MB of RAM, or the exact same amount of RAM if there is more than 128MB.

Realistically, you will want to separate partitions for **/usr**, **/var**, **/home**, and **/tmp** in addition to a root partition. Obviously, you can adjust this equation based on the purpose of the server.

Once you have gone through the steps of adding a partition, and you are comfortable with the variables involved (mount points, sizes, types, devices, and so on), the actual process of editing and deleting partitions is quite simple. Editing an entry means changing the exact same entries that you established when you added the partition, and deleting an entry requires only that you confirm you really want to perform the deletion.

NOTE

One last detail that we have intentionally omitted is the process of adding network drive mounts (NFS). This requires a more complete explanation and is covered in Module 8.

9. Format the newly created partitions.
The screen for formatting partitions will present you with a list of all the newly created partitions. Because you are wiping the disk of previous installations, you want to select all of the partitions to be formatted. (More accurately, Red Hat will be creating a *file system* on it.)

TIP

If you are using an older drive, and you aren't sure about its reliability, click the Check For Bad Blocks While Formatting option, which is below all of the partitions. This will cause the formatting process to take significantly longer, but at least you will know for sure whether the disk is reliable.

10. Install the GRUB boot manager.
GRUB is the *boot manager* for Linux. A boot manager handles the process of actually starting the load process of an operating system. If you're familiar with Windows NT,

you have already dealt with the NT Loader (NTLDR), which presents the menu at boot time, allowing you to select whether you want Windows NT or Windows NT (VGA only).

The Red Hat tool's screen for setting up GRUB has three sections (see Figure 2-6). The top of the screen asks what kind of boot loader that you want to use. I recommend GRUB (see Module 7 for more information on boot loaders).

The middle block of the screen allows you to select whether you want to have GRUB set up on the master boot record (MBR) or the first partition on which Linux resides. The MBR is the very first thing the system will read when booting a system. It is essentially the point where the built-in hardware tests finish and pass off control to the software. If you choose to install GRUB on the MBR, it will prompt you for the OS that you want to bootstrap the next time the computer boots. Of course, if you are running a server, this configuration should be fine.

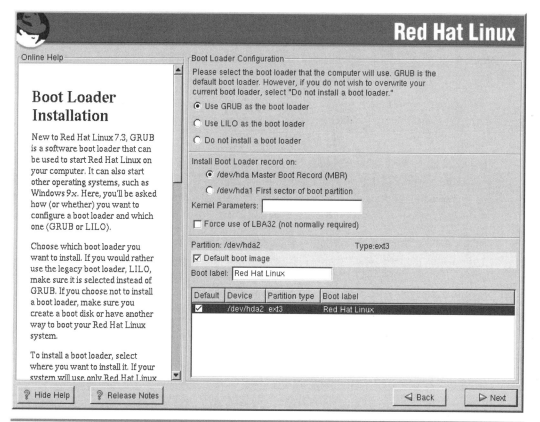

Figure 2-6 Setting up the boot loader

(continued)

If you are already using another boot loader and prefer it, you will want to place GRUB on the first sector of the root partition. This will allow your preferred boot loader to run first and then pass control off to GRUB, should you decide to start Linux.

The last option in the middle block is a box that allows you to enter kernel parameters to be used at boot time. Most people can ignore this box. If the documentation for a particular feature or device requires you to pass a parameter here, add it; otherwise, leave it blank.

Finally, the bottom part of the screen allows you to select which operating systems GRUB will allow you to select at boot time. On a system that is configured to support both Windows and Linux, you will see your choices here. Since your system is set up only for Linux, you will see one choice.

NOTE

The exception is for SMP-based systems that will have two choices. The first choice, Linux, is set up to support multiple processors. In the event this doesn't work out for you, Linux-up will also be available; it will utilize only one processor, but at least it will get you up and going.

11. Configure networking.

Now Red Hat is ready to configure your network interface cards (see Figure 2-7).

Each interface card you have will be listed as a tabbed menu on the top of your screen. Ethernet devices are listed as eth0, eth1, eth2, and so on. For each interface, you can either configure it using DHCP or set the IP address by hand. If you choose to configure by hand, be sure to have the IP, netmask, network, and broadcast addresses ready. Finally, click Activate On Boot if you want the interface to be enabled at boot time.

On the bottom half of the screen, you'll see the configuration choices for giving the machine a host name, gateway, and related DNS information.

NOTE

Even if you are not part of a network, you can fill in the host name. If you don't fill in a host name, your computer will be known as localhost.

Once you have all of this filled in, simply click Next to continue.

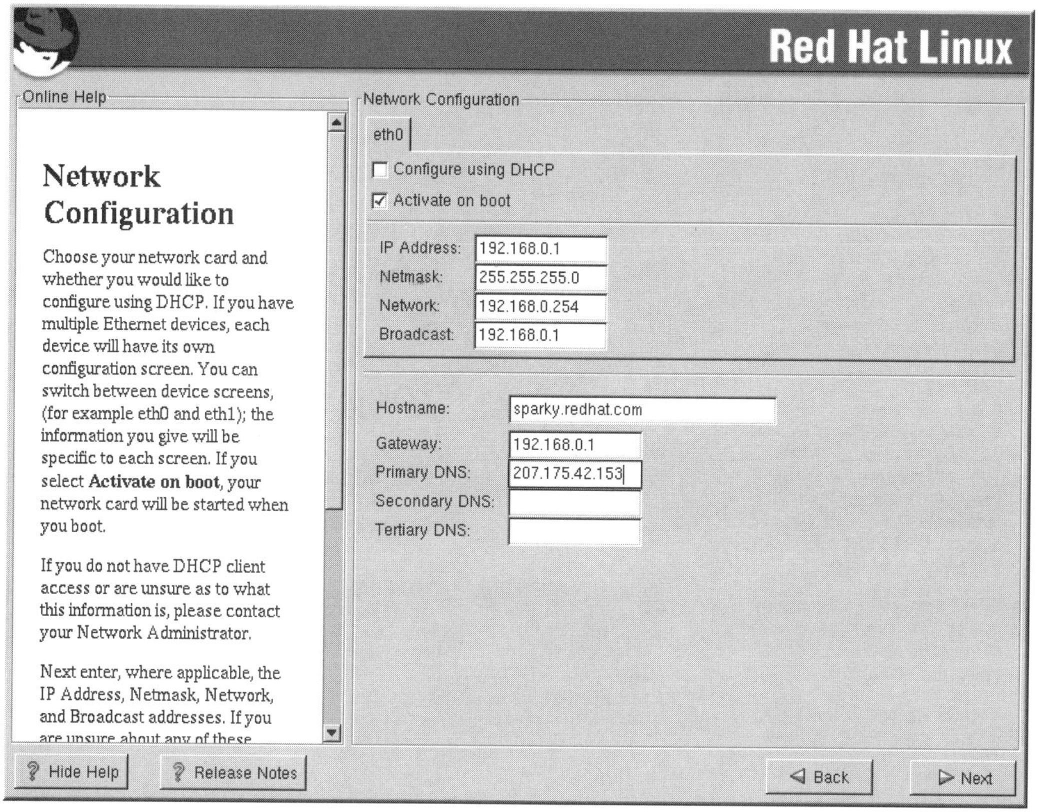

Figure 2-7 Network configuration

12. Configure your time zone information.

The time zone configuration screen (see Figure 2-8) allows you to select in which time zone the machine is located. If your system's hardware clock keeps time in UTC, be sure to click the System Clock Uses UTC button so that Linux can determine the difference between the two and display the correct local time.

13. Create user accounts for your system.

The Red Hat Installation tool creates one account for you, called root. This user account is similar in nature to the Administrator account under Windows NT/2000. The user who is allowed access to this account has full control of the system.

(continued)

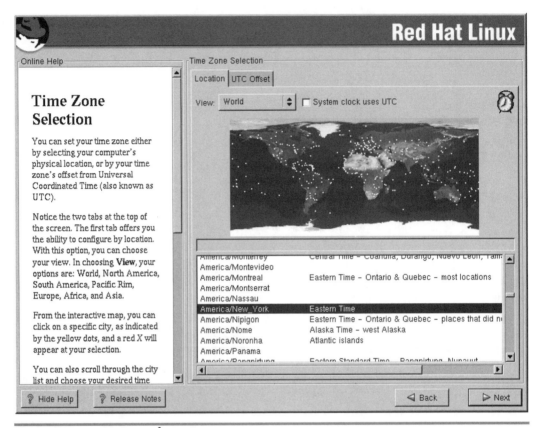

Figure 2-8 Time zone configuration

Thus, it is crucial that you protect this account with a good password. Be sure not to pick dictionary words or names as passwords, as they are easy to guess and crack.

Part of protecting root means not allowing users to log in as the root user over the network. This keeps crackers from being able to guess your root password by using automated login scripts. In order to allow legitimate users to become the root user, you need to log in as yourself, and then use the **su** (switch user) command. Thus, setting the root password isn't enough if you intend to perform remote administration; you will need to set up a real user as well.

In general, it is considered a good idea to set up a normal user to do day-to-day work anyway. This gives you the protection of not being able to accidentally break configuration files or other important components while you're just surfing the Net or performing nonadministrative tasks. The exception to this rule is, of course, certain server configurations where there should never be any users besides the root user (for example, firewalls). Figure 2-9 shows what the Account Configuration screen looks like.

Begin by picking a root password and entering it in the Root Password box at the top of the screen. Enter it again in the Confirm box right below; this protects you from locking yourself out of the system in case you make a typo. The text Root Password Accepted will appear below the password boxes once you have entered a password twice the same way.

NOTE

You do not need to add the root user.

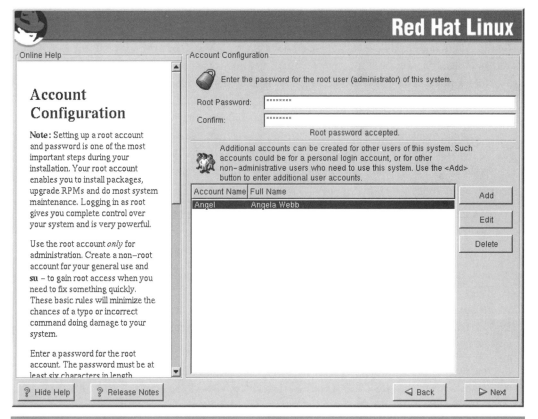

Figure 2-9 Account Configuration screen

(continued)

The remainder of the screen is meant for creating a new user. To do so, click the Add button and fill in the user's information in the window that pops up. When you are done adding users, click the Next button to proceed.

NOTE

If you make any mistakes while adding new users, you can delete and edit them as well.

14. Configure the authentication systems to use.

Linux keeps its list of users in the **/etc/passwd** file. Each system has its own copy of this file, and a user listed in one **/etc/passwd** file cannot log in to another system unless they have an entry in the other **/etc/passwd** file. To allow users to log in to any system in a network of computers, Linux uses the Network Information System (NIS) to handle remote password file issues.

In addition to listing users, the **/etc/passwd** file contains all of the passwords for each user in an encrypted format. For a very long time, this was acceptable since the process of attacking such files to crack passwords was so computationally expensive, it was almost futile to even try. Within the last few years, affordable PCs have gained the necessary computational power to present a threat to this type of security, and therefore a push to use *shadow passwords* has come. With shadow passwords, the actual encrypted password entry is not kept in the **/etc/passwd** file, but rather in an **/etc/shadow** file. The **/etc/passwd** file remains readable by any user in the system, but **/etc/shadow** is readable by the root user only. Obviously, this is a good step up in security.

Another method to arise has been a technique utilizing the MD5 hashing function. (Don't worry about the details of MD5—all you need to concern yourself with is the fact that it is better than the stock method.) Unless you have a specific reason not to do this, be sure to check the options Enable MD5 Passwords and Enable Shadow Passwords at the top of the page.

If your site has an existing NIS infrastructure, enter the relevant NIS domain and server name. If you don't know or if you want to deal with this later, you can safely ignore this step.

Another option is to use a Lightweight Directory Access Protocol (LDAP) server for storing passwords. This is ideal for an environment where you have many thousands of users accessing many servers and NIS doesn't cut it performance-wise. If you aren't sure about LDAP or whether you have an LDAP server, you can skip this step.

Finally, if you are in a Kerberos environment, you will need to enable the Kerberos authentication method. If you go this route, contact your Kerberos administrator for the appropriate realm names, KDC, and admin server. If you aren't sure about what Kerberos is, you probably don't need it.

Once you have selected all checkboxes and filled out the relevant entries in the Authentication configuration, click Next to continue.

15. Select the software packages you want to install.

This is where you can select what packages get installed onto the system. Red Hat categorizes these packages into several high-level descriptions, which allows you to make a quick selection of what type of packages you want installed and safely ignore the details. You can also select to install all of the packages that come with Red Hat, but be warned: a full install can be upwards of 1.5GB of software!

Looking at the choices (see Figure 2-10), you see the menu of top-level groups that Red Hat gives you. You can simply pick the groups that interest you, scroll to the bottom and pick Everything to have all of the packages installed, or click a button at the bottom of the screen labeled Select Individual Packages. Once you have made your decisions, simply click Next.

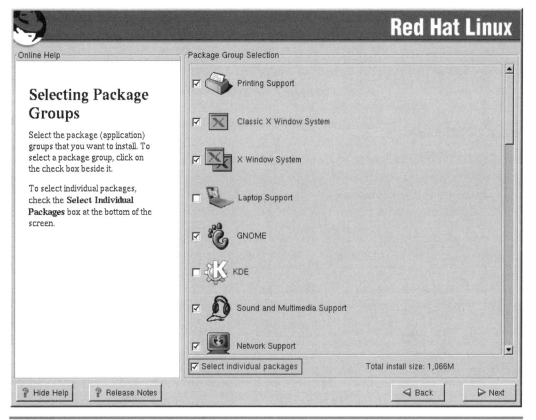

Figure 2-10 Selecting package groups

(continued)

Installing Linux in a Server Configuration

Project 2-1

Installing Red Hat Linux

If you choose Select Individual Packages, you'll see a screen like that shown in Figure 2-11. On the left side of the screen, you'll see the logical groupings of packages, and on the right side of the screen you'll see the packages that exist in that group. When you click a package, the bottom of the screen will show the name of the package and a brief description of it. Right above the description is a button to click if you want that package installed.

If you opted to select individual packages, Red Hat will go through and verify that all of the prerequisites necessary for these packages are met. If any are not met, you will be shown these packages in a new screen. This new screen will prompt you to install these additional packages since you did not specifically choose to install them.

Click Next when you're done picking packages.

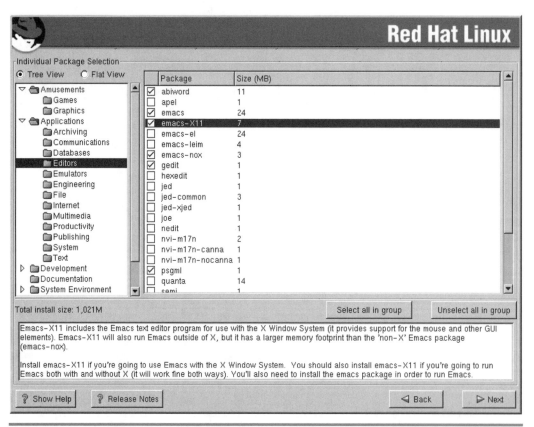

Figure 2-11 Selection of individual packages

16. Configure the X Window System.

The X Window System (also called simply X) is the basis for Linux's graphical user interface. It is what communicates with the actual video hardware. Programs such as KDE and Gnome (which you are more likely to have heard about; if not, read the next module) use X as a standard mechanism for communicating with the hardware.

What makes X interesting is that it is not coupled with the base operating system. In fact, the version of X that Linux uses, XFree86, is also available for many other UNIX-based systems, such as those from Sun. This means it is possible to run a server without ever starting the graphical environment, and as I mentioned earlier in this module, it is often a good idea to do so. By having the GUI turned off, you save memory and system resources that can instead be used for the actual server processes.

Of course, this doesn't change the fact that many nice administrative tools are available under the X Window System only, so getting it set up is still a good idea.

Red Hat will begin by trying to sense the type of video card and monitor you have. If you have a brand name monitor and card, you'll likely have the easiest time. If Linux cannot determine the type of video card and monitor, you will be prompted for the necessary information as shown in Figure 2-12.

TIP

Have the frequency information for your monitor handy. Trying to send your monitor too high a frequency can cause physical damage. I managed to toast my first color monitor this way, back when monitors were far less robust and before X Window System configuration tools existed. Modern monitors will simply not show anything if you overclock the frequency, and X configuration tools reset to the original configuration if the resolution doesn't work.

After the initial video card and monitor configuration, there are five choices under the description of the hardware configuration: Test This Configuration, Customize X Configuration, Use Graphical Login, Skip X Configuration, and a drop-down tab defaulted to Gnome for selecting the default desktop.

The first choice is a button that, when pressed, will immediately test your X Window System configuration. It will let you verify that the settings work. The second is a toggle switch that, when turned on, lets you select your X resolution and colors. By default, Xconfigurator tries to use the highest resolution with the maximum number of colors available. For some people, this resolution setting is too high and makes fonts hard to read.

(continued)

2

Installing Linux in a Server Configuration

Project 2-1

Installing Red Hat Linux

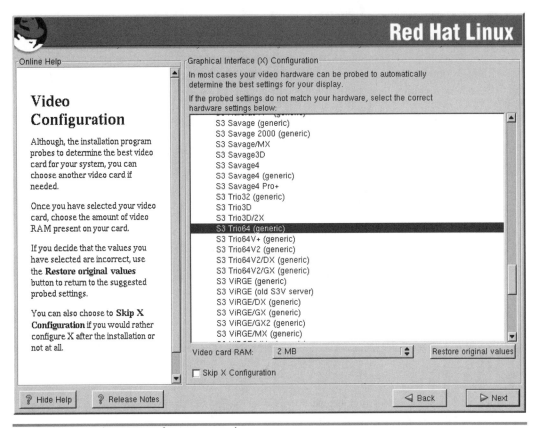

Figure 2-12 Red Hat X configuration tool

The choice of using a graphical login is just that: you can have X automatically start up on boot so that the first login everyone sees is graphical instead of text based. This choice is often nice for the novice user who has a Linux system at their desk.

The next option is if you don't have a need for X or if you want to configure it later. You can click the button to not configure the X Window System.

Finally, if you do want X, you can select your default desktop to be either Gnome or KDE. This, of course, depends on whether you opted to only install one of them earlier in the installation process.

When you're done selecting, click Next to continue. Here you can select the resolution you want to work with. Be sure to test the resolution before continuing. Click Next to continue.

Red Hat will now go through the process of installing all of the packages you have selected as part of the installation process. Depending on the speed of your hard disk, CD-ROM, and machine, this could take from just a few minutes to 20 minutes. A status indicator (see Figure 2-13) will let you know how far the process has gotten and how much longer the system expects to take.

17. Create a boot disk in case of an emergency.

Once the installation process is complete, Red Hat gives you the option of creating a boot disk. Unless you are familiar with recovering a Linux system already, you should take a moment and create one.

Following the directions on the screen, simply insert a blank disk into your drive and click Next. If you don't want to create a boot disk, click the button labeled Skip Boot Disk Creation, and then click Next.

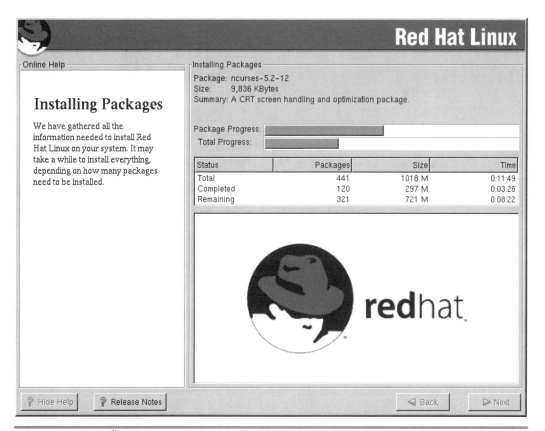

Figure 2-13 Installation status

(continued)

Ask the Expert

Q: Do I really need to create a boot disk?

A: I learned the answer to this the hard way. You should always create a rescue disk. This can get you out of tough spots when you've done something wrong or the computer is in a really bad state. I've been without a boot disk before and spent many hours trying to recover the system. Off the subject, you should *always* create a rescue disk if you run Windows 2000. I can't tell you how many times that would have been handy if I had just paid attention to the suggestion.

Project Summary

That's it! The installation process is over. You'll be prompted to press a key to reboot the system. As the system reboots, be sure to remove any CD-ROMs or floppy disks you have in your system that are capable of booting before your hard disk does.

If you are still having problems with the installation, be sure to visit Red Hat's Web site (http://www.redhat.com/) and take a look at the manuals available for Red Hat 7.3 (http://www.redhat.com/support/manuals/). There you will find the official installation guide for all possible variations in the installation process. You will also find the latest errata, security updates, and notes regarding the Red Hat 7.3 distribution.

✓ *Module 2 Mastery Check*

1. What types of installations can you perform with Red Hat Linux?

2. What is the name of the image that contains the floppy boot disk?

3. What Windows-based program can you use to write the boot image to a floppy drive?

4. Do you have to add the root user on the account configuration screen?

5. What file or files contain the users and their passwords on a Linux system?

6. What other methods of authentication can you use besides the local database?

7. What is the name of the X Window System that Linux uses?

8. Should you create a rescue boot disk during the installation?

9. What is the Swap file system used for?

10. What is the **/home** directory used for typically?

11. What is the Linux device name for the Master IDE drive on the second IDE chain?

12. How many drives can you put on a typical IDE system?

13. How big should the Swap file system be?

14. Where does the GRUB boot loader get installed to?

2

Installing Linux in a Server Configuration

Module 3

GNOME and KDE

GNOME and KDE are the de facto desktops for Linux. It is debatable which desktop environment is better—I would suggest trying out each and seeing which suits your needs best. In this module, we will go over various tips and tricks to make GNOME and KDE work better for you. Since most distributions come with one (or both) preinstalled, you won't have to deal with an installation or configuration process before you can jump in and start using them.

Before we get into the fun stuff, though, we need to step back and understand a little more about the X Window System and how it relates to GNOME and KDE. This will give you a better idea of the big picture of Linux and one of its fundamental architectural differences with Windows NT.

NOTE

This module assumes you are logged in as root. However, all of the changes we talk about here can apply to any user.

CRITICAL SKILL
3.1 Understand the X Window System

The designers of UNIX-based operating systems, like Linux, take a very different view of the world when it comes to user environments than do those behind Microsoft Windows. UNIX folk believe the interface they present the user should be 100% independent of the core operating system. As a result, Linux's kernel is completely decoupled from its user interface. This allows you to select the interface that works best for you, rather than be stuck with the dictated vision of someone else or potentially random "market research."

More important, however, is the stability that comes from having such a large program independent of the core operating system. If the GUI crashes under Windows or MacOS, you have to reboot. Under Linux, you can kill the GUI and restart it without affecting any other services being offered by the system (such as network file services).

In the mid-1980s, an OS-independent foundation for graphical user environments was created and called X Window. X (as it is commonly abbreviated) simply defines the method by which applications can communicate with the graphical hardware. Also established was a well-defined set of functions programmers could call on to perform basic window manipulation.

The simple definition of how windows are drawn and mouse clicks are handled did not include any model of how the windows should look. (In fact, the X Window system in its natural state has no real appearance. It doesn't even draw lines around windows!) Control of appearance was passed off to an external program called a *window manager*. The window manager took care of drawing borders, using color, and making the environment pleasant to the eye. The window manager was required only to use standard calls to the X Window subsystem to draw on the screen. It *did not* dictate how the application itself utilized the windows. This meant application programmers had the flexibility to develop a user interface most intuitive for the application.

Because the window manager was external to the X Window subsystem, and the X Window application program interface (API) was open, any programmer who wanted to develop a new window manager could, and many did. In the context of today, we might associate this form of openness with MP3 players, such as WinAMP, that allow developers to build "skins" for the base player.

The icing on the cake was the relationship between applications and X Window. Typical applications were written to communicate directly with X Window, thereby working with any window manager the user opted to use.

The Downside

As technically interesting and versatile as the X Window System is, it is a pain in the backside to program for. A Windows programmer might equate programming for the X Window System to programming for the original MS Windows prior to the visual tools and MFC libraries. For example, writing a simple program to bring up a window, display the text "Hello World," and then offer a button to allow the user to quit could easily be several hundred lines long under both X and MS Windows!

Here the UNIX folks took a lesson from the Macintosh OS and MS Windows families (who, it should be noted, borrowed their ideas from Xerox's work back in the late 1970s): Failure to offer a reasonably consistent user interface for both the user and the programmer that is easy to use and easy to develop for means a loss of user base.

Commercial UNIX vendors tried to fix this problem with the Common Desktop Environment so their users would get a consistent look and feel. An improved library for X Window, called Motif, was developed as well. For Linux, both of these developments presented a problem, because they went against the ideal of being open source. To make matters even more unpleasant, they weren't much better than what was available before. As of this writing, CDE is being phased out by SUN Microsystems and they are going to use GNOME for the default GUI.

Enter KDE and GNOME

With unfriendly programming environments and unfriendly user interfaces, X Window had the potential to one day turn into a legacy interface. This would be extremely unfortunate, because it offers a design that was (and still is) leaps and bounds beyond other commercial offerings. The protocol is open, which means anyone who wants to write an X client or X server is welcome to. And, of course, one of the best features of the X Window System is that it allows applications to be run on one host but be displayed on another host.

In the late 1990s, two groups came out of the woodwork with solutions to the problems with X Window: GNOME and KDE. KDE offers a new window manager and necessary libraries to make writing applications for it much easier. GNOME offers a general framework for other window managers and applications to work with it. Each has its own ideas for how things should work, but because they both work on top of the X Window System, they aren't entirely incompatible.

NOTE

Despite what you might hear in newsgroups and on Web sites, the two groups are not "at war" with each other. Rather, they welcome the open competition. Each group can feed off of each other's ideas, and in turn, both groups can offer two excellent choices for us, the users.

What This Means for You

The keywords in the previous section were "not entirely incompatible." In order for KDE and GNOME to offer features such as drag and drop, they must offer a uniform way for applications to communicate with each other and a set of developer libraries to do so. Unfortunately, because the two methods are different, they aren't compatible.

What this means for applications can be a little confusing. Depending on the functionality the application calls on from its libraries, it may still work in the other environment as long as the libraries exist. A good example is the **ksysv** program. It was written with KDE in mind, but because the functionality it relies on is 100% available in the library, a system that is running GNOME but has KDE libraries available (such as Red Hat) will allow the application to run without a problem. On the other hand, if an application relied on the KDE window manager itself, the application would not work under GNOME.

As a user, this means that picking one environment over the other has the possibility of locking you out of getting to use certain applications. As of this writing, this hasn't been too much of an issue. In fact, there is work going on between both groups to improve the level of compatibility between them. That leaves you with a choice. If you aren't sure about what you like better, try both and decide for yourself. What anyone else uses is irrelevant. What you like is what matters. And that's what having two competing systems is all about.

CRITICAL SKILL

3.2 Use KDE

KDE is a desktop environment (the K Desktop Environment). It is slightly different from typical window managers that we have mentioned. Instead of just describing how the interface should look, KDE also provides a set of libraries that allow an application to take advantage of some of the special features the window manager has to offer. This includes things like drag-and-drop support, standardized printing support, and so on.

The flip side to this technique of window management is that once an application is designed to run with KDE, it requires KDE in order to work. This is a big change from earlier window managers where applications were independent of the window manager.

From a programmer's point of view, KDE offers a library that is much easier to work with than working directly with the X interface. KDE also offers a standardized object-oriented framework that allows one set of tools to build on another, something that was not available with the X Window System alone.

For this section, we will assume that KDE has already been installed on your system. This is true for Caldera, since it only offers KDE, and, if you opted for using it during the install process, for Red Hat, too.

NOTE

For more details and information on KDE, visit their Web site at http://www.kde.org/.

Starting the X Window System and KDE

When setting up the X Window System, you may have had a choice of starting the system straight into X. If so, all you need to do is log in and you're there—you're using KDE and the X Window System. If that option was not selected, you will have a text-based login prompt. To get into the X environment, simply log in and run **startx**, like so:

```
[root@ford /root]# startx
```

In a few moments, you will be in KDE. Your screen will probably look something like Figure 3-1.

If your screen doesn't look like that, but rather it displays the GNOME banner window on startup, then you need to edit the file that decides which window manager you start. To do this, exit out of GNOME by clicking the bear claw in the lower-left corner of the screen and selecting Logout. This will bring you back into text mode. Edit the **.xinitrc** file using your favorite editor. If you don't have a favorite, try **pico**, like so:

```
[root@ford /root]# pico .xinitrc
```

NOTE

If you aren't familiar with **pico**, don't worry. All of the available commands are always shown at the bottom of the screen. Any command that starts with the caret symbol (^) means you use the CTRL key along with other keys specified. For example, ^X means CTRL-X.

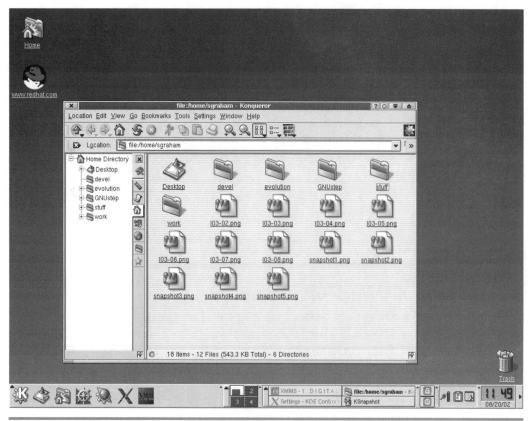

Figure 3-1 The KDE desktop, with the Konqueror Browser/File Manager

Most likely, the file will be empty. If that is the case, simply add the following content:

```
#!/bin/sh
startkde
```

If the file is not empty, go to the very last line. It will probably begin with the string **exec**, which tells the system to execute a program. Change that line so that it reads **startkde** instead.

KDE Basics

KDE shares many qualities with other graphical desktops, such as Windows or MacOS. It has a desktop on which files and folders can exist. One key point to note is that because Linux places all of the hard disks on the system into a unified directory tree, you won't find a special icon allowing you to browse a particular disk like you can under My Computer.

At the bottom of the screen, you will find KDE's *Kpanel*. The leftmost "K" button is the equivalent of the Windows Start button. By clicking it, you will be presented with a menu showing you a number of applications that can be started by simply clicking the appropriate menu entry.

What makes the Kpanel different from the Windows Start menu is that it is also a shortcut bar to commonly used applications. You can configure the bar to have any shortcuts you like by clicking the K button and selecting Panel. Under this menu is a number of configuration options.

If you want to hide the panel altogether, you can do so by clicking the arrows on the far right or the left side of the panel. This will make the panel hide in that direction. Click the arrow again to bring the panel back.

Progress Check

1. What does **startkde** do?

2. What is the Kpanel?

The KDE Control Center

The KDE Control Center is a lot like the Control Panel for Windows, except it is specifically geared toward desktop configuration items (see Figure 3-2).

The Control Center offers an impressive array of tools for configuring KDE to your heart's delight. This includes support for a variety of themes, colors, backgrounds, screen savers, applications, and types of hardware. The best way to see all it has to offer is to go through it and play—this is one of the rare opportunities you have as a system administrator to play with the interface without breaking your system.

In this section, we will step through several common tasks, giving you an idea of what can be done and the typical method for figuring out how to do it. As mentioned earlier, the interface is very Windows-like, so getting around in it should be relatively easy.

---

1. **startkde** starts the KDE desktop.

2. Kpanel is the KDE taskbar that shows up at the bottom of the screen (by default).

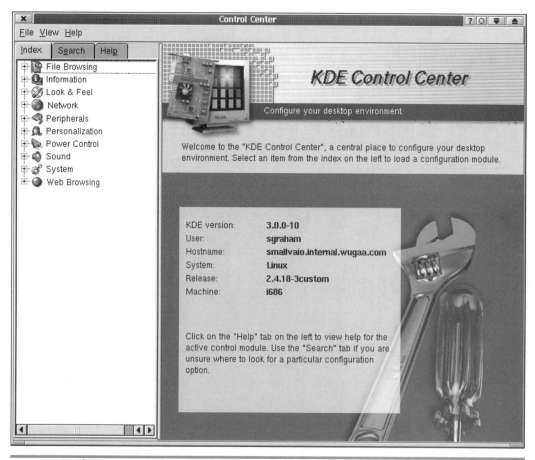

Figure 3-2 The KDE Control Center

Project 3-1 Using Multiple Desktops

One of the most powerful tools you have at your disposal is the virtual desktop. The only dangerous thing about it is your aggravation when you work on systems that don't have this feature.

The essence of virtual desktops is that they allow you to effectively have multiple screens at the same time. All you need to do is select which screen you want to use by clicking the virtual desktop selector at the bottom of the screen. Most KDE installations default to four virtual screens. If you want to adjust that, you can do the following steps.

Step by Step

1. Open the Control Center.

2. Select Look And Feel.

3. Select Desktop.

4. Select Number Of Desktops from the tab-style window on the right side of the Control Center (see Figure 3-3).

5. Move the Number of Desktops slider to the right to increase the number of desktops. (Of course, you can also move it left to reduce the number of desktops.)

6. Click the Apply button at the bottom of the window to make the changes take effect.

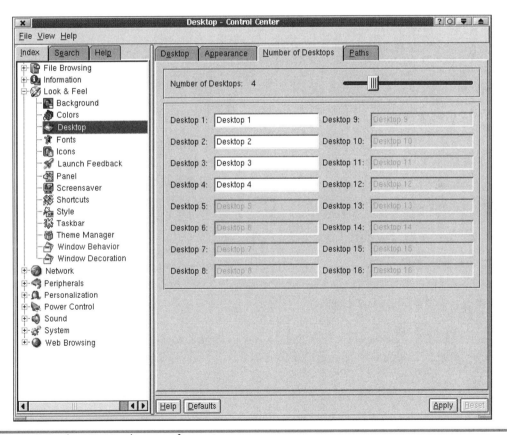

Figure 3-3 The KDE Desktop configuration

(continued)

3

GNOME and KDE

Project
3-1

Using Multiple Desktops

Project Summary

If each desktop has a specific purpose, you can also change the label of the desktop by highlighting it and changing the desktop name field on the same panel. This is one of the strong points of the X Window System—you can have multiple desktops, which means lots of desktop real estate to do your work.

Starting Other Applications

There are multiple ways to start a new application. As a system administrator, you are likely to have a command window up (better known as an *xterm*), so you may find it convenient to simply run the application from there. In fact, most of this book assumes you are running applications from that prompt. Simply open a terminal window box by either clicking the icon of a terminal on the desktop panel or clicking the K menu, selecting Utilities, and then clicking Terminal. This starts up kterm, which is functionally equivalent to an xterm. Once it is open, you can enter the name of the command you wish to run there and press ENTER.

NOTE

Many commands discussed in this book must be run from a terminal window.

Under KDE, you can also bring up the equivalent of the Run option under the Windows Start menu by pressing ALT-F2. This brings up a small window in the center of your screen where you can type in the command you want to run. The window automatically goes away once you press ENTER to execute the command or ESC to abort.

The last way is to search through the directory listing using the file browser and double-clicking the application name you want. This method is, of course, the most tedious, but it can be useful if you can't remember the name of the application. Common directories to check are **/usr/bin**, **/usr/sbin**, **/bin**, **/sbin**, and **/usr/X11R6/bin**.

Changing the Color Scheme

If you're fussy about your desktop environment, you'll probably want to change the appearance of your desktop color scheme. With KDE's Control Center, this is quite easy. Begin by bringing the Control Center up and then clicking the Look And Feel option in the left window.

Changing Your Background   Click the Background menu option under Look And Feel. This will bring up a configuration panel like the one in Figure 3-4. To change your background, simply select either a color or wallpaper from the respective menu. If you choose a wallpaper, you can test what the wallpaper will look like before committing to it by clicking Apply at the

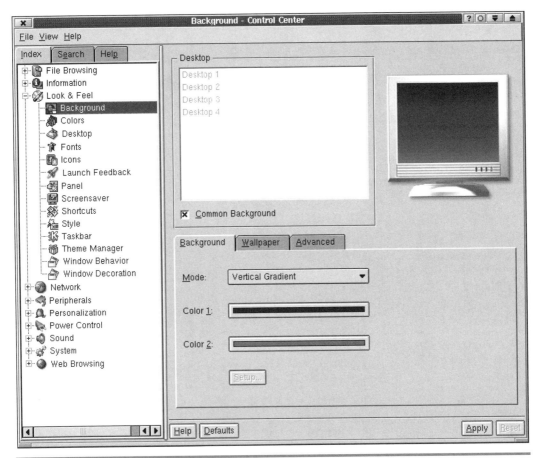

Figure 3-4 The KDE background configuration tool

bottom of the screen. If you like what you see, you can keep the change by clicking OK. If you don't, simply set it back to the original and click Apply again.

Changing Colors   To change the colors, click the Colors menu option under Desktop. This will bring up a configuration panel like the one in Figure 3-5.

Simply click the color combination you like best. If you want to create a new combination, click the Add button underneath the list and give your new settings a name. Highlight this setting and then select the color you want to give each widget in the right side of the panel. For example, to change the color of normal text, open the Widget Color drop-down box. Select Normal

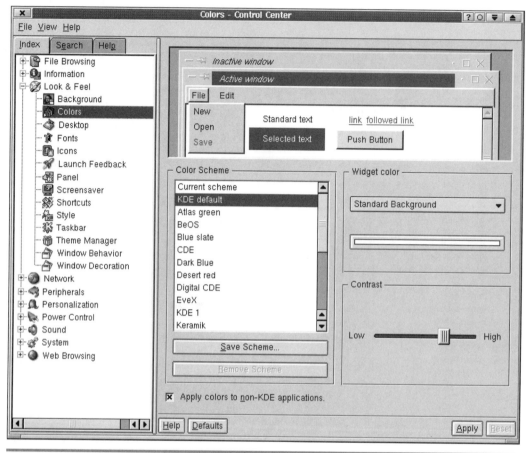

Figure 3-5 Changing the color scheme

Text. The bar underneath the drop-down box will show the current color. Click the bar to bring up a color wheel so you can select the new color you like best.

As always, click Apply once you are done.

Changing the Screen Saver   To change the screen saver, click the Screensaver option under Desktop. This will bring up a configuration panel like the one in Figure 3-6.

In the menu box, select the screen saver you like. A demo of it will appear in the picture of the monitor in the same panel. You can try out a full-screen version of the screen saver by clicking Test. If that screen saver has configuration options, the Setup button will also be available so you can configure it.

Figure 3-6 Selecting your screen saver

From this menu, you can choose to lock your screen in addition to starting the screen saver. This is very handy if you need to leave your workstation in a public location, like an office.

But the most fun feature is the corner activation. Looking at the picture of the monitor carefully, you can see that the four corners of the screen have little gray boxes. Clicking the boxes reveals a menu that lets you pick Ignore, Save Screen, or Lock Screen. The default value is Ignore. However, by selecting either Save Screen or Lock Screen, you can then move the cursor to that corner and immediately cause that action to happen. For example, I have the lower-right corner of my screen set to Save Screen. When I want to immediately activate my screen saver, I simply move my mouse into that corner and the screen saver is active. The lower-left corner is set to Lock Screen. So if I know I'm going away from my desk for a long time, I can immediately lock my screen by moving my mouse into the lower-left corner.

The default behavior for the screen saver is to activate after the number of minutes specified in the screen saver configuration window. Setting any of the corners to activate the screen saver does not invalidate the default behavior.

CRITICAL SKILL
3.3 Use GNOME

Like KDE, GNOME (GNU Network Object Model Environment) offers a complete desktop environment and application framework to make development as well as usage easier. What makes GNOME different is how it achieves these goals. Unlike KDE, GNOME is not a window manager. GNOME provides development libraries and session management—foundation features that we as users don't see. On top of this foundation is a window manager that takes care of the general appearance of the desktop. The default window manager is Sawfish, but there are several choices available.

NOTE

According to the official Web site, the correct pronunciation of "GNOME" is "guh-nome." This is because the G in "GNOME" stands for "GNU," and the correct pronunciation of "GNU" is "guh-new." In the same paragraph, the GNOME team states that no one will be offended if you pronounce it "nome."

From a developer's point of view, GNOME is very interesting. It defines its interfaces with the rest of the world through the CORBA technology. Thus, any development system that can communicate using CORBA can be used to develop GNOME-compliant applications. (For more information, see their developer's Web pages at http://www.gnome.org/.)

For users, this holds the potential for many applications to be developed to take advantage of the features in GNOME. Of course, like KDE, GNOME also works with existing X Window System applications quite nicely.

NOTE

If you do not have GNOME installed, you can download the application and installation directions from the GNOME Web site at http://www.gnome.org/. Precompiled packages for various distributions are also available at their Web site.

Another difference you'll find between GNOME and KDE is that GNOME offers multiple distributions. The base distribution (the one that comes with Red Hat) is quite nice and is what we examine in this section; however, other companies have begun spinning their own versions that have their own benefits. One of the more popular alternatives is Ximian (http://www.ximian.com/), which offers a smoother window manager and upgrade tool (Red Carpet).

Starting the X Window System and GNOME

If you are using Red Hat Linux and have opted for its defaults, you already have GNOME installed as your default GUI. Depending on how the X Window System is configured, you may already have a graphical login prompt. In that case, logging in will automatically place you in the X Window System environment. If you have a text-based login, simply run **startx** in order to bring X up, like so:

```
[root@ford /root]# startx
```

If the default GUI that starts is not GNOME, you can change your personal settings to use GNOME by editing the **.xinitrc** file in your home directory. Begin by trying to exit out of the window manager. If you are in KDE (represented by a big *K* in the lower-left corner), click the *K* to bring up a menu. In that menu should be an option to log out. If you're really stuck, you can also press CTRL-ALT-BACKSPACE to kill the underlying X Window System manager. This will bring you back into text mode. Edit the **.xinitrc** file using your favorite editor. If you don't have a favorite, try **pico**, like so:

```
[root@ford /root]# pico .xinitrc
```

NOTE

If you aren't familiar with **pico**, don't worry. All of the available commands are always shown at the bottom of the screen. Any command that starts with the caret symbol (^) means you use the CTRL key along with other keys specified. For example, ^X means CTRL-X.

Most likely, the file will be empty. If that is the case, simply add the following content:

```
#!/bin/sh
gnome-session
```

If the file is not empty, go to the very last line. It will probably begin with the string **exec**, which tells the system to execute a program. Change that line so that it reads **gnome-session** instead.

GNOME Basics

If you are familiar with GUI interfaces, the GNOME desktop should make you feel right at home. There are two significant differences: the first is that there is no My Computer icon on the desktop. This is because Linux does not have the concept of separate drive letters for each partition. Rather, all of the partitions are made available in a single directory tree, thereby eliminating the need to select a drive.

The second big difference is the panel at the bottom of the screen. This panel is like the MS Windows panel on steroids—it shows what applications are currently running, as well as the date and time, and bear claw button at the left side of the panel is similar to the Start button. The big difference is that this panel is completely configurable. You can move things around in it, dock dynamic applications, set up shortcuts to other applications, and move around your virtual desktops. If you don't want it in the way for a particular task, simply click the right or left arrow buttons at each end of the panel and it will slide out of the way until you click the arrow button again.

By default, the buttons available on the panel are, from left to right, the GNOME Start menu, Screen Locking Tool, help system, a terminal emulation program (sometimes referred to as an xterm), the GNOME Configuration Tool (Start Here), and Netscape Communicator. If you want to change the panel's appearance, click the bear claw in the lower-left corner of your screen and select the Panel menu. It will bring up a series of submenus that allow you to configure various aspects of the panel, including being able to dock running programs into it (applets) and set up new shortcuts (launchers).

The GNOME Configuration Tool

The GNOME Configuration Tool allows you to control the appearance and behavior of GNOME, similar to the way that the Windows Control Panel works. To start the GNOME Configuration Tool, click the panel button that looks like a toolbox.

NOTE

Some of the new Linux distributions don't have a "control panel." All of the configuration is done through the Start Here icon, which uses the Nautilus system to configure the system.

Once started, the GNOME Configuration Tool will look something like Figure 3-7. In this section, we will step through several common tasks. They should give you an idea of what can be done and the typical method for figuring out how to do it. The configuration system looks and behaves as though you are browsing through a directory.

Figure 3-7 The Nautilus GNOME Configuration Tool

Changing the Background

To change your background settings, double-click on the Preferences icon, then the Desktop icon and finally the Background icon. This will bring up a panel that looks similar to the KDE configuration utility.

The Background panel is broken up into two groups, Color and Wallpaper. The Color group allows you to set the background color. If you like, you can select two colors and do a gradient between them, either horizontally or vertically. To select the color itself, click the box immediately underneath the string Color 1 or Color 2. This will bring up a color wheel from which you can choose any color you like.

To change the wallpaper, click the Browse button in the Wallpaper group to see a list of available wallpapers. Once you have found the one you like, simply select it and click Apply to make the change take effect.

Setting the Screen Saver

To set the screen saver under GNOME, click the Desktop icon and the Screensaver icon.

Once there, choosing a screen saver is very easy. Simply select the module you like best from the list shown. A sample of what the screen saver will look like will appear in the Screen Saver Demo, located in the same window. If there are any configuration parameters available for the screen saver, a button will become undimmed immediately beneath the listing of possible screen savers.

The global screen saver settings are on the lower half of the screen saver panel. There, you can select how long the system should wait before starting the screen saver and how long it should wait before it uses advanced power management features to try to turn off the monitor.

Themes

Themes are the way GNOME allows you to configure the appearance of your window manager. These changes go beyond simply changing colors; they can change the appearance of the desktop, windows, borders, and fonts for all applications. (Users of MacOS 8 or WinAMP should be at home with this technology.) If you aren't sure how significant a change you can make, visit the themes Web site at http://www.themes.org/.

The Theme Selector icon is in the same directory as the Background icon. This will bring up a panel that looks like Figure 3-8.

By default, GNOME comes with only the default theme. If you are interested in changing the theme, you can visit http://www.themes.org/ and download new ones.

Once you have a theme selected, you can click the Preview button to see what the theme will look like on your screen before committing to it.

Window Manager

As we mentioned earlier in this section, GNOME does not specify the window manager that must be used with it. All window managers perform the same basic tasks, but the little differences in interface, style, and appearance are what set them apart. The default that ships with Red Hat that works with GNOME is Enlightenment.

To change your window manager from the Control Center, click the Desktop button and then the Window Manager button.

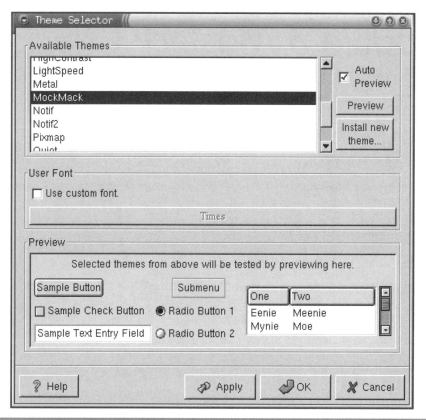

Figure 3-8 The GNOME Theme Selector

If you want to get a better idea of what the screen will look like with a different window manager, you can click the Try button at the bottom of the window. If you decide that the look is not quite what you are interested in, you can go back to your original settings by clicking Revert.

Module 3 Mastery Check

1. What is KDE?

2. What is GNOME?

3. What is the X Window System?

4. What are some advantages of the X Window System over the Windows GUI model?

5. What are some disadvantages of the X Window System compared to the Windows GUI model?

6. What does the **.xinitrc** file do?

7. What do you need to put in **.xinitrc** in order to use the KDE system?

8. What do you need to put in **.xinitrc** in order to use the GNOME system?

9. What does the `startx` command do?

10. Where can you get information on the status of KDE?

11. What are the major sites to get information on GNOME?

Module 4

Installing Software

A great deal of your time will be spent keeping your Linux system up to date with the latest and greatest software. There are three basic methods to installing software on a Linux system. One, use the package manager for the distribution. This is typically the Red Hat Package Manager (RPM). Two, compile the software using the standard GNU compilation method. Three, compile and install the software by hand. We will cover these methods in this module.

When installing software, you typically need to be the root user. (Module 6 will cover how to change user IDs with the **su** command.) In a terminal window, just type **su − root**.

CRITICAL SKILL
4.1 Use the Red Hat Package Manager

The Red Hat Package Manager's primary function is to allow the installation and removal of files (typically, precompiled software). It is wonderfully easy to use, and several graphical interfaces have been built around it to make it even easier. Red Hat, Caldera, and other distributions have started using this tool to distribute their software. In fact, almost all of the software mentioned in this book is available in RPM form. The reason you'll go through the process of compiling software yourself in other modules is so that you can customize the software to your system, as such customizations might not exist in an RPM.

An RPM file is a package that contains files needed for the software to function correctly. These files can be configuration files, binaries, and even pre and post scripts to run while installing the software.

NOTE

In this context, we are assuming that the RPM files contain precompiled binaries.
Several groups, such as Red Hat, also make source code available as an RPM,
but it is uncommon to download and compile source code in this fashion.

The RPM tool performs the installation and uninstallation of RPMs. The tool also maintains a central database of what RPMs you have installed and other information about the package.

In general, software that comes in the form of an RPM is less work to install and maintain than software that needs to be compiled. The tradeoff is that by using an RPM, you accept the default parameters supplied in the RPM. In most cases, these defaults are acceptable. However, if you need to be more intimately aware of what is going on with a service, you may find that compiling the source yourself will prove more educational about what package components exist and how they work together.

Assuming that all you want to do is install a simple package, RPM is perfect. There are several great resources for RPM packages, including the following:

- http://www.rpmfind.net/
- ftp://ftp.redhat.com/
- http://www.linuxapps.com/

Of course, if you are interested in more details about RPM itself, you can visit the RPM Web site at http://www.rpm.org/. RPM comes with Red Hat Linux (and derivatives) as well as Caldera Linux. If you aren't sure if RPM comes with your distribution, check with your vendor.

NOTE

Although the name of the package says "Red Hat," the software can be used with other distributions as well. In fact, RPM has even been ported to other operating systems, such as Solaris and IRIX. The source code to RPM is open-source software, so anyone can take the initiative to make the system work for them.

Installing a New Package

The easiest way to install a new package is to use the **-i** option with RPM. For example, if you downloaded a package called **bc-1.05a-4.i386.rpm** and wanted to install it, you would type:

```
[root@ford /root]# rpm -ivh bc-1.05a-4.i386.rpm
```

If the installation went fine, you would not see any errors or messages. This is the most common method of installing RPMs. On the other hand, if the package already exists, you would see this message:

```
error: package bc-1.05a-4 is already installed
```

Some packages rely on other packages. A game, for example, may depend on SVGA libraries having already been installed. In those instances, you will get a message indicating which packages need to be installed first. Simply install those packages and then come back to the original package.

If you need to upgrade a package that already exists, use the **-U** option, like so:

```
[root@ford /root]# rpm -Uv bc-1.05a-4.i386.rpm
```

Some additional command-line options to RPM are listed in Table 4-1.

Command-Line Option	Description
`--force`	This is the sledgehammer of installation. Typically, you use it when you're knowingly installing an odd or unusual configuration, and RPM's safeguards are trying to keep you from doing so. The `--force` option tells RPM to forego any sanity checks and just do it, even if it thinks you're trying to fit a square peg into a round hole. Be careful with this option.
`-h`	Prints hash marks to indicate progress during an installation. Use with the `-v` option for a pretty display.
`--percent`	Prints the percentage completed to indicate progress. It is handy if you're running RPM from another program, such as a Perl script, and you want to know the status of the install.
`-nodeps`	If RPM is complaining about missing dependency files, but you want the installation to happen anyway, passing this option at the command line will cause RPM to not perform any dependency checks.
`-q`	Queries the RPM system for information.
`--test`	This option does not perform a real installation; it just checks to see whether an installation would succeed. If it anticipates problems, it displays what they'll be.
`-V`	Verifies RPMs or files on the system.
`-v`	Tells RPM to be verbose about its actions.

Table 4-1 RPM Command-Line Options

For example, to force the installation of a package regardless of dependencies or other errors, you would type:

```
[root@ford /root]# rpm -i --force -nodeps packagename.rpm
```

where *packagename.rpm* is the name of the package being installed.

Querying a Package

Sometimes it is handy to know which packages are currently installed and what they do. You can do that with the RPM query options.

To list all installed packages, simply type:

```
[root@ford /root]# rpm -qa
```

Be ready for a long list of packages! If you are looking for a particular package name, you can use the **grep** command to specify the name (or part of the name) of the package, like so:

```
[root@ford /root]# rpm -qa | grep -i 'name'
```

NOTE

The **-i** parameter in **grep** tells it to make its search case-insensitive.

If you just want to view all of the packages one screen at a time, you can use the **more** command, like so:

```
[root@ford /root]# rpm -qa | more
```

To find out which package a particular file belongs to, type:

```
[root@ford /root]# rpm -qf filename
```

where *filename* is the name of the file that you want to check on.

To find out the purpose of a package that is already installed, you must first know the name of the package (taken from the listing in **rpm -qa**) and then specify it, like so:

```
[root@ford /root]# rpm -qi packagename
```

where *packagename* is the name of the package that you want information about.

To find out what files are contained in a package, type:

```
[root@ford /root]# rpm -qlp packagename
```

where *packagename* is the name of the package that you want information about.

Uninstalling a Package

Uninstalling packages with RPM is just as easy as installing them. In most cases, all you will need to type is

```
[root@ford /root]# rpm -e packagename
```

where *packagename* is the name of the package as listed in **rpm -qa**.

Verifying an RPM

A very cool option to the RPM tool is the ability to verify a package. What happens is RPM looks at the package information in its database, which is assumed to be good. It then compares that information with the binaries and files that are on your system. Unfortunately, in today's Internet world, where being hacked is a real possibility, this kind of test should tell you instantly if anyone has done something to your system (see Module 11 for tips on securing your system from attacks). For example, if you want to verify that the **/bin/ls** command is valid, you would type:

```
[root@ford /root]# rpm -Vf /bin/ls
```

If everything is okay with **/bin/ls**, nothing will be displayed to the terminal. If something is wrong, RPM will inform you of what test failed. Some example tests are the MD5 checksum test, file size, and modification times. The moral of the story is: RPM is an ally in finding out what is wrong with your system. If you suspect several things might be wrong, you can verify all installed packages on your system by typing:

```
[root@ford /root]# rpm -Va
```

This command verifies *all* of the packages installed on your system. That's a lot of files, so you might have to give it some time to complete.

GUI RPM Installers

For those who like a good GUI tool to help simplify their lives, there are several package managers included with your distribution. **Gnorpm** is a good GNOME tool that will typically work under KDE as well. It performs all of the functions that the command-line version does without forcing you to remember command-line parameters. Of course, this comes at the price of not being scriptable, but that's why you have the command-line version, too.

Progress Check

1. What does RPM stand for?

2. What command is used to query the RPM database?

---

1. Red Hat Package Manager

2. **rpm -q**

CRITICAL SKILL
4.2 Compile and Install GNU Software

One of the key benefits of open-source software is that you have the source code in your hands. If the developer chooses to stop working on it, you can continue. If you find a problem, you can fix it. In other words, you are in control of the situation and not at the mercy of a commercial developer you can't control. But having the source code means you need to be able to compile it, too. Otherwise all you have is a bunch of text files that can't do much.

Although almost every piece of software in this book is available as an RPM, we will step through the process of compiling it yourself so that you can pick and choose compile time options, which is something you can't do with RPMs. Also, an RPM might be compiled for a specific architecture such as the Intel 486. That code might run better if you compiled it natively on your Intel 686 Pentium III class CPU.

In this section, we will step through the process of compiling the Hello package, a GNU software package that might seem useless at first, but there are reasons for its existence. Most GNU software conforms to a standard method of installing, so let's go ahead and get the package.

Getting and Unpacking the Package

Software that comes in source form is generally made available as a *tarball*—that is, it is archived into a single large file and then compressed. The tools used to do this are **tar** and **gzip**. **tar** handles the process of combining many files into a single large file, and **gzip** is responsible for the compression.

NOTE

Do not confuse **gzip** with WinZip. They are two different programs that use two different (but comparable) methods of compression. It should be noted, though, that WinZip does know how to handle tarballs.

Typically, a single directory is selected in which to build and store tarballs. This allows the system administrator to keep the tarball of each package in a safe place in the event he or she needs to pull something out of it later. It also lets all the administrators know which packages are installed on the system in addition to the base system. A good directory for this is **/usr/local/src**, since software local to a site is generally installed in **/usr/local**.

When unpacked, a tarball will generally create a new directory for all of its files. The hello tarball (**hello-1.3.tar.gz**), for example, creates the subdirectory **hello-1.3**. Most packages follow this standard. If you find a package that does not follow it, it is a good idea to create a subdirectory with a reasonable name and place all the unpacked source files there. This allows multiple builds to occur at the same time without the risk of the two builds conflicting.

First, let's get into the directory we want to compile in:

```
[root@ford /root]# cd /usr/local/src
```

Download the **hello-1.3.tar.gz** file from the GNU FTP site at ftp://ftp.gnu.org/gnu/hello/.
You can type the URL into a browser and download the package or you can use the **ftp**
command-line tool to download the package

```
[root@ford src]# ftp ftp.gnu.org
Connected to ftp.gnu.org
220 GNU FTP server ready.
Name(ftp.gnu.org:root):ftp

330 Please specify the password.
Password:sgraham@cs.ucr.edu (You won't see this when you type it)
ftp>bin
ftp>hash
ftp>cd /gnu/hello
ftp>get hello-1.3.tar.gz
ftp>bye
```

It is a common courtesy to type in your e-mail address as the password. If the **ftp** account
doesn't work you might want to try **anonymous**. Once in the **ftp** command prompt, the **bin**
option tells **ftp** that you want to transfer the files using binary mode. The **hash** option will
print a hash mark for every 1024 bytes of data sent. Finally, you **cd** into the directory and then
issue the FTP **get** command to grab the file. You exit the FTP program by typing **bye**. Then
unpack the tarball with the following command:

```
[root@ford src]# tar -xvzf hello-1.3.tar.gz
```

NOTE

You might encounter files that end with the **.tar.bz2** extension. Bzip2 is a compression
algorithm that is gaining popularity, and GNU **tar** does support decompressing it on
the command line with the **y** or **j** option (instead of the **z** parameter).

The **z** parameter in the **tar** command invokes **gzip** to decompress the file before the
untar process occurs. The **v** parameter tells **tar** to show the name of the file it is **untar**ring
as it goes through the process. This way you'll know the name of the directory where all the
sources are being unpacked. You should now have a directory called **/usr/local/src/hello-1.3**.
You can test this by using the **cd** command to move into it:

```
[root@ford src]# cd /usr/local/src/hello-1.3
```

Looking for Documentation

Once you are inside the directory with all of the source code, begin looking for documentation. *Always read the documentation that comes with the source code!* If there are any special compile directions, notes, or warnings, they will most likely be mentioned here. You will save yourself a great deal of agony by reading the relevant files first.

So then, what are the relevant files? Typically there are two files in a distribution, **README** and **INSTALL**, both of which are located in the root of the source code directory. The **README** file generally includes a description of the package, references to additional documentation (including the installation documentation), and references to the author of the package. The **INSTALL** file typically has directions for compiling and installing the package.

These are not, of course, absolutes. Every package has its quirks. The best way to find out is to simply list the directory contents and look for obvious signs of additional documentation. Some packages use different capitalization: **readme**, **README**, **ReadMe**, and so on. Some introduce variations on a theme, such as **README.1ST** or **README.NOW**, and so on.

Another common place for additional information is a subdirectory that is appropriately called "doc" or "documentation."

To view a text file, use the **more** command:

```
[root@ford hello-1.3]# more README
```

To view the text file in the pico editor, use the **pico** command:

```
[root@ford hello-1.3]# pico README
```

TIP

To get a quick list of all the directories in a source tree, enter the command
[root@ford hello-1.3]# ls -l | grep drwx.

Configuring the Package

Most packages ship with an autoconfiguration script; it is safe to assume they do unless their documentation says otherwise. These scripts are typically named **configure**, and they take parameters. There are a handful of stock parameters that are available across all **configure** scripts, but the interesting stuff occurs on a program-by-program basis. Each package will have a handful of features that can be enabled or disabled or that have special values set at compile time, and they must be set up via **configure**.

To see what **configure** options come with a package, simply run:

```
[root@ford hello-1.3]# ./configure --help
```

Yes, those are two hyphens (--) before the word "help."

One commonly available option is **--prefix**. This option allows you to set the base directory where the package gets installed. By default, most packages use **/usr/local**. Each component in the package will install into the appropriate directory in **/usr/local**.

With all of the options you want set up, a final run of **configure** will create a special type of file called a *makefile*. Makefiles are the foundation of the compilation phase. Generally, if **configure** fails you will not get a makefile. Make sure that the **configure** command did indeed complete without any errors.

Compiling Your Package

Compiling your package is the easy part. All you need to do is run **make**, like so:

```
[root@ford hello-1.3]# make
```

The **make** tool reads all of the makefiles that were created by the **configure** script. These files tell **make** which files to compile and the order in which to compile them—which is crucial since there could be hundreds of source files.

Depending on the speed of your system, the available memory, and how busy it is doing other things, the compilation process could take a while to complete, so don't be surprised.

As **make** is working, it will display each command it is running and all of the parameters associated with it. This output is usually the invocation of the compiler and all of the parameters passed to the compiler—it's pretty tedious stuff that even the programmers were inclined to automate!

If the compile goes through smoothly, you won't see any error messages. Most compiler error messages are very clear and distinct, so don't worry about possibly missing an error. If you do see an error, don't panic. Most error messages don't reflect a problem with the program itself, but usually with the system in some way or another. Typically, these messages are the result of inappropriate file permissions (see the **chmod** command in Module 6) or files that cannot be found. In the latter case, make sure your path has at the very least the **/bin**, **/sbin**, **/usr/bin**, **/usr/sbin**, **/usr/local/bin**, **/usr/local/sbin**, and **/usr/X11R6/bin** directories in it. You can see your path by issuing the following command:

```
[root@ford hello-1.3]# echo $PATH
```

See Module 6 for information on environment variables so that you can set your path correctly.

In general, slow down and read the error message. Even if the format is a little odd, it may explain what is wrong in plain English, thereby allowing you to quickly fix it. If the error is still confusing, look at the documentation that came with the package to see if there is a mailing list or e-mail address you can contact for help. Most developers are more than happy to provide help, but you need to remember to be nice and to the point. (In other words, don't start an e-mail with a rant about why their software is terrible.)

Installing the Package

As with the compile stage, the installation stage typically goes smoothly. In most cases, once the compile is done, all you need to run is

```
[root@ford hello-1.3]# make install
```

This will start the installation script (which is usually embedded in the makefile). Because **make** displays each command as it is executing it, you will see a lot of text fly by. Don't worry about it—it's perfectly normal. Unless you see an error message, the package is installed.

If you do see an error message, it is most likely because of permissions problems. Look at the last file it was trying to install before failure, and then go check on all the permissions required to place a file there. You may need to use the **chmod**, **chown**, and **chgrp** commands for this step; see Module 6 for additional details.

Testing the Software

A common mistake administrators make is to go through all of the process of configuring and compiling and then when they install they don't test out the software. Testing the software also needs be done as a regular user, if the software is to be used by non-root users. In our example, you run the **hello** command to verify the permissions are correct and users won't have problems running the program. You will quickly change users to make sure the software is usable by everyone. We'll cover the **su** command in Module 6.

```
[root@ford /]# su - sgraham
[sgraham@ford ]-> /usr/local/bin/hello

Hello, world!
[sgraham@ford ]-> exit
[root@ford /]#
```

Common Software Problems

The GNU **hello** program might not seem like a very useful tool, for the most part I will agree it is not. But one valuable thing it provides is the ability to test the compiler on your system. If you've just finished the task of upgrading your compiler, compiling this simple program will provide a sanity check that indeed the compiler is working.

One problem you might run into is when the program can't find a file of the type "libsomthing.so" and the program terminates because it can't find the file. This file is what is called a *library*. This is synonymous with DLLs in Windows. These libraries are stored in several locations on the Linux system and typically reside in **/usr/lib/** and **/usr/local/lib/**. If you have installed a software package in a different location than **/usr/local** you will have to configure your system or shell to know where to look for those new libraries.

NOTE

Linux libraries can be located anywhere in your file system. Typically Windows only allows you to store libraries in one location. You'll see that with the use of NFS you can share a directory (in our case, software from one server) and allow any client using that share to use the software residing on the share. With Windows, you're stuck installing the software on each and every machine.

There are two methods for configuring libraries on a Linux system. One is to modify **/etc/ld.conf**, add the path of your new libraries, and use the **ldconfig –m** command to load in the new directories. You can also use the LD_LIBRARY_PATH environment variable to hold a list of library directories to look for library files. Read the man page for **ld.conf** for more information.

Progress Check

1. What is the **README** file used for?

2. What three steps are used to compile a typical GNU software package?

Cleanup

Once the package is installed, you can do some cleanup to get rid of all the temporary files created during the installation. Since you have the original source code tarball, it is okay to simply get rid of the entire directory from which you compiled the source code. In the case of the **hello** program, you would get rid of **/usr/local/src/hello-1.3**. Begin by going one directory level above the directory you want to remove. In this case, that would be **/usr/local/src**.

---

1. The **README** file holds information on how to compile/install and use the software.

2. First **configure**, then **make**, and then **make install**.

```
[root@ford hello-1.3]# cd /usr/local/src
```

Now use the **rm** command to remove the actual directory, like so:

```
[root@ford src]# rm -rf hello-1.3
```

CAUTION

The **rm** command, especially with the **-rf** parameter, is very dangerous. It recursively removes an entire directory without stopping to verify any of the files. When run by the root user, this has the potential to really cause problems on your system. Be very careful and make sure you are erasing what you mean to erase. There is no "undelete" command. I repeat, there is no "undelete" command.

When There Is No configure Script

Sometimes you will download a package and instantly **cd** into a directory and run **./configure**. And you will probably be shocked when you see the message, "No such file or directory." As stated earlier in the module, read the **README** and **INSTALL** files in the distribution. Typically, the authors of the software are courteous enough to provide at least these two files. I don't know how many times I've tried compiling something without first looking at the docs and then come back hours later to find that I missed a step. The first step you take when installing software is to read the documentation. It will probably point out the fact that you need to run **imake** first, then run **make**. You get the idea: always read the documentation first, then proceed to compiling the software.

Project 4-1 Compiling and Installing a GNU Program

In this project, you will download a GNU software package, compile, and install it. I am a big **emacs** fan, so I am going to show how to download and compile it in this project. **emacs** most likely already comes standard on a Linux system, as it is a fairly popular editor. As an administrator, you will be exposed to many editors, such as **vi**, **pico**, and **emacs**. You are always guaranteed to have **vi** on the system. You don't have to install **emacs**, just pick a package that sounds interesting (stay away from **gcc**, though)

Step by Step

1. Change your directory to a scratch space that will allow you to compile (typically **/usr/local/src**).

```
[root@ford /root ]# cd /usr/local/src
```

(continued)

2. Go to the GNU FTP site and download **emacs**. The latest version as of this writing is **emacs-21.2**. The software is located at ftp://ftp.gnu.org/gnu/emacs/.

3. Untar the package.

```
[root@ford /usr/local/src ]# tar -xvzf emacs-21.2.tar.gz
```

4. **cd** into the package directory and read the documentation, notably **README** and **INSTALL**.

```
[root@ford /usr/local/src ]# cd emacs-21.2
[root@ford emacs-21.2]# more README
[root@ford emacs-21.2]# more INSTALL
```

5. Run the **configure** script with the standard options: **--prefix=/usr/local**.

```
[root@ford emacs-21.2]# ./configure --prefix=/usr/local
```

6. Run **make**.

```
[root@ford emacs-21.2]# make
```

7. If the **make** completed without any errors, type **make install**.

```
[root@ford emacs-21.2]# make install
```

8. Make sure that you can run the software as both root and a regular user.

```
[root@ford emacs-21.2]# cd /usr/local/bin
[root@ford bin]# ./emacs
[root@ford bin]# su - sgraham
[sgraham@ford ]->/usr/local/bin/emacs
[sgraham@ford ]->exit
[root@ford bin]#
```

9. Do any cleanup and have a fun time using the software.

```
[root@ford bin]# cd /usr/local/src/emacs-21.2
[root@ford bin]# make clean
```

Project Summary

You have now compiled and installed the **emacs** editor. I usually leave the source sitting around for a while, just in case I need to make some changes to the software. If you are running low on space you might want to do a **make clean** in the package directory to clear out any object files (**.o**) and other files needed for the compilation. Or you can simply delete the directory. Please note that **emacs** is a fairly big package to download and to compile. On a slow system it can take quite a while to compile. You now know how to download and compile software for your system. Luckily, most software is distributed in the GNU format where you just have to type ./**configure**, then **make**, then **make install** to compile and install the software.

✓

Module 4 Mastery Check

1. What is a **.gz** file?

2. What does the **tar** command do?

3. How do you configure a typical GNU software package?

4. What file tells **make** what to do?

5. What command would you issue to install the package **hello-1.3.i386.rpm**?

6. What command would you issue to see all the RPM packages installed on your system?

7. How would you verify all of the RPM packages on your system?

8. What two files should you always look for when installing software?

9. You have just gotten done installing some software by hand. As a regular user, you try running the command and it doesn't work the way you thought. What steps would you take in troubleshooting the problem?

10. How do you become the root user?

11. Name some advantages to using the RPM tool.

12. Name some disadvantages to using the RPM tool.

13. What does the **make** program do?

14. What does the command **make clean** do?

15. What command would you issue to install the software you just got done compiling?

Part II

Single-Host Administration

Module 5

Managing Users

Under Linux, every file and program must be owned by a *user*. Each user has a unique identifier called a *user ID (UID)*. Each user must also belong to at least one *group*, a collection of users established by the system administrator. Users may belong to multiple groups. Like users, groups also have unique identifiers called *group IDs (GIDs)*.

The accessibility of a file or program is based on its UIDs and GIDs. A running program inherits the rights and permissions of the user who invokes it. (SetUID and SetGID, discussed in "Understand SetUID and SetGID Programs" later in this module, create an exception to this rule.) Each user's rights can be defined in one of two ways: a *normal user* or the *root user*. Normal users can access only what they own or have been given permission to run; permission is granted because the user either belongs to the file's group or because the file is accessible to all users. The root user is allowed to access all files and programs in the system, whether or not root owns them. The root user is often called a *superuser*.

If you are accustomed to Windows, you can draw parallels between that system's user management and Linux's user management. Linux UIDs are comparable to Windows SIDs (system IDs), for example. In contrast to Windows NT, you may find the Linux security model maddeningly simplistic: either you're root or you're not. Normal users cannot have root privileges in the same way normal users can be granted administrator access under NT. You'll also notice the distinct absence of Access Control Lists (ACLs) in Linux. Which system is better? Depends on what you want and whom you ask.

In this module, we will examine the technique of managing users for a single host. Managing users over a network will be discussed in Module 19. Let's begin by exploring the actual database files that contain information about users. From there we'll examine the system tools available to manage the files automatically.

CRITICAL SKILL
5.1 Understand User Properties

In Linux, everything has an owner attached to it. Given this, it is impossible for a Linux system to exist without users! At the very least, it needs one root user; however, most Linux distributions ship with several special users set up. These users work well as self-documentation tools since each user owns all of the files related to his or her username—for example, the user www is set up to own all files related to World Wide Web service. These users are configured in such a way that grants access only to a select few, so you do not have to worry about their abuse.

TIP

When possible, run applications without root privileges. (The Apache server, for example, knows how to give up root privileges before it starts accepting connections.) The benefit of doing this is that if an application is found to have a security problem, it cannot be exploited to gain system privileges.

A few things need to be set up for a user's account to work correctly. In this section, we discuss those items and why they need to be there. The actual process of setting up accounts is discussed in "Utilize User Management Tools" later in the module.

Home Directories

Every user who actually logs in to the system needs a place for configuration files that are unique to the user. This place, called a *home directory*, allows each user to work in a customized environment without having to change the environment customized by another user—even if both users are logged in to the system at the same time. In this directory, users are allowed to keep not only their configuration files but their regular work files as well.

For the sake of consistency, most sites place home directories at **/home** and name each user's directory by their login name. Thus, if your login name were sshah, your home directory would be **/home/sshah**. The exception to this is for system accounts, such as a root user's account. Here, home directories are usually set to be either / or something specific to the need for that account (for example, the www account may want its home directory set to **/usr/local/apache** if the Apache Web server is installed). The home directory for root is traditionally / with most variants of UNIX. Many Linux installations use **/root**.

The decision to place home directories under **/home** is strictly arbitrary, but it does make organizational sense. The system really doesn't care where we place home directories so long as the location for each user is specified in the password file (discussed in "The /etc/passwd File" later in this module). You may see some sites use **/u** or break up the **/home** directory by department, thereby creating **/home/engineering**, **/home/accounting**, **/home/admin**, and so on, and then have users located under each department. (For example, Dr. Bosze from engineering would be **/home/engineering/bosze**.)

Passwords

Every account should either have a password or be tagged as impossible to log in to. This is crucial to your system's security—weak passwords are often the cause of a compromised system security.

The original philosophy behind passwords is actually quite interesting, especially since we still rely on a significant part of it today. The idea is simple: instead of relying on protected files to keep passwords a secret, the system would encrypt the password using an AT&T-developed (and National Security Agency–approved) algorithm called Data Encryption Standard (DES) and leave the encrypted value publicly viewable. What originally made this secure was that the encryption algorithm was computationally difficult to break. The best most folks could do is a brute force dictionary attack where automated systems would iterate through a large dictionary and rely on the nature of users to pick English words for their passwords. Many people tried to break DES itself, but since it was an open algorithm that anyone could study, it was made much more bulletproof before it was actually deployed.

When users entered their passwords at a login prompt, the password they entered would be encrypted. The encrypted value would then be compared against the user's password entry. If the two encrypted values matched, the user was allowed to enter the system. The actual algorithm for performing the encryption was computationally cheap enough that a single encryption wouldn't take too long. However, the tens of thousands of encryptions that would be needed for a dictionary attack would take prohibitively long. Along with the encrypted passwords, the password file could then also keep information about the user's home directory, UID, shell, real name, and so on without having to worry about system security being compromised if any application run by any user would be allowed to read it.

But then a problem occurred: Moore's Law on processor speed doubling every 18 months held true, and home computers were becoming fast enough that programs were able to perform a brute force dictionary attack within days rather than weeks or months. Dictionaries got bigger and the software got smarter. The nature of passwords needed to be reevaluated.

Shadow passwords were one solution. In the shadow password scheme, the encrypted password entries were removed from the password file and placed in a separate file called **shadow**. The regular password file would continue to be readable by all users on the system, and the actual encrypted password entries would be readable only by the root user. (The login prompt is run with root permissions.) Why not just make the regular password file readable by root only? Well, it isn't that simple. By having the password file open for so many years, the rest of the system software that grew up around it relied on the fact that the password file was always readable by all users. Changing this would simply cause software to fail.

Another solution has been to improve the algorithm used to perform the encryption of passwords. Some distributions of Linux have followed the path of the FreeBSD operating system and used the MD5 scheme. This has increased the complexity of being able to crack passwords, which, when used in conjunction with shadow passwords, works quite well. (Of course, this is assuming you make your users choose good passwords!)

TIP

Choosing good passwords is always a chore. Your users will inevitably ask, "What then, O Almighty System Administrator, makes a good password?" Here's your answer: a non-language word (not English, not Spanish, not German, not human-language word), preferably with mixed case, numbers, and punctuation—in other words, a string that looks like line noise. Well, this is all nice and wonderful, but if a password is too hard to remember, most people will quickly defeat its purpose by writing it down and keeping it in an easily viewed place. So better make it memorable! I prefer the technique of choosing a phrase and then picking the first letter of every word in the phrase. Thus, the phrase "coffee is VERY GOOD for you and me" becomes ciVG4yam. The phrase is memorable even if the resulting password isn't.

Shells

When users log in to the system, they expect an environment that can help them be productive. This first program that users encounter is called a *shell*. If you're used to the Windows side of the world, you might equate this to command.com, Program Manager, or Windows Explorer (not to be confused with Internet Explorer, which is a Web browser).

Under UNIX, most shells are text based. The shell we discuss in further detail in Module 6 is the default shell for the root user, the Bourne Again Shell, or BASH for short. Linux comes with several shells from which to choose—you can see most of them listed in the **/etc/shells** file. Deciding which shell is right for you is kind of like choosing a favorite beer—what's right for you isn't right for everyone, but, still, everyone tends to get defensive about his or her choice!

What makes UNIX so interesting is that you do not have to stick with the list of shells provided in **/etc/shells**. In the strictest of definitions, the password entry for each user doesn't list what shell to run so much as it lists what program to run first for the user. Of course, most users prefer that the first program run be a shell, such as BASH.

Startup Scripts

Under DOS, you are used to having the **autoexec.bat** and **config.sys** files run automatically when you start up the system. Since DOS is a single-user system, the two programs not only perform system functions such as loading device drivers, but they also set up your working environment.

UNIX, on the other hand, is a multiuser environment. Each user is allowed to have their own configuration files; thus, the system appears to be customized for each particular user, even if other people are logged in at the same time. The configuration file comes in the form of *shell script*—a series of commands executed by the shell that starts when a user logs in. In the case of BASH, it's the file **.bashrc**. (Yes, there is a period in front of the filename—filenames preceded by periods, also called *dot files*, are hidden from normal directory listings unless the user uses a special option to list them.) You can think of shell scripts in the same light as batch files, except shell scripts can be much more capable. The **.bashrc** script in particular is similar in nature to that of **autoexec.bat**.

Most Linux/Unix software likes to store information in directories or files that begin with a **.** in your home directory. Some examples are **.netscape** and **.kde**. Also, there are several files that contain customizable options for some of your favorite applications:

- **.emacs**   The configuration file for **emacs**; venture into this when you would like to start learning Lisp.

- **.bashrc/.profile**   Configuration files for BASH.

- **.tcshrc/.login**   Configuration files for tcsh.

- **.xinitrc**   This script overrides the default script that gets called when you log in to the X Window System.

- **.Xdefaults**   This file contains defaults that you can specify for X Window System applications.

To see all of the files in your home directory, simply type **ls -al**.

When you create a user's account, you should provide a default set of dot files to get the user started. If you use the tools that come with Linux, you don't need to worry about creating these files—the tools automatically do this for you. However, there is nothing stopping you from customizing these files to make them site specific. For example, if you have a special application that requires an environment variable to be set, you can add that to the dot files that are copied to the new user's home directories.

Mail

Creating a new user means not only creating the user's home directory and setting up the environment, it also means making it possible for the user to send and receive e-mail. Setting up a mailbox under Linux is quite easy, and if you use the tools that come with Linux to create the account, you don't even have to do this yourself!

Mailboxes are kept in the **/var/spool/mail** directory. Each user has a mailbox that is based on their login name. Thus, if a user's login is jyom, their mailbox will be **/var/spool/mail/jyom**. All mailboxes should be owned by their respective owners with the permissions set so that others cannot read its contents. (See the **chown**, **chmod**, and **chgrp** commands in Module 6 for details on how to do this.)

An empty mailbox is a zero-length file. To create a zero-length file anywhere in the system, you simply use the **touch** command, like so:

```
[root@ford /root]# touch myfile
```

This will create a new file called **myfile** in the current directory.

CRITICAL SKILL
5.2 # Understand the User Databases

If you're already used to Windows 2000 user management, you're familiar with the Active Directory tool that takes care of the nitty-gritty details of the user database. This tool is convenient, but it makes developing your own administrative tools trickier, since the only other way to read or manipulate user information is through a series of LDAP calls.

In contrast, Linux takes the path of traditional UNIX and keeps all user information in straight text files. This is beneficial for the simple reason that it allows you to make changes to user information without the need of any other tool but a text editor such as **pico**. In many instances, larger sites take advantage of these text files by developing their own user administration tools so that they can not only create new accounts but also automatically make additions to the corporate phone book, Web pages, and so on.

However, users and groups working with UNIX style for the first time may prefer to stick with the basic user management tools that come with the Linux distribution. We'll discuss those tools in "Utilize User Management Tools" later in this module. For now, let's examine how Linux's text files are structured.

The /etc/passwd File

The **/etc/passwd** file stores the user's login, encrypted password entry, UID, default GID, name (sometimes called GECOS), home directory, and login shell. The file keeps one user per line, and each entry for the user is delimited by a colon. For example:

```
sshah:boQavhhaCKaXg:100:102:Steve Shah:/home/sshah:/bin/tcsh
```

NOTE

Although modern distributions of Linux allow for logins to be longer than eight characters, it is generally considered a bad idea to do so. This is because some tools don't work quite right with longer logins, and some versions of UNIX get quite finicky with them.

Earlier in this module, we discussed the details of the password entry. In the code listing above, you can actually see what a DES-encrypted password looks like (the information following the first column). Many sites disable accounts by altering the encrypted password entry so that when the disabled account's user enters their password, it won't match the value in the password file. The guaranteed method of altering passwords for this reason is to insert an asterisk (*) into the entry. The above entry, for example, could be altered to **boQavhhaCKaXg***.

TIP

When disabling accounts in this manner, you may find it helpful not only to add an asterisk character, but also to add a string to indicate why the account was disabled in the first place. For example, if you catch a user downloading pirated software, you could disable his account by changing the encrypted entry to **boQavhhaCKaXg*caught pirating**.

The UID must be unique for every user, with the exception of the UID 0 (zero). Any user who has a UID of 0 has root (administrative) access and thus has full run of the system. Usually, the only user who has this specific UID has the login root. It is considered bad practice to allow any other users or usernames to have a UID of 0. This is notably different from the Windows NT and 2000 models, in which any number of users can have administrative privileges.

NOTE

Some distributions of Linux reserve the UID -1 (or 65535) for the user nobody.

The user's name can be any freeform text entry. Although it is possible for nonprintable characters to exist in this string, it is considered bad practice to use them. Also, the user's name may not span multiple lines.

NOTE

Although the entire line for a user's password entry may not span multiple lines, it may be longer than 80 characters.

The user's home directory appears as discussed earlier in this module. Ditto for the last entry, the user's shell. A complete password file for a system, then, might look like this:

```
root:AgQ/IJgASeW1M:0:0:root:/root:/bin/bash
bin:*:1:1:bin:/bin:
daemon:*:2:2:daemon:/sbin:
adm:*:3:4:adm:/var/adm:
lp:*:4:7:lp:/var/spool/lpd:
sync:*:5:0:sync:/sbin:/bin/sync
shutdown:*:6:0:shutdown:/sbin:/sbin/shutdown
halt:*:7:0:halt:/sbin:/sbin/halt
mail:*:8:12:mail:/var/spool/mail:
news:*:9:13:news:/var/spool/news:
uucp:*:10:14:uucp:/var/spool/uucp:
operator:*:11:0:operator:/root:
games:*:12:100:games:/usr/games:
gopher:*:13:30:gopher:/usr/lib/gopher-data:
ftp:*:14:50:FTP User:/home/ftp:
pop:*:15:15:APOP Admin:/tmp:/bin/tcsh
nobody:*:99:99:Nobody:/:
sshah:Kss9Ere9b1Ejs:500:500:Steve Shah:/home/sshah:/bin/tcsh
hdc:bfCAblvZBIbFM:501:501:H. D. Core:/home/hdc:/bin/bash
jyom:*:502:502:Mr. Yom:/home/jyom:/bin/bash
```

The /etc/shadow File

The speed of home computers began making dictionary attacks against password lists easier for hackers to accomplish. This led to the separation of the encrypted passwords from the **/etc/passwd** file. The **/etc/passwd** file would remain readable by all users, but the passwords kept in the **/etc/shadow** file would be readable only by those programs with root privileges, such as the login program.

In addition to the encrypted password field, the **/etc/shadow** file contains information about password expiration and whether the account is disabled. The format of each line in the **/etc/shadow** file contains the following:

- Login name

- Encrypted password

- Days since January 1, 1970, that the password has been changed

- Days before the password may be changed

- Days after which the password must be changed

- Days before the password is about to expire that the user is warned

- Days after the password is expired that the account is disabled

- Days since January 1, 1970, that the account has been disabled

- Reserved field

Each user has a one-line entry with a colon delimiter. Here's an example:

```
sshah:boQavhhaCKaXg:10750:0:99999:7:-1:-1:134529868
```

Entries with a **-1** imply infinity. In the case where a **-1** appears in the field indicating the number of days before a password expires, you are effectively tagging a user as never having to change their password.

The /etc/group File

As you know, each user belongs to at least one group, that being their default group. Users may then be assigned to additional groups if needed. The **/etc/passwd** file contains each user's default GID. This GID is mapped to the group's name and other members of the group in the **/etc/group** file. The format of each line in the **/etc/group** file is

- Group name

- Encrypted password for the group

- GID number

- Comma-separated list of member users

Again, each field is separated by a colon. An entry looks similar to this:

```
project:baHrElKPNjrPE:102:sshah,hdc
```

Also like the **/etc/passwd** file, the group file must be world-readable so that applications can test for associations between users and groups. Group names should not exceed eight characters, and the GID should be unique for each group. Finally, the comma-separated list of users is used only for users for whom particular groups are not their default group.

If you want to include a group that does not have a password, you can set the entry like this:

```
project:baHrE1KPNjrPE:102:sshah,hdc
```

If you want a group to exist, but you don't want to allow anyone to change their working group to this group (good for applications that need their own group but no valid reason exists for a user to be working inside that group), use an asterisk in the password field. For example:

```
project:*:102:
```

Progress Check

1. What file does BASH use to read a user's settings?

2. Is the password stored in clear text in **/etc/passwd**?

CRITICAL SKILL
5.3 Utilize User Management Tools

The wonderful part about having password database files that have a well-defined format in straight text is that it is easy for anyone to be able to write their own management tools. Indeed, many site administrators have already done this in order to integrate their tools along with the rest of their organization's infrastructure. They can start a new user from the same form that lets them update the corporate phone and e-mail directory, LDAP servers, Web pages, and so on. Of course, not everyone wants to write their own tools, which is why Linux comes with several prewritten tools that do the job for you.

In this section, we discuss user management tools that work from both the command-line interface and the graphical user interface (GUI). Of course, learning how to use both is the preferred route, for you never know under what circumstances you may one day find yourself adding users.

---

1. **~/.bashrc**

2. No, it is stored encrypted in either DES or MD5.

5

Managing Users

Command-Line User Management

You can choose from among six command-line tools to perform the same actions performed by the GUI tool: **useradd**, **userdel**, **usermod**, **groupadd**, **groupdel**, and **groupmod**. The obvious advantage to using the GUI tool is ease of use. However, the disadvantage is that actions that can be performed with it cannot be automated. This is where the command-line tools become very handy.

NOTE

Linux distributions other than Red Hat may have slightly different parameters than the tools used here. To see how your particular installation is different, read the man page for the particular program in question.

useradd

As the name implies, **useradd** allows you to add a single user to the system. Unlike the GUI tool, there are no interactive prompts. Instead, all parameters must be specified on the command line. Here's how you use this tool:

```
useradd [-c comment] [-d homedir] [-e expire date] [-f inactive time]
[-g initial group][-G group[,...]] [-m [-k skeleton dir]] [-M]
[-s shell] [-u uid [-o]] [-n] [-r] login
```

Don't be intimidated by this long list of options! We'll examine them one at a time and discuss their relevance.

Before you dive into these options, take note that anything in the square brackets is optional. Thus, to add a new user with the login sshah, you could issue a command as simple as this:

```
[root@ford /root]# useradd sshah
```

Default values are used for any unspecified values. (To see the default values, simply run **useradd -D**; we will discuss how to change the defaults shortly.) Table 5-1 shows the command options and their descriptions.

Option	Description
-c comment	Allows you to set the user's name in the GECOS field. As with any command-line parameter, if the value includes a space, you will need to put quotes around the text. For example, to set the user's name to Steve Shah, you would have to specify -c "Steve Shah".

Table 5-1 **useradd** Command-Line Options

Option	Description
-d `homedir`	By default, the user's home directory is **/home/***login* (for example, if my login is sshah, my home directory would be **/home/sshah**). When creating a new user, the user's home directory gets created along with the user account. So if you want to change the default to another place, you can specify the new location with this parameter—for example, **-d** `/home/sysadmin/sshah`.
-e `expire-date`	It is possible for an account to expire after a certain date. By default, accounts never expire. To specify a date, be sure to place it in *YYYY MM DD* format. For example, use **-e** `2002 10 28` to expire on October 28, 2002.
-f `inactive-time`	This option specifies the number of days after a password expires that the account is still usable. A value of **0** (zero) indicates that the account is disabled immediately. A value of **-1** will never allow the account to be disabled, even if the password has expired (for example, **-f** `3` will allow an account to exist for three days after a password has expired). The default value is **-1**.
-g `initial-group`	Using this option, you can specify the default group the user has in the password file. You can use a number or name of the group; however, if you use a name of a group, the group must exist in the **/etc/group** file—for example, **-g** `project`.
-G `group[,...]`	This option allows you to specify additional groups to which the new user will belong. If you use the **-G** option, you must specify at least one additional group. You can, however, specify additional groups by separating the list with a comma. For example, to add a user to the project and admin groups, you should specify **-G** `project,admin`.
-m `[-k skel-dir]`	By default, the system automatically creates the user's home directory. This option is the explicit command to create the user's home directory. Part of creating the directory is copying default configuration files into it. These files come from the **/etc/skel** directory by default. You can change this by using the secondary option **-k** `skel dir`. (You must specify **-m** in order to use **-k**.) For example, to specify the **/etc/adminskel** directory, you would use **-m -k** `/etc/adminskel`.
-M	If you used the **-m** option, you cannot use **-M**, and vice versa. This option tells the command *not* to create the user's home directory.
-n	Red Hat Linux creates a new group with the same name as the new user's login as part of the process of adding a user. You can disable this behavior by using this option.

Table 5-1 `useradd` Command-Line Options *(continued)*

Option	Description
`-s shell`	A user's login shell is the first program that runs when a user logs in to a system. This is usually a command-line environment, unless you are logging in from the X Window System login screen. By default, this is the Bourne Again Shell (**/bin/bash**), though some folks like other shells such as the Turbo C Shell (**/bin/tcsh**). This option lets you choose whichever shell you would like to run for the new user upon login. (A list of shells is available in **/etc/shells**.)
`-u uid`	By default, the program will automatically find the next available UID and use it. If for some reason you need to force a new user's UID to be a particular value, you can use this option. Remember that UIDs must be unique for all users.
`Login`	Finally, the only parameter that *isn't* optional! You must specify the new user's login name.

Table 5-1 `useradd` Command-Line Options *(continued)*

For example, to create a new user whose name is H.D. Core, who is a member of the admin and support groups (default group admin), and who prefers using the Turbo C Shell and wants the login name hdc, you would use this line:

```
[root@ford /root]# useradd -c "H. D. Core" -g admin -G support -s /bin/tcsh hdc
```

userdel

userdel does the exact opposite of **useradd**—it removes existing users. This straightforward command has only one optional parameter and one required parameter:

```
userdel [-r] username
```

By running the command with only the user's login specified on the command line, for example, **userdel sshah**, all of the entries in the **/etc/passwd** and **/etc/shadow** files, and references in the **/etc/group** file, are automatically removed. By using the optional parameter (for example, **userdel -r sshah**) all of the files owned by the user in their home directory are removed as well.

usermod

usermod allows you to modify an existing user in the system. It works in much the same way as **useradd**. The exact command-line usage is as follows:

```
usermod [-c comment] [-d homedir] [-m] [-e expire date]
[-f inactive time] [-g initial group]
[-G group[,...]] [-l login] [-s shell]
[-u uid] login
```

Every option you specify when using this command results in that particular parameter being changed about the user. All but one of the parameters listed here are identical to the parameters documented for the **useradd** program. That one option is **-l**.

The **-l** option allows you to change the user's login name. This and the **-u** option are the only options that require special care. Before changing the user's login or UID, you must make sure the user is not logged in to the system or running any processes. Changing this information if the user is logged in or running processes will cause unpredictable results.

Here's an example of using **usermod** to change user hdc so that their comment field reads H.D. Core instead of H.D.C:

```
[root@ford /root]# usermod -c "H.D. Core" hdc
```

groupadd

The group commands are similar to the user commands; however, instead of working on individual users, they work on groups listed in the **/etc/group** file. Note that changing group information does not cause user information to be automatically changed. For example, if you remove a group whose GID is 100 and a user's default group is specified as 100, the user's default group would not be updated to reflect the fact that the group no longer exists.

The **groupadd** command adds groups to the **/etc/group** file. The command-line options for this program are as follows:

```
groupadd [-g gid] [-r] [-f] group
```

Table 5-2 shows command options and their descriptions.

Option	Description
-g gid	Specifies the GID for the new group as *gid*. By default, this value is automatically chosen by finding the first available value.
-r	By default, Red Hat searches for the first GID that is higher than 499. The **-r** options tell **groupadd** that the group being added is a system group and should have the first available GID under 499.
-f	When adding a new group, Red Hat Linux will exit without an error if the specified group to add already exists. By using this option, the program will not change the group setting before exiting. This is useful in scripting cases where you want the script to continue if the group already exists.
group	This option is required. It specifies the name of the group you want to add to be *group*.

Table 5-2 **groupadd** Commands and Options

Suppose, for example, that you want to add a new group called research with the GID 800. To do so, you would type the following command:

```
[root@ford /root]# groupadd -g 800 research
```

groupdel

Even more straightforward than **userdel**, the **groupdel** command removes existing groups specified in the **/etc/group** file. The only usage information needed for this command is

```
groupdel group
```

where *group* is the name of the group to remove. For example, if you wanted to remove the research group, you would issue this command:

```
[root@ford /root]# groupdel research
```

groupmod

The **groupmod** command allows you to modify the parameters of an existing group. The options for this command are

```
groupmod -g gid -n group-name group
```

where the **-g** option allows you to change the GID of the group, and the **-n** option allows you to specify a new name of a group. Additionally, of course, you need to specify the name of the existing group as the last parameter.

For example, if the superman research group wanted to change its name to batman, you would issue the following command:

```
[root@ford /root]# groupmod -n batman superman
```

GUI User Managers

Many of the Linux distributions come with their own GUI user managers. Red Hat comes with a utility called **redhat-config-users** that allows you to add/edit and maintain the users on your system. You can also find **linuxconf** from http://www.solucorp.qc.ca/linuxconf/. It has been my experience that these GUI interfaces work just fine—just be prepared to have to manually change user settings in case the GUI isn't working. Most of these interfaces can be found in the **System Settings** menu under GNOME or KDE.

Project 5-1 Adding/Editing a User

In this project, you will add a user to the system and make sure the user can log in to the system without any problems. When dealing with accounts it is always a good idea to do it right the first time, otherwise you might get the user frustrated because their shell isn't right or their e-mail isn't set up correctly. You will use the following steps to add the user and then change their shell to the **tcsh** shell.

Step by Step

1. First, add the user johndoe to the system with the **adduser** command:

```
[root@ford /root]# useradd -c "John Doe" -g admin -G support johndoe
```

2. Make sure to change the user's password by running the **passwd** program:

```
[root@ford /root]# passwd johndoe
```

3. Try to log in to the system as that user. This will let you know if everything is working correctly for the new user.

4. After getting their new account, the user decides they want **/bin/tcsh** as their shell. You just need to use the **usermod** command to change johndoe's properties:

```
[root@ford /root]# usermod -s /bin/tcsh johndoe
```

Project Summary

This project is simple and straightforward. If you are running your own computer, it is easy to keep all the users on your system in order. When you start having to administer many users, it is helpful to write a script to add many users at a time. There are endless possible customizations that you can make.

CRITICAL SKILL
5.4 Understand SetUID and SetGID Programs

Normally, when a program is run by a user, it inherits all of the rights (or lack thereof) that the user has. If the user can't read the **/var/log/messages** file, neither can the program. Note that this permission can be different than the permissions of the user who owns the program file (usually called *the binary*). For example, the **ls** program (which is used to generate directory listings) is owned by the root user. Its permissions are set so that all users of the system can run the program. Thus, if the user sshah runs **ls**, that instance of **ls** is bound by the permissions granted to the user sshah, not root.

However, there is an exception. Programs can be tagged with what's called a *SetUID bit,* which allows a program to be run with permissions from the program's owner, not the user who is running it. Using **ls** as an example again, setting the SetUID bit on it and having the file owned by root means that if the user sshah runs **ls**, that instance of **ls** will run with root permissions, not with sshah's permissions. The *SetGID bit* works the same way, except instead of applying the file's owner, it is applied to the file's group setting.

To enable the SetUID bit or the SetGID bit, you need to use the **chmod** command, which is covered in detail in Module 6. To make a program SetUID, prefix whatever permission value you are about to assign it with a 4. To make a program SetGID, prefix whatever permission you are about to assign it with a 2. For example, to make the **/bin/ls** a SetUID program (which is a bad idea, by the way), you would use this command:

```
[root@ford /root]# chmod 4755 /bin/ls
```

✓ Module 5 Mastery Check

1. What information is stored in the **/etc/passwd** file?

2. What information is stored in the **/etc/shadow** file?

3. Does Linux use the username or the UID when performing operations pertaining to that user (such as file permissions)?

4. Why can SetUID programs be a bad thing?

5. What is the format of a user entry in the **/etc/passwd** file?

6. What is the GECOS entry?

7. How do you disable a user so they cannot access the system?

8. What information is stored in the **/etc/group** file?

9. What is the format of an entry in the **/etc/group** file?

10. What happens if you forget to add the home directory for a user?

11. Where is the list of available shells listed?

12. What are startup scripts?

Module 6

The Command Line

O ver time, it's been UNIX's command-line options that have given the system its power and flexibility. Casual observers of UNIX gurus are often astounded at the results of a few carefully entered commands. Unfortunately, this power makes UNIX less intuitive to the average user. For this reason, graphical user interfaces (GUIs) have become the de facto standard for many UNIX tools.

More experienced users, however, find that it is difficult for a GUI to present all of the available options. Typically, doing so would make the interface just as complicated as the command-line equivalent. The GUI design is often oversimplified, and experienced users ultimately return to the comprehensive capabilities of the command line.

Before we begin our study of the command-line interface under Linux, understand that this module is far from an exhaustive resource. Rather than trying to cover all the tools without any depth, we have chosen to describe thoroughly a handful of tools we believe to be most critical for day-to-day work.

NOTE

For this module, we assume that you are logged in as root user and have started the X Window System environment. If you are using the GNOME environment (which is the default behavior of the latest versions of Red Hat Linux) you can start an "X terminal." Click the GNOME footprint in the lower-left corner of your screen, select Utilities, and then select Color Xterm. All of the commands you enter in this module should be typed into the window that appears after Color Xterm is selected.

CRITICAL SKILL
6.1 Use the BASH Shell

In Module 5, you learned that one of the parameters for a user's password entry is their *login shell,* which is the first program that runs when a user logs in to a workstation. The shell is comparable to the Windows Program Manager, except that the shell program used, of course, is arbitrary.

A *shell* is simply a program that provides an interface to the system. The Bourne Again Shell (BASH) in particular is a command-line–only interface containing a handful of built-in commands, the ability to launch other programs, and the ability to control programs that have been launched from it (job control). It might seem simple at first, but you will begin to realize that the shell is a very powerful tool.

A variety of shells exist, most with similar features but different means of implementing them. Again for the purpose of comparison, you can think of the various shells as Web browsers; among several different browsers, the basic functionality is the same—displaying content from the Web. In any situation like this, everyone proclaims that their shell is better than the others, but it all really comes down to personal preference.

In this section, we'll examine some of BASH's built-in commands. A complete reference on BASH could easily be a book in itself, so we'll stick with the commands that most affect the daily operations of a systems administrator. However, I do recommend that you eventually study BASH's operations. There's no shortage of excellent books on the topic. As you get accustomed to BASH, you can easily pick up other shells. My personal favorite is **/bin/tcsh**. If you are managing a large site with lots of users, it will be advantageous for you to learn many shells. It is actually fairly easy to pick up another shell, as the differences between them are subtle.

Job Control

When working in the BASH environment, you can start multiple programs from the same prompt. Each program is a *job*. Whenever a job is started, it takes over the *terminal*. (This is a throwback to the days when actual dumb terminals such as VT-100s and Wyse-50s were used to interface with the machine.) On today's machines, the terminal is either the straight-text interface you see when you boot the machine or the window created by the X Window System on which BASH runs. (The terminal interfaces in X Window System are called a pseudo tty, or pty for short.) If a job has control of the terminal, it can issue control codes so that text-only interfaces (the **pine** mail reader, for instance) can be made more attractive. Once the program is done, it gives full control back to BASH, and a prompt is redisplayed for the user.

Not all programs require this kind of terminal control, however. Some, including programs that interface with the user through the X Window System, can be instructed to give up terminal control and allow BASH to present a user prompt, even though the invoked program is still running. In the following example, Netscape Navigator receives such an instruction, represented by the ampersand suffix:

```
[root@ford /root]# netscape &
```

Immediately after you press ENTER, BASH will present a prompt. This is called *backgrounding* the task. Folks who remember Windows NT prior to version 4 will remember having to do something similar with the Start command.

If a program is already running and has control of the terminal, you can make the program give up control by pressing CTRL-Z in the terminal window. This will stop the running job altogether and return control to BASH so that you can enter new commands.

At any given time, you can find out how many jobs BASH is tracking by typing this command:

```
[root@ford /root]# jobs
```

The running programs that are listed will be in one of two states: running or stopped. If a job is stopped, you can start it running in the background, thereby allowing you to keep control of the terminal. Or a stopped job can run in the foreground, which gives control of the terminal back to that program.

To run a job in the background, type

```
[root@ford]# bg number
```

where **number** is the job number you want to background. To run a job in the foreground, type

```
[root@ford]# fg number
```

where **number** is the job number you want in the foreground.

NOTE

You can background any process if you want to. Applications that require terminal input or output will be put into a stopped state if you background them.

Environment Variables

Every instance of a shell, and process for that matter, that is running has its own "environment"— settings that give it a particular look, feel, and, in some cases, behavior. These settings are typically controlled by *environment variables*. Some environment variables have special meanings to the shell, but there is nothing stopping you from defining your own and using them for your own needs. It is with the use of environment variables that most shell scripts are able to do interesting things and remember results from user inputs as well as programs' outputs. If you are already familiar with the concept of environment variables in Windows NT/2000, you'll find that many of the things that you know about them will apply to Linux as well; the only difference is how they are set, viewed, and removed.

Printing Environment Variables

To list all of your environment variables, use the **printenv** command. For example:

```
[root@ford /root]# printenv
```

To show a specific environment variable, specify the variable as a parameter to **printenv**. For example, here is the command to see the environment variable OSTYPE:

```
[root@ford /root]# printenv OSTYPE
```

Setting Environment Variables

To set an environment variable, use the following format:

```
[root@ford /root]# variable=value
```

where *variable* is the variable name, and *value* is the value you want to assign the variable. For example, here is the command to set the environment variable FOO with the value BAR:

```
[root@ford /root]# FOO=BAR
```

Whenever you set environment variables this way, they stay local to the running shell. Once you want that value to be passed to other processes that you launch, use the **export** built-in. The format of the **export** command is as follows:

```
[root@ford /root]# export variable
```

where *variable* is the name of the variable. In the example of setting FOO, you would enter this command:

```
[root@ford /root]# export FOO
```

TIP

You can combine the steps for setting an environment variable with the export command, like so: `[root@ford /root]# export FOO=BAR`

If the value of the environment variable you want to set has spaces in it, surround the variable with quotation marks. Using the above example, to set FOO to "Welcome to the BAR of FOO.", you would enter

```
[root@ford /root]# export FOO="Welcome to the BAR of FOO."
```

Unsetting Environment Variables

To remove an environment variable, use the **unset** command:

```
[root@ford /root]# unset variable
```

where *variable* is the name of the variable you want to remove. For example, here is the command to remove the environment variable FOO:

```
[root@ford]# unset FOO
```

NOTE

This section assumed that you are using BASH. There are many other shells to choose from; the most popular alternatives are C Shell (csh) and its brother Tenex C Shell (tcsh), which use different mechanisms for getting and setting environment variables. We document BASH here since it is the default shell of all new Linux accounts.

Progress Check

1. What is an environment variable?

2. How do you set an environment variable?

3. How do you show the list of running jobs in the shell?

Pipes

Pipes are a mechanism by which the output of one program can be sent as the input to another program. Individual programs can be chained together to become extremely powerful tools.

Let's use the **grep** program to provide a simple example of pipes usage. The **grep** utility, given a stream of input, will try to match the line with the parameter supplied to it and display only matching lines. For example, if you were looking for all environment variables containing the string "OSTYPE," you could enter this command:

```
[root@ford /root]# printenv | grep "OSTYPE"
```

The vertical bar (|) character represents the pipe between **printenv** and **grep**.

The command shell under Windows also utilizes the pipe function. The primary difference is that all commands in a Linux pipe are executed concurrently, whereas Windows runs each program in order, using temporary files to hold intermediate results.

Redirection

Through *redirection,* you can take the output of a program and have it automatically sent to a file. The shell rather than the program itself handles this process, thereby providing a standard mechanism for performing the task. (Using redirection is much easier than having to remember how to do this for every single program!)

Redirection comes in three classes: output to a file, append to a file, and send a file as input.

To collect the output of a program into a file, end the command line with the greater than symbol (>) and the name of the file to which you want the output redirected. If you are redirecting to an existing file and you want to append additional data to it, use two > symbols (>>) followed by the filename. For example, here is the command to collect the output of a directory listing into a file called **/tmp/directory_listing**:

```
[root@ford /root]# ls > /tmp/directory_listing
```

---

1. An environment variable is a globally available variable that belongs to the current running process.

2. **EXPORT VARIABLE='value'**

3. Use the **jobs** command.

Continuing this example with the directory listing, you could append the string "Directory Listing" to the end of the **/tmp/directory_listing** file by typing this command:

```
[root@ford /root]# echo "Directory Listing" >> /tmp/directory_listing
```

The third class of redirection, using a file as input, is done by using the less than sign (<) followed by the name of the file. For example, here is the command to feed the **/etc/passwd** file into the **grep** program:

```
[root@ford /root]# grep 'root' < /etc/passwd
```

Command-Line Shortcuts

One of the difficulties in moving to a command-line interface, especially from command-line tools such as command.com, is working with a shell that has a good number of shortcuts. These refinements may surprise you if you're not careful. This section explains the most common of the BASH shortcuts and their behaviors.

Filename Expansion

Under UNIX-based shells such as BASH, wildcards on the command line are expanded *before* being passed as a parameter to the application. This is in sharp contrast to the default mode of operation for DOS-based tools, which often have to perform their own wildcard expansion. The UNIX method also means that you must be careful where you use the wildcard characters.

The wildcard characters themselves in BASH are identical to those in command.com: the asterisk (*) matches against all filenames, and the question mark (?) matches against single characters. If you need to use these characters as part of another parameter for whatever reason, you can *escape* them by preceding them with a backslash (\ ) character. This causes the shell to interpret the asterisk and question mark as regular characters instead of wildcards.

NOTE

Most UNIX documentation refers to wildcards as regular expressions. The distinction is important since regular expressions are substantially more powerful than just wildcards alone. All of the shells that come with Linux support regular expressions. You can read more about them in either the shell's manual page or in the book *Mastering Regular Expressions*, 2nd Edition, by Jeffrey E. F. Friedl (O'Reilly & Associates, 2002).

Environment Variables as Parameters

Under BASH, you can use environment variables as parameters on the command line. (Although command.com does this as well, it's not a common practice and thus is an often forgotten convention.) For example, issuing the parameter **$FOO** will cause the value of the FOO environment variable to be passed rather than the string "$FOO".

Multiple Commands

Under BASH, multiple commands can be executed on the same line by separating the commands with semicolons (;). For example, to execute this sequence of commands on a single line

```
[root@ford /root]# ls -l
[root@ford /root]# cat /etc/passwd
```

you could instead type the following:

```
[root@ford /root]# ls -l ;cat /etc/passwd
```

Since the shell is also a programming language, you can run commands serially only if the first command succeeds:

```
[root@ford /root]# make && make install
```

The previous command will run the **make** command and only run **make install** if the first command succeeds.

Finding Help

There are two help systems available under Linux—one is the *man page system* and the other is the *texinfo*, or *info system*. Both are fairly similar in usage, but info has a little more usability because it has the ability to hyperlink to other documents and sections of the current document. Using man is simple; just type **man** and then the filename or subject you need help on:

```
[root@ford /root]# man man
```

If you want to read help pages for **emacs**, issue the following command:

```
[root@ford /root]# man emacs
```

You will see references throughout this book referring you to look at the man pages, which you can do by using the **man** command.

CRITICAL SKILL
6.2 Understand File Listings,
Ownerships, and Permissions

Managing files under Linux is different than managing files under Windows NT/2000, and radically different from managing files under Windows 95/98. In this section, we discuss basic file management tools for Linux. We'll start with specifics on some useful general-purpose commands, and then step back and look at some background information.

Listing Files: ls

The `ls` command is used to list all the files in a directory. Of more than 26 available options, the ones listed here are the most commonly used. The options can be used in any combination.

Option for `ls`	Description
-1	Long listing. In addition to the filename, shows the file size, date/time, permissions, ownership, and group information.
-a	All files. Shows all files in the directory, including hidden files. Names of hidden files begin with a period.
-t	Lists in order of last modified time.
-r	Reverses the listing.
-1	Single column listing.
-R	Recursively lists all files and subdirectories.

To list all files in a directory with a long listing, type this command:

```
[root@ford /root]# ls -la
```

To list a directory's non-hidden files that start with *A*, type this:

```
[root@ford /root]# ls A*
```

File and Directory Types

Under Linux (and UNIX in general), almost everything is abstracted to a file. Originally this was done to simplify the programmer's job. Instead of having to communicate directly with device drivers, special files (which look like ordinary files to the application) are used as a bridge. Several types of files accommodate all these file uses.

Normal Files

Normal files are just that—normal. They contain data or executables, and the operating system makes no assumptions about their contents.

Directories

Directory files are a special instance of normal files. Directory files list the location of other files, some of which may be other directories. (This is similar to folders in Windows.) In general, the contents of directory files won't be of importance to your daily operations, unless you need to open and read the file yourself rather than using existing applications to navigate directories. (This would be similar to trying to read the DOS File Allocation Table directly rather than using command.com to navigate directories, or using the findfirst/findnext system calls.)

Hard Links

Each file in the Linux file system gets its own *i-node*. An i-node keeps track of a file's attributes and its location on the disk. If you need to be able to refer to a single file using two separate filenames, you can create a *hard link*. The hard link will have the same i-node as the original file and will therefore look and behave just like the original. With every hard link that is created, a *reference count* is incremented. When a hard link is removed, the reference count is decremented. Until the reference count reaches zero, the file will remain on disk.

NOTE

A hard link cannot exist between two files on separate partitions. This is because the hard link refers to the original file by i-node, and a file's i-node may differ among file systems.

Symbolic Links

Unlike hard links, which point to a file by its i-node, a *symbolic link* points to another file by its name. This allows symbolic links (often abbreviated *symlinks*) to point to files located on other partitions, even other network drives.

Block Devices

Since all device drivers are accessed through the file system, files of type *block device* are used to interface with devices such as disks. A block device file has three identifying traits:

- It has a major number.

- It has a minor number.

- When viewed using the **ls -l** command, it shows **b** as the first character of the permissions.

For example:

```
[root@ford /root]# ls -l /dev/hda
brw-rw----   1 root       disk        3,    0 May  5  1998 /dev/hda
```

Note the **b** at the beginning of the file's permissions; the **3** is the major number, and the **0** is the minor number.

A block device file's major number identifies the represented device driver. When this file is accessed, the minor number is passed to the device driver as a parameter telling it which device it is accessing. For example, if there are two serial ports, they will share the same device driver and thus the same major number, but each serial port will have a unique minor number.

Character Devices

Similar to block devices, character devices are special files that allow you to access devices through the file system. The obvious difference between block and character devices is that block devices communicate with the actual devices in large blocks, whereas character devices work one character at a time. (A hard disk is a block device; a modem is a character device.) Character device permissions start with a **c**, and the file has a major and a minor number. For example:

```
[root@ford /root]# ls -l /dev/ttyS0
crw-------   1 root       tty         4,   64 May  5  1998 /dev/ttyS0
```

Named Pipes

Named pipes are a special type of file that allows for interprocess communication. Using the **mknod** command (discussed later in this module), you can create a named pipe file that one process can open for reading and another process can open for writing, thus allowing the two to communicate with one another. This works especially well when a program refuses to take input from a command-line pipe, but another program needs to feed the other one data and you don't have the disk space for a temporary file.

For a named pipe file, the first character of its file permissions is a **p**. For example:

```
[root@ford /root]# ls -l mypipe
prw-r--r--   1 root       root              0 Jun 16 10:47 mypipe
```

Progress Check

1. What is output redirection?

2. What is the difference between a block device and a character device?

Change Ownership: chown

The **chown** command allows you to change the ownership of a file to someone else. Only the root user can do this. (Normal users may not give away file ownership or steal ownership from another user.) The format of the command is as follows:

```
[root@ford /root]# chown [-R] username filename
```

where **username** is the login of the user to whom you want to assign ownership, and **filename** is the name of the file in question. The **filename** may be a directory as well.

The **-R** option applies when the specified **filename** is a directory name. This option tells the command to recursively descend through the directory tree and apply the new ownership not only to the directory itself, but to all of the files and directories within it.

TIP

Linux allows you to use a special notation with **chown** to also supply the group to **chgrp** the files to. The format of the command becomes **chown username.groupname filename**.

Change Group: chgrp

The **chgrp** command-line utility lets you change the group settings of a file. It works much like **chown**. Here is the format:

```
[root@ford /root]# chgrp [-R] groupname filename
```

where **groupname** is the name of the group to which you want to assign **filename** ownership. The **filename** may be a directory as well.

---

1. Output redirection is when you write the output of a command to another file decriptor.

2. A block device reads and writes blocks of data, whereas a character device reads and writes data one character at a time.

The **-R** option applies when the specified *filename* is a directory name. As with **chown,** the **-R** option tells the command to recursively descend through the directory tree and apply the new ownership not only to the directory itself, but also to all of the files and directories within it.

Change Mode: chmod

Directories and files within the Linux system have permissions associated with them. By default, permissions are set for the owner of the file, the group associated with the file, and everyone else who can access the file (also known as Owner, Group, Other). When you list files or directories, you see the permissions in the first column of the output. Permissions are divided into four parts. The first part is represented by the first character of the permission. Normal files have no special value and are represented with a hyphen (**-**) character. If the file has a special attribute, it is represented by a letter. The two special attributes we are most interested in here are directories (**d**) and symbolic links (**1**).

The second, third, and fourth parts of a permission are represented in three-character chunks. The first part indicates the file owner's permission. The second part indicates the group permission. The last part indicates the world permission. In the context of UNIX, "world" means all users in the system, regardless of their group settings.

Following are the letters used to represent permissions and their corresponding values. When you combine attributes, you add their values. The **chmod** command is used to set permission values.

Letter	Permission	Value
R	Read	4
W	Write	2
X	Execute	1

Using the numeric command mode is typically known as the octal permissions since the value can range from 0–7. To change permissions on a file, you simply add these values together for each permission you want to apply to. For example, if you want to make it so that just the user can have full access (RWX) to the file, you would type the following:

```
[root@ford /root]# chmod 700 foo
```

What is important to note is that using the octal mode you always *replace* any permissions that were set. So if there was a file in **/usr/local** that was SetUID and you ran the command **chmod -R 700 /usr/local**, that file will no longer be SetUID. If you want to change certain bits, you should use the symbolic mode of **chmod**. This mode turns out to be much easier to remember and you can add, subtract, or overwrite permissions.

The symbolic form of **chmod** allows you to set the bits of either the owner, group, or others. You can also set the bits for all. For example, if you want to change a file so that it is executable for the owner, you can run the following command:

```
[root@ford /root]# chmod u+x foobar.sh
```

If you want to change the group's bit to execute also, use the following:

```
[root@ford /root]# chmod ug+x foobar.sh
```

If you need to specify different permissions for others, just add a comma and its permission symbols:

```
[root@ford /root]# chmod ug+x,o-rwx foobar.sh
```

If you do not want to add or subtract a permission bit, you can use the = sign instead of **+** or **-**. This will write the specific bits to the file and erase any other bit for that permission. In the previous examples, we used **+** to add the execute bit to the user and group fields. If you *only* want the execute bit, you would replace the **+** with **=**. There is also a forth character you can use: **a**. This will apply the permission bits to all of the fields.

Following are the most common combinations of the three permissions. Other combinations, such as **-wx**, do exist, but they are rarely used.

Letter	Permission	Value
---	No permissions	0
r--	Read only	4
rw-	Read and write	6
rwx	Read, write, and execute	7
r-x	Read and execute	5
--x	Execute only	1

For each file, three of these three-letter chunks are grouped together. The first chunk represents the permissions for the owner of the file, the second chunk represents the permissions for file's group, and the last chunk represents the permissions for all users on the system. Table 6-1 describes some common file permission setups.

Permission	Numeric Equivalent	Symbolic Equivalent	Description
-rw-------	600	u=rw	Owner has read and write permissions. Set for most files.
-rw-r--r--	644	u=rw,g=r,o=r	Owner has read and write permissions; group and world have read only permission. Be sure you want to let other people read this file.
-rw-rw-rw-	666	a=rw	Everyone has read and write permissions. Not recommended; this combination allows the file to be accessed and changed by anyone, anywhere on the system.
-rwx------	700	u=rwx	Owner has read, write, and execute permissions. Best combination for programs the owner wishes to run (files that result from compiling a C or C++ program).
-rwxr-xr-x	755	u=rwx,go=rx	Owner has read, write, and execute permissions. Everyone else has read and execute permissions.
-rwxrwxrwx	777	a=rwx	Everyone has read, write, and execute privileges. Like the 666 setting, this combination should be avoided.
-rwx--x--x	711	u=rwx,go=x	Owner has read, write, and execute permissions; everyone else has execute only permissions. Useful for programs that you want to let others run but not copy.

Table 6-1 File Permission Combinations

Permission	Numeric Equivalent	Symbolic Equivalent	Description
drwx------	700	u=rwx	This is a directory created with the **mkdir** command. Only the owner can read and write into this directory. Note that all directories must have the executable bit set.
drwxr-xr-x	755	u=rwx,go=rx	This directory can be changed only by the owner, but everyone else can view its contents.
drwx--x--x	711	u=rwx,go=x	A handy combination for keeping a directory world-readable but restricted from access by the **ls** command. File can be read only by someone who knows the filename.

Table 6-1 File Permission Combinations *(continued)*

CRITICAL SKILL
6.3 Manage Files

This section covers the basic command-line tools for managing files and directories. Most of this will be familiar to anyone who has used a command-line interface—same old functions, but new commands to execute.

Copy Files: cp

The **cp** command is used to copy files and has a substantial number of options. See its man page for additional details. By default, this command works silently, only displaying status information if an error condition occurs. Following are the most common options for **cp**:

Option for cp	Description
-f	Forces copy; does not ask for verification
-I	Interactive copy; before each file is copied, verifies with user

To copy **index.html** to **index-orig.html**, use the following command:

```
[root@ford /root]# cp index.html index-orig.html
```

To interactively copy all files ending in **.html** to the **/tmp** directory, type this command:

```
[root@ford /root]# cp -i *.html /tmp
```

Move Files: mv

The **mv** command is used to move files from one location to another. Files can be moved across partitions as well. That requires a copy operation to occur, so that move command may take longer. Following are the most common options for **mv**:

Option for mv	Description
-f	Forces move
-I	Interactive move

To move a file from **/usr/src/myprog/bin/*** to **/usr/bin**, use this command:

```
[root@ford /root]# mv /usr/src/myprog/bin/* /usr/bin
```

There is no explicit rename tool, so you can use **mv**. To rename **/tmp/blah** to **/tmp/bleck**, type this command:

```
[root@ford /root]# mv /tmp/bleck /tmp/blah
```

Link Files: ln

The **ln** command lets you establish hard links and soft links. (See "File and Directory Types" earlier in this module.) The general format of **ln** is as follows:

```
[root@ford /root]# ln original_file new_file
```

Although **ln** has many options, you'll never need to use most of them. The most common option, **-s**, creates a symbolic link instead of a hard link.

To create a symbolic link so that **/usr/bin/myadduser** points to **/usr/local/bin/myadduser**, issue this command:

```
[root@ford /root]# ln -s /usr/local/bin/myadduser /usr/bin/myadduser
```

Find a File: find

The **find** command lets you search for files based on various criteria. Like the tools we have already discussed, **find** has a large number of options that you can read about on its man page. Here is the general format of **find**:

```
[root@ford /root]# find start_dir [options]
```

where **start_dir** is the directory from which the search should start.

To find all files in **/tmp** that have not been accessed in at least seven days, use the following command:

```
[root@ford /root]# find /tmp -atime 7 -print
```

Type this command to find all files in **/usr/src** whose names are core and to remove them:

```
[root@ford /root]# find /usr/src -name core -exec rm {} \;
```

To find all files in **/home** that end in .jpg and are over 100K in size, issue this command:

```
[root@ford /root]# find /home -name "*.jpg" -size 100k
```

File Compression: gzip

In the original distributions of UNIX, the tool to compress files was appropriately called **compress**. Unfortunately, the algorithm was patented by someone hoping to make a great deal of money. Instead of paying out, most sites sought and found another compression tool with a patent-free algorithm: **gzip**. Even better, **gzip** consistently achieves better compression ratios than **compress** does. Another bonus: recent changes have allowed **gzip** to uncompress files that were compressed using the **compress** command.

TIP

The filename extension usually identifies a file compressed with **gzip**. These files typically end in .GZ (files compressed with **compress** end in .Z).

Note that **gzip** compresses the file in place, meaning that after the compression process, the original file is removed, and the only thing left is the compressed file.

To compress a file and then decompress it, use this command:

```
[root@ford /root]# gzip myfile
[root@ford /root]# gzip -d myfile.gz
```

Issue this command to compress all files ending in **.html** using the best compression possible:

```
[root@ford /root]# gzip -9 *.html
```

bzip2

If you have noticed files with a .bz extension, these have been compressed with the **bzip2** compression utility. **bzip2** uses a different compression algorithm that usually turns out smaller files than **gzip**. **bzip2** uses semantics that are similar to **gzip**; for more information, read the man page on **bzip2**.

Create a Directory: mkdir

The **mkdir** command in Linux is identical to the same command in other flavors of UNIX, as well as in MS-DOS. The only option available is **-p**, which will create parent directories if none exist. For example, if you need to create **/tmp/bigdir/subdir/mydir** and the only directory that exists is **/tmp,** using **-p** will cause **bigdir** and **subdir** to be automatically created along with **mydir**.

To create a directory called **mydir**, use this command:

```
[root@ford /root]# mkdir mydir
```

NOTE The **mkdir** command cannot be abbreviated to **md** as it can under DOS.

Remove Directory: rmdir

The **rmdir** command offers no surprises for those familiar with the DOS version of the command; it simply removes an existing directory. The only command-line parameter available for this is **-p**, which removes parent directories as well. For example, in a directory named **/tmp/bigdir/subdit/mydir**, if you want to get rid of all the directories from **bigdir** to **mydir**, you'd issue this command alone:

```
[root@ford /tmp]# rmdir -p bigdir/subdir/mydir
```

To remove a directory called **mydir**, you'd type this:

```
[root@ford /root]# rmdir mydir
```

NOTE

The **rmdir** command cannot be abbreviated to **rd** as it can under DOS.

Show Present Working Directory: pwd

It is inevitable that you will sit down in front of an already logged in workstation and not know where you are in the directory tree. To get this information, you need the **pwd** command. It has no parameters, and its only task is to print the current working directory. The DOS equivalent is typing **cd** alone on the command line; however, the BASH **cd** command takes you back to your home directory.

To get the current working directory, use this command:

```
[root@ford src]# pwd /usr/local/src
```

Tape Archive: tar

If you are familiar with the PKZip program, you are accustomed to the fact that the compression tool reduces file size but also consolidates files into compressed archives. Under Linux, this process is separated into two tools: **gzip** and **tar**.

The **tar** program combines multiple files into a single large file. It is separate from the compression tool, so it allows you to select which compression tool to use or whether you even want compression. Additionally, **tar** is able to read and write to devices in much the same way **dd** can, thus making **tar** a good tool for backing up to tape devices.

NOTE

Although the name of the **tar** program includes the word "tape," it isn't necessary to read or write to a tape drive when creating archives. In fact, you'll rarely use **tar** with a tape drive in day-to-day situations (backups aside). The reason it was named **tar** in the first place was that when it was originally created, limited disk space meant that tape was the most logical place to put archives. Typically, the **-f** option in **tar** would be used to specify the tape device file, rather than a traditional UNIX file. You should be aware, however, that you can still **tar** straight to a device.

Here's the structure of the **tar** command, its most common options, and several examples of its use:

```
[root@ford /root]# tar [commands and options] filename
```

Option for `tar`	Description
`-c`	Creates a new archive
`-t`	Views the contents of an archive
`-x`	Extracts the contents of an archive
`-f`	Specifies the name of the file (or device) in which the archive is located
`-v`	Provides verbose descriptions during operations
`-I`	Decompresses with the `bzip2` algorithm on the fly
`-z`	Assumes the file is already (or will be) compressed with `gzip`

To create an archive called **apache.tar** containing all the files from **/usr/src/apache**, use this command:

```
[root@ford src]# tar -cf apache.tar /usr/src/apache
```

To create an archive called **apache.tar** containing all the files from **/usr/src/apache**, and to show what is happening as it happens, enter the following:

```
[root@ford src]# tar -cvf apache.tar /usr/src/apache
```

To create a **gzip** compressed archive called **apache.tar.gz** containing all of the files from **/usr/src/apache**, and to show what is happening as it happens, issue this command:

```
[root@ford src]# tar -cvzf apache.tar.gz /usr/src/apache
```

To extract the contents of a **gzip**ped **tar** archive called **apache.tar.gz**, and to show what is happening as it happens, use this command:

```
[root@ford /root]# tar -xvzf apache.tar.gz
```

If you like, you can also specify a physical device to **tar** to and from. This is handy when you need to transfer a set of files from one system to another and for some reason you cannot create a file system on the device. (Or sometimes it's just more entertaining to do it this way.) To create an archive on the first floppy device, you would enter this:

```
[root@ford /root]# tar -cvzf /dev/fd0 /usr/src/apache
```

To pull that archive off of a disk, you would type

```
[root@ford src]# tar -xvzf /dev/fd0
```

Concatenate Files: cat

The **cat** program fills an extremely simple role: to display files. More creative things can be done with it, but nearly all of its usage will be in the form of simply displaying the contents of text files—much like the **type** command under DOS. Because multiple filenames can be specified on the command line, it's possible to concatenate files into a single, large continuous file. This is different from **tar** in that the resulting file has no control information to show the boundaries of different files.

To display the **/etc/passwd** file, use this command:

```
[root@ford /root]# cat /etc/passwd
```

To display the **/etc/passwd** file and the **/etc/group** file, issue this command:

```
[root@ford /root]# cat /etc/passwd /etc/group
```

Type this command to concatenate **/etc/passwd** with **/etc/group** into the file **/tmp/complete**:

```
[root@ford /root]# cat /etc/passwd /etc/group > /tmp/complete
```

To concatenate the **/etc/passwd** file to an existing file called **/tmp/orb**, use this:

```
[root@ford /root]# cat /etc/passwd >> /tmp/orb
```

NOTE

If you want to **cat** a file in reverse, you can use the **tac** command.

Display a File One Screen at a Time: more

The **more** command works in much the same way the DOS version of the program does. It takes an input file and displays it one screen at a time. The input file can either come from its **stdin** or from a command-line parameter.

Additional command-line parameters, though rarely used, can be found in the man page.

To view the **/etc/passwd** file one screen at a time, use this command:

```
[root@ford /root]# more /etc/passwd
```

To view the directory listing generated by the **ls** command one screen at a time, enter this:

```
[root@ford /root]# ls | more
```

Disk Utilization: du

You will often need to determine where and by whom disk space is being consumed, especially when you're running low on it! The **du** command allows you to determine the disk utilization on a directory-by-directory basis. Here are some of the options available:

Option for du	Description
-c	Produces a grand total at the end of the run.
-h	Prints sizes in human-readable format.
-k	Prints sizes in kilobytes rather than block sizes. (Note: Under Linux, one block is equal to 1K, but this is not true for all UNIX.)
-s	Summarizes. Prints only one output for each argument.

To display the amount of space each directory in **/home** is taking up in human-readable format, use this command:

```
[root@ford /root]# du -sh /home/*
```

Show the Directory Location of a File: which

The **which** command searches your entire path to find the name of the file specified on the command line. If the file is found, the command output includes the actual path of the file. This command is used to locate fully qualified paths.

Use the following command to find out which directory the **ls** command is in:

```
[root@ford /root]# which ls
```

You may find this similar to the **find** command. The difference here is that since **which** only searches the path, it is much faster. Of course, it is also much more limiting than **find**, but if all you're looking for is a program, you'll find it to be a better choice of commands.

Locating a Command: whereis

The **whereis** tool searches your path and displays the name of the program and its absolute directory, the source file (if available), and the man page for the command (again, if available).

To find the location of the program, source, and manual page for the command **grep**, use this:

```
[root@ford /root]# whereis grep
```

Disk Free: df

The **df** program displays the amount of free space, partition by partition. The drives/partitions must be mounted in order to get this information. NFS information can be gathered this way, as well. Some parameters for **df** are listed here; additional (rarely used) options are listed in the **df** manual page.

Option for df	Description
-h	Generates free space amount in human-readable numbers rather than free blocks.
-1	Lists only the local mounted file systems. Does not display any information about network mounted file systems.

To show the free space for all locally mounted drivers, use this command:

```
[root@ford /root]# df -l
```

To show the free space in a human-readable format, for the file system in which your current working directory is located, enter

```
[root@ford /root]# df -h .
```

To show the free space in a human-readable format for the file system on which **/tmp** is located, type this command:

```
[root@ford /root]# df -h /tmp
```

Synchronize Disks: sync

Like most other modern operating systems, Linux maintains a disk cache to improve efficiency. The drawback, of course, is that not everything you want written to disk will have been written to disk at any given moment.

To schedule the disk cache to be written out to disk, you use the **sync** command. If **sync** detects that writing the cache out to disk has already been scheduled, the kernel is instructed to immediately flush the cache. This command takes no command-line parameters.

Type this command to ensure the disk cache has been flushed:

```
[root@ford /root]# sync ;   sync
```

Project 6-1   Moving a User and its Home Directory

This project will demonstrate how to put together all of the topics covered so far in this module. The elegant design of UNIX and Linux allows you to combine simple commands to perform advanced operations. This project will cover the process of moving a user's home directory and changing a user's UID. Sometimes in the course of administration you might have to move a user around. Also, some companies have a policy to move the user's UID if they move into a new group (such as from marketing to engineering). In this project, you are going to move the user sgraham from his home directory **/export/home/sgraham** to **/export2/home/eng**, and change his UID from 1000 to 2000.

Step by Step

1. Check the disk usage on **/export2** to make sure there is enough space on the partition for sgraham's home directory:

```
[root@ford /]# du -sk /export2
```

2. Move sgraham's home directory over to **/export2** by using the **tar** command with a pipe:

```
[root@ford /]# cd /export/home
[root@ford /export/home]# tar -cf - sgraham |
                        (cd /export2/home/eng;tar -xvpf -)
```

3. Edit the **/etc/passwd** file and change sgraham's UID from 1000 to 2000 using the command **vipw** or **vi /etc/passwd**:

```
[root@ford /]# vipw
```

4. Since you changed the UID, you need to change the owner on **/export2/home/eng/sgraham** to sgraham's new UID (2000):

```
[root@ford /]# chown -R sgraham /export2/home/eng/sgraham
```

5. Make sure that the permissions are correct by issuing an **ls -l** on the new directory:

```
[root@ford /]# ls -l /export2/home/eng/sgraham
```

6. Log in to the sgraham account and see that everything is working. You should be able to see sgraham's files, and the shell should operate correctly. Use the **su** command (see usage later in this module):

```
[root@ford /]# su - sgraham
```

Project
6-1

Moving a User and its Home Directory

Project Summary

After you have tested access to the new directory, everything should be good to go for sgraham. Always double-check the permissions and make sure that the home directory has been moved correctly. It really does pay to do it right the first time. As good practice, I usually leave the old home directory for a couple of weeks to make sure nothing was lost in the transition (remember, **tar** only copies a folder's contents).

CRITICAL SKILL
6.4
Manipulate Processes

Under Linux (and UNIX in general), each running program comprises at least one process. From the operating system's standpoint, each process is independent of the others. Unless it specifically asks to share resources with other processes, a process is confined to the memory and CPU allocation assigned to it. Processes that overstep their memory allocation (which could potentially corrupt another running program and make the system unstable) are immediately killed. This method of handling processes has been a major contributor to the stability of UNIX systems. User applications cannot corrupt other user programs or the operating system.

This section describes the tools used to list and manipulate processes. They are very important elements of a system administrator's daily work.

List Processes: ps

The **ps** command lists all the processes in a system, their state, size, name, owner, CPU time, wall clock time, and much more. There are many command-line parameters available, and the ones most often used are described in Table 6-2.

The most common set of parameters used with the **ps** command is **-auxww**. These parameters show all the processes (regardless of whether they have a controlling terminal), each process's owners, and all the processes' command-line parameters. Let's examine the output of an invocation of **ps -auxww**.

```
USER       PID %CPU %MEM   VSZ  RSS TTY     STAT START   TIME COMMAND
root         1  0.0  0.3  1096  476 ?       S    Jun10   0:04 init
root         2  0.0  0.0     0    0 ?       SW   Jun10   0:00 [kflushd]
root         3  0.0  0.0     0    0 ?       SW   Jun10   0:00 [kpiod]
root         4  0.0  0.0     0    0 ?       SW   Jun10   0:00 [kswapd]
root         5  0.0  0.0     0    0 ?       SW<  NJun10  0:00 [mdrecoveryd]

bin        253  0.0  0.2  1088  288 ?       S    Jun10   0:00 portmap
root       300  0.0  0.4  1272  548 ?       S    Jun10   0:00 syslogd -m 0
root       311  0.0  0.5  1376  668 ?       S    Jun10   0:00 klogd
daemon     325  0.0  0.2  1112  284 ?       S    Jun10   0:00 /usr/sbin/atd
root       339  0.0  0.4  1284  532 ?       S    Jun10   0:00 crond
root       357  0.0  0.3  1232  508 ?       S    Jun10   0:00 inetd
root       371  0.0  1.1  2528 1424 ?       S    Jun10   0:00 named
```

Option for `ps`	Description
`-a`	Shows all processes with a controlling terminal, not just the current user's processes
`-r`	Shows only running processes (see the description of process states later in this section)
`-x`	Shows processes that do not have a controlling terminal
`-u`	Shows the process owners
`-f`	Displays parent/child relationships among processes
`-l`	Produces a list in long format
`-w`	Shows a process's command-line parameters (up to half a line)
`-ww`	Shows all of a process's command-line parameters, despite length

Table 6-2 Command-Line Options for ps

The very first line of the output provides column headers for the listing, as follows:

- **USER**   Who owns what process.

- **PID**   Process identification number.

- **%CPU**   Percentage of the CPU taken up by a process. Note: For a system with multiple processors, this column will add up to more than 100%.

- **%MEM**   Percentage of memory taken up by a process.

- **VSZ**   The amount of virtual memory a process is taking.

- **RSS**   The amount of actual (resident) memory a process is taking.

- **TTY**   The controlling terminal for a process. A question mark in this column means the process is no longer connected to a controlling terminal.

- **STAT**   The state of the process:

  - **S**   Process is sleeping. All processes that are ready to run (that is, being multitasked, and the CPU is currently focused elsewhere) will be asleep.

  - **R**   Process is actually on the CPU.

  - **D**   Uninterruptible sleep (usually I/O related).

  - **T**   Process is being traced by a debugger or has been stopped.

  - **Z**   Process has gone zombie. This means either (1) the parent process has not acknowledged the death of its child using the **wait** system call, or (2) the parent was improperly **kill**ed, and until the parent is completely **kill**ed, the **init** process (see Module 9) cannot reap the child itself. A zombied process usually indicates poorly written software.

In addition, the STAT entry for each process can take one of the following modifiers: W = No resident pages in memory (it has been completely swapped out); < = High-priority process; N = Low-priority task; L = Pages in memory are locked there (usually signifying the need for real-time functionality).

- **START**   Date the process was started.

- **TIME**   Amount of time the process has spent on the CPU.

- **COMMAND**   Name of the process and its command-line parameters.

Show an Interactive List of Processes: top

The **top** command is an interactive version of **ps**. Instead of giving a static view of what is going on, **top** refreshes the screen with a list of processes every 2 to 3 seconds (user adjustable). From this list, you can reprioritize processes or **kill** them. Figure 6-1 shows a **top** screen.

The **top** program's main disadvantage is that it's a CPU hog. On a congested system, this program tends to complicate system management issues. Users start running **top** to see what's going on, only to find several other people running the program as well, slowing down the system even more.

By default, **top** is shipped so that everyone can use it. You may find it prudent, depending on your environment, to restrict **top** to root only. To do this, change the program's permissions with the following command:

```
[root@ford /root]# chmod 0700 /usr/bin/top
```

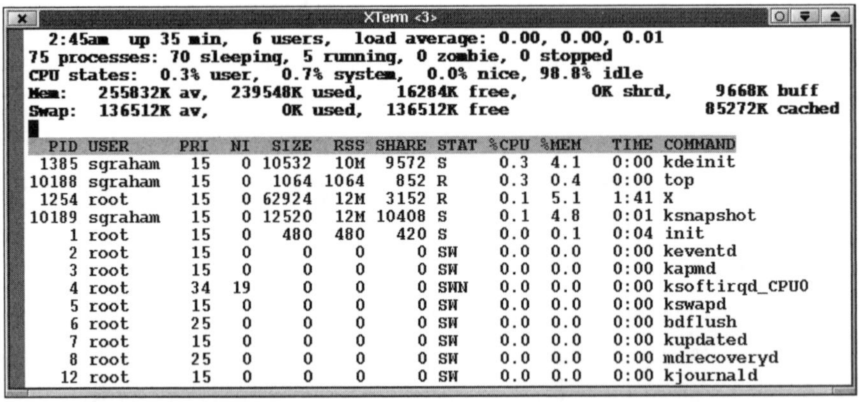

```
                                  XTerm <3>
   2:45am  up 35 min,  6 users,  load average: 0.00, 0.00, 0.01
 75 processes: 70 sleeping, 5 running, 0 zombie, 0 stopped
 CPU states:  0.3% user,  0.7% system,  0.0% nice, 98.8% idle
 Mem:    255832K av,  239548K used,    16284K free,      OK shrd,    9668K buff
 Swap:   136512K av,      OK used,   136512K free                  85272K cached

   PID USER     PRI  NI   SIZE  RSS SHARE STAT %CPU %MEM   TIME COMMAND
  1385 sgraham   15   0  10532  10M  9572 S    0.3  4.1   0:00 kdeinit
 10188 sgraham   15   0   1064 1064   852 R    0.3  0.4   0:00 top
  1254 root      15   0  62924  12M  3152 R    0.1  5.1   1:41 X
 10189 sgraham   15   0  12520  12M 10408 S    0.1  4.8   0:01 ksnapshot
     1 root      15   0    480  480   420 S    0.0  0.1   0:04 init
     2 root      15   0      0    0     0 SW   0.0  0.0   0:00 keventd
     3 root      15   0      0    0     0 SW   0.0  0.0   0:00 kapmd
     4 root      34  19      0    0     0 SWN  0.0  0.0   0:00 ksoftirqd_CPU0
     5 root      15   0      0    0     0 SW   0.0  0.0   0:00 kswapd
     6 root      25   0      0    0     0 SW   0.0  0.0   0:00 bdflush
     7 root      15   0      0    0     0 SW   0.0  0.0   0:00 kupdated
     8 root      25   0      0    0     0 SW   0.0  0.0   0:00 mdrecoveryd
    12 root      15   0      0    0     0 SW   0.0  0.0   0:00 kjournald
```

Figure 6-1 Output of the **top** command

Send a Signal to a Process: kill

This program's name is misleading: it doesn't really kill processes. What it *does* do is send *signals* to running processes. The operating system, by default, supplies each process a standard set of *signal handlers* to deal with incoming signals. From a system administrator's standpoint, the most important handler is for signals 9 and 15, kill process and terminate process, respectively. When **kill** is invoked, it requires at least one parameter: the process identification number (PID) as derived from the **ps** command. When passed only the PID, **kill** sends signal 15. Some programs intercept this signal and perform a number of actions so that they can shut down cleanly. Others just stop running in their tracks. Either way, **kill** isn't a guaranteed method for making a process stop.

Signals

The optional parameter available for **kill** is **-*n***, where the ***n*** represents a signal number. As a system administrator, you are most interested in signals 9 (kill) and 1 (hang up).

The kill signal, 9, is the impolite way of stopping a process. Rather than asking a process to stop, the operating system simply kills the process. The only time this will fail is when the process is in the middle of a system call (such as a request to open a file), in which case the process will die once it returns from the system call.

The hang-up signal, 1, is a bit of a throwback to the VT-100 terminal days of UNIX. When a user's terminal connection dropped in the middle of a session, all of that terminal's running processes would receive a hang-up signal (often called a SIGHUP or HUP). This gave the processes an opportunity to perform a clean shutdown or, in the case of background processes, to ignore the signal. These days, a HUP is used to tell certain server applications to go and reread their configuration files (you'll see this in action in several of the later modules). Most applications simply ignore the signal.

Security Issues

The power to terminate a process is obviously a very powerful one, making security precautions important. Users may only kill processes they have permission to kill. If nonroot users attempt to send signals to processes other than their own, error messages are returned. The root user is the exception to this limitation; root may send signals to all processes in the system. Of course, this means root needs to exercise great care when using the **kill** command.

Examples of kill

Use this command to terminate process number 2059:

```
[root@ford /root]# kill 2059
```

For an almost guaranteed kill of process number 593, issue this command:

```
[root@ford /root]# kill -9 593
```

Type the following to send the HUP signal to the **init** program (which is always PID 1):

```
[root@ford /root]# kill -1 1
```

CRITICAL SKILL

6.5 Use Common Linux Tools

The following tools don't fall into any specific category we've covered in this module. They all make important contributions to daily system administration chores.

Who Is Logged In: who

On systems that allow users to log in to other users' machines or special servers, you will want to know who is logged in. You can generate such a report by using the **who** command:

```
[root@ford /root]# who
```

The **who** report looks like this:

```
sshah     tty1      Jun 14 18:22
root      pts/9     Jun 14 18:29 (:0)
root      pts/11    Jun 14 21:12 (:0)
root      pts/12    Jun 14 23:38 (:0)
```

Switch User: su

Once you have logged in to the system as one user, you need not log out and back in again in order to assume another identity (root user, for instance). Instead, use the **su** command to switch. This command has only two command-line parameters, both of which are optional.

Running **su** without any parameters will automatically try to make you the root user. You'll be prompted for the root password and, if you enter it correctly, will drop down to a root shell. If you are already the root user and want to switch to another ID, you don't need to enter the new password when you use this command.

For example, if you're logged in as yourself and want to switch to the root user, type this command:

```
[sshah@ford ~]$ su
```

If you're logged in as root and want to switch to, say, user sshah, enter this command:

```
[root@ford /root]# su sshah
```

The optional hyphen (**-**) parameter tells **su** to switch identities and run the login scripts for that user. For example, if you're logged in as root and want to switch over to user sshah with all of his login and shell configurations, type this command:

```
[root@ford /root]# su - sshah
```

Networking Tools

If you are starting your experience with Linux in an already networked environment, you may find some of these tools handy for getting around. However, if you need to configure your network first, you should read Module 23.

Mail Preferences: mail, pine, and mutt

Like everyone else, Linux folk need to read their e-mail. And as you can imagine, you have plenty of choices with which you can do so. We discuss some GUI-based POP mail readers in Appendix C; here, we give mention to command-line tools.

The one tool that you will always be able to find is called—you guessed it—**mail**. Simply run **mail** from the command line, like so:

```
[sshah@ford ~]$ mail
```

and you'll see what mail you have available to read. Because this tool does not require any screen formatting, it is well suited for those instances where you are troubleshooting a host so broken it has no terminal control.

To exit the **mail** program, type **q** and press ENTER. If you want more information about **mail**, check out its man page. As you'll see, for a tool that looks very simple, it actually offers quite a bit of capability.

Another popular tool is **pine**, which actually takes control of your terminal window and makes the display look much nicer. Being a fully menu-driven program where all of your options are always listed on a menu in front of you, **pine** tends to be a very popular choice for people new to UNIX.

From a practical point of view, **pine** is ideal for communicating with people who use all sorts of other mail tools since it understands all of the popular standards in use today (such as MIME attachments). **pine** also offers a very powerful filing system with which you can archive your mail easily and find it again at a later date.

For those of you who like **vi** and lightweight mail readers, **mutt** is the e-mail reader for you. If you have users who have several thousand messages in their inbox, **mutt** can quickly handle these messages. Other readers such as **pine** have been known to choke on large mail files. (My philosophy is you shouldn't have that much mail in the first place.)

CRITICAL SKILL
6.6 Use Linux Editors

Editors are by far the bulkiest of common tools, but they are also the most useful. Without them, making any kind of change to a text file would be a tremendous undertaking. Regardless of your Linux distribution, you will have gotten a few editors. You should take a few moments to get comfortable with them before you're busy fighting another problem.

NOTE

Not all distributions come with all of the editors listed here.

vi

The **vi** editor has been around UNIX-based systems since the 1970s, and its interface shows it. It is arguably one of the last editors to actually use a separate command mode and data entry mode; as a result, most newcomers find it unpleasant to use. But before you give **vi** the cold shoulder, take some time to get comfortable with it. In difficult situations, you may not have a pretty graphical editor at your disposal, and **vi** is ubiquitous across all UNIX systems.

The version of **vi** that ships with Linux distributions is **VIM** (VI iMproved). It has a lot of what made **vi** popular in the first place and many features that make it useful in today's typical environments (including a graphical interface if the X Window System is running).

To start **vi**, simply type

```
[root@ford /root]# vi
```

The easiest way to learn more about **vi** is to start it and enter **:help**. If you ever find yourself stuck in **vi**, press the ESC key several times and then type **:qu!** to force an exit without saving. If you want to save the file, type **:wq**.

emacs

It has been argued that **emacs** is an operating system all by itself. It's big, feature-rich, expandable, programmable, and all-around amazing. If you're coming from a GUI background, you'll probably find **emacs** a pleasant environment to work with at first. On its cover, it works like Notepad in terms of its interface. Yet underneath is a complete interface to the GNU development environment, a mail reader, a news reader, a Web browser, and even a psychiatrist (well, not exactly).

To start **emacs**, simply type

```
[root@ford /root]# emacs
```

Once **emacs** has started, you can visit the psychiatrist by pressing ESC-X and then typing **doctor**. To get help using **emacs**, press CRTL-H. The **emacs** tutorial will walk you through the basics of using the editor.

pico

pico is another editor inspired by simplicity. Typically used in conjunction with the **pine** mail reading system, **pico** can also be used as a standalone editor. Like **joe**, it can work in a manner similar to Notepad, but **pico** uses its own set of key combinations. Thankfully, all available key combinations are always shown at the bottom of the screen.

To start **pico**, simply type

```
[root@ford /root]# pico
```

pico is the editor used by **pine** by default. You can set up **pine** so that it uses another editor if you like. Don't let any other admins know that you use **pico**—you will catch all kinds of grief since **emacs** is the better text editor!

A Note on Holy Wars

You will note that in the last paragraph I stated that **emacs** is a better editor than **pico**. While I will probably get a ton of e-mail stating that **pico** is superior to **emacs**, that is my opinion. If you read newsgroups and Slashdot you'll sometimes come across what is known as a Holy War. These are flaming e-mails describing why a certain tool is better than anything else in the world. These wars range from Linux vs. Windows to Emacs vs. Vi, Perl vs. Python, and the list goes on and on. My advice is to get familiar with the editor of your choice. I personally love to use the **emacs** editor, yet I know how to use **pico**, **vi**, and a host of other editors, mostly because I've had to help others use their editor of choice. Once you are comfortable with one, stick with it and learn it well. Don't let other people's opinions dictate your decisions.

Module 6 Mastery Check

1. What is **vi**?

2. What is **pine**?

3. What does the **su** command do?

4. How do you send a process a signal?

5. What command lists all of the running processes?

6. What is the effect of the following command?

   ```
   [root@ford ]# chmod 0744 /root/foo
   ```

7. What is the effect of the following command?

   ```
   [root@ford ]# chmod -R ug+rx,o=rx /usr/local
   ```

8. Why would you want to use the symbolic form of the **chmod** command over the octal form?

9. What section of the man pages would cover the **/etc/exports** file?

10. How do you print out all of the environment variables in the shell?

11. What is the notion of job control?

12. Which is the better editor, **emacs** or **vi**?

13. What does the **tar** command do?

14. What does the **cat** command do?

Module 7

Booting and Shutting Down

A s operating systems have become more complex, the process of starting up and shutting down has become more comprehensive. Anyone who has undergone the transition from a straight DOS-based system to a Windows 2000-based system has experienced this transition firsthand. Not only is the core operating system brought up and shut down, but also an impressive list of services must be started and stopped. Like Windows 2000, Linux comprises an impressive list of services that are turned on as part of the boot procedure.

In this module, we discuss the bootstrapping of the Linux operating system with LILO and GRUB. We will then step through the processes of starting up and shutting down the Linux environment. We discuss the scripts that automate this process as well as the parts of the process for which modification is acceptable.

CAUTION

Apply a liberal dose of common sense in following this module with a real system. As you experiment with modifying startup and shutdown scripts, bear in mind that it is possible to bring your system to a nonfunctional state that cannot be recovered by rebooting. Don't try new processes on production systems; make backups of all the files you wish to change; and most important, have a boot disk ready in case you make an irreversible change.

CRITICAL SKILL
7.1 Understand Boot Loaders

For any operating system to boot on standard PC hardware you need what is called a *boot loader*. If you have only installed Windows on a PC, you have probably never seen a boot loader. Typically, the boot loader will reside in the MBR, and it knows how to get the operating system up and running. Linux can be booted with any of several boot loaders; it just has to support booting Linux. Partition Magic comes with a tool called Boot Magic that supports Linux. The main choices that come with Linux distributions are the LILO (Linux Loader) and GRUB (the Grand Unified Bootloader). We will cover LILO first since it has a long history of being the only boot loader for Linux. Then we will cover GRUB, which is becoming very popular since it has more features than LILO and, like LILO, can boot several other operating systems.

NOTE

Usually in the process of installation you will be prompted with the choice to use LILO or GRUB. I would suggest using GRUB if at all possible; we will discuss why later in the module. Red Hat 7.3 now uses the GRUB boot loader as the default. Mandrake has also been using GRUB for some time.

CRITICAL SKILL
7.2 Understand LILO

LILO, short for Linux Loader, is a boot manager. It allows you to boot multiple operating systems, provided each system exists on its own partition. (Under PC-based systems, the *entire* boot partition must also exist beneath the 1,024-cylinder boundary.) In addition to booting multiple operating systems, with LILO you can choose various kernel configurations or versions to boot. This is especially handy when you're trying kernel upgrades before adopting them.

The big picture with LILO is straightforward: a configuration file (**/etc/lilo.conf**) specifies which partitions are bootable and, if a partition is Linux, which kernel to load. When the **/sbin/lilo** program runs, it takes this partition information and rewrites the boot sector with the necessary code to present the options as specified in the configuration file. At boot time, a prompt (usually **lilo:**) is displayed, and you have the option of specifying the operating system. (Usually, a default can be selected after a timeout period.) LILO loads the necessary code, the kernel, from the selected partition and passes full control over to it.

LILO is what is known as a two-stage boot loader. The first stage loads LILO itself into memory and prompts you for booting instructions with the **lilo:** prompt. Once you enter the OS to boot, LILO enters the second stage, booting the Linux operating system.

NOTE

If you are familiar with the NT boot process, you can think of LILO as comparable to the OS loader (NTLDR). Similarly, the LILO configuration file, **/etc/lilo.conf**, is comparable to **BOOT.INI** (which is typically hidden from view).

CRITICAL SKILL
7.3 Configure LILO

The LILO configuration file is **/etc/lilo.conf**. In most cases, you won't need to modify the file in any significant way. When you do need to change this file, the options are quite plain and simple to follow. Let's begin by reviewing a simple configuration. The file shown here is probably quite similar to what is already in your default **lilo.conf** file:

```
boot=/dev/hda
prompt
timeout=50
image=/boot/vmlinuz-2.2.5-15
        label=linux
        root=/dev/hda2
        read-only
other = /dev/hda1
        label = dos
        table = /dev/hda
```

Ask the Expert

Q: What are the steps of the booting process on a dual boot system?

A: With a system that doesn't contain LILO, the DOS MBR is used. First, your PC will do a POST (power-on self-test) to make sure you have a CPU, memory, and so on. Then the BIOS will try to find the boot sector of the first boot device, which can be the floppy drive, CD-ROM, or hard drive. In our example, we have just the hard drive. BIOS will then load the DOS-MBR. The DOS-MBR then loads the boot sector from the active partition. This active partition is typically Windows. If it is LILO (installed on **/dev/hda1**, for example), then it will load LILO and LILO will take over. The DOS-MBR is the master boot record to boot Microsoft Windows and DOS.

If a system has LILO installed on the MBR, BIOS will load LILO from the MBR and then LILO will let you load the operating system of your choice. You typically want to install LILO or GRUB on the MBR, unless you are using another boot loader, in which case you will want to install LILO on a Linux partition that is below the 1,024th cylinder.

Q: On what partitions can I put LILO?

A: You can put LILO on the MBR or any Linux partition that is below the 1,024th cylinder. You do *not* want to install LILO on the partition that Windows is installed on. This will overwrite the Windows loader and you won't be able to boot Windows without a lot of work.

Q: If I install Linux on the MBR, will I still be able to boot Windows?

A: Yes. Most modern distributions set this up for you. LILO can be configured to boot Windows; it just needs to know the partition and the type of OS.

Q: LILO is totally broken on my system and I can't boot. How do I fix this?

A: There are a couple of things you can do. First, you can use the rescue disks that you created when you installed Linux. You did create them, right? If not, you can boot the distribution CDs into rescue mode and run LILO again to fix the MBR. If all else fails,

(continued)

you can use a DOS-formatted floppy disk that has the DOS **fdisk** utility. Just boot the floppy disk and run the following command:

```
A:> fdisk /MBR
```

This will write the DOS-MBR to the hard disk.

Q: **If I have to install the DOS-MBR, will I lose the ability to boot Windows and Linux?**

A: You will lose the ability to boot Linux (off of the hard drive), but you will not lose the ability to boot Windows. In fact, Windows will boot automatically. Remember, the DOS-MBR will load the boot sector from the active partition, which is usually Windows. You will have to reinstall LILO or boot off of a floppy disk to get Linux booted.

When you want another program (such as the NT OS loader) to handle the MBR, you can specify that the boot sector be written to another partition. Then control can be passed to this partition from the code specified in the MBR.

The first line, **boot=/dev/hda**, tells LILO where to write the boot sector. Usually, this is the first sector of the boot drive: **/dev/hda** for IDE-based disks, and **/dev/sda** for SCSI-based disks. This sector is better known as the *master boot record (MBR)*. The purpose of the MBR is to inform PC designers what to load first to start the operating system. Once loaded, the program stored in the MBR is expected to take over the boot process.

Returning to the configuration file, you see the next command is **prompt**. This instruction tells LILO to give the **lilo:** prompt at boot time. At this prompt, the user can either type in the name of the boot image that is to start or press TAB to list the available options. By default, LILO will wait indefinitely for user input unless a timeout command is specified.

The **timeout=50** command tells LILO to wait for 50 deciseconds (5 seconds) before selecting the default boot image and starting the boot process.

The next line begins a small block. With the following line, you are indicating a specific boot image:

```
image=/boot/vmlinuz-2.2.5-15
```

This being the first block, it will be the default boot image. The image to boot is the file **/boot/vmlinuz-2.2.5-15**, which is a Linux kernel. Inside the block is the line **label=linux**, which is the name that is displayed if the user asks for a list of available boot options at the **lilo:** prompt.

Also inside the block is the line:

```
root=/dev/hda2
```

which tells LILO the partition on which the **/boot/vmlinuz-2.2.5-15** file is located.

If you aren't sure which partition holds your kernel, go to the kernel's directory and enter:

```
df .
```

This will produce a response similar to the following:

```
[root@ford /boot]# df .
Filesystem          1k-blocks       Used Available Use% Mounted on
/dev/hda2             108870       56119     47129  54% /
```

The first column, where the entry begins with a **/dev**, is the device where your kernel is located. In this example, the kernel (which is located in the **/boot** directory) exists on the **/dev/hda2** partition. (See Module 8 for more information about partitions.)

The last option in the block is **read-only**, which tells LILO to mount the root file system with read-only permissions when starting the kernel. This is necessary so that the root file system can check itself for corruption during the boot process. Once this is done, the root file system is automatically remounted with read/write access.

This ends the first block. A block is separated from the next block by a line beginning with either **image=** or **other=**. In our example, the next block starts with **other=/ dev/hda1**. For this example, the **/dev/hda1** partition, as it turns out, is set up with a complete DOS installation. (This could just as well be Windows 95/98, Windows NT, or Windows 2000.) As in the preceding block, you see the **label=** line; however, that's where the similarities end. The next line is **table=/dev/hda**, which specifies where table information can be found for the operating system on the partition you are trying to boot (**/dev/hda1**).

NOTE

Although DOS and Windows are the most common "other" operating systems in a dual-boot configuration, they are not the only options you have. LILO can be used to boot any other operating system that understands partitions.

Additional LILO Options

In addition to the options discussed above, a number of other options can be placed in the **lilo.conf** file. This section describes the most common options. With these, you should be able to configure most (if not all) of your systems without a problem. For those rare situations requiring additional configuration, you can read the man page on **lilo.conf**; it gives a brief rundown of all the available options.

Global Options in lilo.conf

The following global options are applicable to the entire configuration file, not just one particular block.

`default=name`	Specifies the default operating system that should boot. If this is not specified, the first block is the default.
`message=message-file`	You can specify that a message (whose text is in *message-file*) be displayed before presenting a `lilo:` prompt. This message cannot be longer than 64K, and if it is changed, the map file must be rebuilt. (See the upcoming section "Run LILO.")
`prompt`	Forces LILO to display a `lilo:` prompt and wait for user response. Automated reboots cannot be done if this option is specified and the `timeout` option is not.
`timeout=deciseconds`	Specifies the number of deciseconds (tenths of a second) to wait at a prompt before selecting the `default` boot option and continuing with the boot process.

Per-Block Options

The options listed in this section apply only to specific blocks that designate bootable operating systems.

`image=image name`	Specifies which Linux kernel to boot.
`other=image name`	Specifies other arbitrary operating systems to boot.
`table=device name`	For a particular block, specifies which device stores the partition table.
`label=name`	The name of the block that should be displayed if the user requests a list at the `lilo:` prompt. This label should be unique across all blocks.
`password=password`	Indicates that an image should be booted only if the *password* is correctly specified by the user.
`restricted`	User must enter a password if any command-line parameters are passed to the kernel. (This is especially important if you need to password-protect the single-user mode environment.)

NOTE

If you opt to use either the **password** or **restricted** option, you should set the permissions on your **/etc/lilo.conf** file so that only root can read it. With the default permission setup, the file can only be changed by root, but anyone can read it. The command to set the read permission to root only is
`[root@ford /root]# `**`chmod 600 / etc/lilo.conf`**`.`

Kernel Options

Options can be passed to the kernel from LILO. Such options may include the request to boot into single-user mode (the most common usage of this feature). If you need to pass kernel options only once in a while (such as requesting to go into single-user mode), you can pass these parameters at the **lilo:** prompt. For example, at **lilo:** you might enter **linux s** to start the kernel image with the **linux** label and pass the parameter **s** to it. This boots Linux into single-user mode. Obviously, these options apply to Linux kernels only.

append=*string*	Append ***string*** to any command-line parameter the user specifies.
literal=*string*	Similar to **append**, except ***string*** replaces the passed parameters of a user's command line rather than being appended.
read-only	Specifies that the root file system should be mounted as read-only. After the kernel loads and runs a check on it using the **fsck** tool, the root file system is remounted as read/write.

Progress Check

1. What is LILO?

2. What is a POST?

3. What is the MBR?

4. What is a boot loader?

CRITICAL SKILL
7.4 Run LILO

Now that you are familiar with your **/etc/lilo.conf** file, it's time to actually run the LILO boot manager program and let it do its important work. Usually this is a relatively uneventful process.

---

1. LILO is the Linux Loader.
2. A POST is the computer's power-on self-test.
3. The MBR is the master boot record. The BIOS uses this to bootstrap the operating system.
4. A boot loader is a program that loads an operating system's kernel into memory and starts the OS.

In most cases, you will simply need to run LILO without any parameters. The result will look something like this:

```
[root@ford /boot]# lilo
Added linux *
Added dos
```

LILO has taken the information from **/etc/lilo.conf** and written it into the appropriate boot sector.

Viewing the man page on LILO reveals many command-line options. Most of them, however, have **lilo.conf** equivalents, so we won't examine them here. Table 7-1 lists the most important options for the **lilo** command.

7.5 Understand GRUB

Most of the modern distributions are using GRUB as the default boot loader during installation. Red Hat is now doing this and Mandrake has been using GRUB for some time. GRUB is a three-stage boot loader and has many advantages over LILO.

NOTE

You might notice that GRUB is a pre-1.0 release of software, also known as *alpha* software. Don't be frightened by this. If a distribution like Red Hat or Mandrake is using it in their installations, it is probably quality "alpha" code.

LILO Command Option	Description
`-t`	Tests the configuration without actually loading it. The **-t** option alone doesn't tell you much, but when used with the **-v** option (defined in this table), you can see exactly what LILO would do.
`-C config-file`	By default, LILO looks for the **/etc/lilo.conf** configuration file. You can specify an alternate file with this command-line option.
`-r root-directory`	Tells LILO to **chroot** to the specified directory before doing anything. The **chroot** command will change the root directory to the directory specified in **root-directory**. Typically, this option is used when booting from a floppy to repair a broken system, so that LILO knows which directories to search for files. (For example, if you boot from a floppy and mount the root file system to the **/mnt** directory, you will probably want to run LILO as **lilo -r /mnt**.)
`-v`	Makes LILO verbose about what it's doing.

Table 7-1 Command-Line Options to LILO

GRUB has a second-stage process that allows it to mount several file systems and grab its configuration file from disk. If you look in **/boot/grub**, you will see several files of the form **x_stage_1_5**, where *x* can be one of **e2fs**, **reiserfs**, or **xfs**. In the final stage, GRUB, like LILO, allows you to select from a list what operating system to load. Unlike LILO, though, you can break into the GRUB CLI and boot another kernel that is not in the configuration file. This feature alone is priceless. Sometimes you can configure a new kernel, put the kernel in **/boot** install a new version of LILO on the MBR and forget to keep your old kernel configuration around. If the kernel fails to boot, you are stuck booting off of a floppy disk or CD-ROM. With GRUB, you can simply get into the cli and load the original known working kernel and boot successfully. Also, GRUB is only installed once. Any modifications are stored in a text file, and any changes don't need to be written to the MBR or partition like LILO needs.

Installing GRUB

If you have installed a distribution and used GRUB, you can skip this section. Once you have installed GRUB on the MBR, you do not have to perform this procedure every time you make a kernel change. The first step to installing GRUB is to create a boot floppy disk. This will allow you to boot using the floppy disk and use GRUB to write itself to the MBR. Once you have booted, you will write the boot information and be able to boot off of the hard drive.

The GRUB Floppy Disk

You need to first locate the GRUB images, located by default in **/usr/share/grub/i386-redhat** on a Red Hat system. Then you will use the **dd** command to write the **stage1** and **stage2** images to the floppy disk:

```
[root@ford i386-redhat]# dd if=stage1 of=/dev/fd0 bs=512 count=1
```

This writes the file **stage1** to the first 512 bytes of the floppy disk. Then you will write the **stage2** image right after the first image:

```
[root@ford i386-redhat]# dd if=stage2 of=/dev/fd0 bs=512 seek=1
```

Now you can boot off of this floppy so you can install the GRUB boot loader.

Installing GRUB on the MBR

If you are going to install GRUB on the MBR, you need to set the root device for GRUB; this is where GRUB can find the kernel. To do this, run the **grub** command and enter in the following commands:

```
grub> root (hd0,0)
```

Now you can write GRUB to the MBR by using the **setup** command:

```
grub> setup (hd0,0)
```

Configuring GRUB

Since you only have to install GRUB once on the MBR or partition of your choice, you have the luxury of simply editing a text file, **/boot/grub/menu.1st**. When you are done editing this file, you can simply reboot and select the new kernel that you added to the configuration. The configuration file looks like the following:

```
grub.conf generated by anaconda
#
# Note that you do not have to rerun grub after making changes to this file
# NOTICE:  You have a /boot partition.  This means that
#          all kernel and initrd paths are relative to /boot/, eg.
#          root (hd0,1)
#          kernel /vmlinuz-version ro root=/dev/hda6
#          initrd /initrd-version.img
#boot=/dev/hda
default=1
timeout=10
splashimage=(hd0,1)/grub/splash.xpm.gz
title Red Hat Linux (2.4.18-0.13)
        root (hd0,1)
        kernel /vmlinuz-2.4.18-0.13 ro root=/dev/hda6 hdd=ide-scsi
        initrd /initrd-2.4.18-0.13.img
title Windows XP
        rootnoverify (hd0,0)
        chainloader +1
```

After looking at the LILO configuration file, these options should make sense. The only difference is that GRUB uses a different naming convention for the partitions. In the above listing, your Linux kernel (in **/boot**) is on the second partition of the first hard drive. Windows XP is on the first partition of the first hard drive. The **splashimage** option is to show an image on the screen when you select which operating system to boot. The **initrd** option allows you to load kernel modules from an image, not the modules from **/lib/modules**. See the GRUB **info** pages, available through the **info** command, for more information on the configuration options.

NOTE

You might be wondering what the **initrd** option is really for. Basically, this allows distributions to use a generic kernel that only supports the native Linux file system, which is currently **ext3**. The problem that occurs is that you might need a file system module to load all of your new modules—if you chose to install the ReiserFS file system, for example. This is a chicken before the egg problem. The solution is to provide the kernel with an image that contains necessary loadable modules to get the rest of the modules.

Project 7-1 Adding a New Kernel to Boot with LILO

In Module 10, we discuss the process of compiling new kernels to boot with. Part of that process requires adding an entry into the **/etc/lilo.conf** file so that LILO knows about the new kernel. More important, this entry allows you to keep the existing, working configuration in case the new kernel doesn't work as you'd like it to. You can always reboot and select an older kernel that does work.

Module 10 has a project that involves compiling a 2.4.18 kernel with the 802.11b wireless networking support. You will either use LILO or GRUB to load this new kernel. This project will cover using the LILO boot loader. If you are using the GRUB boot loader, see Project 7-2.

Step by Step

1. Copy the new kernel into the **/boot** directory and name it **/boot/vmlinuz-2.4.18-wireless**. I prefer to name my custom kernel with a meaningful name so I don't forget what kernel is used for what. You will add the following to **/etc/lilo.conf**:

```
image=/boot/vmlinuz-2.4.18-wireless
    label=linux-wireless
    root=/dev/hda2
    read-only
```

NOTE

root is **/dev/hda2** in the example system. Set the root variable to whatever the root file system is on your system.

2. If you want this kernel to be the default kernel, you need to change the default variable at the beginning of the configuration file to the following:

```
default=vmlinux-2.4.18-wireless
```

3. Examine the final configuration file:

```
default=vmlinux-2.4.18-wireless
boot=/dev/hda
prompt
timeout=50
image=/boot/vmlinuz-2.2.5-15
        label=linux
        root=/dev/hda2
        read-only
```

```
other = /dev/hda1
        label = dos
        table = /dev/hda
image=/boot/vmlinuz-2.4.18-wireless
        label=linux-wireless
        root=/dev/hda2
        read-only
```

4. Now run the **lilo** command to save the configuration to the MBR.

5. Reboot your system to verify that the kernel works.

Project Summary

In this project, you added the ability to boot a new kernel. The process is straightforward and usually involves little heartache. Just keep in mind that the first rule of thumb is to *always* keep a backup kernel that you know is working. That way, when you try out your new kernel and realize you forgot to compile in support for your file systems (yes, it can be done, believe me), you can simply boot into the known working configuration and recompile your kernel the right way.

Project 7-2 Adding a New Kernel to Boot with GRUB

Project
7-2

Adding a New Kernel to Boot with GRUB

For this project, you will use the GRUB boot loader to boot your new 802.11b kernel. The steps will be similar to Project 7-1, although the configuration and operation of GRUB is different.

Step by Step

1. Copy the new kernel into the **/boot** directory and name it **/boot/vmlinuz-2.4.18-wireless**. I prefer to name my custom kernel with a meaningful name so I don't forget what kernel is used for what. You will add the following to **/boot/grub/menu.1st**:

```
title Wireless Red Hat Linux (2.4.18-wireless)
        root (hd0,1)
        kernel /vmlinuz-2.4.18-wireless ro root=/dev/hda6 hdd=ide-scsi
```

NOTE

The **root** variable is for an example system. Set the **root** variable to whatever your root file system is on your system.

(continued)

2. If you want this kernel to be the default kernel, you need to change the default variable at the beginning of the configuration file to the number corresponding to the configuration block. Since your configuration block is the third one, you'll use 2 (the count starts from 0):

```
default=2
```

3. Examine the GRUB configuration file:

```
default=2
timeout=10
splashimage=(hd0,1)/grub/splash.xpm.gz
title Red Hat Linux (2.4.18-0.13)
        root (hd0,1)
        kernel /vmlinuz-2.4.18-0.13 ro root=/dev/hda6 hdd=ide-scsi
        initrd /initrd-2.4.18-0.13.img
title Windows XP
        rootnoverify (hd0,0)
        chainloader +1
title Wireless Red Hat Linux (2.4.18-wireless)
        root (hd0,1)
        kernel /vmlinuz-2.4.18-wireless ro root=/dev/hda6 hdd=ide-scsi
```

4. Notice that you don't need to run the **grub** command to write the configuration. Unlike LILO, GRUB will read this file after it has reached the second stage.

5. Reboot your system to verify that the new kernel works.

Project Summary

This project is very similar to the first project in this module. One thing to note is that you don't need to run GRUB after modifying the configuration file, since it is smarter than LILO. Also remember to always have your old kernel sitting around in case you need to boot it. GRUB lets you get away with removing a good configuration from the **menu.1st** file since you can tell GRUB to load a kernel through its cli upon bootup.

CRITICAL SKILL

7.6 Understand Bootstrapping

In this section, I'll assume you are already familiar with the boot process of other operating systems and thus already know the boot cycle of your hardware. This section will cover the process of bootstrapping the operating system. We'll begin with the Linux boot loader (usually LILO for PCs).

Kernel Loading

Once LILO has started and you have selected Linux as the operating system to boot, the very first thing to get loaded is the kernel. Keep in mind that no operating system exists in memory at this point, and PCs (by their unfortunate design) have no easy way to access all of their memory. Thus, the kernel must load completely into the first megabyte of available RAM. In order to accomplish this, the kernel is compressed. The head of the file contains the code necessary to bring the CPU into protected mode (thereby removing the memory restriction) and decompress the remainder of the kernel.

Kernel Execution

With the kernel in memory, it can begin executing. It knows only whatever functionality is built into it, which means any parts of the kernel compiled as modules are useless at this point. At the very minimum, the kernel must have enough code to set up its virtual memory subsystem and root file system (usually, the **ext3** file system). Once the kernel has started, a hardware probe determines what device drivers should be initialized. From here, the kernel can *mount* the root file system. (You could draw a parallel of this process to that of Windows being able to recognize and access its C drive.) The kernel mounts the root file system and starts a program called **init**.

NOTE

Obviously, we've omitted discussion of the many details of Linux kernel startup; these details are really only of interest to kernel developers. However, if you are curious you can visit the Kernel Hackers Guide at http://www.redhat.com:8080.

The init Process

The **init** process (which we'll examine more closely in Module 9) is the first non-kernel process that is started, and therefore it always gets the process ID number of 1. **init** reads its configuration file, **/etc/inittab**, and determines the *runlevel* where it should start. Essentially, a runlevel dictates the system's behavior. Each level (designated by an integer between 0 and 6) serves a specific purpose. A runlevel of **initdefault** is selected if it exists; otherwise you are prompted to supply a runlevel value.

The runlevel values are as follows:

0	Halt the system
1	Enter single-user mode (no networking is enabled)
2	Multiuser mode, but without NFS
3	Full multiuser mode (normal operation)
4	Unused
5	Same as runlevel 3, except using an X Window System login rather than a text-based login
6	Reboot the system

When it is told to enter a runlevel, **init** executes a script as dictated by the **/etc/ inittab** file. The default runlevel depends on whether you indicated the system should start with a text-based or X Window System login during the installation phase.

rc Scripts

In the preceding section, we mentioned that the **/etc/inittab** file specifies which scripts to run when runlevels change. These scripts are responsible for either starting or stopping the services that are particular to the runlevel.

Because of the number of services that need to be managed, **rc** scripts are used. The main one, **/etc/rc.d/rc**, is responsible for calling the appropriate scripts in the correct order for each runlevel. As you can imagine, such a script could easily become extremely uncontrollable! To keep this from happening, a slightly more elaborate system is used.

For each runlevel, a subdirectory exists in the **/etc/rc.d** directory. These runlevel subdirectories follow the naming scheme of **rcX.d**, where *X* is the runlevel. For example, all the scripts for runlevel 3 are in **/etc/rc.d/rc3.d**.

In the runlevel directories, symbolic links are made to scripts in the **/etc/rc.d/init.d** directory. Instead of using the name of the script as it exists in the **/etc/rc.d/init.d** directory, however, the symbolic links are prefixed with an **S** if the script is to start a service, or with a **K** if the script is to stop (or kill) a service. (See Module 6 for information on symbolic links.) Note that these two letters are case sensitive. You must use uppercase letters or the startup scripts will not recognize them.

In many cases, the order in which these scripts are run makes a difference. (You can't use DNS to resolve hostnames if you haven't yet configured a network interface!) To enforce order, a two-digit number is suffixed to the **S** or **K**. Lower numbers execute before higher numbers; for example, **/etc/rc.d/rc3.d/S50inet** runs before **/etc/rc.d/rc3.d/S55named** (**S50inet** configures the network settings, and **S55named** starts the DNS server).

The scripts pointed to in the **/etc/rc.d/init.d** directory are the workhorses; they perform the actual process of starting and stopping services. When **/etc/rc.d/rc** runs through a specific runlevel's directory, it invokes each script in numerical order. It first runs the scripts that begin with a **K**, and then the scripts that begin with an **S**. For scripts starting with **K**, a parameter of **stop** is passed. Likewise, for scripts starting with S, the parameter **start** is passed.

Let's peer into the **/etc/rc.d/rc2.d** directory and see what's there:

```
[root@ford rc2.d]# ls -l
total 0
lrwxrwxrwx   1 root     root            15 Aug 11  1998
 K15httpd ->> ../init.d/httpd
lrwxrwxrwx   1 root     root            15 Jul 29  1998
 K15sound ->> ../init.d/sound
lrwxrwxrwx   1 root     root            16 Jun 10 09:36
```

```
K20rstatd ->> ../init.d/rstatd
lrwxrwxrwx   1 root      root             13 Jun 10 09:39
S90xfs ->> ../init.d/xfs
lrwxrwxrwx   1 root      root             19 Jun 10 09:34
S99linuxconf ->> ../init.d/linuxconf
lrwxrwxrwx   1 root      root             11 Jul 29  1998
S99local ->> ../rc.local
```

Thus, when **K15sound** is invoked, it really starts the following instead:

```
/etc/rc.d/init.d/sound stop
```

If **S90xfs** is invoked, the following is what really gets run:

```
/etc/rc.d/init.d/xfs start
```

Writing Your Own rc Script

In the course of keeping a Linux system running, at some point you will need to modify the startup or shutdown script. There are two roads you can take to doing this:

- If your change is to be affected at boot time only, and the change is small, you may want to simply edit the **/etc/rc.d/rc.local** script. This script gets run at the very end of the boot process.

- On the other hand, if your addition is more elaborate and/or requires that the shutdown process explicitly stop, you should add a script to the **/etc/rc.d/init.d** directory. This script should take the parameters **start** and **stop** and act accordingly.

Of course, the first option, editing the **/etc/rc.d/rc.local** script, is the easier of the two. To make additions to this script, simply open it in your editor of choice and append the commands you want run at the end. This is good for simple one- or two-line changes.

If you do need a separate script, however, you will need to take the second option. The process of writing an **rc** script is not as difficult as it may seem. Let's step through it using an example, to see how it works. (You can use our example as a skeleton script, by the way, changing it to add anything you need.)

Assume you want to start a special program that pops up a message every 60 minutes and reminds you that you need to take a break from the keyboard (a good idea if you don't want to get carpal tunnel syndrome!). The script to start this program will include the following:

- A description of the script's purpose (so you don't forget it a year later)

- Verification that the program really exists before trying to start it

- Acceptance of the **start** and **stop** parameters and performance of the required actions

Given these parameters, here's the script we will write. Notice that lines starting with a number sign (#) are only comments and not part of the script's actions, except for the first line.

```sh
#!/bin/sh
#
# Carpal          Start/Stop the Carpal Notice Daemon
#
# description: Carpald is a program which wakes up every 60 minutes and
#              tells us that we need to take a break from the keyboard
#              or we'll lose all functionality of our wrists and never
#              be able to type again as long as we live.
# processname: carpald

# Source function library.
. /etc/rc.d/init.d/functions

[ -f /usr/local/sbin/carpald ] || exit 0

# See how we were called.
case "$1" in
  start)
        echo -n "Starting carpald: "
        daemon carpald

        echo
        touch /var/lock/subsys/carpald
        ;;
  stop)
        echo -n "Stopping carpald services: "
        killproc carpald

        echo
        rm -f /var/lock/subsys/carpald
        ;;
  status)
        status carpald
        ;;
  restart|reload)
        $0 stop
        $0 start
        ;;
  *)
        echo "Usage: carpald start|stop|status|restart|reload"
        exit 1
esac

exit 0
```

NOTE

Even though the #! line shows that this script is **/bin/sh**, it should be noted that **/bin/sh** is a symbolic link to **/bin/bash**. This is not the case on other UNIX systems.

Once you have a new script written, simply add the necessary symbolic links (symlinks, as described in Module 6) from the appropriate runlevel directory to have the script either start or stop. In our sample script, we want it to start only in either runlevel 3 or runlevel 5. This is because we are assuming these are the only two runlevels during which we will do normal day-to-day work. Lastly, we want the daemon to be shut down when we go to runlevel 6 (reboot). Here are the commands we enter to create the required symlinks:

```
[root@ford /root]# cd /etc/rc.d/rc3.d
[root@ford rc3.d]# ln -s ../init.d/carpal S99carpal
[root@ford rc3.d]# cd ../rc5.d
[root@ford rc5.d]# ln -s ../init.d/carpal S99carpal
[root@ford rc5.d]# cd ../rc6.d
[root@ford rc6.d]# ln -s ../init.d/carpal K00carpal
```

Notice that for runlevels 3 and 5, we used the number 99 after the **S** prefix; this ensures that the script will be one of the last things to get started as part of the boot process. For runlevel 6, we wanted the opposite—**carpald** should shut down before the rest of the components. (The sequence for starting components generally goes from most critical to least critical, whereas shutting components down goes from least critical to most critical.)

Seems rather elaborate, doesn't it? Well, the good news is that because you've set up this **rc** script, you won't ever need to do it again. More important, the script will automatically run during startup and shutdown and be able to manage itself. The overhead up front is well worth the long-term benefits.

Enabling and Disabling Services

At times, you may find that you simply don't need a particular service to be started at boot time. This is especially true if you are considering Linux as a replacement for a Windows NT File and Print server.

As described in the preceding sections, you can cause a service not to be started by simply renaming the symbolic link in a particular runlevel directory; rename it to start with a **K** instead of an **S**. Once you are comfortable with working the command line and the symbolic links, you'll find this to be the quickest way of enabling and disabling services.

7

Booting and Shutting Down

Although a GUI tool is a nice way to do this task, you may find yourself in a situation where there is no graphical interface (for example, you have logged in to a co-located server and cannot redirect the X Window System through the firewall). In that case, you will need to move the symlinks by hand in the **/etc/rc.d** directory.

Disabling a Service

To disable a service, you must first find out two things: the name of the service and the runlevel at which it starts. More than likely, you'll already know the name of it, and also more than likely, the service is started in both runlevels 3 and 5. If you aren't sure about the runlevel, use the **find** command (see Module 6) to find it. For example,

```
[root@ford rc.d]# find . -name "*nfs*" -print
```

will find all files containing the string "nfs". You'll likely get three hits (locations containing the sought file), the first being in the **init.d** directory. Recall that this is the main script that does the work, though it is not directly called. You do not want to remove this script in case you want to enable it again in the future. Going back to the results of the **find** command, you'll see that you got two hits in the **rc3.d** and **rc5.d** directories.

To remove the service, simply **cd** into those directories and rename the symlink so that instead of starting with an **S**, it starts with a **K**. By renaming the symlink, you'll be able to come back later and easily enable it without having to try and figure out the correct order that entry should be in (for example, should it be **S35nfs** or **S45nfs**?).

Enabling a Service

Enabling a service works just like disabling a service. You find the scripts that actually run at the appropriate runlevels, except instead of changing them from an **S** to a **K**, you'll change them *to* an **S** from a **K**.

If the symlink you are looking for does not exist, but the appropriate script in the **init.d** directory does exist, you can simply add a new symlink in the **rc3.d** and **rc5.d** directories. Be sure to use the correct format for the filename (see previous sections for details).

Odds and Ends of Booting and Shutting Down

Starting up and shutting down a Linux server is always troubling. This is because typical Linux servers run for very long periods of time without needing a reboot and thus, when they do need a reboot, something bad has usually happened.

Thankfully, Linux does an excellent job of self-recovery. It is rare to have to deal with a system that will not boot correctly, but that is not to say that it'll never happen—and that's what this section is all about.

fsck!

The File System Check (**fsck**) tool is automatically run on every boot. Its purpose is similar to that of Windows Scandisk: to check and repair any damage on the file system before continuing the boot process. Because of its critical nature, **fsck** is traditionally placed very early in the boot sequence.

If you were able to do a clean shutdown, **fsck** will run without incident. However, if for some reason you had to perform a hard shutdown (such as having to press the reset button), **fsck** will need to run through all of the local disks listed in the **/etc/fstab** file and check them. (And it isn't uncommon for the system administrator to be cursing through the process.)

If **fsck** does need to run, don't panic. It is unlikely you'll have any problems. However, if something does arise, **fsck** will prompt you with information about the problem and ask whether you want to repair it. See Module 8 for more details on the repair process. In general, you'll find that answering "yes, go ahead and repair it" is the right thing to do.

In the eight years I have administered UNIX systems, the only disks that **fsck** could not repair were those that were physically damaged or improperly terminated on a SCSI chain.

If you are running the new **ext3** or **reiserfs** file systems, you will not need to run **fsck** on them since they are journaled file systems. Because of this, the boot time will be greatly increased. The only tradeoff with running a journaled file system is the overhead involved in keeping the journal.

I Only See "LI" When I Boot! What Happened?

This is one of the more aggravating situations because it seems like you did everything right—what the heck happened? Thankfully, LILO makes an effort to tell you where the problem is, based on the number of characters it prints of the "LILO" string.

The most common of these errors is when LILO only prints the first two characters of the string ("LI") and then stops. When this happens, it is usually the case that the entire boot partition does not exist in the first 1,024 cylinders. Unfortunately, that means having to repartition your disk and reinstalling Linux.

As you are installing Linux again, be sure that the first partition you select to boot from exists completely below the 1,024-cylinder mark. This is due to a limitation in LILO that has been corrected in newer versions but has not been widely made available in new Linux distributions such as Red Hat.

Booting into Single-User ("Recovery") Mode

Under Windows, the concept of "Recovery Mode" was borrowed from a long-time UNIX feature of booting into single-user mode. What this means for you under Linux is that if something gets broken in the startup scripts that affects the booting process of a host, it is possible for you to boot into this mode, make the fix, and then allow the system to boot into complete multiuser mode (normal behavior).

To boot into single-user mode, you must be at the **lilo:** prompt that is presented to you at boot time. When there, press the TAB key so that your choices of kernels are presented to you. The first kernel listed is your default kernel that is booted. Enter the name of the kernel followed by a space and the keyword **single**. For example:

```
lilo: linux single
```

If you are using the GRUB boot loader, the steps are a little different. First you need to select the Linux OS that you want to boot and press the E key. You will see a menu listing of several kernels to boot. Usually you will use the arrow keys to select the menu item labeled Kernel. Then press the E key again. Now you can add the keyword **single** to the end of the line. Press ENTER to go back to the GRUB boot menu, then press B to boot the kernel into single-user mode.

When you boot into single-user mode, the Linux kernel will boot as normal, except when it gets to the point where it starts the **init** program, it will only go through runlevel 1 and then stop. (See previous sections in this module for a description of all the runlevels.) Depending on the system configuration, you will either be prompted for the root password or simply given a shell prompt. If prompted for a password, enter the root password and press ENTER, and you will get the shell prompt.

NOTE
Red Hat 7 users who have the graphical boot manager will need to press CTRL-X in order to switch back to text mode where there will be a **boot:** prompt. From there, you can enter the name of the kernel followed by an **s** to get into single-user mode.

At this time, you'll find that almost all the services that are normally started are not running. This includes network configuration. So if you need to change the IP address, gateway, netmask, or any network-related configuration file, you can. This is also a good time to run **fsck** manually on any partitions that could not be automatically checked and recovered. (The **fsck** program will tell you which partitions are misbehaving, if any.) A common problem that is easy to fix at this point is getting the DNS client-side configuration fixed right. (A typical symptom of bad client DNS configuration is that the system seems to hang for minutes on starting up services like Sendmail and NFS.) Simply edit the **/etc/resolv.conf** file and enter the correct IP address of your DNS server, and you're off.

NOTE

In single-user mode of many Linux distributions, only the root partition will be automatically mounted for you (Red Hat 7 will try to mount all of the partitions for you). If you need to access any other partitions, you will need to mount them yourself using the **mount** command. You can see all of the partitions that you can mount in the **/etc/fstab** file.

Once you have made any changes you need to make, simply press CTRL-D. This will exit single-user mode and continue with the booting process. Multiuser mode should run (runlevel 3 or 5, depending on whether you have the X Window System set to automatically come up).

If you need to reboot instead of continuing the boot process, remember that you need to unmount all of your disks by hand using the **unmount** command. Once you get to the point where the root partition is the only one left, simply remount it with read-only access like so:

```
[root@ford /root]# mount -o ro /
```

Then to reboot, simply run the **reboot** command.

Module 7 Mastery Check

1. What is LILO?

2. What is GRUB?

3. Is LILO a two- or three-stage boot loader?

4. What is a three-stage boot loader?

5. What is better, a three-stage boot loader or a two-stage boot loader?

6. What is the default **rc** directory for runlevel 5?

7. How are scripts in the **rc** directories called?

8. How do you disable a service that starts in runlevel 3?

9. If you disable a service that starts in runlevel 3, do you need to disable it in runlevel 5?

10. What is runlevel 6?

11. How do you boot into single-user mode?

12. What is single-user mode?

13. What is the configuration file for **init**?

14. How do you make the system boot into runlevel 5 by default?

Module 8

File Systems

L inux is built upon the foundation of *file systems*. They are the mechanisms by which the disk gets organized, providing all of the abstraction layers above sectors and cylinders. In this module, we'll discuss the composition and management of these abstraction layers supported by the default Linux file system, ext2.

We will also cover the many aspects of managing disks. This includes creating partitions, establishing file systems, automating the process by which they are mounted at boot time, and dealing with them after a system crash.

NOTE

Before beginning your study of this module, you should already be familiar with files, directories, permissions, and owners in the Linux environment. If you haven't yet read Module 6, it's best to read that module before continuing.

CRITICAL SKILL
8.1 Understand the Makeup of File Systems

Let's begin by going over the structure of file systems under Linux. It will help to clarify your understanding of the concept and let you see more easily how to take advantage of the architecture.

i-Nodes

The most fundamental building block of many UNIX file systems (including Linux's ext2) is the *i-node*. An i-node is a control structure that points to either other i-nodes or to data blocks.

The control information in the i-node includes the file's owner, permissions, size, time of last access, creation time, group ID, and so on. (For the truly curious, the entire kernel data structure is available in **/usr/src/linux/include/linux/ext2_fs.h**—assuming, of course, that you have the source tree installed in the **/usr/src** directory.) The one thing an i-node *does not* keep is the file's name.

As mentioned in Module 6, directories themselves are special instances of files. This means each directory gets an i-node, and the i-node points to data blocks containing information (filenames and i-nodes) about the files in the directory. Figure 8-1 illustrates the organization of i-nodes and data blocks in the ext2 file system.

Ask the Expert

Q: Why does it take a long time to move a big directory to another file system, yet when I move a directory within a file system it takes only seconds?

A: Since filenames are stored in the directory i-node, a copy within the file system simply involves updating the directory i-node to point to the i-node containing the data. When you copy across file systems, i-nodes don't transfer, so you have to create all of the i-nodes of the original file or files.

As you can see in Figure 8-1, the i-nodes are used to provide *indirection* so that more data blocks can be pointed to—which is why each i-node does not contain the filename. (Only one i-node works as a representative for the entire file; thus, it would be a waste of space if every i-node contained filename information.) For example, my 6GB disk contains 1,079,304 i-nodes. If every i-node consumed 256 bytes to store the filename, a total of about 33MB would be wasted in storing filenames, even if they weren't being used!

Each indirect block can point in turn to other indirect blocks if necessary. With up to three layers of indirection, it is possible to store files as large as 2GB on an ext2 file system.

NOTE

With the 2.4 kernel series, or patches to the 2.2 series, you can get files that are well above 2GB. One pitfall is that you have to recompile libc so that it will be able to seek into a file of that size. libc is a major undertaking and shouldn't be taken lightly.

TIP

2GB for a file system is usually enough space for day-to-day operations. When you start to run a database you might hit this problem, since it is quite possible and normal to see files of this size. The trick is to plan ahead and make sure you implement the large file support. Some commercial databases also use their own proprietary file system, so you might not see this problem.

Superblocks

The very first piece of information read from a disk is its *superblock*. This small data structure reveals several key pieces of information, including the disk's geometry, the amount of

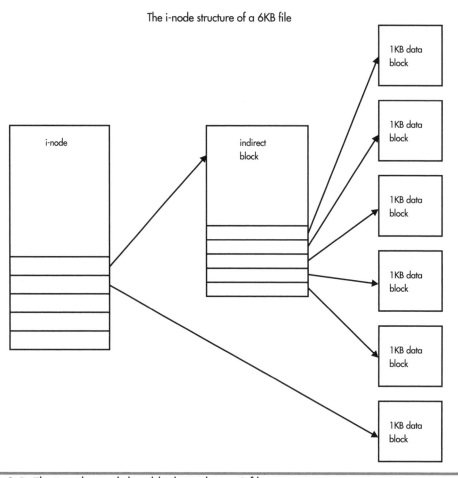

The i-node structure of a 6KB file

Figure 8-1 The i-nodes and data blocks in the ext2 file system

available space, and, most important, the location of the first i-node. Without a superblock, a file system is useless.

Something as important as the superblock is not left to chance. Multiple copies of this data structure are scattered all over the disk to provide backup in case the first one is damaged. Under Linux's ext2 file system, a superblock is placed after every *group* of blocks, which contains i-nodes and data. One group consists of 8192 blocks; thus, the first redundant superblock is at 8193, the second at 16385, and so on. The designers of the ext2 and ext3 file systems smartly put this superblock redundancy into the file system. Other UNIXes don't support this and you are left to restoring the file system from tape.

ext3 and ReiserFS

As of this writing, the ext2 file system is somewhere around nine years old. This means two things for us as system administrators. First and foremost, ext2 is rock solid. It is a well tested subsystem of Linux and has had the time to be very well optimized. Second, other file systems that were considered experimental when ext2 was created have matured and become available to Linux.

The two file systems that are the current candidates to replace ext2 in the next few years are ext3 and ReiserFS. Both offer significant improvements in performance and stability, but the most important component of both of them is that they have moved to a new way of getting the data to the disk. This new method is called *journaling.* Traditional file systems (such as ext2) must search through the directory structure, find the right place on disk to lay out the data, and then lay out the data. (Linux can also cache the whole process, including the directory updates, thereby making the process appear faster to the user.) New versions of Red Hat starting with 7.3 are using the ext3 file system by default. Other distributions such as Mandrake allow you to choose ext3 or ReiserFS upon installation (along with many other file systems).

The problem with not having a journaling file system is that in the event of an unexpected crash, the **fsck** program has to follow up on all of the files on the disk to make sure they don't contain any dangling references (for example, i-nodes that point to other, invalid i-nodes or datablocks). As disks expand in size and shrink in price, the availability of these large capacity disks means more of us will have to deal with the aftermath of having to **fsck** a large disk. And as anyone who has had to do that before can tell you, it isn't fun. The process can take a long time to complete, and that means downtime for your users.

With journaling file systems, the new way of getting data out to disk, instead of finding the right place, the file system simply writes the data out in any order it can, as fast as it can. Each time, it logs the location of these datablocks. You can think of it like using the same spiral notebook for multiple classes without pre-partitioning the notebook. It would be wiser to simply take notes for each class in chronological order instead of grouping all of one class together. A journaled file system is like such a notebook, with the beginning of the notebook containing an index telling you which pages contain all the notes for a single class. Once the data is written, the file system can go move things around to make them optimal for reading without risking the integrity of the file.

What this means to you as a system administrator is that the amount of time it takes for the disk to write out data is much less, while at the same time the safety of getting the data written out to disk quickly means that in the event of a system crash, you won't need to run **fsck**. Think of how much faster you could recover a system if you didn't have to run **fsck** on a 70G disk! (Haven't had to run **fsck** on a big disk before? Think about how long it takes to run Scandisk under Windows on large disks.)

If you want to learn more about the ext2 file system, I highly recommend taking a look at *Linux Kernel Internals*, edited by Michael Beck (Addison-Wesley, 1998). Although the book is a bit dated in many aspects of the kernel (it was written for the 2.0 series), the parts about the ext2 file system still hold true since ext2 is the base of the ext3 file system. When you look at the structure definition, you'll even notice that there are ACL stubs in the structure.

Which File System to Use?

You might be asking by now, which file system should I use? As of this writing, the current trend is to shift toward ext3. Most likely this will become the standard file system of choice. As with all things Linux, the choice is yours. I've run ReiserFS and haven't had any problems whatsoever, even after unplugging the power on purpose (don't try this unless you are prepared to deal with the consequences!). Your best bet is to try many file systems and see how they perform with the application you are using the system for. Journaling can add overhead, so you just might want to stay with an ext2 file system.

CRITICAL SKILL
8.2 Manage File Systems

The process of managing file systems is trivial—that is, the management becomes trivial *after* you have memorized all aspects of your networked servers, disks, backups, and size requirements with the condition that they will never again have to change. In other words, managing file systems isn't trivial at all.

There aren't many technical issues involved in file systems. Once the systems have been created, deployed, and added to the backup cycle, they do tend to take care of themselves for the most part. What makes them tricky to manage are the administrative issues—such as users who refuse to do housekeeping on their disks, and cumbersome management policies dictating who can share what disk and under what condition, depending, of course, on the account under which the disk was purchased, and . . . (It sounds frighteningly like a *Dilbert* cartoon strip, but there is a good deal of truth behind that statement.)

Unfortunately, there's no cookbook solution available for dealing with office politics, so in this section we'll stick to the technical issues involved in managing file systems—that is, the process of mounting and unmounting partitions, dealing with the **/etc/fstab** file, and performing file-system recovery with the **fsck** tool.

Mounting and Unmounting Local Disks

Linux's strong points include its flexibility and the way it lends itself to seamless management of file locations. Partitions are mounted so that they appear as just another subdirectory. Even a substantial number of file systems look, to the user, like one large directory tree.

This characteristic is especially helpful to the administrator, who can relocate partitions to various servers but can have the partitions still mounted to the same location in the directory tree; users of the file system need not know about the move at all.

The file system management process begins with the root directory. The partition containing the kernel and core directory structure is mounted at boot time. This single partition needs to have all the required utilities and configuration files to bring the system up to single-user mode. Many of the directories on this partition are empty.

As the boot scripts run, additional partitions are mounted, adding to the structure of the file system. The mount process overlays a single subdirectory with the directory tree of the partition it is trying to mount. For example, let's say that **/dev/hda1** is the root partition. It has the directory **/usr,** which contains no files. The partition **/dev/hda3** contains all the files that you want in **/usr,** so you mount **/dev/hda3** to the directory **/usr**. Users can now simply change directories to **/usr** to see all the files from that partition. The user doesn't need to know that **/usr** is actually a separate partition.

Keep in mind that when a new directory is mounted, the **mount** process hides all the contents of the previously mounted directory. So in our **/usr** example, if the root partition did have files in **/usr** before mounting **/dev/hda3,** those **/usr** files would no longer be visible. (They're not erased, of course—once **/dev/hda3** is unmounted, the **/usr** files would become visible again.)

Using the mount Command

Like many command-line tools, the **mount** command has a plethora of options, most of which you won't be using in daily work. You can get full details on these options from the **mount** man page. In this section, we'll explore the most common uses of the command.

The structure of the **mount** command is as follows:

```
mount [options] device directory
```

where **[options]** may be any of those shown in Table 8-1.

Option for mount	Description
-a	Mounts all the file systems listed in **/etc/fstab** (this file is examined later in this section).
-t fstype	Specifies the type of file system being mounted. Linux can mount file systems other than the ext2 standard, most notably FAT, VFAT, and FAT32. The **mount** command can usually sense this information on its own.
-o options	Specifies **options** applying to this **mount** process. These are usually options specific to the file system type (options for mounting network file systems may not apply to mounting local file systems).

Table 8-1 Options Available for the **mount** Command

Option for the `mount -o` Parameter (for Local Partitions)	Description
`ro`	Mounts the partition as read-only.
`rw`	Mounts the partition as read-write (default).
`exec`	Permits the execution of binaries (default).
`noatime`	Disables update of the access time on i-nodes. For partitions where the access time doesn't matter (such as news spools), this improves performance.
`noauto`	Disables automatic mount of this partition when the `-a` option is specified (applies only to the **/etc/fstab** file).
`nosuid`	Disallows application of `setuid` program bits to the mounted partition.
`sb=n`	Tells **mount** to use block **n** as the superblock on an ext2 file system.

Table 8-2 Options Available for Use with the `mount -o` Parameter

The options available for use with the **mount -o** parameter are shown in Table 8-2.

The following **mount** command mounts the **/dev/hda3** partition to the **/usr** directory with read-only privileges:

```
[root@ford /root]# mount -o ro /dev/hda3 /usr
```

Unmounting File Systems

To unmount a file system, use the **umount** command. Here's the command format:

```
umount [-f] directory
```

where **directory** is the directory to be unmounted. For example:

```
[root@ford /root]# umount /usr
```

unmounts the partition mounted on the **/usr** directory.

When the File System Is in Use   There's a catch to **umount**: if the file system is in use (that is, when someone has a file open on that partition), you won't be able to unmount that file system. To get around this, you have the following three choices:

File Systems

- You can use the **lsof** program (available at **ftp://vic.cc.purdue.edu/pub/ tools/unix/lsof**) or **fuser** to determine which processes are keeping the files open, and then kill them off or ask the process owners to stop what they're doing. (Read about the **kill** parameter in **fuser** on the **fuser** man page.) If you choose to kill the processes, be sure you understand the repercussions of doing so (read: don't get fired for doing this).

- You can use the **-f** option with **umount** to force the unmount process. Any processes with open files on the partition will be left hanging, and data may be lost.

- The safest and most proper alternative is to bring the system down to single-user mode and then unmount the file system. In reality, of course, you don't always get this luxury.

The /etc/fstab File

As mentioned earlier, **/etc/fstab** is a configuration file that **mount** can use. This file contains a list of all partitions known to the system. During the boot process, this list is read and the items in it are automatically mounted.

Here's the format of entries in the **/etc/fstab** file:

```
/dev/device /dir/to/mount       fstype    parameters    fs_freq        fs_passno
```

Following is a sample **/etc/fstab** file:

```
/dev/hda2               /                ext2    defaults    1 1
/dev/hda8               /home            ext2    defaults    1 2
/dev/hda7               /tmp             ext2    defaults    1 2
/dev/hda5               /usr             ext2    defaults    1 2
/dev/hda6               /var             ext2    defaults    1 2
/dev/hda1               /usr/local       ext2    defaults    1 2
/dev/hda3               swap             swap    defaults    0 0
/dev/fd0                /mnt/floppy      ext2    noauto      0 0
/dev/cdrom              /mnt/cdrom       iso9660 noauto,ro   0 0
/dev/hdc                /mnt/cdrom2      iso9660 noauto,ro   0 0
none                    /proc            proc    defaults    0 0
none                    /dev/pts         devpts  mode=0622   0 0
```

NOTE

You might notice with newer distributions that the device has been replaced with a token that looks like the following: **LABEL=/**. When you did the initial installation, the disk partitioning program set the label on the partition. Upon boot up, the system scans the partition tables and looks for these labels. Where this comes in *really* handy is when you are using SCSI. Typically, SCSI has a set SCSI ID. With this system, you can move the disk around and change the SCSI ID, and the system will still know how to mount the file system even though the device might have changed from **/dev/sda10** to **/dev/sdb10**.

Let's take a look at a few details of **/etc/fstab** that haven't been mentioned yet, most notably the entry of **swap** for **/dev/hda3**, and **none** for **/proc** and **/dev/pts**. In general, you'll never have to touch these file systems once the system is installed, so don't worry about them.

- The **/dev/hda3** partition is where virtual memory resides. In Linux, the virtual memory can be kept on a separate partition from the root partition. This is done to improve performance, since the swap partition can obey rules different than a normal file system. Since the partition doesn't need to be backed up or checked with **fsck** at boot time, the last two parameters on it are zeroed out. (Note that a swap partition can be kept in a normal disk file as well. See the man page on **mkswap** for additional information.)

- The **none** entry in conjunction with **/proc** is for the **/proc** file system. This is a special file system that provides an interface to kernel parameters through what looks like any other file system. Although it appears to exist on disk, it really doesn't—all the files represent something that is in the kernel. Most notable is **/dev/kcore**, which is the system memory abstracted as a file. People new to the **/proc** file system often mistake this for a large unnecessary file and accidentally remove it, which will cause the system to malfunction in many glorious ways. Unless you are sure you know what you are doing, it's a safe bet to leave all the files in **/proc** alone.

- The last entry in a **/etc/fstab** file, **/dev/pts** is for a new mechanism to improve implementation for network terminal support (**ptys**). This entry is necessary if you intend to allow remote login to your host via **rsh**, **telnet**, **rlogin**, or **ssh**.

If you use the Linuxconf configuration tool, you don't have to edit this **/etc/fstab** file directly. However, like anything else in system management, you should know how this file is organized in case you need to edit it by hand.

TIP

When mounting partitions with the **/etc/fstab** configured, you can run the **mount** command with only one parameter: the directory you wish to mount to. The **mount** command checks **/etc/fstab** for that directory; if found, **mount** will use all parameters that have already been established there. For example, here's the command to mount a CD-ROM given the **/etc/fstab** shown earlier:
[root@ford /root]# **mount /mnt/cdrom**.

Using fsck

The **fsck** tool, short for File System ChecK, is used to diagnose and repair file systems that may have become damaged in the course of daily operations. Such repairs are usually necessary after a system crash in which the system did not get a chance to fully flush all of its internal buffers to disk. (Although this tool's name bears a striking resemblance to one of the expressions often uttered after a system crash, that this tool is part of the recovery process is *strictly* coincidence.)

Usually, the system runs the **fsck** tool automatically during the boot process (much in the same way Windows runs Scandisk) if it detects a partition that was not cleanly unmounted. Linux makes an impressive effort to automatically repair any problems it runs across and, in most instances, does take care of itself. The robust nature of the ext2 file system helps in such situations. Nevertheless, it may happen that you get this message:

```
*** An error occurred during the file system check.
*** Dropping you to a shell; the system will reboot
*** when you leave the shell.
```

At this point, you need to run **fsck** by hand and answer its prompts yourself.

If you do find that a file system is not behaving as it should (log messages are excellent hints to this situation), you may want to run **fsck** yourself on a running system. The only downside is that the file system in question must be unmounted in order for this to work. If you choose to take this path, be sure to remount the file system when you are done.

fsck isn't the proper title for the ext2 repair tool; it's actually just a wrapper. The **fsck** wrapper tries to determine what kind of file system needs to be repaired and then runs the appropriate repair tool, passing any parameters that were passed to **fsck**. In ext2, the real tool is called **e2fsck** or **fsck.ext2**. When a system crash occurs, you may need to call **e2fsck** directly rather than relying on other applications to call it for you automatically.

For example, to run **e2fsck** on the **/dev/hda3** file system, you would run:

```
[root@ford /root]# e2fsck /dev/hda3
```

To force a check and automatically answer Yes to any prompts that come up, you would enter this command:

```
[root@ford]# e2fsck -f -y /dev/hda3
```

What If I Get Errors?

First, relax. The **fsck** check rarely finds problems that it cannot correct by itself. When it does ask for human intervention, telling **fsck** to execute its default suggestion is often enough. Very rarely does a single pass of **e2fsck** not clear up all problems.

On the rare occasions when a second run is needed, it *should not* turn up any more errors. If it does, you are most likely facing a hardware failure. Remember to start with the obvious: check for reliable power and well-connected cables. Anyone running SCSI systems should verify that they're using the correct type of terminator, that cables aren't too long, that SCSI

IDs aren't conflicting, and that cable quality is adequate. (SCSI is especially fussy about the quality of the cables.)

The lost+found Directory

Another rare situation is when **e2fsck** finds segments of files that it cannot rejoin with the original file. In those cases, it will place the fragment in the partition's **lost+found** directory. This directory is located where the partition is mounted, so if **/dev/hda3** is mounted on **/usr**, then **/usr/lost+found** correlates to **/dev/hda3**.

Anything can go into a **lost+found** directory—file fragments, directories, and even special files. When normal files wind up there, a file owner should be attached, and you can contact the owner and see if they need the data (typically, they won't). If you encounter a directory in **lost+found**, you'll most likely want to try and restore it from the most recent backups rather than trying to reconstruct it from **lost+found**.

At the very least, **lost+found** tells you if anything became dislocated. Again, such errors are extraordinarily rare.

CRITICAL SKILL
8.3 Add and Partition a Disk

The process of adding a disk under Linux on the Intel (x86) platform is relatively easy. Assuming you are adding a disk that is of similar type to your existing disks (for example, adding an IDE disk to a system that already has IDE drives or adding a SCSI disk to a system that already has SCSI drives), the system should automatically detect the new disk at boot time. All that is left is partitioning it and creating a file system on it.

If you are adding a new type of disk (like a SCSI disk on a system that only has IDE drives), you may need to compile in support for your SCSI card to the kernel. Note that most Linux distributions come with support for many popular SCSI cards as part of the standard installation. If you didn't recompile the kernel from the original installation, it is unlikely that you will need to recompile the kernel to add support. To compile in support for a new type of disk, see Module 10. Be sure to step through all of the relevant menus and mark the appropriate driver to be compiled either into the base kernel or as a module (assuming it can be compiled as a module).

Once the disk is in place, simply boot the system and you're ready to go. If you aren't sure about whether the system can see the new disk, run the **dmesg** command and see whether the driver loaded and was able to find your disk. For example:

```
[root@ford /root]# dmesg | more
```

Overview of Partitions

For the sake of clarity, and in case you need to know what a partition is and how it works, let's do a brief review of this subject. Every disk must be *partitioned. Partitions* divide up the disk, and each segment acts as a complete disk by itself. Once a partition is filled, it cannot automatically overflow onto another partition. Usually, the process of partitioning a disk accomplishes one of two goals. Either the user needs two different operating systems installed and each operating system requires its own partition, or it may be prudent that the usage of space on one partition not interfere with space dedicated to other tasks on other partitions.

An example of the latter occurs in user home directories. When users of the system are not the administrators of the system, the administrator must ensure that users don't consume the entire disk for their personal files. This takes up room needed for logging purposes and temporary files, causing the system to misbehave. To prevent this, a special partition is created for user files so that they don't overflow into protected system space.

NOTE

It is acceptable to partition a disk so that only one large partition is taking up the entire disk. But beware: if this is the boot partition, the entire partition must fit within the 1024 cylinder boundary or you will not be able to boot. See the LILO module (Module 7) for more information.

Where Disks Exist

Under Linux, each disk is given its own device name. IDE disks start with the name **/dev/hd***X*, where *X* can range from *a* through *z,* with each letter representing a physical device. For example, in an IDE-only system with one hard disk and one CD-ROM, both on the same IDE chain, the hard disk would be **/dev/hda** and the CD-ROM would be **/dev/hdb**. Disk devices are automatically created during system installation.

When partitions are created, new devices are used. They take the form of **/dev/hd***XY*, where *X* is the device letter (as described just above), and *Y* is the partition number. Thus, the first partition on the **/dev/hda** disk is **/dev/hda1**, the second partition would be **/dev/hda2**, and so on.

SCSI disks follow the same basic scheme as IDE, except instead of starting with **/dev/hd**, they start with **/dev/sd**. Therefore, the first partition on the first SCSI disk would be **/dev/sda1**, the second partition on the third SCSI disk would be **/dev/sdc2**, and so on.

Progress Check

1. What is the naming convention for IDE hard drives under Linux?

2. What task does the **/etc/fstab** file perform?

Creating Partitions

During the installation process, you probably used a "pretty" tool to create partitions. Unfortunately, Linux platforms don't ship with a standard utility for creating and managing partitions. A basic mechanism that does exist on all Linux distributions is **fdisk**. Though it's small and somewhat awkward, it's a reliable partitioning tool. Furthermore, in the event you need to troubleshoot a system that has gone really wrong, you should be familiar with basics such as **fdisk**. The only real downside to **fdisk** is its lack of a user interface.

CAUTION

The process of creating partitions is irrevocably destructive to the data already on the disk. Before creating, changing, or removing partitions on any disk, you must be very sure of what's on the disk being modified, and you need to have a backup if that data is still needed.

NOTE

An easier-to-use wrapper called **cfdisk** exists as well. However, this tool may not be available in an emergency situation, so it's best to learn how to use **fdisk** despite its awkwardness.

For this sample run, let's assume that we want to partition the **/dev/hdb** device, a 340MB IDE hard disk. (Yes, they do still exist.) We begin by running **fdisk** with the **/dev/hdb** parameter:

```
[root@ford /root]# fdisk /dev/hdb
```

---

1. IDE hard drives are named in the format of **/dev/hd***XY*, where *X* is the device letter and *Y* is the partition number.

2. The **/etc/fstab** file tells the system what file systems to mount upon startup. It also stores information for the **dump** and **fsck** commands.

which outputs a simple prompt:

```
Command (m for help):
```

Let's use **m** to see what our options are. This menu is reasonably self-explanatory:

```
Command (m for help): m
Command action
   a   toggle a bootable flag
   b   edit bsd disklabel
   c   toggle the dos compatibility flag
   d   delete a partition
   l   list known partition types
   m   print this menu
   n   add a new partition
   o   create a new empty DOS partition table
   p   print the partition table
   q   quit without saving changes
   s   create a new empty Sun disklabel
   t   change a partition's system id
   u   change display/entry units
   v   verify the partition table
   w   write table to disk and exit
   x   extra functionality (experts only)
Command (m for help):
```

We begin by looking at the existing partition, using the **p** command (print the partition table):

```
Command (m for help): p
Disk /dev/hdb: 16 heads, 63 sectors, 665 cylinders
Units = cylinders of 1008 * 512 bytes
   Device Boot    Start      End     Blocks   Id  System
/dev/hdb1   *         1      664    334624+    6  FAT16
Command (m for help):
```

We have a little legacy system here, don't you think? Time to upgrade this disk—we start by removing the existing partition using the **d** command (delete a partition):

```
Command (m for help): d
Partition number (1-4): 1
Command (m for help):
```

And we use the **p** (print the partition table) command to verify the results:

```
Command (m for help): p
Disk /dev/hdb: 16 heads, 63 sectors, 665 cylinders
```

```
Units = cylinders of 1008 * 512 bytes
   Device Boot    Start      End    Blocks   Id  System
Command (m for help):
```

No partition there. Time to start creating partitions. For the sake of discussion, we'll pretend this disk is large enough to accommodate a full workstation configuration. To set this up, we need to create the partitions shown in Table 8-3.

So now that we know which partitions to create, let's do it! We start with the root partition. Given that we have only 340MB to work with, we'll keep root small—only 25MB.

```
Command (m for help): n
Command action
   e   extended
   p   primary partition (1-4)
p
Partition number (1-4): 1
First cylinder (1-665, default 1): 1
Last cylinder or +size or +sizeM or +sizeK (1-665, default 665): +25M
Command (m for help):
```

Notice the first prompt is for whether we want a primary or extended partition. This is because of a goofy mess created long ago when hard disks were so small that no one thought more than four partitions would ever be needed. When disks got bigger and backward-compatibility was an issue, a trick was required to accommodate more partitions. The last partition would be an "extended" partition, unseen by the user but able to contain additional partitions.

The next question: which partition number? You can see the limit of four primary partitions as part of the question. We start with one, picking the default starting cylinder, and then specify that we want 25MB allocated to it.

To create the second partition for swap, we type the following:

```
Command (m for help): n
Command action
   e   extended
   p   primary partition (1-4)
p
Partition number (1-4): 2
First cylinder (52-665, default 52): 52
Last cylinder or +size or +sizeM or +sizeK (52-665, default 665): +16M
Command (m for help):
```

Partition	Description
/	The root partition is for those core system files necessary to bring a system to single-user mode. Once established, the partition's contents shouldn't vary at all and definitely shouldn't need to grow. The intent is to isolate this file system from other file systems, to prevent interference with core operations.
/usr	This partition is used for system software such as user tools, compilers, X Window System, and so forth. Because we may one day need to find a bigger home for our system software, we put this in a separate partition.
/var	The **/var** partition is used to hold files that change a lot—this usually includes spool directories (mail, print, and so on) and log files. What makes this partition worrisome is that external events can make its contents grow beyond allocated space. Log files from a Web server, for instance, can grow quickly and beyond your control. To keep these files from spilling over into the rest of your system, it's wise to keep this partition separate. (A type of attack via the network can be mounted by artificially generating so much activity on your server that the disk fills up with system logs and the system behaves unreliably.)
/tmp	Similar to **/var**, files in **/tmp** can unexpectedly consume substantial space. This can occur when users leave files unattended or application programs create large temporary files. Either way, maintaining this partition is a good safety mechanism.
/home	If you need to store home directories on your disk, especially for users whose disk consumption needs to be restricted, you'll definitely want to have this separate partition.
swap	The swap partition is necessary to hold virtual memory. Although it isn't required, swap is often a good idea in case you do exhaust all your physical RAM. In general, you'll want this partition to be the same size as your RAM.

Table 8-3 Disk Partitions and Their Typical Purpose

This time, the prompts are identical to those used for the previous partition, with slightly different numbers. However, by default, **fdisk** is creating ext2 partitions. We need this partition to be of type **swap**. To do this, we use the **t** (change partition type) command:

```
Command (m for help): t
Partition number (1-4): 2
Hex code (type L to list codes): L
  0   Empty           16   Hidden FAT16     61   SpeedStor        a6   OpenBSD
  1   FAT12           17   Hidden HPFS/NTF  63   GNU HURD or Sys  a7   NeXTSTEP
  2   XENIX root      18   AST Windows swa  64   Novell Netware   b7   BSDI fs
  3   XENIX usr       24   NEC DOS          65   Novell Netware   b8   BSDI swap
  4   FAT16 <32 <N    3c   PartitionMagic   70   DiskSecure Mult  c1   DRDOS/secFAT-
```

```
  5   Extended          40  Venix 80286      75  PC/IX            c4 DRDOS/secFAT-
  6   FAT16             41  PPC PReP Boot     80  Old Minix        c6 DRDOS/secFAT-
  7   HPFS/NTFS         42  SFS               81  Minix / old Lin  c7 Syrinx
  8   AIX               4d  QNX4.x            82  Linux swap       db CP/M / CTOS .
  9   AIX bootable      4e  QNX4.x 2nd part   83  Linux            e1 DOS access
  a   OS/2 Boot Manag   4f  QNX4.x 3rd part   84  OS/2 hidden C:   e3 DOS R/O
  b   Win95 FAT32       50  OnTrack DM        85  Linux extended   e4 SpeedStor
  c   Win95 FAT32 (LB   51  OnTrack DM6 Aux   86  NTFS volume set  eb BeOS fs
  e   Win95 FAT16 (LB   52  CP/M              87  NTFS volume set  f1 SpeedStor
  f   Win95 Ext'd (LB   53  OnTrack DM6 Aux   93  Amoeba           f4 SpeedStor
 10   OPUS              54  OnTrackDM6        94  Amoeba BBT       f2 DOS secondary
 11   Hidden FAT12      55  EZ-Drive         a0  IBM Thinkpad hi   fe LANstep
 12   Compaq diagnost   56  Golden Bow       a5  BSD/386          ff BBT
 14   Hidden FAT16      5c  Priam Edisk
Hex code (type L to list codes): 82
Changed system type of partition 2 to 82 (Linux swap)
Command (m for help):
```

The first question is, of course, what partition number do we want to change to? Since we want the second partition to be the swap, we entered **2**. The next prompt is a bit more cryptic: the hexadecimal code for the correct partition. My wife has to remind me what day it is sometimes, so you can imagine that I don't remember all these hexadecimal codes. The **L** command lists all available partition types. We spot 82 for Linux Swap, so we enter that, and we're done.

NOTE

It used to be that Linux's swap partition was limited to 128M. This is no longer the case. You can create a swap partition as large as 2GB.

Now for creating **/usr**. We'll make it 100MB in size:

```
Command (m for help): n
Command action
   e   extended
   p   primary partition (1-4)
p
Partition number (1-4): 3
First cylinder (85-665, default 85): 85
Last cylinder or +size or +sizeM or +sizeK (85-665, default 665): +100M
Command (m for help):
```

So at this point, we have three partitions: **root**, **swap**, and **/usr**. We can see them by entering the **p** command:

```
Command (m for help): p
Disk /dev/hdb: 16 heads, 63 sectors, 665 cylinders
Units = cylinders of 1008 * 512 bytes
   Device Boot    Start       End   Blocks   Id  System
/dev/hdb1              1        51   25672+   83  Linux
/dev/hdb2             52        84   16632    82  Linux swap
/dev/hdb3             85       288  102816    83  Linux
Command (m for help):
```

Now we need to create the extended partition to accommodate **/tmp**, **/var**, and **/home**. We do so using the **n** command, just as for any other new partition:

```
Command (m for help): n
Command action
   e   extended
   p   primary partition (1-4)
e
Partition number (1-4): 4
First cylinder (289-665, default 289): 289
Last cylinder or +size or +sizeM or +sizeK (289-665, default 665): 665
Command (m for help):
```

Instead of designating a megabyte value for the size of this partition, we enter the last cylinder number, thus taking up the remainder of the disk. Let's see what this looks like:

```
Command (m for help): p
Disk /dev/hdb: 16 heads, 63 sectors, 665 cylinders
Units = cylinders of 1008 * 512 bytes
   Device Boot    Start       End   Blocks   Id  System
/dev/hdb1              1        51   25672+   83  Linux
/dev/hdb2             52        84   16632    82  Linux swap
/dev/hdb3             85       288  102816    83  Linux
/dev/hdb4            289       665  190008     5  Extended
Command (m for help):
```

Now we're ready to create the last three partitions:

```
Command (m for help): n
First cylinder (289-665, default 289): 289
Last cylinder or +size or +sizeM or +sizeK (289-665, default 665): +100M
Command (m for help): n
First cylinder (493-665, default 493): 493
Last cylinder or +size or +sizeM or +sizeK (493-665, default 665): +45M
Command (m for help): n
```

```
First cylinder (585-665, default 585): 585
Last cylinder or +size or +sizeM or +sizeK (585-665, default 665): 665
Command (m for help):
```

Note that for the very last partition, we again specified the last cylinder instead of a megabyte value so that we are sure that we have allocated the entire disk. One last **p** command shows us what our partitions now look like:

```
Command (m for help): p
Disk /dev/hdb: 16 heads, 63 sectors, 665 cylinders
Units = cylinders of 1008 * 512 bytes
    Device Boot    Start        End     Blocks   Id  System
/dev/hdb1              1         51      25672+  83  Linux
/dev/hdb2             52         84      16632   82  Linux swap
/dev/hdb3             85        288     102816   83  Linux
/dev/hdb4            289        665     190008    5  Extended
/dev/hdb5            289        492     102784+  83  Linux
/dev/hdb6            493        584      46336+  83  Linux
/dev/hdb7            585        665      40792+  83  Linux
Command (m for help):
```

Perfect. We commit the changes to disk and quit the **fdisk** utility by using the **w** (write table to disk and exit) command:

```
Command (m for help): w
The partition table has been altered!
Calling ioctl() to re-read partition table.
Syncing disks.
WARNING: If you have created or modified any DOS 6.x
partitions, please see the fdisk manual page for additional
information.
[root@ford /root]#
```

If we needed to write an **/etc/fstab** file ourselves for this configuration, it would look something like this:

```
/dev/hdb1        /           ext2      defaults    1 1
/dev/hdb2        swap        swap      defaults    0 0
/dev/hdb3        /usr        ext2      defaults    1 2
/dev/hdb5        /home       ext2      defaults    1 2
/dev/hdb6        /var        ext2      defaults    1 2
/dev/hdb7        /tmp        ext2      defaults    1 2
none             /proc       proc      defaults    0 0
none             /dev/pts    devpts    mode=0622   0 0
```

Converting an ext2 File System to an ext3 File System

At this point, you might be asking why there weren't any ext3 options when you created the file system. The reason is because the ext3 extensions are built upon the ext2 file system. To convert to the ext3 file system, you must be running a kernel that supports the ext3 file system (as of this writing, most recent distributions contain support for ext3). To switch to the ext3 file system, enter the following command on the device you want to change:

```
[root@ford /root]# tunefs -j /dev/hda1
```

If you decide you want to revert back to the ext2 file system, simply issue the following command:

```
[root@ford /root]# tunefs -O has_journal /dev/hda1
```

This will clear the **has_journal** bit in the file system. The man page for **tunefs** recommends that you run an **fsck** on the file system to return it to a known state. Also, there are bits set in the file system that tell Linux when to do a forced **fsck** on the disks. Since ext3 doesn't need this, you can run the following command to turn off forced checks:

```
[root@ford /root]# tunefs -i 0 -c 0 /dev/hda1
```

Project 8-1   Making File Systems

With the partitions created, you need to put file systems on them. (If you're accustomed to Microsoft Windows, this is akin to formatting the disk once you've partitioned it.)

Under Linux, you use two tools for this process: **mke2fs** to create ext2 file systems, and **mkswap** to create swap file systems. There are many command-line parameters available for the **mke2fs** tool, many of which are needed only if you have an unusual situation. And if you have such an unusual need, I'm confident you don't need this text for guidance on creating file systems!

Step by Step

1. The only command-line parameter you'll usually have to set is the partition onto which the file system should go. To create a file system on the **/dev/hdb3** partition, you would issue the command

```
[root@ford /root]# mke2fs /dev/hdb3
```

and the result would look something like this:

```
[root@ford /root]# mke2fs /dev/hdb3
mke2fs 1.14, 9-Jan-1999 for EXT2 FS 0.5b, 95/08/09
```

(continued)

```
Linux ext2 file system format
File system label=
25792 inodes, 102816 blocks
5140 blocks (5.00%) reserved for the super user
First data block=1
Block size=1024 (log=0)
Fragment size=1024 (log=0)
13 block groups
8192 blocks per group, 8192 fragments per group
1984 inodes per group
Superblock backups stored on blocks:
        8193, 16385, 24577, 32769, 40961, 49153, 57345, 65537,
        73729, 81921, 90113, 98305
Writing inode tables: done
Writing superblocks and file system accounting information: done
[root@ford /root]#
```

2. Setting up swap space with the **mkswap** command is equally straightforward. The only parameter needed is the partition onto which the swap space will be created. To create swap space on **/dev/hdb2**, you would use

```
[root@ford /root]# mkswap /dev/hdb2
```

and the result would look something like this:

```
[root@ford /root]# mkswap /dev/hdb2
Setting up swapspace version 0, size = 17027072 bytes
[root@ford /root]#
```

3. Mount the file system with the **mount** command to see if everything worked:

```
[root@ford /root]# mount /dev/hdb3 /mnt
```

4. Add the file system permanently to **/etc/fstab** so that it gets mounted at boot time.

Project Summary

With this project, you can successfully create and add new partitions and file systems to your system. The good news is that adding disks isn't the most frequent thing that is going to happen. The bad news is that when you do have to add a new disk, you always have to yank out the books to remember how. I would recommend walking through the process at least once, so when the time does come that you need to create another partition you at least know what is supposed to happen.

Network File Systems

Network file systems make it possible for you to dedicate systems to serving disks while letting clients handle the computer-intensive tasks of users. Centralized disks mean easier backup solutions and ready physical security. Under Linux (and UNIX as a whole), disk centralization is accomplished through the Network File System (NFS). See Module 18 for more information on NFS.

✓

Module 8 Mastery Check

1. What partition code is the native Linux file system?

2. What partition code is the Linux swap file system?

3. What file contains file system device and mount point information?

4. What does the **fsck** program do?

5. How do you force a file system to be checked?

6. What function does the **mount** command perform?

7. What is a superblock?

8. What is the main difference between the ext2 and ext3 file systems?

9. What does the following command perform?

   ```
   [root@ford /root]# mke2fs /dev/hdb3
   ```

10. How do you convert an ext2 file system to an ext3 file system?

11. How do you format a partition for use as a swap?

12. What is an i-node?

13. What is a journaling file system?

Module 9

Core System Services

Regardless of distribution, network configuration, and overall system design, every Linux system has five core services: **init**, **inetd**, **xinetd**, **syslogd**, and **cron**. The functions performed by these services may be simple, but they are also fundamental. Without their presence, a great deal of Linux's power would be missed.

In this module, we'll discuss each one of the core services, its corresponding configuration file, and the suggested method of deployment (if appropriate). You'll find that the sections covering these simple services are not terribly long, but don't neglect this material. We highly recommend taking some time to get familiar with their implications (perhaps during those lovely commutes through traffic every morning). Many creative solutions have been realized through the use of these services. Hopefully, this module will inspire a few more.

CRITICAL SKILL
9.1 Understand the init Service

The **init** process is the patron of all processes. *Always* the first process that gets started in any UNIX-based system (such as Linux), **init**'s process ID is always 1. Should **init** ever fail, the rest of the system will most definitely follow suit.

The **init** process serves two roles. The first is being the ultimate parent process. Because **init** never dies, the system can always be sure of its presence and, if necessary, make reference to it. The need to refer to **init** usually happens when a process dies before all of its spawned children processes have completed. This causes the children to inherit **init** as their parent process. A quick execution of the **ps -af** command will show a number of processes that will have a parent process ID (PPID) of 1.

The second job for **init** is to handle the various runlevels by executing the appropriate programs when a particular runlevel is reached. This behavior is defined by the **/etc/inittab** file.

The /etc/inittab File

The **/etc/inittab** file contains all the information **init** needs for starting runlevels. The format of each line in this file is as follows:

```
id:runlevels:action:process
```

NOTE

Lines beginning with the number symbol (#) are comments. Take a peek at your own **/etc/inittab**, and you'll find that it's already liberally commented. If you ever do need to make a change to **/etc/inittab** (and it's unlikely that you'll ever need to), you'll do yourself a favor by including liberal comments to explain what you've done.

Table 9-1 explains the significance of each of the four items in the **/etc/inittab** file's line format.

/etc/inittab Item	Description
`id`	A unique sequence of 1–4 characters that identifies this entry in the **/etc/inittab** file.
`runlevels`	The runlevels at which the process should be invoked. Some events are special enough that they can be trapped at all runlevels (for instance, the CTRL-ALT-DEL key combination to reboot). To indicate that an event is applicable to all runlevels, leave **runlevels** blank. If you want something to occur at multiple runlevels, simply list all of them in this field. For example, the **runlevels** entry **123** specifies something that runs at runlevels 1, 2, and 3.
`action`	Describes what action should be taken. Options for this field are explained in Table 9-2.
`process`	Names the process (program) to execute when the runlevel is entered.

Table 9-1 /etc/inittab Line Entry Format

Table 9-2 defines the options available for the **action** field in the **/etc/inittab** file.

Values for `action` Field in /etc/inittab File	Description
`respawn`	The process will be restarted whenever it terminates.
`wait`	The process will be started once when the runlevel is entered, and **init** will wait for its completion.
`once`	The process will be started once when the runlevel is entered; however, **init** won't wait for termination of the process before possibly executing additional programs to be run at that particular runlevel.
`boot`	The process will be executed at system boot. The **runlevels** field is ignored in this case.
`bootwait`	The process will be executed at system boot, and **init** will wait for completion of the boot before advancing to the next process to be run.
`ondemand`	The process will be executed when a specific runlevel request occurs. (These runlevels are **a**, **b**, and **c**.) No change in runlevel occurs.
`initdefault`	Specifies the default runlevel for **init** on startup. If no default is specified, the user is prompted for a runlevel on console.
`sysinit`	The process will be executed during system boot, before any of the **boot** or **bootwait** entries.

Table 9-2 Options Available for the **action** Field in the **/etc/inittab** File

Values for *action* Field in /etc/inittab File	Description
powerwait	If **init** receives a signal from another process that there are problems with the power, this process will be run. Before continuing, **init** will wait for this process to finish.
powerfail	Same as **powerwait**, except that **init** will not wait for the process to finish.
powerokwait	If **init** receives the same type of signal as **powerwait**, when a file called **/etc/powerstatus** exists with the string "OK" in it, this process will be executed, and **init** will wait for its completion.
ctrlaltdel	The process is executed when **init** receives a signal indicating that the user has pressed CTRL-ALT-DEL. Keep in mind that most X Window System servers capture this key combination, and thus **init** will not receive this signal if the X Window System is active.

Table 9-2   Options Available for the *action* Field in the **/etc/inittab** File *(continued)*

Now let's look at a sample line from an **/etc/inittab** file:

```
# If power was restored before the shutdown kicked in, cancel it.
pr:12345:powerokwait:/sbin/shutdown -c "Power Restored; Shutdown Cancelled"
```

In this case:

- **pr** is the unique identifier

- **1, 2, 3, 4**, and **5** are the runlevels from which this process can be activated

- **powerokwait** is the condition under which the process is run

- The **/sbin/shutdown** . . . command is the process

The telinit Command

It's time to 'fess up: the mysterious force that tells **init** when to change runlevels is actually the **telinit** command. This command takes two command-line parameters. One is the desired runlevel that **init** needs to know about, and the other is **-t *sec***, where ***sec*** is the number of seconds to wait before telling **init**.

NOTE

Whether **init** actually changes runlevels is its decision. Obviously, it usually does, or this command wouldn't be terribly useful.

It is extremely rare that you'll ever have to run the **telinit** command yourself. Usually, this is all handled for you by the startup and shutdown scripts.

NOTE

Under most UNIX implementations (including Linux), the **telinit** command is really just a symbolic link to the **init** program. Because of this, some folks prefer running **init** with the runlevel they want rather than using **telinit**. Personally, I find that using **telinit** to change runlevels self-documents much more nicely.

Progress Check

1. What does the **telinit** program do?

2. What is the purpose of the **/etc/inittab** file?

3. What is **init**?

CRITICAL SKILL
9.2 Learn the inetd and xinetd Processes

The **inetd** and **xinetd** programs are daemon processes. You probably know that daemons are special programs that, after starting, voluntarily release control of the terminal from which they started. The only mechanism by which daemons can interface with the rest of the system is through interprocess communication (IPC) channels, by sending entries to the system-wide log file, or by appending to a disk file.

The role of **inetd** is as a "superserver" for other network server-related processes, such as **telnet** and **ftp**. It's a simple philosophy: Not all server processes (including those that accept new **telnet** and **ftp** connections) are called upon so often that they require a program to be running in memory all the time. So instead of constantly maintaining potentially dozens of services loaded in memory waiting to be used, they are all listed in **inetd**'s configuration file, **/etc/inetd.conf**. On their behalf, **inetd** listens for incoming connections. Thus only a single process needs to be in memory.

---

1. The **telinit** program allows you to switch runlevels and display which run level you are currently at.

2. The **/etc/inittab** file tells **init** what to do at each run level.

3. **init** is the master process. It is the first process spawned after the kernel is booted, and it is responsible for getting the system up and running.

A secondary benefit of **inetd** falls to those processes needing network connectivity but whose programmers do not want to have to write it into the system. The **inetd** program will handle the network code and pass incoming network streams into the process as its standard-in (**stdin**). Any of the process's output (**stdout**) is sent back to the host that has connected to the process.

NOTE

Unless you are programming, you don't have to be concerned with **inetd**'s **stdin/stdout** feature. On the other hand, for someone who wants to write a simple script and make it available through the network, it's worth exploring this very powerful tool.

As a general rule of thumb, low-volume services (such as Telnet) are usually best run through the **inetd**, whereas higher-volume services (such as Web servers) are better run as a standalone process that is always in memory ready to handle requests.

Current distributions of Red Hat and Mandrake started using a newer version of **inetd** called **xinetd**. The **xinetd** program accomplishes the same task as the regular **inetd** program, yet it includes a new configuration file format and some additional features.

Unfortunately, **xinetd** uses a format that is very different than the classic **inetd** configuration file format. (Most other variants of UNIX, including Solaris and FreeBSD, use the classic **inetd** format.) This means that if you have an application that relies on **inetd**, you may need to provide some hand adjustments to make it work. Of course, you should definitely contact the developers of the application and let them know of the change so that they can release a newer version that works with the new **xinetd** configuration format, as well.

In this section, we will cover the new **xinetd** daemon. If your system uses **inetd**, you should be able to read **/etc/inetd.conf** and see the similarities between **inetd** and **xinetd**.

The /etc/xinetd.conf File

The **/etc/xinetd.conf** file consists of a series of blocks that take the following format:

```
blockname
{
    variable = value
}
```

where **blockname** is the name of the block that is being defined, **variable** is the name of a variable being defined within the context of the block, and **value** is the value assigned to the **variable**. Every block can have multiple variables defined within.

One special block exists which is called "**defaults**." Whatever variables are defined within this block are applied to all other blocks that are defined in the file.

An exception to the block format is the **includedir** directive, which tells **xinetd** to go read all the files in a directory and consider them to be part of the **/etc/xinetd.conf** file.

Any line that begins with a number sign (#) is the start of a comment. The stock **/etc/inetd.conf** file that ships with Red Hat 7.3 looks like this:

```
#
# Simple configuration file for xinetd
#
# Some defaults, and include /etc/xinetd.d/

defaults
{
        instances               = 60
        log_type                = SYSLOG authpriv
        log_on_success          = HOST PID
        log_on_failure          = HOST RECORD
}

includedir /etc/xinetd.d
```

Don't worry if all of the variables and values aren't familiar to you yet; we will go over those in a moment. Let's first make sure you understand the format of the file.

In this example, the first four lines of the file are comments explaining what the file is and what it does. After the comments, you see the first block: **defaults**. The first variable that is defined in this block is **instances**, which is set to the value of 60. Four variables in total are defined in this block, the last one being **log_on_failure**. Since this block is titled **defaults**, the variables that are set within it will apply to all future blocks that are defined. Finally, the last line of the file specifies that the **/etc/xinetd.d** directory must be examined for other files that contain more configuration information. This will cause **xinetd** to read all of the files in that directory and parse them as if they were part of the **/etc/xinetd.conf** file.

Variables and Their Meanings

The variable names that are supported by **xinetd** are as follows:

Variable	Description
id	This attribute is used to uniquely identify a service. This is useful because services exist that can use different protocols and need to be described with different entries in the configuration file. By default, the service ID is the same as the service name.

Variable	Description
type	Any combination of the following values may be used: **RPC** if this is an RPC service, **INTERNAL** if this service is provided by **xinetd**, or **UNLISTED** if this is a service not listed in the **/etc/services** file.
disable	This is either the value **yes** or **no**. A **yes** value means that although the service is defined, it is not available for use.
socket_type	Valid values for this variable are **stream** to indicate that this service is a stream-based service, **dgram** to indicate that this service is a datagram, or **raw** to indicate that this service uses raw IP datagrams. The **stream** value refers to connection-oriented (TCP) data streams (for example, Telnet and FTP). The **dgram** value refers to datagram (UDP) streams (for example, the TFTP service is a datagram-based protocol). Other protocols outside the scope of TCP/IP do exist; however, you'll rarely encounter them.
protocol	Determines the type of protocol (either **tcp** or **udp**) for the connection type.
wait	If this is set to **yes**, only one connection will be processed at a time. If this is set to **no**, multiple connections will be allowed by running the appropriate service daemon multiple times.
user	Specifies the username under which this service will run. The username must exist in the **/etc/passwd** file.
group	Specifies the group name under which this service will run. The group must exist in the **/etc/group** file.
instances	Specifies the maximum number of concurrent connections this service is allowed to handle. The default is no limit if the **wait** variable is set to **nowait**.
server	The name of the program to run when this service is connected.
server_args	The arguments passed to the server. In contrast to **inetd**, the name of the server should not be included in **server_args**.
only_from	Specifies the networks from which a valid connection may arrive. (This is the built-in TCP Wrappers functionality.) You can specify this in one of three ways: a numeric address, a host name, or a network address with netmask. The numeric address can take the form of a complete IP address to indicate a specific host (such as 192.168.1.1). However, if any of the ending octets are zeros, the address will be treated like a network where all of the octets that are zero are wildcards (such as 192.168.1.0 means any host that starts with the numbers 192.168.1). Alternately, you can specify the number of bits in the netmask after a slash (for example, 192.168.1.0/24 means a network address of 192.168.1.0 with a netmask of 255.255.255.0).

Variable	Description
no_access	The opposite of **only_from** in that instead of specifying the addresses from which a connection is valid, this variable specifies the addresses from which a connection is invalid. It can take the same type of parameters as **only_from**.

log_type	Determines where logging information for that service will go. There are two valid values: **SYSLOG** and **FILE**. If **SYSLOG** is specified, you must specify to which syslog facility to log as well (see "Gain Knowledge of the syslogd Daemon," later in this module, for more information on facilities). For example, you can specify:
	
	`log_type = SYSLOG local0`
	
	Optionally, you can include the log level, as well. For example:
	
	`log_type = SYSLOG local0 info`
	
	If **FILE** is specified, you must specify which filename to log. Optionally, you can also specify the soft limit on the file size. The soft limit on a file size is where an extra log message indicating that the file has gotten too large will be generated. If the soft limit is specified, a hard limit can also be specified. At the hard limit, no additional logging will be done. If the hard limit is not explicitly defined, it is set to be 1% higher than the soft limit. An example of the **FILE** option is as follows:
	
	`log_type = FILE /var/log/mylog`

log_on_success	Specifies which information is logged on a connection success. The options include **PID** to log the process ID of the service that processed the request, **HOST** to specify the remote host connecting to the service, **USERID** to log the remote username (if available), **EXIT** to log the exit status or termination signal of the process, or **DURATION** to log the length of the connection.
port	Specifies the network port under which the service will run. If the service is listed in **/etc/services**, this port number must equal the value specified there.
interface	Allows a service to bind to a specific interface and only be available there. The value is the IP address of the interface that you wish this service to be bound to. An example of this is binding less secure services (such as Telnet) to an internal and physically secure interface on a firewall and not allowing it the external, more vulnerable interface outside the firewall.
cps	The first argument specifies the maximum number of connections per second this service is allowed to handle. If the rate exceeds this value, the service is temporarily disabled for the second argument number of seconds. For example: `cps = 10 30` This will disable a service for 30 seconds if the connection rate ever exceeds 10 connections per second.

You do not need to specify all of the variables in defining a service. The only required ones are:

- socket_type

- user

- server

- wait

An Example of a Simple Service Entry

Using the **finger** service as an example, let's take a look at one of the simplest entries possible with **xinetd**:

```
# default: on
# description: The finger server answers finger requests. Finger is \
#        a protocol that allows remote users to see information such \
#        as login name and last login time for local users.
service finger
{
        socket_type     = stream
        wait            = no
        user            = nobody
        server          = /usr/sbin/in.fingerd
}
```

In Red Hat 7.3, you can find this file in **/etc/xinetd.d/finger**.

Progress Check

1. What is **xinetd** used for?

2. What services are typically in the **xinetd** configuration files?

---

1. **xinetd** is used to call upon network services only when needed.
2. TCP and UDP network services such as Telnet and Finger.

Project 9-1 Enabling/Disabling the Telnet Service

This project walks you through the process of disabling services that are run through the **inetd/xinetd** daemon. If you want a secure system, chances are you will run with very few services—I know some people who don't even run **xinetd** at all! I typically will enable a service so I can do some quick maintenance, like compile SSH, then disable the insecure service. It takes three steps to disable a service: disable the service in the **inetd/xinetd** configuration file, restart the **inetd/xinetd** service, and finally test to make sure the service is indeed down. To enable a service is just the opposite procedure.

Step by Step

1. Edit the file **/etc/xinetd.d/telnet** and change the parameter **disable** to yes:

```
# default: on
# description: The telnet server serves telnet sessions; it uses \
#        unencrypted username/password pairs for authentication.
service telnet
{
        flags           = REUSE
        socket_type     = stream
        wait            = no
        user            = root
        server          = /usr/sbin/in.telnetd
        log_on_failure  += USERID
        disable         = yes
}
```

2. Restart the **xinetd** server.

3. Telnet to the box and see if the Telnet service is indeed down.

Project Summary

This project walked you through disabling a service with the **xinetd** configuration files. If you need to create another service to run under **xinetd**, just copy an existing one to a new filename and modify it for your needs. The process is simple to enable or disable a service. It is just a matter of testing and making sure that the services is either disabled or enabled. You don't want to think that you have disabled Telnet and have it still be running.

Gain Knowledge of the syslogd Daemon

With so much going on at any one time, especially with services that are disconnected from a terminal window, it's necessary to provide a standard mechanism by which special events and messages can be logged. Linux uses the **syslogd** daemon to provide this service.

The **syslogd** daemon provides a standardized means of performing logging. Many other UNIXs employ a compatible daemon, thus providing a means for cross-platform logging over the network. This is especially valuable in a large heterogeneous environment where it's necessary to centralize the collection of log entries to gain an accurate picture of what's going on. You could equate this system of logging facilities to the Windows NT System Logger.

The log files that **syslogd** stores to are straight text files, usually stored in the **/var/log** directory. Each log entry consists of a single line containing the date, time, host name, process name, PID, and the message from that process. A system-wide function in the standard C library provides an easy mechanism for generating log messages. If you don't feel like writing code but want to generate entries in the logs, you have the option of using the **logger** command.

As you can imagine, a tool with **syslogd**'s importance is something that gets started as part of the boot scripts. Every Linux distribution you would use in a server environment will already do this for you.

Invoke syslogd

If you do find a need to either start **syslogd** manually or modify the script that starts it up at boot, you'll need to be aware of **syslogd**'s command-line parameters, shown in Table 9-3.

The /etc/syslog.conf File

The **/etc/syslog.conf** file contains the configuration information that **syslogd** needs to run. This file's format is a little unusual, but the default configuration file you have will probably suffice unless you begin needing to seek out specific information in specific files or sent to remote logging machines.

Log Message Classifications

Before you can understand the **/etc/syslog.conf** file format itself, you have to understand how log messages get classified. Each message has a *facility* and a *priority*. The facility tells you from which subsystem the message originated, and the priority tells you how important the message is. These two values are separated by a period.

Both values have string equivalents, making them easier to remember. The string equivalents for facility and priority are listed in Tables 9-4 and 9-5, respectively.

Parameter	Description
-d	Debug mode. Normally, at startup, **syslogd** detaches itself from the current terminal and starts running in the background. With the **-d** option, **syslogd** retains control of the terminal and prints debugging information as messages are logged. It's extremely unlikely that you'll need this option.
-f *config*	Specifies a configuration file as an alternative to the default **/etc/syslog.conf**.
-h	By default, **syslogd** does not forward messages sent to it that were really destined for another host. Caution: If you use this parameter, you run the risk of being used as part of a denial-of-service attack.
-l hostlist	This option lets you list the hosts for which you are willing to perform logging. Each host name should be its simple name, not its fully qualified domain name (FQDN). You can list multiple hosts, as long as they are separated by a colon; for example, **-l toybox:ford:oid**.
-m interval	By default, **syslogd** generates a log entry every 20 minutes as a "just so you know, I'm running" message. This is for systems that may not be busy. (If you're watching the system log and don't see a single message in over 20 minutes, you'll know for a fact that something has gone wrong.) By specifying a numeric value for interval, you can indicate the number of minutes **syslogd** should wait before generating another message.
-r	By default, as a security precaution, the **syslogd** daemon refuses messages sent to it from the network. This command-line parameter enables this feature.
-s domainlist	If you are receiving **syslogd** entries that show the entire FQDN, you can have **syslogd** strip off the domain name and leave just the host name. Simply list the domain names to remove in a colon-separated list as the parameter to the **-s** option. For example: `-s x-files.com:conspiracy.com:wealthy.com`

Table 9-3 **syslogd** Command-Line Parameters

Facility String Equivalent	Description
auth	Authentication messages.
authpriv	Essentially the same as **auth**.
cron	Messages generated by the **cron** subsystem (see "Learn How to Use the cron Program," later in this module).

Table 9-4 Facility Values for **syslogd**

Facility String Equivalent	Description
`daemon`	Generic classification for service daemons.
`kern`	Kernel messages.
`lpr`	Printer subsystem messages.
`mail`	Mail subsystem messages (including per mail logs).
`mark`	Obsolete, but you may find some books that discuss it; `syslogd` simply ignores it.
`news`	Messages through the NNTP subsystem.
`security`	Same thing as `auth`; should not be used.
`syslog`	Internal messages from `syslog` itself.
`user`	Generic messages from user programs.
`uucp`	Messages from the UUCP (UNIX to UNIX copy) subsystem.
`local0 - local9`	Generic facility levels whose importance can be decided based on your needs.

Table 9-4 Facility Values for `syslogd` (continued)

Priority String Equivalent	Description
`debug`	Debugging statements.
`info`	Miscellaneous information.
`notice`	Important statements, but not necessarily bad news.
`warning`	Potentially dangerous situation.
`warn`	Same as `warning`; should not be used.
`err`	An error condition.
`error`	Same as `err`; should not be used.
`crit`	Critical situation.
`alert`	A message indicating an important occurrence.
`emerg`	An emergency situation.

Table 9-5 Priority Values for `syslogd`

NOTE

The priority levels are in the order of severity according to **syslogd**. Thus **debug** is not considered severe at all, and **emerg** is the most crucial. For example, the combination facility-and-priority string **mail.crit** indicates there is a critical error in the mail subsystem (for example, it has run out of disk space). **syslogd** considers this message more important than **mail.info**, which may simply note the arrival of another message.

In addition to the following table of priority levels, **syslogd** also understands wildcards. Thus, you can define a whole class of messages; for instance, **mail.*** refers to all messages related to the mail subsystem.

Format of /etc/syslog.conf

Here is the format of each line in the configuration file:

```
facility/priority combinations separated by commas    file/process/host to log to
```

For example:

```
kern.info, kern.emerg /var/log/kerneld
```

The location to which **syslogd** can send log messages is also quite flexible. It can save messages to files and send messages to FIFOs, to a list of users, or (in the case of centralized logging for a large site) to a master log host. To differentiate these location elements, the following rules are applied to the location entry:

- If the location begins with a slash (/), the message is going to a file.
- If the location begins with a pipe (|), the message is going to a FIFO.
- If the location begins with an @, the message is going to a host.

Table 9-6 shows examples of location entries according to these rules.

Location Style	Description
/var/log/logfile	A file. Note: If you prefix the filename with a dash, **syslogd** will not synchronize the file system after the write. This means you run the risk of losing some data if there is a crash before the system gets a chance to flush its buffers. On the other hand, if an application is being overly verbose about its logging, you'll gain performance using this option. Remember: If you want messages sent to the console, you need to specify **/dev/console**.

Table 9-6 Examples of Location Entries

Location Style	Description
|/tmp/mypipe	A pipe. This type of file is created with the **mknod** command. With **syslogd** feeding one side of the pipe, you can have another program running that reads the other side of the pipe. This is an effective way to have programs parsing log output, looking for critical situations, so that you can be paged if necessary.
@loghost	A host name. This example will send the message to **loghost**. The **syslogd** daemon on **loghost** will then record the message.

Table 9-6 Examples of Location Entries *(continued)*

If you enter no special character before the location entry, **syslogd** assumes that the location is a comma-separated list of users who will have the message written to their screen.

If you use an asterisk (*), **syslogd** will send the message to all of the users who are logged in. As usual, any line that begins with a number symbol (#) is a comment.

Now let's look at some examples of configuration file entries:

```
# Log all the mail messages in one place.
mail.* /var/log/maillog
```

This example shows that all priorities in the mail facility should have their messages placed in the **/var/log/maillog** file.

Consider the next example:

```
# Everybody gets emergency messages, plus log them on another
# machine.
*.emerg        @loghost,sshah,hdc,root
```

In this example, you see that any facility with a log level of **emerg** is sent to another system running **syslogd** called **loghost**. Also, if the user hdc, sshah, or root is logged in, the message being logged is written to the user's console.

You can also specify multiple selectors on a single line for a single event. For example:

```
*.info;mail.none;authpriv.none                    /var/log/messages
```

Sample /etc/syslog.conf File

Following is a complete **syslog.conf** file:

```
# Log all kernel messages to the console.
# Logging much else clutters up the screen.
#kern.*                                       /dev/console

# Log anything (except mail) of level info or higher.
# Don't log private authentication messages!
*.info;mail.none;authpriv.none                /var/log/messages

# The authpriv file has restricted access.
authpriv.*                                    /var/log/secure

# Log all the mail messages in one place.
mail.*                                        /var/log/maillog
# Everybody gets emergency messages, plus log them on another
# machine.
*.emerg                                               *

# Save mail and news errors of level err and higher in a
# special file.
uucp,news.crit                                /var/log/spooler

# Save boot messages also to boot.log
local7.*                                      /var/log/boot.log
```

CRITICAL SKILL
9.4 Learn How to Use the cron Program

The **cron** program allows any user in the system to schedule a program to run on any date, at any time, or on a particular day of week, down to the minute. Using **cron** is an extremely efficient way to automate your system, generate reports on a regular basis, and perform other periodic chores. (Not-so-honest uses of **cron** include having it invoke a system to have you paged when you want to get out of a meeting!)

Like the other services we've discussed in this module, **cron** is started by the boot scripts and is most likely already configured for you. A quick check of the process listing should show it quietly running in the background:

```
[root@ford /root]# ps auxw | grep cron | grep -v grep
root        341  0.0  0.0  1284   112 ?          S    Jun21    0:00 crond
[root@ford /root]#
```

The **cron** service works by waking up once a minute and checking each user's **crontab** file. This file contains the user's list of events that they want executed at a particular date and time. Any events that match the current date and time are executed.

The **crond** command itself requires no command-line parameters or special signals to indicate a change in status.

The crontab File

The tool that allows you to edit entries to be executed by **crond** is **crontab**. Essentially, all it does is verify your permission to modify your **cron** settings and then invoke a text editor so you can make your changes. Once you're done, **crontab** places the file in the right location and brings you back to a prompt.

Whether or not you have appropriate permission is determined by **crontab** by checking the **/etc/cron.allow** and **/etc/cron.deny** files. If either of these files exists, you must be explicitly listed there for your actions to be effected. For example, if the **/etc/cron.allow** file exists, your username must be listed in that file in order for you to be able to edit your **cron** entries. On the other hand, if the only file that exists is **/etc/cron.deny**, unless your username is listed there, you are implicitly allowed to edit your **cron** settings.

The file listing your cron jobs (often referred to as the **crontab** file) is formatted as follows. All values must be listed as integers.

```
Minute Hour Day Month DayOfWeek Command
```

If you want to have multiple entries for a particular column (for instance, you want a program to run at 4:00 A.M., 12:00 P.M., and 5:00 P.M.), then you need to have each of these time values in a comma-separated list. Be sure not to type any spaces in the list. For the program running at 4:00 A.M., 12:00 P.M., and 5:00 P.M., the **Hour** values list would read **4,12,17**. Newer versions of **cron** allow you to use a shorter notation for supplying fields. For example if you want to run a process every two minutes, you just need to put **/2** as the first entry. Notice that **cron** uses military time format.

For the **DayOfWeek** entry, 0 represents Sunday, 1 represents Monday, and so on, all the way to 6 representing Saturday.

Any entry that has a single asterisk (*) wildcard will match any minute, hour, day, month, or day of week when used in the corresponding column.

When the dates and times in the file match the current date and time, the command is run as the user who set the **crontab**. Any output generated is e-mailed back to the user. Obviously, this can result in a mailbox full of messages, so it is important to be thrifty with your reporting. A good way to keep a handle on volume is to output only error conditions and have any unavoidable output sent to **/dev/null**.

Let's look at some examples. The following entry runs the program **/usr/bin/ping -c** 5 zaphod every four hours:

```
0 0,4,8,12,16,20 * * * /usr/bin/ping -c 5 zaphod
```

or using the shorthand method:

```
0 */4 * * * /usr/bin/ping -c 5 zaphod
```

Here is an entry that runs the program **/usr/local/scripts/backup_level_0** at 10:00 P.M. every Friday night:

```
0 22 * * 5 /usr/local/scripts/backup_level_0
```

And finally, here's a script to send out an e-mail at 4:01 A.M. on April 1 (whatever day that may be):

```
1 4 1 4 * /bin/mail dad@domain.com < /home/sshah/joke
```

NOTE

When **crond** executes commands, it does so with the **sh** shell. Thus, any environment variables that you might be used to may not work within **cron**.

Edit the crontab File

Now that you know the format of the **crontab** configuration file you need to edit the file. You don't do this by editing the file directly; you use the **crontab** command to edit your **crontab**:

```
[root@ford /root]# crontab -e
```

To list what is in your current **crontab** file just give **crontab** the **-l** argument to concatenate the file to your terminal.

✓ Module 9 Mastery Check

1. What process has the process ID of 1?

2. What is the **/etc/inittab** file used for?

3. What line would you change to make the system boot into runlevel 3 by default?

4. What two commands could you issue to reboot the system?

5. Why is it a bad idea to kill the **init** process?

6. How would you let the **xinetd** server know you have changed the configuration file?

7. Why would you not want to use **inetd/xinetd** for high-volume servers?

8. What does the **cron** program do?

9. How would you schedule the script **/root/scripts/foo.sh** to run every five minutes every day of the month using **cron**?

10. How would a user modify his or her **crontab** file?

11. What file is used by **cron** for the system-wide **crontab**?

12. What is **syslog**?

13. Where is the configuration file for **syslogd** located?

14. Why would you want to send **syslog** messages to another **syslog** server?

15. Is **syslog** a reliable logging mechanism?

Module 10

Compiling the Linux Kernel

One of Linux's greatest strengths is that its source code is available to anyone who wishes to peer inside. The GNU GPL (general public license) under which Linux is distributed even allows you to tinker with the source code and distribute your changes! Real changes to the source code (at least, those to be taken seriously) go through the process of joining the official kernel tree. This requires extensive testing and proof that the changes will benefit Linux as a whole. At the very end of the approval process, the code gets a final yes or no from a core group of the Linux project's original developers who have the trust of Linus Torvalds. It is this extensive review process that keeps the quality of Linux's code so noteworthy.

NOTE

Linux's core development group is geographically quite diverse. Key people include Alan Cox in the U.K., Alexey Kuznetsov in Moscow, and Linus himself in California's Silicon Valley.

For systems administrators who have used other operating systems, this approach to code control is a significant departure from the philosophy of waiting for the company to release a patch, service release, or some sort of "hot fix." Instead of having to wade through public relations, sales engineers, and other front-end units, you have the option of contacting the author of the subsystem directly and explaining your problem. A patch can be created and sent to you before the next official release of the kernel, and get you up and running.

Of course, the flip side of this working arrangement is that you need to be able to compile a kernel yourself rather than rely on someone else to supply precompiled code. And, of course, you won't have to do this often, because production environments, once stable, rarely need a kernel compile. But if need be, you should know what to do. Luckily, it's not difficult.

NOTE

Not so long ago, most commercial UNIX-based operating systems required that their kernels be relinked whenever configuration changes were made. The process of relinking the kernel essentially involves taking all of the individual components of the kernel and gluing them together. This allows sites to add and remove components should they decide to make more efficient use of their available hardware. (Note that the individual components that were linked together were precompiled modules, not source code.) However, since the advent of dynamically loaded modules (discussed in more detail later in this module), most UNIX systems have removed the need for this step.

In this module, we'll walk through the process of acquiring a kernel source tree, configuring it, compiling it, and finally, installing the result.

CAUTION

The kernel is the first thing that loads when a Linux system is booted. If the kernel doesn't work right, it's unlikely that the rest of the system will boot. Be sure to have an emergency boot disk handy in case you need to revert to an old configuration. Also see the section on GRUB in Module 7.

CRITICAL SKILL
 10.1 Understand the Kernel

Before we jump into the process of compiling, let's back up a step and make sure you're clear on the concept of what a kernel is and the role it plays in the system. Most often, a reference to Linux is generally a reference to a Linux *distribution*. As discussed in Module 1, a distribution comprises everything necessary to get Linux to exist as a functional operating system in a networked environment. (For example, Red Hat Linux is a distribution.) Distributions contain code from projects that are independent of Linux; in fact, many of these projects can exist on other UNIX-like platforms as well. The GNU C Compiler, for example, which comes with all Linux distributions, also exists on many other operating systems (probably more systems than most people realize exist).

So, then, what *does* make up the pure definition of Linux? The *kernel*. The kernel of any operating system is the core of all the system's software. The only thing more fundamental than the kernel is the hardware itself.

The kernel has many jobs. The essence of its work is to abstract the underlying hardware from the software and provide a running environment for application software, through system calls. Specifically, the environment must handle issues such as networking, disk access, virtual memory, and multitasking—a complete list of these tasks would take up a module in itself! Today's Linux kernel (2.4.18) contains roughly 2.8 million lines of code (including device drivers). By comparison, the sixth edition of UNIX from Bell Labs in 1976 had roughly 9,000 lines. Figure 10-1 illustrates the kernel's position in a complete system.

Although the kernel is a small part of a complete Linux system, it is by far the most critical element. If the kernel fails or crashes, the rest of the system goes with it. Happily, Linux can boast its kernel stability. *Uptimes* (the length of time in between reboots) for Linux systems are often expressed in years. Indeed, UNIX systems in general regularly claim significantly long uptimes.

CRITICAL SKILL
10.2 Find the Kernel Source Code

Your distribution of Linux probably has the source code to the specific kernel it installed, whatever version that may be. If you find a need to download a different (possibly newer)

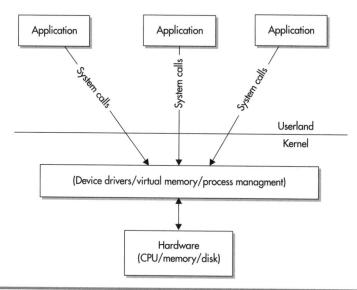

Figure 10-1 A visual representation of how the Linux kernel fits into a complete system

version, the first place to look for the source code is at the official kernel Web site: http://www.kernel.org/. This site contains a listing of Web sites mirroring the kernel source as well as several free tools and general-purpose utilities.

Under the site's link for downloading the kernel, you'll find a list of mirror Web sites based on country codes. Although you can connect to any of them, you'll most likely get the best performance by sticking to your own country. Go to http://www.*xx*.kernel.org/, where *xx* is the Internet country code for your country. For the United States, this address is http://www.us.kernel.org/.

NOTE

Because of how the online information system distributes load across multiple sites, you may see a different Web page every time you visit. Don't be concerned—all the sites are synchronized every night. Simply follow the links to the directory that stores copies of the kernel in which you're interested.

Get the Correct Version

The Web site listing of kernels available will contain folders for v1.0, v1.1, and so forth, and v2.2, v2.3, and so forth. Before you follow your natural inclination to get the latest version, make sure you understand how the Linux kernel versioning system works.

Because Linux's development model encourages public contributions, the latest version of the kernel must be accessible to everyone, all the time. This presents a problem, however: software that is undergoing significant updates may be unstable and not of production quality.

To circumvent this problem, early Linux developers adopted a system of using odd-numbered kernels (1.1, 1.3, 2.1, 2.3, and so on) to indicate a design-and-development cycle. Thus, the odd-numbered kernels carry the disclaimer that they may not be stable and should not be used for situations in which reliability is a must. These kernels typically come out at a very high rate since there is so much development activity—new versions of development kernels can be released as often as twice a week! Of course, this is a good thing for developers, because it allows them to keep careful watch of how things are progressing on all fronts.

On the other hand, even-numbered kernels (1.0, 1.2, 2.0, 2.2, and so on) are considered ready-for-production systems. They have been allowed to mature under the public's usage (and scrutiny). Unlike development kernels, production kernels are released at a much slower rate and only contain bug fixes. It is rare that an even-numbered kernel contains a new feature.

The version of the kernel that we are going to use is 2.4.18, available at http://www.kernel .org/linux/kernel/v2.4/linux-2.4.18.tar.gz.

Unpack the Kernel Source Code

Until now, you've probably seen most packages come in files with the .RPM extension, and you're most likely accustomed to using one of the tools that came with the system (such as **glint** or **gnoRPM**) to install the package. Kernel source code is a little different and requires some user participation. Let's go through the steps to unpack the kernel.

You'll start by renaming the existing tree so that you can revert back to it if the new version doesn't work out. Once the old tree is safe, you'll create a new directory for the version of Linux you're going to unpack. Only then are you ready to unpack it. Overall, it's really a straightforward process.

For the remainder of this module, we'll assume you are working out of the **/usr/src** directory. This is the traditional location of the kernel source tree.

Save the Current Source Tree

Before unpacking the new source tree, save and rename the current one. In the directory tree in **/usr/src**, you'll see a directory called **linux**:

```
[root@ford src]# ls -l
total 2
drwxr-xr-x   3 root     root        1024 Oct 16 09:33 linux
-rw-------   1 root     root    99502080 Oct 16 21:34 linux-2.4.18.tar.gz
drwxr-xr-x   7 root     root        1024 Oct 16 09:36 redhat
[root@ford src]#
```

In the **linux** directory is the current source tree. (Note that some distributions, including Red Hat, do not install the entire source tree by default. Only the necessary files for development purposes are installed.) The safe path to upgrading is to rename the existing tree with a suffix indicating its associated version number. Find out the current version number with the **uname** command, like so:

```
[root@ford src]# uname -r
2.4.18-3
[root@ford src]#
```

In this case, you want to rename the **linux** directory **linux-2.4.18-3**:

```
[root@ford src]# mv linux linux-2.4.18-3
```

NOTE

If someone has previously updated the running kernel, it's possible that the running kernel does not match the sources in **/usr/src/linux**. In this situation, you can find out the version of the kernel by looking at the file **makefile** in the **/usr/src/linux** directory. At the top of the file, you'll see lines indicating version, patch level, and sublevel. If version = 2, patch level = 3, and sublevel = 30, you have kernel version 2.3.30.

Modify the Directory Structure

Now take the opportunity to add some clarity to your directory structure. In our example, we had to use the **uname** command to find out the current version of the kernel and thus what to name the **linux** directory. This works acceptably well the first time around. However, in the event that you need to upgrade multiple times and wish to keep your older kernel source codes, you'll want to find a better way of tracking the association between directories and kernel versions.

So instead of creating a new directory called **linux**, we'll take advantage of the fact that we know we're working with the 2.4.18 kernel. We'll name the directory **linux-2.4.18**.

There is a slight catch to this naming convention. The kernel we've downloaded will automatically unpack into a directory called **linux**. Additionally, development tools that already exist in the system are expecting certain files to be in **/usr/src/linux**, not **/usr/src/linux-2.4.18**. Thus we use a symbolic link, as follows:

```
[root@ford src]# mkdir linux-2.4.18
[root@ford src]# ln -s linux-2.4.18 linux
```

```
[root@ford src]# ls -l
total 3
lrwxrwxrwx   1 root     root         12 Oct 12 21:23 linux -> linux-2.4.18
drwx------   2 root     root       1024 Oct 12 21:23 linux-2.4.18
drwxr-xr-x   3 root     root       1024 Oct 16 09:33 linux-2.4.18-3
-rw-------   1 root     root    9502080 Oct 16 21:34 linux-2.4.18.tar.gz
drwxr-xr-x   7 root     root       1024 Oct 16 09:36 redhat
[root@ford src]#
```

Unpack the Kernel

Now for the big finish: unpacking the kernel itself. This is done using the **tar** command:

```
[root@ford src]# tar -xzf linux-2.4.18.tar.gz
```

You'll hear your hard disk whirl for a bit—it is, after all, a large file! On a Pentium II 350MHz with a reasonably quick IDE drive, this step takes just under two minutes.

TIP

Take a moment to check out what's inside of the kernel source tree. At the very least, you'll get a chance to see what kind of documentation ships with a stock kernel. Developers can also take this opportunity to learn more about how Linux's innards work.

CRITICAL SKILL
10.3 Build the Kernel

So now you have an unpacked kernel tree just waiting to be configured. In this section, we're going to review the process of configuring a kernel. This is in contrast to operating systems such as Windows 2000, which come preconfigured and therefore contain support for many features you may not want.

The Linux design philosophy allows the individual to decide about the important parts of the kernel. (If you don't have a SCSI subsystem, what's the point in wasting memory to support it?) This individualized design has the important benefit of letting you thin down the feature list so that Linux can run on less-powerful systems with the same excellent performance. You may find that a box incapable of supporting Windows 2000 Server is more than enough for a Linux server.

Two steps are required in building a kernel: configuring and compiling. We won't get into the specifics of configuration in this module, which would be difficult because of the fast-paced evolution of Linux kernel distributions. However, once you understand the basic process, you should be able to apply it from version to version. For the sake of discussion, we'll cite examples from the v2.4.18 kernel that we unpacked in the previous section.

The make xconfig Process

The first step in building the kernel is configuring its features. Usually your desired feature list will be based on whatever hardware you need to support. This, of course, means that you'll need a list of that hardware. The following command will list all hardware connected to the system via the PCI bus:

```
[root@ford src]# cat /proc/pci
```

NOTE

Looking at the contents of the **/proc/pci** file is not the only way to probe your hardware. I highly recommend taking a look at what else is in the **/proc** file system.

With this list of hardware, you're ready to start configuring the kernel. Begin by starting the X Window System with the **startx** command. Once X is up and running, open a terminal window and enter these commands:

```
[root@ford /root]# cd /usr/src/linux
[root@ford linux]# make xconfig
```

The second command invokes the **make** utility. This development tool helps you create scripts describing all the steps necessary for compiling a program, but other uses for **make** (and many other well-designed tools for UNIX) have been found. One of these uses is to compile and execute the GUI configuration tool. Non-GUI tools exist as well and can be started with the **make config** or **make menuconfig** command.

The **make xconfig** command displays a window like that shown in Figure 10-2. In this opening window, you'll see all the top-level configuration menus. By clicking the buttons, you can open submenus listing all the specific features that you can enable. A default setting exists for most options, but it is recommended that you review all settings to make sure they're set as desired. When you've worked your way through all the menus, click the Save And Exit button.

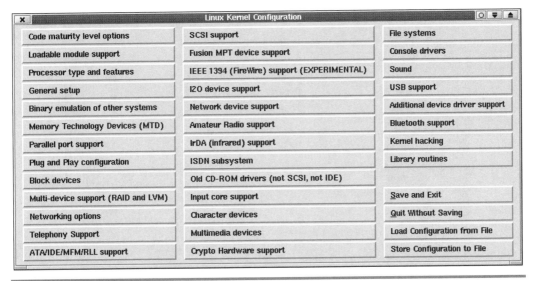

Figure 10-2 Main Linux kernel configuration window

Progress Check

1. How do you start the kernel configuration process?

2. In what directory is the Linux kernel typically stored?

Kernel Features and Modules

The General Setup submenu in the configuration utility is shown in Figure 10-3. The first three columns contain the option buttons Y (Yes), M (Module), and N (No). The fourth column contains the name of the option in question, and the fifth column offers a Help button that will bring up a related window explaining the feature.

---

1. `make xconfig`

2. **/usr/src/linux**

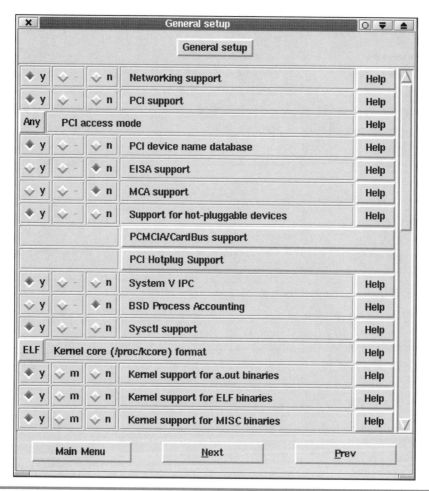

Figure 10-3 General Setup submenu

Answering Yes or No to enable or disable a kernel feature is simple enough, but let's take a closer look at the very cool *module configuration* option. As a systems administrator, you will find situations where you need a kernel feature only for extremely short periods of time. (An example is support for floppy disks; you'll rarely need this feature, but it's a good idea to have it nonetheless. Enabling that support, on the other hand, means the kernel requires more room in memory, which means less room for applications.)

With the module system, the kernel designers have created a way for parts of the kernel, called *modules*, to be dynamically loaded and unloaded from the kernel as needed. Features not often used can thus be enabled but won't waste memory when they aren't being used.

Thankfully, the kernel can automatically determine what to load and when; you enjoy the benefits of streamlined running without the burden of having additional management tasks.

NOTE

Traditionally, kernels have been written to require that all components reside in memory at all times, regardless of frequency of use. However, today's typical operating systems (including Linux) only keep in memory the absolute core of the system, which is always needed. Device drivers and certain networking features are now supported as modules.

Naturally, not everything is eligible to be compiled as a module. The kernel must know a few things before it can load and unload modules, such as how to access the hard disk and parse through the file system. If you aren't sure whether a particular feature can be compiled as a module, try it and see. As long as you have a way of accessing the system configuration (which we'll discuss later in this section), you can always go back and select Yes instead of Module for any configuration option.

The standard procedure in compiling the kernel is to walk through each of the top-level menu items and pick and choose which options you want to compile in to your kernel. The following project will cover how to compile the kernel after you have gone through the configuration of the kernel.

Project 10-1 Compiling the Kernel

This stage of the kernel-building process is by far the easiest, but it also takes the most time. The compile itself works in three stages. The first stage creates the *dependency tree*, which is a fancy way of saying that the system determines which files need to be compiled and which can be ignored. The second stage is the cleanup. Any previous compiles in this particular tree get tidied up, and old files are removed. Even if the tree is brand new, including this cleanup step never hurts. The last step is the compile itself. Once started, this last step doesn't need any attendance.

Because of the amount of code that needs to be compiled, be ready to wait a few minutes at the very least. A fast Pentium-based system may take upward of four to five minutes to churn through the entire source code.

Step by Step

1. After configuring the kernel, you need to run the following:

   ```
   [root@ford linux]# make dep; make clean
   ```

2. Now you need to make the kernel by typing:

   ```
   [root@ford linux]# make bzImage
   ```

(continued)

3. One last thing you need to do is compile all of the modules:

```
[root@ford linux]# make modules
```

Project Summary

If everything went smoothly, you should have a kernel waiting in **/usr/src/linux/arch/i386/boot**. We will cover the installation of the kernel and modules in the next project. When you start to compile the kernel a lot (and you know the build won't fail), you can combine the last three steps into one:

```
[root@ford linux]# make dep && make clean && make bzImage && make modules
```

This command will perform each step and make sure there are no errors in the process. So if **make dep** fails, nothing else will execute.

Project 10-2 Installing the Kernel

So now you have a fully compiled kernel just waiting to be installed. You probably have a couple of questions: Just where *is* the compiled kernel, and where the heck do I install it?

The first question is easy to answer. Assuming you have a PC and are working out of the **/usr/src/linux** directory, the compiled kernel will be called **/usr/src/linux/arch/i386/boot/ bzImage**. The map file for this will be **/usr/src/linux/System.map**. You'll need both files for the install phase. (If you did a **make zImage** instead of **make bzImage**, the compiled kernel will be **/usr/src/linux/arch/i386/zImage**).

Step by Step

1. Copy the **bzImage** file into **/boot**, renaming **bzImage** to:

vmlinuz-*x.x.xx*

where ***x.x.xx*** is the version number of the kernel. For the sample kernel you're using in this module, the filename would be **vmlinuz-2.4.18**. So the exact command for this example is as follows:

```
[root@ford linux]# cp /usr/src/linux/arch/i386/boot/bzImage /boot/vmlinuz-2.4.18
```

NOTE

The decision to name the kernel image **vmlinuz-2.4.18** is somewhat arbitrary. It's convenient because kernel images are commonly referred to as **vmlinuz**, and the suffix of the version number is useful when you have multiple kernels available. Of course, if you want to have multiple versions of the same kernel (for instance, one with SCSI support and the other without it), then you will need to design with a more representative name. For example, on my laptop I just compiled in 802.11b wireless support and named the new kernel: **vmlinuz-wireless**.

2. Now that the kernel image is in place, copy over the **System.map** file. This file is useful when the kernel is misbehaving and generating "Oops" messages. These messages include a lot of detail about the current state of the system, including a lot of hexadecimal numbers. **System.map** gives Linux a chance to turn those hexadecimal numbers into readable names, making debugging easier. Though this is mostly for the benefit of developers, it can be handy when you're reporting a problem.

3. Using the same convention as the kernel image itself, copy the **System.map** file like so:

```
[root@ford linux]# cp /usr/src/linux/System.map /boot/System.map-2.4.18
```

4. With the kernel in place, install the modules that you compiled earlier by running the following command:

```
[root@ford linux]# make modules_install
```

This will create a directory under the **/lib/modules** directory based on the version of the kernel being compiled and install the appropriate modules there.

5. With the proper files in place, edit the **/boot/grub/menu.1st** file so that the system recognizes these kernels as options when booting. Refer to Module 7 for details on the **menu.1st** file format. Let's consider a vanilla configuration in which this kernel is to be labeled **linux-2.4.18**, and the **df /boot** command (see Module 6) tells you that the images are located on the **/dev/hda1** partition. You would insert the following lines in the **/boot/grub/menu.1st** file:

```
title My New Kernel
     root(hda,0)
     kernel /boot/vmlinuz-2.4.18
```

6. If you are running GRUB, simply reboot and select the kernel you want when the prompt shows up. When you are confident that this is the kernel you will always want to boot with, you can change the line that says **default** accordingly to where you added your

Project 10-2

Installing the Kernel

(continued)

configuration. For example, if you added your new options to **/boot/grub/menu.1st** at the end of the file and you only have two kernels, you would change **default=0** to **default=1**.

NOTE

For full details on GRUB, see Module 7.

Project Summary

If everything went successfully, you should have a new kernel with a new feature that you wanted to add. Compiling the kernel is not a difficult process, and most of the time you get new features when you compile a new kernel.

It Didn't Work!

The kernel *didn't* fly, you say? It froze in the middle of booting? Or it booted all the way and then nothing worked right? First and foremost, *don't panic*. This kind of problem happens to everyone, even the pros. After all, they're more likely to try untested software first. So don't worry, the situation is most definitely reparable.

First, notice that when you added a new entry in the **/boot/grub/menu.1st** file, you *did not* remove the previous entry. You'll use that now. Reboot, and at the GRUB: prompt enter the name of the previous kernel that was known to work. This is probably called **linux**. This action should bring you back to a known system state.

Now go back to the kernel configuration and verify that all the options you selected will work for your system. For example, did you accidentally enable support for the Sun UFS file system instead of Linux's ext2 file system? Did you set any options that depended on other options being set? Remember to use the Help buttons beside each kernel option in the configuration interface, making sure that you understand what each option does and what you need to do to make it work right.

When you're sure you have your settings right, step through the compilation process again and reinstall the kernel. Remember, if you are using lilo you need to rerun `lilo` so that the changes take effect. If you are running GRUB, you simply need to edit **/boot/grub/menu.1st** and then reboot and try again.

Don't worry, each time you compile a kernel, you'll get better at it. When you do make a mistake, it'll be easier to go back, find it, and fix it.

✓

Module 10 Mastery Check

1. Would the kernel linux-2.5.23.tar.gz be classified as stable or as a beta kernel?

2. Where can you find the latest kernel on the Internet?

3. Where is the source to the Linux kernel stored on the file system?

4. How can you tell what version of the kernel you are currently running?

5. What command do you issue to configure the Linux kernel through a GUI interface?

6. After configuring the kernel, what commands need to be run to compile the new kernel?

7. Where is the kernel stored after you are done compiling it?

8. Do you have to make any changes to lilo or GRUB after you install a new kernel?

9. What is a loadable module?

10. How can you tell what devices are currently on the system?

11. What command is used to install the new modules?

Module 11

Securing an Individual Server

You don't have to look hard to find that someone has discovered yet another new and exciting way to break into your systems. Sites such as http://www.securityfocus.com/ and mailing lists such as BugTraq regularly announce such new exploits for the public to consume. And to make the situation even more troublesome for system administrators is the proliferation of "script kiddies." These individuals do not themselves possess the technical knowledge to break into other sites; they use pre-built scripts instead, usually for the sole purpose of impressing friends and being a nuisance. The positive result of this behavior is the Linux community being very responsive to security issues that come up. It's not unheard of to have security patches released in less than 24 hours of their announcement.

In this module, we discuss basic techniques for securing your server. If you follow these tips, you'll be more likely to keep out the script kiddies. But be advised: no system is perfect. New holes are discovered daily, and new tools to launch attacks come out more often than we'd like to imagine. Securing your systems is much like fighting off disease—as long as you maintain basic hygiene, you're likely to be okay, but you'll never be invulnerable.

Nearly all network administration texts today have chapters like this one, explaining which of the neat, network-friendly features you have to turn off so that crackers can't abuse them. Because of cracker-friendly programs such as Back Orifice, IT managers must constantly remain vigilant about protecting their Windows NT/2000 systems from unauthorized access. Unfortunately, it's a sad reality we have to deal with.

CRITICAL SKILL
11.1 Understand TCP/IP and Network Security

This module assumes you have experience configuring a system for use on a TCP/IP network. Because the focus here is on network security and not an introduction to networking, this section discusses only those parts of TCP/IP affecting your system's security.

The Importance of Port Numbers

Every host on an IP-based network has at least one IP address. In addition, every Linux-based host has many individual processes running. Each process has the potential to be a network client, a network server, or both. Obviously, if a packet's destination were identified with the IP address alone, the operating system would have no way of knowing to which process the packet's contents should be delivered.

To solve this problem, TCP/IP adds a component identifying a TCP (or UDP) *port*. Every connection from one host to another has a *source port* and a *destination port*. Each port is labeled with an integer between 0 and 65535.

In order to identify every unique connection possible between two hosts, the operating system keeps track of four pieces of information: the source IP address, the destination IP address, the source port number, and the destination port number. The combination of these four values is guaranteed to be unique for all host-to-host connections. (Actually, the operating system tracks a myriad of connection information, but only these four elements are needed to uniquely identify a connection.)

The host initiating a connection specifies the destination IP address and port number. Obviously, the source IP address is already known. But the source port number, the value that will make the connection unique, is assigned by the source operating system. It searches through its list of already open connections and assigns the next available port number. By convention, this number is always greater than 1024 (port numbers from 0 to 1023 are reserved for system uses). Technically, the source host can also select its source port number. In order to do this, however, another process cannot have already taken that port. Generally, most applications let the operating system pick the source port number for them.

Knowing this arrangement, we can see how source Host A can open multiple connections to a single service on destination Host B. Host B's IP address and port number will always be constant, but Host A's port number will be different for every connection. The combination of source and destination IPs and port numbers (a 4-tuple) is therefore unique, and both systems can have multiple independent data streams (connections) between each other.

For a server to offer services, it must run programs that listen to specific port numbers. Many of these port numbers are called *well-known services* because the port number associated with a service is an approved standard. For example, port 80 is the well-known service port for the HTTP protocol.

In "Using the netstat Command," later in this module, we'll look at the **netstat** command as an important tool for network security. When you have a firm understanding of what port numbers represent, you'll be able to easily identify and interpret the network security statistics provided by the **netstat** command.

For More Information on TCP/IP

There are many great books that discuss TCP/IP in greater detail. The *Network Administrators Reference* by Tere Parnell and Christopher Null (McGraw-Hill/Osborne, 1998) is a good place to start. This book discusses network administration from a high-level point of view and is a solid text all by itself (despite being very NT-centric). It discusses TCP/IP, but doesn't get too far into the nuts and bolts.

The ultimate TCP/IP bible (referenced by network developers and administrators around the world) is W. Richard Stevens's *TCP/IP Illustrated* series (Addison-Wesley, 1994–96). These books step you through TCP/IP and related services in painstaking detail. As a systems administrator, you'll be interested mostly in *Volume 1: The Protocols*, which addresses the suite of protocols and gives a strong explanation of IP stacks. If there's a kernel-hacker inside you who's curious about TCP/IP implementation, check out Stevens's line-by-line analysis of the BSD network code in *Volume 2: The Implementation.* (Although there's little resemblance between Linux's networking code and the code documented in *Volume 2*, the general guidance and philosophy therein is still invaluable.)

Another excellent book, *TCP/IP Network Administration*, by Craig Hunt (O'Reilly & Associates, 1998), is a solid network administration reference. It has a much greater breadth of topics (but less technical depth) than Stevens's *Volume 1*.

Finally, if you're responsible for implementing a firewall (and I recommend you do), the O'Reilly & Associates text on firewall design, *Building Internet Firewalls* (*2000x*), edited by D. Brent Chapman et al, is a good one. And from Cheswick and Bellovin (who built AT&T's first firewall), there's *Firewalls and Internet Security* (Addison-Wesley, 1994).

CRITICAL SKILL
11.2 Track Services

The services provided by a server are what make it a server. These services are accomplished by processes that bind to network ports and listen to the requests coming in. For example, a Web server might start a process that binds to port 80 and listens for requests to download the pages of a site. Unless a process exists to listen to a specific port, Linux will simply ignore packets sent to that port.

NOTE

Remember that when a process makes a request to another server, it opens a connection on a port, as well. The process is, in effect, listening to data coming in from that port. However, on the client the process knows to whom it's talking because it initiated the request. The client process will automatically ignore any packets sent to it that do not originate from the server to which it's connected.

This section discusses the usage of the **netstat** command, a tool for tracking network connections (among other things) in your system. It is, without a doubt, one of the most useful debugging tools in your arsenal for troubleshooting security and day-to-day network problems.

Using the netstat Command

To track what ports are open and what ports have processes listening to them, you use the **netstat** command. For example:

```
[root@ford /root]# netstat -natu
Active Internet connections (servers and established)
Proto Recv-Q Send-Q Local Address          Foreign Address        State

tcp       1      0 209.179.251.53:1297    199.184.252.5:80   CLOSE_WAIT
```

```
tcp       1       0 209.179.251.53:1296     199.184.252.5:80   CLOSE_WAIT
tcp      57       0 209.179.158.93:1167     199.97.226.1:21    CLOSE_WAIT
tcp       0       0 192.168.1.1:6000        192.168.1.1:1052   ESTABLISHED
tcp       0       0 192.168.1.1:1052        192.168.1.1:6000   ESTABLISHED

[root@ford /root]#
```

By default (with no parameters), **netstat** will provide all established connections for both network and domain sockets. That means you'll see not only the connections that are actually working over the network, but also the interprocess communications (which, from a security monitoring standpoint, are not useful). So in the command illustrated above, we have asked **netstat** to show us all ports (**-a**)—whether they are listening or actually connected—for TCP (**-t**) and UDP (**-u**). We have told **netstat** not to spend any time resolving host names from IP addresses (**-n**).

In the **netstat** output, each line represents either a TCP or UDP network port, as indicated by the first column of the output. The Recv-Q (receive queue) column lists the number of bytes received by the kernel but not read by the process. Next, the Send-Q column tells us the number of bytes sent to the other side of the connection but not acknowledged.

The fourth, fifth, and sixth columns are the most interesting in terms of system security. The Local Address column tells us our own server's IP address and port number. Remember that your server recognizes itself as 127.0.0.1 and 0.0.0.0 as well as its normal IP address. In the case of multiple interfaces, each port being listened to will show up on both interfaces and thus as two separate IP addresses. The port number is separated from the IP address by a colon. In the output from the **netstat** example shown above, one Ethernet device has the IP address 192.168.1.1, and the PPP connection has the address 209.179.251.53. (Your IP addresses will vary depending on your setup.)

The fifth column, Foreign Address, identifies the other side of the connection. In the case of a port that is being listened to for new connections, the default value will be 0.0.0.0:*. This IP address means nothing since we're still waiting for a remote host to connect to us!

The sixth column tells us the State of the connection. The man page for **netstat** lists all of the states, but the two you'll see most often are LISTEN and ESTABLISHED. The LISTEN state means there is a process on your server listening to the port and ready to accept new connections. The ESTABLISHED state means just that—a connection is established between a client and server.

Security Implications of netstat's Output

By listing all of the available connections, you can get a snapshot of what the system is doing. You should be able to explain and justify *all* ports listed. If your system is listening to a port that you cannot explain, this should raise suspicions.

If you've been using your memory cells for other purposes and haven't memorized the services and their associated port numbers, you can look up the matching info you need in the **/etc/services** file. However, some services (most notably those that use the portmapper) don't have set port numbers but are valid services. To see which process is associated with a port, use the **-p** option with **netstat**. Be on the lookout for odd or unusual processes using the network. For example, if the BASH shell is listening to a network port, you can be fairly certain that something odd is going on.

Finally, remember that you are only interested in the destination port of a connection; this tells you which service is being connected to and whether it is legitimate. Unfortunately, **netstat** doesn't explicitly tell who originated a connection, but you can usually figure it out if you give it a little thought. Of course, becoming familiar with the applications that you do run and their use of network ports is the best way to determine who originated a connection to where. In general, you'll find that the rule of thumb is that the side whose port number is greater than 1024 is the side that originated the connection. Obviously, this general rule doesn't apply to services typically running on ports higher than 1024, such as the X Window System (port 6000).

Shutting Down Services

One purpose for the **netstat** command is to determine what services are enabled on your servers. Making Linux easier to install and manage right out of the box has led to more and more default settings that are unsafe, so keeping track of services is especially important.

When you're evaluating which services should stay and which should go, answer the following questions:

1. *Do we need the service?* The answer to this question is very important. In most situations, you should be able to disable a great number of services that start up by default. A standalone Web server, for example, should not need to run NFS.

2. *If we do need the service, is the default setting secure?* This question can also help you eliminate some services—if they aren't secure and they can't be made secure, then chances are they should be removed. The Telnet service, for instance, is often a candidate for early removal because it requires that passwords be sent over the Internet without encryption.

3. *Does the service software need updates?* All software needs updates from time to time, such as that on Web and FTP servers. This is because as features get added, new security problems creep in. So be sure to remember to track the server software's development and get upgrades installed as soon as security bulletins are posted.

Shutting Down xinetd and inetd Services

To shut down a service that is started via the **xinetd** program, simply edit the service's configuration file in **/etc/xinetd** and set disable equal to Yes. If you are using a stock **inetd**, edit the **/etc/inetd.conf** file and comment out the service you no longer want. To designate the service as a comment, start the line with a number sign (#). See Module 9 for more information on **xinetd** and **inetd**.

Remember to send the HUP signal to **inetd** once you've made any changes to the **/etc/inetd.conf** file and a SIGUSR2 signal to **xinetd**. If you are using Red Hat Linux, you can also type the following command:

```
[root@ford /root]# /etc/rc.d/init.d/xinetd reload
```

Shutting Down Non-inetd Services

If a service is not run by **inetd**, then a process that is probably started at boot time is running it. The easiest way to stop that from happening is to change the symlink. Go to the **/etc/rc.d/** directory and in one of the **rc*.d** directories, find the symlinks that point to the startup script. (See Module 7 for information on startup scripts.) Rename the symlink to start with an X instead of S. If you decide to restart a service, it's easy to rename it again starting with an S. If you have renamed the startup script but want to stop the currently running process, use the **ps** command to find the process ID number and then the **kill** command to actually terminate the process. For example, here are the commands to kill a **portmap** process, and the resulting output:

```
[root@ford /root]# ps auxw | grep portmap
bin       255  0.0  0.1  1084  364 ?        S    Jul08  0:00 portmap
root      6634  0.0  0.1  1152  440 pts/0    S    01:55  0:00 grep portmap
[root@ford /root]# kill 255
```

NOTE

As always, be sure of what you're killing before you kill it, especially on a production server.

A Note About the syslogd Service

One non-**inetd** service that will pop up on **netstat** output but can be safely ignored is **syslogd**. This service has historically defaulted to binding to a network port and listening for network messages to log. Because of the danger of logging arbitrary messages from a network, Linux developers have added a mechanism whereby **syslogd** only logs requests sent from other hosts if it has been started with the **-r** option. By default, **syslogd** does not start with **-r**, so you can safely let it remain on your system.

Progress Check

1. What does **netstat** allow you to view?

2. How do I restart the **xinetd** daemon?

Project 11-1   Shutting Down Services

This project will guide you through shutting down services on your system and possibly making it more secure. Basically, you want to kill any services that you don't want running, make sure they are not going to start up after you reboot, and finally test to make sure the service is no longer running. This project will cover turning off the Telnet server.

Step by Step

1. Determine where Telnet is being run from. By default, it will be run from **xinetd**.

2. Edit the file **/etc/xinetd.d/telnet** and set the disable keyword to **yes**:

```
disable = yes
```

3. Restart the **xinetd** daemon:

```
[root@ford /]# /etc/init.d/xinetd restart
```

4. Try to Telnet to the local host to see if it fails. You should get a connection refused error.

Project Summary

There are many ways to secure your server. The simplest way is to simply not allow a service to run, in this case the **telentd:** server. I personally don't run Telnet at all and completely rely on SSH. The other popular way to secure a service is to attach SSL to it, such as HTTPS and SPOP. You could also put up a firewall to disallow access to certain hosts on the network. Just remember, the most secure computer is one that isn't plugged into the network.

---

1. It allows you to view many things, one of which is the open ports on the system.
2. **killall -HUP xinetd**

CRITICAL SKILL

11.3 Monitor Your System

The process of tying down your server's security isn't just for the sake of securing your server. It also gives you the opportunity to see clearly what normal server behavior should look like. After all, once you know what normal behavior is, unusual behavior will stick out like a sore thumb. For instance, if you turned off your Telnet service when setting up the server, seeing a log entry for Telnet means something is very wrong!

Commercial packages that perform monitoring do exist and may be worth checking out for your site as a whole, but we'll leave the discussions of their capabilities to *Network World* or *PC Week*. Here, we'll take a look at a variety of other excellent tools that help you accomplish the monitoring of your system. Some of these tools come with all Linux distributions; some don't. All are free and easily acquired.

Making the Best Use of syslog

In Module 9, we explored syslog, the system logger that saves messages from various programs into a set of text files for record-keeping purposes. By now, you've probably seen the type of log messages you get with syslog. These include security-related messages such as who has logged in to the system, when they logged in, and so forth.

As you can imagine, it's possible to analyze these logs to build a time-lapse image of the utilization of your system services. This data can also point out questionable activity. For example, why was the host crackerboy.nothing-better-to-do.net sending so many Web requests in such a short period of time? What was he looking for? Has he found a hole in the system?

Log Parsing

Doing periodic checks on the system's log files is an important part of maintaining security. Unfortunately, scrolling through an entire day's worth of logs is a time-consuming and unerringly boring task that reveals few meaningful events. To ease the drudgery, pick up a text on a scripting language (such as Perl) and write small scripts to parse out the logs. A well-designed script works by throwing away what it recognizes as normal behavior and showing everything else. This can reduce thousands of log entries for a day's worth of activities down to a manageable few dozen. This is an effective way to detect attempted break-ins and possible security gaps. Hopefully, it'll become entertaining to watch the script kiddies trying and failing to break down your walls.

Storing Log Entries

Unfortunately, log parsing may not be enough. If someone breaks into your system, it's likely that your log files will be promptly erased—which means all those wonderful scripts won't be able to tell you a thing. To get around this, consider dedicating a single host on your network to storing log entries. Configure your **/etc/syslog.conf** file to send all of its messages to this single host, and configure the host so that it's listening only to the syslog port (514). In most instances, this should be enough to gather, in a centralized place, the evidence of any bad things happening.

If you're *really* feeling paranoid, consider attaching a DOS-based PC to the serial port of the loghost and using a terminal emulation package such as Telix to record all of the messages sent to the loghost. (You can also use another Linux box running **minicom** in log mode—just be sure *not* to network this second Linux machine.) Have **/etc/syslog.conf** configured to send all messages to a **/dev/ttyS0** if you're using COM1 or **/dev/ttyS1** if you're using COM2. And, of course, do *not* connect the DOS system to the network. This way, in the event the loghost also gets attacked, the log files won't be destroyed. The log files will be safe residing on the DOS system, which is impossible to log in to without physical access.

For the highest degree of monitoring capability, connect a parallel-port printer to the DOS system and have the terminal emulation package echo everything it receives on the serial port to the printer. Thus, if the DOS system fails or is damaged in some way by an attack, you'll have a hard copy of the logs. (Note that a serious drawback to using the printer for logging is that you cannot easily search through the logs. If you choose to set up this arrangement, consider also keeping an electronic copy for easier searching.)

TIP

Consider using a package like **swatch** to page you when it sees a log entry that indicates trouble. You can find out more about it at http://www.stanford.edu/~atkins/swatch/.

Monitoring Bandwidth with MRTG

Monitoring the amount of bandwidth being used on your servers produces some very useful information. The most practical use for it is justifying the need for upgrades. By showing system utilization levels to your managers, you'll be providing hard numbers to back up your claims. Your data can be easily turned into a graph, too—and managers like graphs! Another useful aspect of monitoring bandwidth is to identify bottlenecks in the system, thus helping you to better balance the system load. But the most useful aspect of graphing your bandwidth is to identify when things go wrong.

Once you've installed a package such as MRTG (Multi-Router Traffic Grapher, available at http://www.mrtg.org/) to monitor bandwidth, you will quickly get a criterion for what "normal" looks like on your site. A substantial drop or increase in utilization is something to investigate. Check your logs, and look for configuration files with odd or unusual entries.

COPS

The COPS tool (Computer Oracle and Password System) provides a simple and automated way of checking for unusual settings in the system. Such checks include looking for SetUID programs in home directories, unusual permission settings on home directories, configuration files that expose your system to outside access without authorization, and so on.

One of the most significant features of COPS is that it is designed to be automatically run from a **cron** entry (see Module 9 for more about **cron**) every night. The report, if there is anything to report, is e-mailed to you.

You can research and download the latest and greatest version of COPS at ftp://ftp.cert.org/pub/tools/.

TripWire

TripWire, now a commercial package, takes a very paranoid approach to security: If something changes, TripWire tells you. This comprehensive protection removes the opportunity for someone to place a "backdoor" or "time bomb" in your system.

TripWire generates MD5 checksums of every file on your system and saves them in an encrypted format. When you want to check on differences, you can recall the saved checksums and compare all of the files on the system to their known good MD5 checksum. Differences are reported.

The idea here is for you to perform an install and then ready a system for network deployment. But before actually putting the system onto the network, you run the TripWire tool to generate and store all of the checksums. You can be confident that your list of MD5 checksums is safe in its encrypted domicile.

The process of setting up a TripWire arrangement is, of course, time consuming. However, short of cutting off network connectivity, it's hard to tighten up a system any more than this.

RPM

If your system is using RPM you can use that tool to quickly verify if a file has been modified. RPM uses the known file sizes and checksums of the files and compares them to the ones that are on disk. If they differ, someone has tampered with your files. Suspect services and files are usually the following: **telnetd**, **login**, **/bin/ls**, **bash**, **last**, and **syslog**. A typical script kiddy is going to try to replace binaries that hide what they are doing.

NOTE

A favorite for script kiddies is to use directories with the filename "..." As you can see, it is not that hard to mistake "..." for ".." which is the parent directory. On top of that, they will replace **/bin/ls** so that it won't even display these directories. Once upon a time, I was cleaning up some directories on a system and noticed that the file system still had a huge amount of data. Upon further investigation (by issuing the command **echo** *) I had found that someone had stored several MBs of data in a directory called "..." If you think that something is awry, drop into a mode of discovery, use other tools to list the directory, and see what is going on.

SATAN

SATAN, the System Administrators Tool for Analyzing Networks, was released in the mid-1990s to a flurry of press suggestions that it was a hacker's toolkit. SATAN's author, Dan Farmer, more or less declared that it *was* a hacker's toolkit—but for system administrators rather than evildoers.

SATAN works by probing your network for potential security holes. This program is especially interesting because it can be run from both inside your network (for you) and outside your network (against you). It's an effective way of exposing firewall gaps when you run it from the outside, and an excellent investigation of internal weaknesses when run from an inside host.

Although SATAN is a bit older and doesn't identify many of the newer attacks that are employed today, it does do many of the "twist the door handle and see if it's open" checks that are no less important. You should assume that others will run SATAN against you, so be sure you know where your own weaknesses are and get them fixed as quickly as possible.

Like COPS, SATAN is available from ftp://ftp.cert.org/pub/tools/.

Module 11 Mastery Check

1. What command is used to list all of the ports that are open on your system?

2. If you are not using a service that is enabled in **inetd/xinetd**, should you disable it?

3. How does one go about disabling a service in **xinetd**?

4. Why would you want to look at your syslog files periodically?

5. What is SATAN?

6. Why would bandwidth usage be an indicator of something wrong?

7. If someone has physical access to a Linux computer, can they compromise it?

8. What would be the benefit of running TripWire on your system?

9. What RPM command could you use to verify that a file has not changed?

Part III

Internet Services

Module 12

DNS

The need to map those long numerical IP addresses into people-friendly format has been an issue with TCP/IP since its creation in the 1970s. Although this translation isn't mandatory, it does make the network much more useful and easy to work with for most of us.

Initially, IP address-to-name mapping was done through the maintenance of a **hosts.txt** file that was distributed via FTP to all the machines on the Internet. As the number of hosts grew (starting back in the early 1980s), it was soon clear that a single person maintaining a single file of all of those hosts was not a realistic way of managing the association of IP addresses to host names. To solve this problem, a distributed system was devised in which each site would maintain information about its own hosts. One host at each site would be considered "authoritative," and that single host address would be kept in a master table that could be queried by all other sites. This is the essence of DNS, the *Domain Name Service*.

For example, if Host A wanted to contact Host B, the following queries would occur:

1. Host A would ask who was authoritative for all of the host names at Site B.

2. Host A would receive an answer such as "Nameserver B."

3. Host A would then ask Nameserver B, "What is Host B's IP address?"

4. Nameserver B would answer with Host B's IP address.

5. With the IP address of Host B in hand, Host A could begin direct communication with Host B.

If this seems like a lot of extra work to get something as simple as another host's IP address, realize that the only other choice would be to have a central site maintaining a master list of all hosts (numbering in the tens of millions) and having to update those host names tens of thousands of times a day—simply impossible! Even more important to consider are the needs of each site. One site may need to maintain a private DNS server because its firewall requires that IP addresses not be visible to outside networks, yet the inside network must be able to find hosts on the Internet. If you're stunned by the prospect of having to manage this for every host on the Internet, then you're getting the picture.

NOTE

In this module, you will see the terms "DNS server" and "name server" used interchangeably. Technically, "name server" is a little ambiguous because it can apply to any number of naming schemes that resolve a name to a number and vice versa. In the context of this module, "name server" will always mean a DNS server unless otherwise stated.

In this module, we will discuss DNS in depth, so you'll have what you need to configure and deploy your own DNS servers for whatever your needs may be.

CAUTION

This module uses as examples many host names, domain names, and IP addresses that really do exist. Please be kind and do *not* configure your DNS server with their settings!

CRITICAL SKILL
12.1 Understand Naming Services

Not all sites run DNS servers. Not all systems need DNS servers. In sufficiently small sites with no Internet connectivity, it's reasonable for each host to keep its own copy of a table matching all of the host names in the local network with their corresponding IP addresses. This table is stored in the **/etc/hosts** file.

TIP

Even in hosts that have access to a DNS server, you may want to keep a hosts file locally, where a particular host can look up an IP address before going out to the DNS server. Typically, this is done so that the system can keep track of hosts it needs for booting so that even if the DNS server may become unavailable, the system can still boot. Less obvious might be the simple reason that you want to give a host a name but you don't want to (or can't) add an entry to your DNS server.

The **/etc/hosts** file keeps its information in a simple tabular format, and is a basic naming service. The IP address is in the first column, and all the related host names are in the second column. Only white space separates the entries. Pound symbols (#) at the beginning of a line represent comments. Here's an example:

```
#
# Host table for Steve's Internal network
#
127.0.0.1    localhost   localhost.localdomain
192.168.1.1  ford        # Steve's Linux box
192.168.1.3  toybox      # Heidi's Mac (MacOS 9/X)
192.168.1.6  tinymac     # Mac Duo 2400 (MacOS 9/PPC Linux)
192.168.1.7  assimilator # Win2k / Linux
192.168.1.8  trillian    # Firewall/Router (Linux)
192.168.1.9  arthur      # FreeBSD toy
192.168.1.20 zaphod      # Printer
```

In general, your **/etc/hosts** file should contain at the very least the necessary host-to-IP mappings to allow your system to boot up if the DNS server is not responding. A more robust naming service is the DNS system. The rest of this module will cover the use of the DNS name service.

CRITICAL SKILL
12.2 Understand How DNS Works

In this section, we'll explore some background material necessary to your understanding of the installation and configuration of a DNS server and client.

Domains and Hosts

Until now, you've most likely referenced sites by their *fully qualified domain name* (FQDN), like this one: www.hyperreal.org. Each string between the periods in this FQDN is significant. Starting from the right end and moving to the left, you have first the top-level domain (.org, .com, .net, .mil, .gov, .edu, .int, and the two-letter country codes such as .us for the United States).

NOTE

Getting a new top-level domain approved is a difficult process. As of this writing, several new top-level domains have been given a go (such as .tv). The new top-level domains are going for a hefty price of three thousand dollars a pop. You can easily get a .com or .org domain for two years at thirty dollars.

From these top-level domains come actual organizational boundaries. Companies, ISPs, educational communities, and nonprofit groups typically acquire unique names under one or more of the domains. Here are a few examples: redhat.com, caldera.com, planetoid.org, hyperreal.org, theorb.com, spinway.com, and arraynetworks.net. Assignment of these names is done by companies like register.com and networksolutions.com under the authority of the IANA (Internet Assigned Naming Authority).

Visually, you can imagine the DNS format as an upside-down tree (see Figure 12-1). The root of the tree is a simple period; this is the period that's supposed to occur after every FQDN. Thus, the proper FQDN for www.planetoid.org is really www.planetoid.org. (with the root period at the end). Most applications have come to assume that the user will not place the suffixing period.

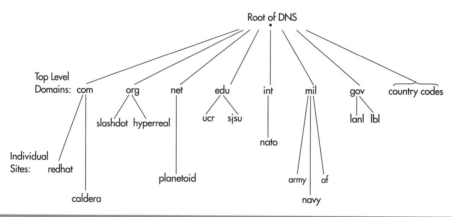

Figure 12-1 The DNS tree, two layers deep

All domains are placed in *root servers*, DNS servers scattered around the entire world. Each server contains the entire mapping of domain names up to two layers deep (planetoid.org, redhat.com, and so on) to their *primary name servers*. A primary name server for a domain is simply a DNS server that knows about all hosts and subdomains existing under its domain. For example, the root servers know that the primary name server for planetoid.org is 207.126.116.254. That's all the root server knows about planetoid.org. To find out about the hosts existing inside of planetoid.org, you have to ask the DNS server at 207.126.116.254. When asked about planetoid.org, the DNS server at 207.126.116.254 knows only about the hosts inside planetoid.org—and nothing else. If you ask it about whitehouse.gov, it will turn around and ask the primary name server for whitehouse.gov. (See the information about caching name servers in "Configure DNS Servers" later in this module.)

By keeping DNS distributed in this manner, the task of keeping track of all the hosts connected to the Internet is delegated to each site taking care of its own information. The central repository listing of all the primary name servers, called the *root server*, is the only list of existing domains. Obviously, a list of such critical nature is itself mirrored across multiple servers and multiple geographic regions. For example, an earthquake in Japan may destroy the root server for Asia, but all the other root servers around the world can take up the slack until it comes back online. The only difference noticeable to users is likely to be a slightly higher latency in resolving domain names. Pretty amazing, isn't it?

So now that you know how domains get resolved, you can begin to see the separation of hosts and domains. The host name is the very first word before the first period in an FQDN. For example, in the FQDN taz.hyperreal.org, the host name is taz, and the domain name is hyperreal.org. When a user sitting somewhere far away (in Internet terms) asks, "What's the IP address of taz.hyperreal.org?" the root servers will tell the user to ask ns.hyperreal.org. When ns.hyperreal.org is asked the same question, it can authoritatively answer "209.133.83.16."

Subdomains

"But I just saw the site www.cs.ucr.edu!" you say. "What's the host name component, and what's the domain name component?"

Welcome to the wild and mysterious world of *subdomains*. A subdomain exhibits all the properties of a domain, except that it has delegated a subsection of the domain instead of all the hosts at a site. Using the ucr.edu site as an example, the subdomain for the Department of Computer Science is cs.ucr.edu. When the primary name server for ucr.edu receives a request for a host name whose FQDN ends in cs.ucr.edu, the primary forwards the request down to the primary name server for cs.ucr.edu. Only the primary name server for cs.ucr.edu knows all the hosts existing beneath it.

Figure 12-2 shows you the relationship from the root servers down to ucr.edu, and then to cs.ucr.edu. The "www" is, of course, the host name.

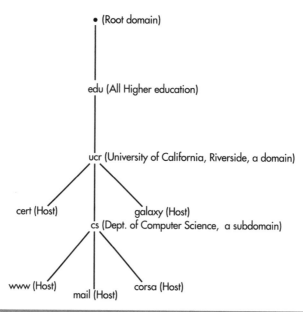

Figure 12-2 Delegation of subdomains

To make this clearer, let's follow the path of a DNS request. A query starts with the top-level domain edu. Within edu is ucr.edu, and five authoritative DNS servers for ucr.edu are found. Let's pick (at random) the blue.ucr.edu server to be contacted and ask about www.cs.ucr.edu. blue.ucr.edu's DNS configuration is such that for anything ending with a cs.ucr.edu, the server must contact momo.cs.ucr.edu to get an authoritative answer. The request for www.cs.ucr.edu is then passed on to momo.cs.ucr.edu, which returns 138.23.169.15.

Note that when a site name appears to reflect the presence of subdomains, it doesn't mean subdomains in fact exist. Although the host name specification rules do not allow periods, the BIND name server has always allowed them (BIND is described in the upcoming section "Install a DNS Server"). Thus, from time to time, you will see periods used in host names. Whether or not a subdomain exists is handled by the configuration of the DNS server for the site. For example, www.cert.ucr.edu does not mean cert.ucr.edu is a subdomain. Rather, it means www.cert is the host name of a system in the ucr.edu domain.

in-addr.arpa Domain

DNS allows resolution to work in both directions. *Forward resolution* converts names into IP addresses, and *reverse resolution* converts IP addresses back into host names. The process of reverse resolution relies on the *in-addr.arpa* domain.

As explained in the preceding section, domain names are resolved by looking at each component from right to left, with the suffixing period indicating the root of the DNS tree. Very few top-level domains exist, but each level going down the tree fans out. Following this logic, IP addresses must have a top-level domain as well. This domain is called the in-addr.arpa.

Unlike FQDNs, IP addresses are resolved from left to right once they're under the in-addr.arpa domain. Each octet further narrows down the possible host names. Figure 12-3 gives you a visual example of reverse resolution of the IP address 138.23.169.15.

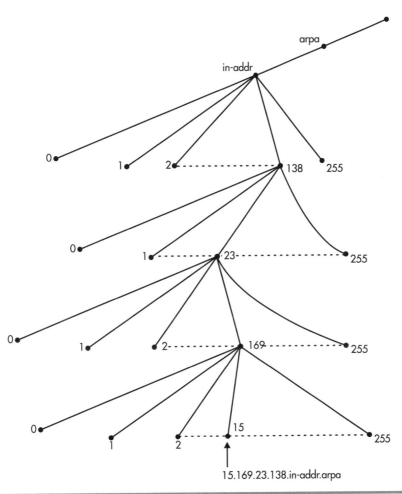

Figure 12-3 Reverse DNS resolution of 138.23.169.15

Types of Servers

DNS servers come in three flavors: primary, secondary, and caching. *Primary servers* are the ones considered authoritative for a particular domain. An *authoritative server* is the one on which the domain's configuration files reside. When updates to the domain's DNS tables occur, they are done on this server.

Secondary servers work as backups and as load distributors for the primary name servers. Primary servers know of the existence of secondaries and send them periodic updates to the tables. When a site queries a secondary name server, the secondary responds with authority. However, because it's possible for a secondary to be queried before its primary can alert it to the latest changes, some people refer to secondaries as "not quite authoritative." Realistically speaking, you can generally trust secondaries to have correct information. (Besides, unless you know which is which, you cannot tell the difference between a query response from a primary and one received from a secondary.)

Caching servers are just that: caching servers. They contain no configuration files for any particular domain. Rather, when a client host requests a caching server to resolve a name, that server will check its own local cache first. If it cannot find a match, it will find the primary server and ask it. This response is then cached. Practically speaking, caching servers work quite well because of the temporal nature of DNS requests. That is, if you've asked for the IP address to hyperreal.org, you are likely to do so again in the near future. (The Web has made this even more likely.) Clients can tell the difference between a caching server and a primary or secondary server, because when a caching server answers a request, it answers it "nonauthoritatively."

NOTE

A DNS server can be configured to act with a specific level of authority for a particular domain. For example, a server can be primary for domain.com but be secondary for example.net. All DNS servers act as caching servers, even if they are also primary or secondary for any other domains.

CRITICAL SKILL
12.3 Install a DNS Server

Most Linux distributions come with the option to install a DNS server when the system is installed for the first time. The DNS server of choice for Linux and for almost all UNIX servers is BIND, the Berkeley Internet Name Domain server. (At one point, a rumor floated around the Internet that Windows NT's name server bore striking similarity to BIND. This rumor was never confirmed or denied.) As of this writing, the latest BIND version is 9.0.

NOTE

Because of the critical nature of the BIND software, it was taken over by the Internet Software Consortium (ISC) to ensure its continued development. You can find out more about the ISC at http://www.isc.org/. As of this writing, the ISC is in charge of development of a DHCP server as well as the INN news server.

Because of the timing between writing this book and the release of new distributions, it is unlikely you have the latest version of BIND. If you're a Win2K administrator, you should be quite familiar with this since most Win2K books to date have been written for prereleases rather than the official release. (Ah, the exciting world of frequent updates…) But if you are running the last official release of BIND (8.3.3), don't worry. There were no known security problems with 8.3.3, so you should be safe on that front. Plus, those configuration keywords that were correct for 8.3.3 are still correct for 9.0.

NOTE

If you are running Red Hat Linux with the DNS server that shipped with it, you can skip to the "Configure DNS Servers" section. All you need to know is that the default location for the **named.conf** file is **/etc**, and the default location for the records files is **/var/named**. However, it is always a good idea to keep up with the latest versions of BIND, so going through the steps of downloading and compiling BIND 9 is likely to be the better choice.

The great news is that once BIND is configured, you'll rarely need to concern yourself with its operation. Nevertheless, keep an eye out for new releases. New bugs and security issues are discovered from time to time and should be corrected. Of course, new features are released as well, but unless you have a need for them, those releases are less critical. All new BIND releases are available at http://www.isc.org/.

In this section, we'll discuss the process of downloading and compiling BIND. If your distribution uses package management software, you may want to look for the precompiled versions of the BIND software. If you do go with a precompiled version, however, be sure to download it from a trusted source.

NOTE

Although freely available with full source code to anyone who wishes to download it, BIND has the benefit of the ISC's commercial-quality management and support. Of course, you'll have to pay for the commercial-level support, but the software supported by their commercial-level contracts is the same software you can download for free.

Obtaining BIND

The first big difference you'll see between BIND 8.*x* and BIND 9.2.1 is the packaging. BIND 8 is distributed in three separate files: **bind-contrib.tar.gz**, **bind-doc.tar.gz**, and **bind-src.tar.gz** for user-contributed code, documentation, and source code, respectively. The new version of

BIND ships with all three of these packages in one handy tarball: **bind-9.2.1.tar.gz**. You can download this from ftp://ftp.isc.org/isc/bind9/9.2.1/bind-9.2.1.tar.gz.

You will want to download the tarball into a directory that has plenty of free space. For this example, I'm using **/usr/local/src**. As the root user (see the **su** command in Module 6), start by unpacking the archive as follows:

```
[root@ford src]# tar -xvzf bind-9.2.1.tar.gz
```

This will create a subdirectory called **bind-9.2.1** and place all of the files inside of it.

Unlike previous versions of BIND that used a build script based on what operating system you had, the new version uses the GNU autoconf scripts to automatically make those determinations and pick the appropriate configuration. To configure BIND, enter the directory created when unpacking the BIND source tree and run **configure** as follows:

```
[root@ford src]# cd bind-9.2.1
[root@ford bind-9.2.1]# ./configure
```

This will allow BIND to automatically determine the configuration of your machine and place all the configuration files relative to the **/usr/local** directory. (If you want to stick to the Red Hat locations, you should run **./configure --prefix=/usr** instead. For this module, however, we will assume that BIND has been installed relative to **/usr/local**. If you install it the Red Hat way, be sure you adjust your path names accordingly in the remaining examples.)

Once BIND has been configured, you need to compile it by running the **make** command, like so:

```
[root@ford bind-9.2.1]# make
```

The **make** command will take a few minutes to run depending on the speed of your system. You should see a lot of commands fly across your screen—this is okay. It is simply **make** giving you a play-by-play commentary of what's going on.

Once it is done compiling, you will need to install the packages. This is done with the **make install** command:

```
[root@ford bind-9.2.1]# make install
```

Once this command finishes, you are ready to begin configuring the server and running the DNS server.

If BIND Doesn't Compile

First, don't worry. BIND is extremely unlikely to fail. I have successfully compiled BIND several times already without any problems. However, if for some reason it did not work, try removing the **bind-9.0.0** directory (see the `rmdir` command in Module 6) and start again. Once you have gone through the steps, you'll see that starting from scratch takes only a few extra minutes. This may seem naive, but more than likely there was simply a problem in the unpacking process, or the `configure` command was not able to find things. Be sure you are doing this as the root user (see the `su` command in Module 6).

If it is still not working, send a copy of the last screen of output from `make` to the developers of BIND at bind9-bugs@isc.org. Remember to include as much information as you can about your configuration and the messages that you got. And, of course, be nice. You'll be talking to the actual developers here—starting your message with a rant about how BIND is not a good way to get help.

What Was Installed

Many tools come with the BIND distribution. The three tools that we are interested in are as follows:

Tool	Description
/usr/local/bin/host	Performs a simple query on a name server
/usr/local/bin/dig	Traces the path of a name server
/usr/local/sbin/named	The DNS server itself

The remainder of the module will discuss each of these tools, their configurations, and their usage.

Starting DNS at Boot Time

If you are using the Red Hat–supplied DNS server, you only need to check that there exists a symlink in the **/etc/rc.d/rc3.d** directory that points to the **/etc/rc.d/init.d/named** script and that the symlink's name starts with an **S**. (See Module 7 for more information about startup scripts.) If this symlink is there, the Red Hat–supplied server is already in place and ready to go.

If you have installed Red Hat's server but performed the upgrade to BIND 9.0, then you will need to change the **/etc/rc.d/init.d/named** script. Using your favorite text editor, change the script so that instead of running **/usr/sbin/named**, it will run **/usr/ loal/sbin/named**. (Remember to adjust the path name if you installed BIND in a different location using the `--prefix` option at configure time.) Also, adjust the location of the **named.conf** file.

Note that the Red Hat script for starting and stopping BIND was originally for BIND 8.*x*. This is fine, and it will continue to start and stop the BIND 9.0 installation without a problem so long as the path names have been adjusted. However, the original script also has the feature of getting status information from BIND. The method that it used is no longer valid, and thus you cannot run **/etc/rc.d/init.d/named status** to get status information. Since the `start` and `stop` parameters do work, the script will properly start the server at boot time.

If you aren't using Red Hat, you'll find that most of the preceding comments regarding Red Hat's methods will probably work for you, too. Note, however, that you cannot simply start **named** from the **rc.local** script at the very end. This is because many other services (such as Sendmail) rely on DNS to be properly functioning in order for them to start. Be sure that BIND starts as the first network service after the IP address gets set.

CRITICAL SKILL
12.4 Configure DNS Clients

In this section and the next, we'll delve into the wild and exciting process of configuring DNS clients and servers! Okay, maybe they're not that exciting—but there's no denying their significance to the infrastructure of any networked site, so you'd best be able to get a few warm and fuzzy feelings about DNS configurations.

The Resolver

So far, we've been studying servers and the DNS tree as a whole. The other part of this equation is, of course, the client—the host that's contacting the DNS server to resolve a host name into an IP address.

Under Linux, the *resolver* handles the client side of DNS. This is actually part of a library of C programming functions that get *linked* to a program when the program is started. Because all of this happens automatically and transparently, the user doesn't have to know anything about it. It's simply a little bit of magic that lets them start browsing the Internet.

From the system administrator's perspective, configuring the DNS client isn't magic, but it's very straightforward. There are only two files involved: **/etc/resolv.conf** and **/etc/nsswitch.conf**.

The /etc/resolv.conf file

The **/etc/resolv.conf** file contains the information necessary for the client to know what its local DNS server is. (Every site should have, at the very least, its own caching DNS server.) This file has two lines. The first indicates the default search domain, and the second line indicates the IP address of the host's name server.

The *default search domain* applies mostly to sites that have their own local servers. When the default search domain is specified, the client side will automatically append this domain name to the requested site and check that first. For example, if you specify your default domain to be yahoo.com and then try to connect to the host name my, the client software will automatically try contacting my.yahoo.com. Using the same default, if you try to contact the host www.stat.net, the software will try www.stat.net.yahoo.com (a perfectly legal host name), find that it doesn't exist, and then try www.stat.net alone (which does exist).

Of course, you may supply multiple default domains. However, doing so will slow the query process a bit, because each domain will need to be checked. For instance, if both yahoo.com and stanford.edu are specified, and you perform a query on www.stat.net, you'll get three queries: www.stat.net.yahoo.com, www.stat.net.stanford.edu, and www.stat.net.

The format of the **/etc/resolv.conf** file is as follows:

```
search domainname
nameserver IP-address
```

where **domainname** is the default domain name to search, and **IP-address** is the IP address of your DNS server. For example, here's my **/etc/resolv.conf**:

```
search planetoid.org
nameserver 127.0.0.1
```

Thus, when I contact zaphod.planetoid.org, I only need to specify zaphod as the host name. Since I run a name server on my own machine, I specify the local host address.

The /etc/nsswitch.conf file

The **/etc/nsswitch.conf** file tells the system where it should look up certain kinds of configuration information (*services*). When multiple locations are identified, the **/etc/nsswitch.conf** file also specifies the order in which the information can best be found. Typical configuration files that are set up to use **/etc/nsswitch.conf** include the password file, group file, and hosts file. (To see a complete list, open the file in your favorite text editor.)

The format of the **/etc/nsswitch.conf** file is simple. The service name comes first on a line (note that **/etc/nsswitch.conf** applies to more than just host name lookups), followed by a colon. Then come the locations that contain the information. If multiple locations are identified, the entries are listed in the order in which the system needs to perform the search. Valid entries for locations are files, **nis**, **dns**, **[NOTFOUND]**, and **NISPLUS**. Comments begin with a pound symbol (#).

For example, if you open the file with your favorite editor, you'll see a line similar to this:

```
hosts:      files nisplus nis dns
```

This line tells the system that all host name lookups should first start with the **/etc/hosts** file. If the entry cannot be found there, NISPLUS is checked. If the host cannot be found via NISPLUS, regular NIS is checked, and so on. It's possible that NISPLUS isn't running at your site and you want the system to check DNS records before it checks NIS records. In this case, you'd change the line to

```
hosts:      files dns nis
```

And that's it. Save your file, and the system automatically detects the change.

The only recommendation for this line is that the hosts file (**files**) should always come first in the lookup order.

What's the preferred order for NIS and DNS? This is very much dependent on the site. Whether you want to resolve host names with DNS before trying NIS will depend on whether the DNS server is closer than the NIS server in terms of network connectivity, if one server is faster than another, firewall issues, site policy issues, and other such factors.

Using [NOTFOUND]

In the **/etc/nsswitch.conf** file, you'll see entries that end in **[NOTFOUND]**. This is a special directive that allows you to stop the process of searching for information after the system has failed all prior entries. For example, if your file contains the line **hosts: files [NOTFOUND] dns nis**, the system will try to look up host information in the **/etc/hosts** file only. If the requested information isn't there, NIS and DNS won't be searched.

Progress Check

1. What is the resolver?

2. What is a subdomain?

Project 12-1 Configuring the Client

This project will step through the process of setting up the Linux client to use the DNS system.

Step by Step

1. Edit **/etc/resolv.conf** and set the **nameserver** entry to point to your DNS server. Per our example:

```
search planetoid.org
nameserver 127.0.0.1
```

2. Edit **/etc/nsswitch.conf** to make it perform name lookups.

```
hosts:      files dns nis
```

3. Test the configuration with the **ping** utility or **nslookup**.

Project Summary

Setting up the Linux client to perform name lookups is not a hard task. The thing to watch out for is making sure that you test any changes to the configuration that you use. If you forget to make changes to **/etc/nsswitch.conf**, you might never use DNS even if the resolver is configured correctly.

---

1. The resolver is the client-side library that performs name lookups.

2. A subdomain is a subsection of a domain. An example is that cs.ucr.edu is a subdomain of ucr.edu.

The **named.conf** file is the main configuration file for BIND. Based on this file's specifications, BIND determines how it should behave and what additional configuration files, if any, must be read. If you've read any other books about DNS and BIND, you may be thinking that I've made a typo and what I *really* mean is **named.boot**. Not at all—the **named.boot** file is used by older versions of BIND (4.*x,* the latest of which is 4.9.3). The ISC has since stopped support for this series and now supports only the 8.*x* and 9.*x* series of BIND, which uses a completely new file format—and thus the new filename.

This section of the module covers what you need to know to set up a general purpose DNS server. You'll find a complete guide to the new configuration file format in the **html** directory of BIND's documentation.

The general format of the **named.conf** file is as follows:

```
statement {
    options;      // comments
};
```

The **statement** keyword tells BIND we're about to describe a particular facet of its operation, and **options** are the specific commands applying to that statement. The curly braces are required so that BIND knows which options are related to which statements; there's a semicolon after every option and after the closing curly brace.

An example of this is as follows:

```
options {
    directory "/var/named";    // put config files in /var/named
};
```

The location of the **named.conf** file depends on what you specified the **--prefix** line to be when configuring BIND. If you left it to the default, BIND will look for it in the **/usr/local/etc** directory. However, if you have a Red Hat installation, you will find it by default to be in the **/etc** directory. I personally prefer keeping all host specific configuration files in the **/etc** directory, so I created a symlink (see Module 6) from **/usr/ local/etc/ named.conf** to **named.conf**.

The Specifics

This section documents the most common statements you will see in a **named.conf** file. The best way to tackle this is to give it a skim but then treat it as a reference guide for later sections. If some of the directives seem bizarre or don't quite make sense to you during the first pass, don't worry. Once you see them in use in later sections, the hows and whys will quickly fall into place.

NOTE

I can almost hear you saying it: "Why is this stuff so ugly to configure? Don't they have a GUI for this? Can't this be simplified!?" Well, yes and no. The hard part here is not the configuration file, but the concepts. And no GUI can simplify that for you. But once you understand the concepts, the configuration file will feel much more sane. If you feel lost while you're glancing through this section, you may just want to skip to the next section and see these files in action. Then come back and actually see what the files are doing in better detail.

Comments

Comments may be in one of the following formats:

Format	Indicates
//	C++-style comments
/*...*/	C-style comments
#	Perl and UNIX shell script-style comments

In the case of the first and last styles (C++ and Perl/UNIX shell), once a comment begins, it continues until the end of the line. In regular C-style comments, the closing ***/** is required to indicate the end of a comment. This makes C-style comments easier for multiline comments. In general, however, you can pick the comment format that you like best and stick with it. No one style is better than another.

statement Keywords

You can use the following **statement** keywords:

Keyword	Description
acl	Access Control List—determines what kind of access others have to your DNS server.
include	Allows you to include another file and have that file treated like part of the normal **named.conf** file.
logging	Specifies what information gets logged and what gets ignored. For logged information, you can also specify where the information is logged.
options	Addresses global server configuration issues.
controls	Allows you to declare control channels for use by the **ndc** utility.
server	Sets server-specific configuration options.
zone	Defines a DNS zone (discussed in further detail in "Zones" later in the module).

The include Statement

If you find that your configuration file is starting to grow unwieldy, you may want to consider breaking up the file into smaller components. Each file can then be included into the main **named.conf** file. Note that you cannot use the **include** statement inside another statement.

Here's an example of an **include** statement:

```
include "/var/named/acl.conf";
```

CAUTION

To all you C and C++ programmers out there: Be sure not to begin **include** lines with the pound symbol (#), despite what your instincts tell you! That symbol is used to start comments in the **named.conf** file. (Believe me when I say this error is a very frustrating bug to track down!)

The logging Statement

The **logging** statement is used to specify what information you want logged, and where. When this statement is used in conjunction with the **syslog** facility, you get an extremely powerful and configurable logging system. The items logged are a number of statistics about the status of **named**. By default, they are logged to the **/var/log/messages** file.

Unfortunately, the configurability of this logging statement comes at the price of some additional complexity, but the default logging set up by **named** is good enough for most uses. If you want to reconfigure the logging process, read the BIND Administrators Reference Manual.

The server Statement

The **server** statement tells BIND specific information about other name servers it might be dealing with. The format of the **server** statement is as follows:

```
server ip-address {
      bogus yes/no;
      transfer-format one-answer/many-answers;
};
```

where **ip-address** is the IP address of the server in question.

The first item in the statement, **bogus**, tells the server whether or not the other server is sending bad information. This is useful in the event you are dealing with another site that may be sending you bad information due to a misconfiguration. The second item, **transfer-format**, tells BIND whether this server can accept multiple answers in a single query response. As far as we know, the only servers that can handle multiple responses are BIND version 8.*x* servers.

A sample **server** entry might look like this:

```
server 192.168.3.12 {
      bogus no;
      transfer-format many-answers;
};
```

Zones

The **zone** statement allows you to define a DNS zone—the definition of which is often confused. Here is the fine print: *a DNS zone is not the same thing as a DNS domain.* The difference is subtle, but important.

Let's review: Domains are designated along organizational boundaries. A single organization can be separated into smaller administrative subdomains. Each subdomain gets its own zone. All of the zones collectively form the entire domain.

For example, .bigcompany.com is a domain. Within it are the subdomains .engr.bigcompany.com, .marketing.bigcompany.com, .sales.bigcompany.com, and .admin.bigcompany.com. Each of the four subdomains has its own zone. And .bigcompany.com has some hosts within it that do not fall under any of the subdomains, thus it has a zone of its own. As a result, .bigcompany.com is actually composed of five zones in total.

In the simplest model, where a single domain has no subdomains, the definition of zone and domain are the same in terms of information regarding hosts, configurations, and so on.

The process of setting up zones in the **named.conf** file is discussed in the following section.

Configure DNS Servers

Time for Big Fun: configuring a name server! Oh, you don't think it's fun? Well, wait until you find out how much people get paid for knowing this stuff.

Earlier, you learned about the differences between primary, secondary, and caching name servers. Briefly, primary name servers contain the databases with the latest DNS information for a zone. When a zone administrator wants to update these databases, the primary name server gets the update first, and the rest of the world asks it for updates. Secondaries explicitly keep track of primaries, and primaries notify the secondaries when changes occur. Primaries and secondaries are considered equally authoritative in their answers. Caching name servers have no authoritative records, only cached entries.

Updating the named.conf File for a Primary Zone

The most basic syntax for a zone entry is as follows:

```
zone domain-name  {
      type master;
      file path-name;
};
```

The **path-name** refers to the file containing the database information for the zone in question. For example, to create a zone for the domain planetoid.org, where the database file is located in **/var/named/planetoid.org.db**, you would use the following:

```
zone "planetoid.org" {
     type master;
     file "planetoid.org.db";
};
```

Note that the **directory** option for the **named.conf** file will automatically prefix the **planetoid.org.db** filename. So if you designated **directory /var/named;**, the server software will automatically look for planetoid.org's information in **/var/named/ planetoid.org.db.**

Now that's just the *forward reference*—the mechanism by which others can look up a name and get the IP address. It's proper Net behavior to also supply an IP-to-host name mapping (also necessary if you want to send e-mail to some sites). To do this, you provide an entry in the in-addr.arpa domain.

The format of an in-addr.arpa entry is the first three octets of your IP address, reversed, followed by in-addr.arpa. Assuming that the network address for planetoid.org is 192.168.1, the in-addr.arpa domain would be 1.168.192.in-addr.arpa. Thus, the **zone** statement in the **named.conf** file would be as follows:

```
zone "1.168.192.in-addr.arpa" {
     type master;
     file "planetoid.org.rev";
};
```

Now that you have your **named.conf** entries ready, it's time to actually write the **planetoid.org.db** and **planetoid.org.rev** files.

Updating the named.conf for a Secondary Zone

The zone entry format for secondary servers is very similar to that of master servers. For forward resolution, here is the format:

```
zone domain-name {
     type slave;
     masters  IP-address-list; ;
};
```

where the **domain-name** is the exact same name as the primary name server, and the **IP-address-list** is the list of IP addresses where the primary name server for that zone exists.

A recommended additional option you can list in a secondary zone configuration is

```
file path-name;
```

where ***path-name*** is the full path location of where the server will keep copies of the primary's zone files. By keeping a local copy, you can reduce bandwidth needs for updates and improve performance.

Additional Options

A secondary zone configuration may also use some of the configuration choices from the **options** statement. These options are

- **check-names**
- **allow-update**
- **allow-query**
- **allow-transfer**
- **max-transfer-time-in**
- **notify**
- **also-notify**

Updating the named.conf File for a Caching Zone

A caching configuration is the easiest of all configurations. It's also required for every DNS server configuration, even if you are running a primary or secondary server. This is necessary in order for the server to recursively search the DNS tree to find other hosts on the Internet.

The two zone entries you need are for the cache, and making the local-host entry primary for itself. Here's the first entry:

```
zone "." {
     type hint;
     file "named.ca";
};
```

The line **type hint**; specifies that this is a caching zone entry, and the line **file** "**named.ca**"; specifies the file that will prime the cache with entries pointing to the root servers. (This **named.ca** file comes with the BIND package. You can also find the latest file at ftp://rs.internic.net.)

The second zone entry is as follows:

```
zone "0.0.127.in-addr.arpa"  {
     type master;
     file "named.local";
};
```

This is the reverse entry for resolving the local host address back to the local host name. The **named.local** file contains the following:

```
$TTL 86400
@       IN      SOA     localhost. root.localhost. (
                                1997022700 ; Serial
                                28800      ; Refresh
                                14400      ; Retry
                                3600000    ; Expire
                                86400 )    ; Minimum
                IN      NS      localhost.

1       IN      PTR     localhost.
```

If this doesn't make sense to you yet, don't worry. Just know that this is enough for a caching server. The following sections will help you make sense of this file.

DNS Records Types

Okay, I kind of lied. You *aren't* ready to create the **planetoid.org.db** and **planetoid.org.rev** files—not quite yet. First, you need to understand all the record types for DNS: SOA, NS, A, PTR, CNAME, MX, TXT, and RP.

SOA: Start of Authority

The SOA record starts the description of a site's DNS entries. The format of this entry is as follows:

```
domain.com. IN SOA ns.domain.com. hostmaster.domain.com. (
     1999080801        ; serial number
     10800             ; refresh rate in seconds (3 hours)
     1800              ; retry in seconds (30 minutes)
     1209600           ; expire in seconds (2 weeks)
     604800     )      ; minimum in seconds (1 week)
```

The first line contains some details you need to pay attention to:

- **domain.com.** is of course to be replaced with your domain name. Notice that last period at the end of **domain.com.**? It's supposed to be there—indeed, the DNS configuration files are extremely picky about it. The ending period is necessary for the sever to differentiate relative host names from fully qualified domain names (FQDNs); for example, the difference between oid and oid.planetoid.org.

- **IN** tells the name server that this is an Internet record. There are other types of records, but it's been years since anyone has had a need for them. You can safely ignore them.

- **SOA** tells the name server this is the Start of Authority record.

- **ns.domain.com.** is the FQDN for the name server for this domain (that would be the server where this file will finally reside). Again, watch out and don't miss that trailing period.

- **hostmaster.domain.com.** is the e-mail address for the domain administrator. Notice the lack of an @ in this address. The @ symbol is replaced with a period. Thus, the e-mail address referred to in this example is hostmaster@domain.com. The trailing period is used here, too.

The remainder of the record starts after the opening parenthesis on the first line. The first line is the serial number. It's used to tell the name server when the file has been updated. Watch out—forgetting to increment this number when you make a change is a mistake frequently made in the process of managing DNS records. (Forgetting to put a period in the right place is another common error.)

TIP

To maintain serial numbers in a sensible way, use the date formatted in the following order: YYYYMMDDxx. The tail-end xx is an additional two-digit number starting with 00, so if you make multiple updates in a day, you can still tell which is which.

The second line in the list of values is the refresh rate in seconds. This value tells the secondary DNS servers how often they should query the primary server to see if the records have been updated.

The third value is the retry rate in seconds. If the secondary server tries but cannot contact the primary DNS server to check for updates, the secondary server tries again after the specified number of seconds.

The fourth value is intended for secondary servers that have cached the zone data. It tells these servers that if they cannot contact the primary server for an update, they should discard the value after the specified number of seconds. One to two weeks is a good value for this interval.

The final value, minimum, tells caching servers how long they should wait before expiring an entry if they cannot contact the primary DNS server. Five to seven days is a good guideline for this entry.

NOTE

Don't forget to place the closing parenthesis after the final value.

NS: Name Server

The NS record is used for specifying which name servers maintain records for this zone. The format of this record is as follows:

```
IN NS          ns1.domain.com.
IN NS          ns2.domain.com.
```

You can have as many backup name servers as you'd like for a domain—at least two is a good idea. Most ISPs are willing to act as secondary DNS servers if they provide connectivity for you.

A: Address Record

The A record is used for providing a mapping from host name to IP address. The format of an A address is simple:

```
host name          IN A          IP-Address
```

For example, an A record for the host oid.planetoid.org, whose IP address is 192.168.1.2, would look like this:

```
oid               IN A          192.168.1.2
```

Note that any host name is automatically suffixed with the domain name listed in the SOA record, unless this host name ends with a period. In the foregoing example for oid, if the SOA record above it is for planetoid.org, then oid is understood to be oid.planetoid.org. If you were to change this to oid.planetoid.org (without a trailing period), the name server would understand it to be oid.planetoid.org.planetoid.org. So if you want to use the FQDN, be sure to suffix it with a period.

PTR: Pointer Record

The PTR record is for performing reverse name resolution, thereby allowing someone to specify an IP address and determine the corresponding host name. The format for this record is very similar to the A record, except with the values reversed:

```
IP-Address          IN PTR          host name
```

The **IP-address** can take one of two forms: just the last octet of the IP address (leaving the name server to automatically suffix it with the information it has from the in-addr.arpa domain name); or the full IP address, which is suffixed with a period. The **host name** must have the complete FQDN. For example, the PTR record for the host oid would be as follows:

```
192.168.1.2.      IN PTR          oid.planetoid.org.
```

MX: Mail Exchanger

The MX record is in charge of telling other sites about your zone's mail server. If a host on your network generated an outgoing mail with its host name on it, someone returning a message would not send it back directly to that host. Instead, the replying mail server would look up the MX record for that site and send the message there instead.

When Internet sites were primarily composed of UNIX-based systems, with Sendmail configured as a NULL host forwarding to a mail hub, lack of an MX record was okay. But as more non-UNIX systems joined the Net, MX records became crucial. If pc.domain.com sends a message using its PC-based mail reader (which cannot accept SMTP mail), it's important that the replying party have a reliable way of knowing the identity of pc.domain.com's mail server.

The format of the MX record is as follows:

```
domainname.  IN MX weight host name
```

where **domainname.** is the domain name of the site (with a period at the end, of course); the **weight** is the importance of the mail server (if multiple mail servers exist, the one with the smallest number has precedence over those with larger numbers); and the **host name** is, of course, the name of the mail server. It is important that the **host name** have an A record, as well.

Here's an example entry:

```
domain.com.     IN MX 10 mailserver1
                IN MX 20 mailserverbackup
```

Typically, MX records occur at the top of DNS configuration files. If a domain name is not specified, the default name is pulled from the SOA record.

CNAME: Canonical Name

CNAME records allow you to create aliases for host names. This is useful when you want to provide a highly available service with an easy-to-remember name, but still give the host a real name.

Another popular use for CNAMEs is to "create" a new server with an easy-to-remember name without having to invest in a new server at all. An example: A site has a mail server named mailhost in a UNIX-like tradition. As non-UNIX people come into the Internet picture, they assume the mail server will be called mail; to accommodate this assumption, a CNAME is created rather than renaming the server so that all requests to the host named mail will transparently resolve to mailhost.

Here's the format for the CNAME record:

```
new host name   IN CNAME   old host name
```

For example, for the mail-to-mailhost mapping mentioned just above, our entries might look like this:

```
mailhost      IN A        192.168.1.10
mail          IN CNAME    mailhost
```

CAUTION

It is a bad, bad, bad practice to point an MX record to a CNAME record. The official DNS specification document explicitly prohibits this. BIND will allow it, but only to keep backward compatibility with a broken feature from the past.

Progress Check

1. What is an A record?

2. What is a CNAME record?

Project 12-2 Setting Up the BIND Database Files

So now you have the entries you need in the **named.conf** file, and you know about all the DNS record types. It's time to create the actual database that will feed the server.

The database file format is not too strict, but some conventions have jelled over time. Sticking to these conventions will make your life easier and will smooth the way for the administrator who takes over your creation.

TIP

Comment liberally. In this file, comment lines begin with a semicolon. Although there isn't a lot of mystery about what's going on in a DNS database file, a history of the changes is a useful reference about what was being accomplished and why.

Every database file must start with a $TTL entry. This entry tells BIND what the time-to-live value is for each individual record. (The TTL in the SOA record is for the SOA record only.) After the $TTL entry is the SOA record and at least one NS record. Everything else is optional. (Of course, "everything else" is what makes the file useful!) You may find the following general format helpful to follow:

```
$TTL
SOA record
NS records
MX records
A and CNAME records
```

(continued)

Project
12-2

Setting Up the BIND Database Files

---

1. An A record is a mapping of a host name to an IP address.

2. A CNAME is an alias record for a host name.

Step by Step

Here is a complete zone configuration file for a single domain with four hosts and a time-to-live setting of 604,800 seconds (1 week):

```
$TTL 604800
@          IN     SOA     domain.com.   hostmaster.domain.com. (
                          1999022300 ; serial number
                          10800    ;Refresh every 3 hours
                          1800     ;Retry every 30 minutes
                          1209600 ;Expire in 2 weeks
                          604800 ) ;Minimum 1 week
           IN     NS      ns.domain.com.
           IN     MX 10   mail.domain.com.
imp        IN     A       192.168.1.1    ; Internet gateway
mail       IN     A       192.168.1.2    ; mail server
technics   IN     A       192.168.1.3    ; web server
www        IN     CNAME   technics
ns         IN     A       192.168.1.4    ; name server
peanutbutter IN   A       192.168.1.5    ; firewall
```

Set up the corresponding reverse lookup file for domain.com. It should look like the following file:

```
$TTL 604800
@   IN    SOA 1.168.192.in-addr.arpa.  hostmaster.domain.com. (
                          1999010501        ; Serial
                          10800             ; Refresh rate (3 hours)
                          1800              ; Retry (30 minutes)
                          1209600           ; Expire (2 weeks)
                          604800 )          ; Minimum (1 week)
           IN     NS      ns.domain.com.
1          IN     PTR     imp.domain.com.
2          IN     PTR     mail.domain.com
3          IN     PTR     technics.domain.com
4          IN     PTR     ns.domain.com
5          IN     PTR     peanutbutter.domain.com.
```

Project Summary

The database files are your most important configuration files. It is easy to create the forward lookup databases; what usually gets left out are the reverse lookups. Some tools like Sendmail and TCPWrappers will perform reverse lookups on IP addresses to see where people are coming from. So it is a common courtesy to have this information.

A Complete Configuration

So far, we've given you snippets of configuration files. Hopefully that has been enough to give you the big DNS picture and provide plenty of guidance for coming up with your own configuration file. Then again, a nice example never hurts.

Following is a complete configuration for a primary domain (domain.com) that also acts as a secondary to a friend, example.com. In exchange, the example.com domain acts as your secondary. You allow zone transfers to occur between your two sites, but not with any other sites. The domain.com site's ISP provides DNS service, as well, to which you forward requests when you cannot resolve information yourself.

Here is the **named.conf** file:

```
options {
  directory "/var/named";
  forwarders {
              192.168.2.1;
              192.168.2.2;
  };
  allow-transfer  {
              10.0.0.1;    // ns1.example.com
              10.0.0.2;    // ns2.example.com
  };
};

//
// a caching only name server config
//
zone "." {
        type hint;
        file "named.ca";
};

zone "0.0.127.in-addr.arpa" {
        type master;
        file "named.local";
};

//
// our primary information
//
zone "domain.com"  {
        type master;
        file "named.domain.com.";
};
```

```
zone "1.168.192.in-addr.arpa" {
        type master;
        file "named.rev";
};

//
// our secondary information for example.com
//
zone "example.com" {
        type slave;
        file "example.com.cache";
        masters  { 10.0.0.1; 10.0.0.2; };
};
```

Here is the **/var/named/named.local** file:

```
$TTL 86400
@       IN      SOA     localhost. root.localhost.  (
                                        1997022700 ; Serial
                                        28800      ; Refresh
                                        14400      ; Retry
                                        3600000    ; Expire
                                        86400 )    ; Minimum
                IN      NS      localhost.

1       IN      PTR     localhost.
```

Here is the **/var/named/named.domain.com** file:

```
$TTL 86400
@       IN      SOA     domain.com.  hostmaster.domain.com. (
                        1999022300 ; serial number
                        10800   ;Refresh every 3 hours
                        1800    ;Retry every 30 minutes
                        1209600 ;Expire in 2 weeks
                        604800 ) ;Minimum 1 week
                IN      NS      ns.domain.com.
                IN      MX 10   mail.domain.com.
imp             IN      A       192.168.1.1   ; Internet gateway
mail            IN      A       192.168.1.2   ; mail server
technics        IN      A       192.168.1.3   ; web server
www             IN      CNAME   technics
ns              IN      A       192.168.1.4   ; name server
peanutbutter    IN      A       192.168.1.5   ; firewall
```

Here is the **/var/named/named.rev** file:

```
$TTL 604800
@   IN   SOA 1.168.192.in-addr.arpa.  hostmaster.domain.com. (
                        1999010501      ; Serial
                        10800           ; Refresh rate (3 hours)
                        1800            ; Retry (30 minutes)
                        1209600         ; Expire (2 weeks)
                        604800 )        ; Minimum (1 week)
             IN    NS      ns.domain.com.
1            IN    PTR     imp.domain.com.
2            IN    PTR     mail.domain.com
3            IN    PTR     technics.domain.com
4            IN    PTR     ns.domain.com
5            IN    PTR     peanutbutter.domain.com.
```

You don't have to create any files to be secondary for example.com. You only need to add the entries you already have in the **named.conf** file.

CRITICAL SKILL

12.7 Use DNS Tools

This section describes a few tools that you'll want to get acquainted with as you work with DNS. They'll help you troubleshoot problems more quickly.

kill -HUP

If you have changed BIND's configuration files, you will need to tell it to reread them by sending the named process a HUP signal. Begin by finding the process ID for the **named** process. This can be done by looking for it in **/usr/local/var/run/named.pid** or in **/var/run/named.pid**. If you do not see it in either place, you can run the following command to get it:

```
[root@ford /root]# ps -C named
```

This will produce output that looks something like this:

```
PID TTY          TIME CMD
14880 ?        00:00:00 named
14881 ?        00:00:00 named
14882 ?        00:00:00 named
14883 ?        00:00:00 named
14884 ?        00:00:00 named
```

Look for the lowest number in the first column and use it to send a HUP signal, like this:

```
[root@ford /root]# kill -HUP 14880
```

Of course, replace "14880" with the correct process ID from your output. Under BIND 9 you'll need to send the process the USR2 signal to tell it to reload its configuration files.

The ndc Tool

BIND also comes with a tool called **ndc**. This tool is very handy for controlling the name server and also debugging problems with the name server. The most often used feature of **ndc** is its ability to tell named to reread its configuration files. To do so, simply run the following command:

```
[root@ford /root]# ndc reload
```

After running this command, named will reread its configuration files. You should verify that any changes you made did indeed take effect.

NOTE ndc no longer ships with BIND 9.X. Because you are more likely to see bind 8.X servers, this command is handy to know.

host

The **host** tool is really the master of all DNS tools. By learning all of the features **host** has to offer, you can eliminate the need to learn several of the smaller tools that come with BIND. Long-time users of **nslookup** may be surprised to see their old friend being put away. Well, the news isn't as bad as you think—the BIND team is simply trying to leave less overlap between their tools.

In its simplest use, **host** allows you to resolve host names into IP addresses from the command line. For example:

```
[root@ford root]# host theorb.com
theorb.com has address 209.133.83.16
```

You can also use **host** to perform reverse lookups. For example:

```
[root@ford root]# host 209.133.83.16
16.83.133.209.IN-ADDR.ARPA domain name pointer taz.hyperreal.org
```

This can lead to all kinds of interesting discoveries. In this case, you see that theorb.com is the same as taz.hyperreal.org. It's likely that taz.hyperreal.org is also "virtually hosting" other domains, as well.

TIP

If you are familiar with **nslookup**, don't worry—it's still there. However, since the BIND group is trying to move people away from it, consider using the **dig** tool (discussed next) instead when you need to find out about records other than A and PTR, or when you need to query servers other than your own.

dig

The domain information gopher, **dig**, is a great tool for gathering information about DNS servers. The typical format of the **dig** command is

```
[root@ford /root]# dig @server domain query-type
```

where **@server** is the name of the DNS server you want to query, **domain** is the domain name you are interested in querying, and **query-type** is the name of the record you are trying to get (A, MX, NS, SOA, HINFO, TXT, or any).

For example, to get the **mx** record for the domain whitehouse.gov from the DNS server ns1.ucsd.edu, you would run:

```
[root@ford /root]# dig @ns1.ucsd.edu whitehouse.gov mx
```

dig is an incredibly powerful program. You should read the man page that was installed with **dig** to learn how to use some of its more advanced features.

✔ Module 12 Mastery Check

1. What is the format of the **/etc/resolv.conf** file?

2. What function does the **/etc/nsswitch.conf** file perform?

3. What is a PTR record?

4. What is an A record?

5. What is the resolver?

6. Where can you obtain BIND?

7. What is the main configuration file for BIND?

8. What is an NS record?

9. What is the SOA for?

10. What is an MX record?

11. What is a caching name server?

12. How do you tell **named** to reload its configuration files and databases?

13. What does the **whois** command do?

14. How would you test your name server to make sure it is working correctly?

15. What is the in-addr.arpa domain?

Module 13

FTP

The File Transfer Protocol (FTP) has existed for the Internet since around 1971. Remarkably, the protocol has undergone very little change since then. Clients and servers, on the other hand, have been almost constantly improved and refined. This module covers the FTP software package ProFTPD.

The ProFTPD software is a fairly popular FTP server and is being used by debian.org, kernel.org, redhat.com, and sourceforge.net. The fact that these sites run the software can attest to its robustness and security.

CAUTION

Like most other services, ProFTPD is only as secure as you make it. The authors of the program have provided all of the necessary tools to make your site secure, but a bad configuration can cause your site to become open. Remember to double-check your configuration and test it out before going live. Also remember to check the ProFTPD Web site frequently for any software updates.

In this module, we will discuss how to download, compile, and install the latest version of ProFTPD. We will also show how to configure it for private access as well as anonymous access. And finally, we will show how to use the **ftp** client and test out your new FTP server.

CRITICAL SKILL
13.1 Understand the Mechanics of FTP

The act of transferring a file from one computer to another may seem trivial, but in reality it is not—at least, not if you're doing it right. In this section, we step through the details of the FTP client/server interaction. While this information isn't crucial to being able to get an FTP server up and running, it is important when you need to consider security issues as well as troubleshooting issues—especially troubleshooting issues that don't clearly manifest themselves as FTP-related. ("Is it the network, or is it FTP?")

Client/Server Interactions

When an FTP client wants to connect to an FTP server, it takes a random high port (a port number greater than 1024) as its source and port number 21 as its destination on the FTP server. (Port 21 is the ubiquitous FTP server port defined in the FTP standard.) Once the connection is established, the client can log in and issue commands to go through the FTP server's directories.

When the client makes a request to transfer a file, the server grabs another random high port and begins listening for connections on it. It sends this new port number to the FTP client over the existing connection. The FTP client takes this port number and initiates a new connection from one of its random high ports to the port number the server provided. The original connection is left open so that the client and server can send additional "out of band" messages to each other (for example, to abort the transfer).

This design, conceived in the early 1970s, assumed something that was reasonable for a long period of time on the Internet: Internet users are a friendly bunch who know better. This was indirectly protected by the fact that the National Science Foundation (NSF) funded the Internet backbone, and therefore no commercial organizations were allowed onto it unless they were working in conjunction with a research institute. Academic- and government-funded research labs made up most of the users.

Around 1990–91, the NSF stopped footing the bill for the Internet backbone, and the Internet went commercial. At first, it wasn't a big deal. Then the World Wide Web came along and the Net's population exploded—along with its security problems.

Many sites have now taken to using firewalls to protect their internal networks from the Big Bad Internet. Firewalls, however, consider arbitrary connections from high ports on the Internet to high ports on the internal network to be a very bad thing (rightfully so). As a result, many firewalls implement application-level proxies for FTP, which keep track of FTP requests and open up those high ports when needed to receive data from a remote site.

Of course, not all firewalls are that smart. Many sites rely on packet filtering firewalls, which don't really understand the data going through them, but know that data being sent to arbitrary high ports is bad and thus bounces it out. This type of firewall promptly breaks FTP, because FTP relies on being able to open a connection back with the client on a high port. A typical symptom of this behavior occurring is when a client appears to be able to connect to the server without a problem, but the connection seems to hang whenever an attempt to transfer data occurs.

Now think back to when FTP was originally created and bandwidth was at a premium. When someone wanted to get a file transferred from host A to host B while sitting at host C, the process of transferring the file from host A to C and then from C to B would end up wasting an incredible amount of bandwidth. So the designers of the FTP protocol came up with a solution: make it possible for someone sitting on host C to transfer a file from host A to host B directly. This was done via a *passive transfer*.

Passive transfers are accomplished by having the client side rather than the server side initiate the connection for data transfer. From the standpoint of firewalls, this allows the client to remain securely behind a firewall without the need for complex rules for allowing connections back in.

Now that you know how FTP works, the remaining sections of this module will cover the installation of the FTP server and how to use the **ftp** client to access the FTP server. First we will cover the process of downloading and installing the ProFTPD server.

CRITICAL SKILL
13.2 Install ProFTPD

ProFTPD (the **proftp** daemon) is available from the ProFTPD Web site at http://www
.proftpd.org/. Any further information that you need regarding ProFTPD can be found within
their documentation tree at http://www.proftd.org/docs/. The current version of ProFTPD is
1.2.6 as of this writing. After downloading the package, untar it in **/usr/local/src**:

```
[root@ford /usr/local/src]# tar -xvjf proftpd-1.2.6.tar.bz2
```

 NOTE

Linux versions of tar support the **-j** option, which allows you to decompress **bz2** files
on the fly just like the **-z** (gzip) option.

Be sure to read the README and INSTAL files located in the root software directory.
The developers of the software wisely used the standard GNU configuration methodology,
so to configure the software you simply have to issue the following command:

```
[root@ford /usr/local/src/proftpd-1.2.6/]# ./configure
```

By default, the **configure** script will use **/usr/local** as its prefix and install most of the
ProFTPD binaries in this directory. Now use **make** to compile the software:

```
[root@ford /usr/local/src/proftpd-1.2.6/]# make
```

Once everything has compiled cleanly, issue the command **make install** to complete
the installation. The **make install** process installs a total of four binaries on your system.
ftpcount and **ftpwho** are installed in **/usr/local/bin**. **proftpd** and **ftpshut** are installed in
/usr/local/sbin/. The **ftpcount** utility counts how many FTP users you have logged into the
system. The **ftpwho** utility displays the usernames of all the users logged into the system.
Finally, the **proftpd** binary is the FTP daemon itself, which does all the hard work. Since we
have configured and installed the software, we can move on to configuring ProFTPD.

CRITICAL SKILL
13.3 Configure the ProFTPD Server

By default, the configuration file for ProFTPD is in the directory **/usr/local/etc/**; the file is
named **proftpd.conf**. If you have installed ProFTPD with the prefix set to /, the file will be
/etc/proftpd.conf. The following is the example configuration file that comes with ProFTPD.

There are not many changes that need to be made, and the format looks strikingly familiar to the Apache Web server configuration file format.

```
# This is a basic ProFTPD configuration file (rename it to
# 'proftpd.conf' for actual use.  It establishes a single server
# and a single anonymous login.  It assumes that you have a user/group
# "nobody" and "ftp" for normal operation and anon.
ServerName                      "ProFTPD Default Installation"
ServerType                      standalone

DefaultServer                   on
# Port 21 is the standard FTP port.
Port                            21
# Umask 022 is a good standard umask to prevent new dirs and files
# from being group and world writable.
Umask                           022
# To prevent DoS attacks, set the maximum number of child processes
# to 30.  If you need to allow more than 30 concurrent connections
# at once, simply increase this value.  Note that this ONLY works
# in standalone mode, in inetd mode you should use an inetd server
# that allows you to limit maximum number of processes per service
# (such as xinetd)
MaxInstances                    30
# Set the user and group that the server normally runs at.
User                            nobody
Group                           nogroup
# Normally, we want files to be overwriteable.
<Directory /*>
  AllowOverwrite                on
</Directory>
# A basic anonymous configuration, no upload directories.
<Anonymous ~ftp>
  User                          ftp
  Group                         ftp
  # We want clients to be able to login with "anonymous" as well as "ftp"
  UserAlias                     anonymous ftp
  # Limit the maximum number of anonymous logins
  MaxClients                    10
  # We want 'welcome.msg' displayed at login, and '.message' displayed
  # in each newly chdired directory.
  DisplayLogin                  welcome.msg
  DisplayFirstChdir             .message
  # Limit WRITE everywhere in the anonymous chroot
  <Limit WRITE>
    DenyAll
  </Limit>
</Anonymous>
```

You'll want to change the **ServerName** directive to whatever you would like. **ServerType** should be set to **inetd** in our example. If you choose to run ProFTPD in standalone mode, you can leave the directive as **standalone**. You will notice globally that there are **User** and **Group** directives. This tells the server what user and group to run as. It is safe to set both of these to **nobody**—you should be sure you know what you're doing if you change these users.

NOTE

Make sure that the user nobody and group nobody exist on your system. ProFTPD will fail to work if the users you specify don't exist.

Now you get to the **Anonymous** directive, noted by the following line:

```
<Anonymous ~ftp>
```

This lets you configure different parameters for anonymous access to your FTP server. By default, the **User** and **Group** directives are different from the global user and group. This allows the server process handling anonymous users to run as the user ftp and group ftp. Since you have configured anonymous access this way, the ftp user's home directory will be used for anonymous access. Check your local password file to see where ftp's home directory lies. On Red Hat 7.3, the default is **/var/ftp**. The remaining parameters specify various options to control the number of anonymous users and customizable options. The final directive of note is the **<Limit WRITE>** directive, which tells the FTP server not to allow the anonymous user to write anything on the server. The **<Limit>** directive will also allow you to control other forms of access to the FTP server.

Progress Check

1. What does the **ftpcount** utility do?

2. Where is the ProFTPD configuration file?

---

1. The **ftpcount** utility counts how many users are logged into the FTP server.
2. The ProFTPD configuration file resides at **/usr/local/etc/proftpd.conf**.

Controlling Access to FTP

There are two types of access that you can grant to the **ftp** daemon. The first is anonymous, and the second is allowing a user to log into his or her home directory via FTP. How you set up your FTP server is up to you—you can allow only anonymous access, both anonymous and user access, or only user access.

Allowing Both Valid and Anonymous Users to Log In

The default configuration file provided will allow both anonymous and regular users of your system to log in via ProFTPD. By default, ProFTPD is configured to use the **/etc/passwd** and **/etc/shadow** files for user authentication. If you are adventurous, you can look at the ProFTPD documentation to use other forms of authentication, from SQL to LDAP.

Allowing Only Anonymous Access

To allow only the ftp user or anonymous access to your FTP server, you need to use the **<Limit LOGIN>** directive. Globally, you set the **Limit** directive to the following:

```
<Limit LOGIN>
      DenyAll
</Limit>
```

This directive tells the FTP server not allow any logins for normal users. Under the **<Anonymous>** directive, you need to override the global **<Limit LOGIN>** directive as follows:

```
<Anonymous ~ftp>
<Limit LOGIN>
      AllowAll
</Limit>
...
```

Allowing Only Users to Log In

Allowing users is just the opposite logic from the above example. You need to set the **<Limit LOGIN>** directive to **DenyAll** in the **<Anonymous>** directive block.

After making these changes, you need to test out the server and verify that indeed normal users cannot log into the system and only the anonymous user is allowed. Now that we have the ProFTPD configuration file covered, we can move to setting up your system to actually listen on the FTP port by using **xinetd**.

Adding FTP to xinetd

To have ProFTPD run with **xinetd**, you should add a file in **/etc/xinetd.d/** that will describe what service to start for FTP. The following is an example **xinetd** configuration file, **/etc/xinetd.d/ ftp**:

```
service ftp
{
        flags       = REUSE
        socket_type = stream
        instances   = 50
        wait        = no
        user        = root
        server      = /usr/local/sbin/proftpd
        bind        = 192.168.1.101
}
```

NOTE

The bind IP address should be the address that exists on your server.

After you have made your configuration changes and configured **xinetd.conf**, you need to restart **xinetd** so it will listen for FTP requests. This is done by simply restarting **xinetd** through the **rc** scripts:

```
[root@ford /]# /etc/init.d/xinetd restart
```

Now that everything is configured, it is time to test out your new FTP server by using the **ftp** command-line utility. The next section will cover how to use the command-line utility and any tips and tricks associated with using the FTP protocol.

CRITICAL SKILL

13.4 Use the FTP Client

FTP is pretty easy to use and chances are you've already used the protocol to download various packages over the Internet. Typically, most users use a Web browser to download FTP content. Under Linux you can do the same or choose to use the command-line utility. Since using a browser is fairly straightforward, we will cover using the **ftp** command-line utility in the following sections.

TIP

If for some reason the FTP server is not working, you should take a look at your log files to see what is going on. This will be the first place to look for problems, as usually the log message will plainly tell you what is wrong. I find running **tail -f /var/log/messages** in another window while configuring new services to be a handy tool.

Project 13-1   Using the ftp Command-Line Utility

To get started, you can use the **ftp** command in various ways. In its most simple way, you can issue the command with the name of the host you want to connect to. This project will cover the basic use of the **ftp** command-line utility.

Step by Step

1. Start by typing **ftp** and passing the hostname that you want to connect to as the argument:

```
[root@ford /]# ftp localhost
```

NOTE

This is assuming that you are trying to connect to the server that you are currently logged into.

You will be prompted with a message like the following:

```
Connected to smallvaio.internal.wugaa.com.
220 ProFTPD 1.2.6 Server (ProFTPD Default Installation)
[smallvaio.internal.wugaa.com]
Name (192.168.1.101:sgraham):
```

2. Login as the user ftp or anonymous:

```
Name (192.168.1.101:sgraham): ftp
331 Anonymous login ok, send your complete email address as your password.
Password:
```

3. Enter your e-mail address as your password. (The password will not be echoed back to you on the screen.)

(continued)

13

FTP

Project
13-1

Using the ftp Command-Line Utility

After you have given your password, you will be given the standard FTP prompt as follows:

```
230-Hello
 Welcome to my FTP server
230 Anonymous access granted, restrictions apply.
Remote system type is UNIX.
Using binary mode to transfer files.
ftp> ls
500 EPSV not understood.
227 Entering Passive Mode (192,168,1,101,4,30).
150 Opening ASCII mode data connection for file list
-rwxr-xr-x    1 root      root           37 Sep  8 22:17 welcome.msg
226 Transfer complete.
ftp>
```

4. Type **ls** to list the contents of the current directory.

You will notice that the only thing in the **ftp** directory is the file **welcome.msg**, which is actually printed out the screen. It contains the line "Welcome to my FTP Server."

5. To download the **welcome.msg** file, simply type **get welcome.msg** at the FTP command prompt.

6. Type **bye** to exit out of the **ftp** command.

Project Summary

The **ftp** command is pretty simple to use. In this project, you simply got the **welcome.msg** file from the FTP server. In a typical environment, files you want to grab will be located in **/pub** on the FTP server.

Table 13-1 lists some common FTP commands. Overall you will notice some of the commands mimic the Linux shell commands.

We have covered downloading and installing the ProFTPD server and testing it out with the standard Linux FTP client. You'll probably want to add more content to your FTP server. Typically, sites store public information in **/pub**. If you don't like the **ftp** utility, you can try the **ncftp** utility, which offers tab completion and better status reporting when downloading files. Of course, you could always use Mozilla to download through FTP with a nice GUI.

Command	Description
`help`	Prints out the list of commands the server supports.
`help cmd`	Prints out the help for a specific command.
`ls`	Performs a directory listing.
`cd dir`	Changes the current working directory.
`get`	Performs the FTP **get** and downloads to the current local directory you are in.
`mget`	Performs a multiple **get**. This allows you to download several files at once.
`lcd dir`	Changes the local (client) directory to the directory specified. Handy for switching to **/tmp** without exiting FTP.
`prompt`	Turns off prompting you if you want to download a file when using **mget**.
`bin`	Sets the transfer mode to binary. Most clients set this automatically.
`hash`	Prints out a hash character for every 1024 bytes. Good for getting status of the download.

Table 13-1 Common FTP Commands

✓ Module 13 Mastery Check

1. What is the configuration file for ProFTPD?

2. What does the FTP **get** command do?

3. How do you download multiple files with FTP?

4. Why would you want to use the binary transfer mode?

5. How do you change the client current working directory from the **ftp** utility?

6. Why would you want to run the ProFTPD server as the user nobody?

7. How do you disable the ability for the anonymous user to write files?

8. How do you disallow users the ability to log in to FTP?

9. What are the standard FTP ports?

10. What does the **bind** option in the **xinetd** configuration file do?

11. How do you tell how many users are logged into the ProFTPD server?

12. How do you find out who is logged into the ProFTPD server?

13. What is the purpose of the **welcome.msg** file?

Module 14

Setting Up Your Web Server Using Apache

In this module, we discuss the process of installing and configuring the *Apache HTTP server* (http://www.apache.org/) on your Linux server. Apache is free software released under the GNU GPL. According to one of the most respected statistics on the Net (published by Netcraft Ltd., http://www.netcraft.co.uk/), Apache has a market share of more than 50%. This level of respect from the Internet community comes from the following benefits and advantages provided by the Apache server software:

- It is stable.

- Several major Web sites, including Amazon.com and IBM are using it.

- The entire program and related components are open source.

- It works on a large number of platforms (all popular variants of UNIX, some of the not-so-popular variants of UNIX, and even Windows 2000/NT).

- It is extremely flexible.

- It has proved to be secure.

Before we get into the steps necessary to configure Apache, we will review some of the fundamentals of the HTTP protocol as well as some of the internals of Apache, such as its process ownership model. This information will help you understand why Apache is set up to work the way it does.

CRITICAL SKILL
14.1 Understand the HTTP Protocol

HTTP (Hypertext Transfer Protocol) is, of course, a significant portion of the foundation for the World Wide Web, and Apache is the server implementation of the HTTP protocol. Browsers such as Netscape Navigator and Microsoft Internet Explorer are client implementations of HTTP.

As of this writing, the HTTP protocol is at version 1.1 and is documented in RFC 2616 (for details, go to ftp://ftp.isi.edu/in-notes/rfc2616.txt).

Headers

When a Web client connects to a Web server, the client's default method of making this connection is to contact the server's TCP port 80. Once connected, the Web server says nothing; it's up to the client to issue HTTP-compliant commands for its requests to the server. Along with each command comes a *request header* including information about the client.

For example, when using Netscape Navigator under Linux as a client, a Web server will receive the following information from a client:

```
GET / HTTP/1.0
Connection: Keep-Alive
User-Agent: Mozilla/4.06 [en] (X11; U; Linux 2.2.5-15 i686)
Host: localhost:8000
Accept: image/gif, image/x-xbitmap, image/jpeg, image/pjpeg,
image/png, /
Accept-Encoding: gzip
Accept-Language: en
Accept-Charset: iso-8859-1,*,utf-8
```

The first line contains the HTTP **GET** command, which asks the server to fetch a file. The remainder of the information makes up the header, which tells the server about the client, the kind of file formats the client will accept, and so forth. Many servers use this information to determine what can and cannot be sent to the client, as well as for logging purposes.

Along with the request header, additional headers may be sent. For example, when a client uses a hyperlink to get to the server site, a header entry showing the client's originating site will also appear in the header.

When it receives a blank line, the server knows a request header is complete. Once the request header is received, it responds with the actual requested content, prefixed by a server header. The server header tells the client information about the server, the amount of data the client is about to receive, and the type of data coming in. For example, the request header shown just above, when sent to an HTTP server, results in the following server response header:

```
HTTP/1.1 200 OK
Date: Wed, 01 May 2002 08:57:44 GMT
Server: Apache/1.3.24 (Unix)
Content-Location: index.html.en
Vary: negotiate,accept-language,accept-charset
TCN: choice
Last-Modified: Fri, 04 May 2001 00:00:38 GMT
ETag: "835b7-5b0-3af1f126;3ccfadb0"
Accept-Ranges: bytes
Content-Length: 1456
Content-Type: text/html
Content-Language: en
```

A blank line and then the actual content of the transmission follow the response header.

Ask the Expert

Q: What is the major difference between HTTP/1.0 and HTTP/1.1?

A: There are many differences between HTTP/1.0 and HTTP/1.1. The major difference is the ability to run multiple requests over the same TCP connection in HTTP/1.1. Overall, you want to run a server that supports HTTP/1.1. Browsers will take advantage of the better protocol and reduce download times since the clients typically will not have to reestablish a TCP connection for each request.

Nonstandard Ports

The default port for HTTP requests is port 80, but you can also configure a Web server to use a different (arbitrarily chosen) port that is not in use by another service. This allows sites to run multiple Web servers on the same host, each server on a different port. Some sites use this arrangement for multiple configurations of their Web servers, to support various types of client requests.

When a site runs a Web server on a nonstandard port, you can see that port number in the site's URL. For example, the address http://www.redhat.com/ with an added port number would read http://www.redhat.com:80/.

CAUTION

Don't make the mistake of going for "security through obscurity." If your server is on a nonstandard port, that doesn't guarantee that Internet troublemakers won't find your site. Because of the automated nature of tools used to attack a site, it takes fewer than 100 lines of C code to scan a server and find which ports are running Web servers. Using a nonstandard port does not keep your site secure.

Process Ownership and Security

As discussed in other modules, running a Web server under UNIX forces you to deal with the Linux (and UNIX in general) model. In terms of permissions, that means each process has an owner, and that owner has limited rights on the system.

Whenever a program (process) is started, it inherits the permissions of its parent process. For example, if you're logged in as root, the shell in which you're doing all your work has all the same rights as the root user. In addition, any process you start from this shell will inherit all the permissions of that root. Processes may give up rights, but they cannot gain rights.

NOTE

There is an exception to the Linux inheritance principle. Programs configured with the SetUID bit (see the **chmod** command in Module 6) do not inherit rights from their parent process, but rather start with the rights specified by the owner of the file itself. For example, the file containing the program **su** (**/bin/su**) is owned by root and has the SetUID bit set. If the user sshah runs the program **su**, that program doesn't inherit the rights of sshah, but instead will start with the rights of root.

How Apache Processes Ownership

To do network setups, the Apache HTTP server must start with root permissions. Specifically, it needs to bind itself to port 80 so that it can listen for requests and accept connections. Once it does this, Apache can give up its rights and run as a nonroot user, as specified in its configuration files. By default, this is the user *nobody*.

As user nobody, Apache can read only the files that user nobody has permission to read. Thus, if a file's permissions are set so that they are readable only by the file's owner, the owner must be nobody. For any file that you want available to user nobody, set that file's permission to world readable:

```
chmod a+r filename
```

where *filename* is the name of the file.

Security is especially important for sites that use CGI scripts. By limiting the permissions of the Web server, you decrease the likelihood that someone can send a malicious request to the server. The server processes and corresponding CGI scripts can break only what they can access. As user nobody, the scripts and processes don't have access to the same key files that root can access. (Remember that root can access everything, no matter what the permissions.)

CAUTION

In the event that you decide to allow CGI scripts on your server, pay strict attention to how they are written. Be sure it isn't possible for input coming in over the network to make the CGI script do something it shouldn't. Although there are no statistics on this, most successful attacks on sites are possible because of improperly configured Web servers and/or poorly written CGI scripts.

Progress Check

1. What port does the Apache HTTP server use?

2. What are HTTP headers used for?

<hr>

Project 14-1   Installing the Apache HTTP Server

Although most distributions of Linux come with the Apache HTTP server already installed, you may need to perform an upgrade or adjust the configuration. This section walks you through the process of downloading the Apache source code, compiling it, and finally installing it. Apache configuration commands are covered in later sections.

If you want to stick with your Linux distribution's default Apache installation, you can skip this section. All you'll need to know are the locations of the Apache configuration files and the top-level pages, and how to restart the server. For Red Hat 7 and higher, these are as follows:

Configuration files	/etc/httpd/conf
Top-level pages	/var/www
Server restart	/etc/rc.d/init.d/httpd restart

The latest version of the Apache HTTP server is always located at http://httpd.apache .org/dist/. As of this writing, the latest stable version is Apache 2.0.43, available in the **httpd-2.0.43.tar.gz** archive file.

Step by Step

1. Download the latest version from http://httpd.apache.org/.

2. Extract the tar archive.

```
[root@ford /root]# cd /usr/local/src
[root@ford src]# tar -xvzf httpd-2.0.43.tar.gz
```

3. Run the **configure** script.

```
[root@ford src]# cd httpd-2.0.43
[root@ford httpd-2.0.43]# ./configure--prefix=/usr/local/http-2.0.43
```

4. Run **make**.

<hr>

1. By default, Apache uses the standard HTTP port: 80.

2. HTTP headers are used to convey status and information about the current request or response.

```
[root@ford http-2.0.43]# make
```

5. Run **make install**, if step 4 didn't have any errors.

```
[root@ford httpd-2.0.43]# make install
```

6. Quickly check the configuration file for any needed changes.

7. Start the server.

```
[root@ford http-2.0.43]# cd /usr/local/http-2.0.43/bin
[root@ford bin]# ./httpdctl start
```

Project Summary

This project quickly covered the compilation and installation of the httpd server. The Apache group conforms to the GNU software package standard, so compilation was easy and straightforward. Keep in mind if you need to enable modules, you will have to rerun the **configure** script and recompile your software. The basic configuration should work for most things, but you will most likely want to customize your configuration to conform to your site. The upcoming section covers the configuration of httpd.

Apache Modules

Part of what makes Apache so powerful and flexible is that its design allows extensions through modules. Apache comes with many modules by default and automatically includes them in the default installation.

If you are interested in extending Apache's capability, visit http://httpd.apache.org/docs/ to see what other modules are available for inclusion as well as directions on adding them to your installation.

To give you some idea of what kinds of things people are doing with modules, visit http://modules.apache.org/. There you will find modules like the LDAP Authentication Module to let your users authenticate against a LDAP server, **mod_backhand** to perform load balancing across multiple Web servers, and **mod_frontpage** to provide Front Page extensions to Apache.

Make Sure Nobody Is There!

As mentioned earlier, Apache runs by default as user nobody. Make sure this user exists by viewing the **/etc/passwd** file and looking for the entry. (If you need to, review Module 5 for instructions on confirming whether a particular user exists.)

14

Setting Up Your Web Server Using Apache

Project 14-1

Installing the Apache HTTP Server

Starting Up and Shutting Down Apache

One of the nicest features of Linux is the ability to start up and shut down system services without needing to reboot. This is easy to do in the Apache server.

To start Apache, use this command:

```
[root@ford root]# /usr/local/httpd-2.0.43/bin/httpdctl start
```

To shut down Apache, enter this command:

```
[root@ford root]# /usr/local/httpd-2.0.43/bin/httpdctl stop
```

Starting Apache at Boot Time

Since so many distributions of Linux come with Apache installed, you'll need to disable the existing configuration if you want to run your newly compiled version. To do this, check the **rc.d** directories and find the symbolic links that point to existing Apache startup scripts. Existing scripts are likely to be called **httpd** or **apache**.

For example, under Red Hat Linux, the **/etc/rc.d/rc3.d/S85httpd** script points to **/etc/rc.d/init.d/httpd**, which starts up the default installation of Apache. To change this so that a recently compiled version runs instead, you would replace the link to point to **/usr/local/httpd-2.0.43/bin/httpdctl**.

Under Red Hat Linux, the commands to accomplish this update are as follows:

```
[root@ford root]# cd /etc/rc.d/rc3.d
[root@ford rc3.d]# rm S85httpd
[root@ford rc3.d]# ln -s /usr/local/httpd-2.0.43/bin/httpdctl S85httpd
```

Don't forget to do the same for shutdown scripts. Here are the appropriate commands under Red Hat Linux:

```
[root@ford rc3.d]# cd /etc/rc.d/rc6.d
[root@ford rc6.d]# rm K15httpd
[root@ford rc6.d]# ln -s /usr/local/httpd-2.0.43/bin/httpdctl K15httpd
```

For details on startup and shutdown scripts, see Module 7.

Progress Check

1. What command is used to control the HTTP server?

2. Where can you find modules for the Apache HTTP server?

Testing Your Installation

You can perform a quick test on your Apache installation using a default home page. To do this, start up the server (if necessary) using the following command:

```
[root@ford /root]# /usr/local/httpd-2.0.43/bin/httpdctl start
```

Apache comes with a default home page, **index.html**, located in **/usr/local/httpd-2.0.43/ htdocs**. To find out if your Apache installation went smoothly, start a Web browser and tell it to visit your machine. For example, for a machine with the host name franklin.domain.com, you would visit http://franklin.domain.com/. There you should see a simple Web page whose title is "It Worked!" If you don't, retrace your Apache installation steps and make sure you didn't encounter any errors in the process. (Linux error messages are sometimes very terse, making them easy to miss.)

CRITICAL SKILL
14.2 Configure Apache

Apache supports a rich set of configuration options that are sensible and easy to follow. This makes it a simple task to set up the Web server in various configurations.

This section walks through a basic configuration. The default configuration is actually quite good and (believe it or not) works right out of the box, so if the default is acceptable

---

1. The **httpdctl** command will let you control the Apache Web server. (This command is **apachectl** in the 1.3.x series of Apache.)

2. http://modules.apache.org/

to you, simply start creating your HTML documents! Apache allows several common customizations. After we step through creating a simple Web page, we'll show how you can make those common customizations in the Apache configuration files.

Creating a Simple Root-Level Page

If you like, you can start adding files to Apache right away in the **/usr/local/httpd-2.0.43/ htdocs** directory for top-level pages. Any files placed in that directory must be world readable.

As mentioned earlier, Apache's default Web page is **index.html**. Let's take a closer look at changing the default home page so that it reads "Welcome to ford.planetoid.org." Here are the commands:

```
[root@ford]# cd /usr/local/httpd-2.0.43/htdocs
[root@ford]# echo "Welcome to ford.planetoid.org" >> index.html
[root@ford]# chmod 644 index.html
```

You could also use an editor such as **vi** or **pico** to edit the **index.html** file and make it more interesting and correct.

Creating Home Pages

Users who want to create home pages have to take only the following steps:

```
[sshah@ford]$ cd
[sshah@ford]$ chmod a+x .
[sshah@ford]$ mkdir public_html
[sshah@ford]$ chmod a+x public_html
```

As a result of these commands, files placed in the **public_html** directory for a particular user and set to world readable will be on the Web with the URL http://*yourhostname .domain.com*/~*username*, where *yourhostname.domain.com* is the user machine's fully qualified domain name, and *username* is the login of the user who created the Web page. The default filename that loads is **index.html**.

For example, user sshah would enter the following to create a home page:

```
[sshah@ford]$ cd ~/public_html
[sshah@ford]$ echo "Welcome to Steve's Homepage" >> index.html
[sshah@ford]$ chmod 644 index.html
```

If sshah's site name is ford.domain.com, his URL would be http://ford.domain.com/ ~sshah. (One hopes, of course, that he'll eventually go back and edit the **index.html** file to contain something more interesting.)

Apache Configuration Files

The configuration files for Apache are located in the **/usr/local/apache/conf** directory. There you will see the three files **srm.conf**, **access.conf**, and **httpd.conf**.

 NOTE

The first two config files, **srm.conf** and **access.conf**, are stub files only and are no longer used; essentially, they're artifacts from when Apache was originally just a set of patches against the NCSA Web server many years ago. They contain only a note saying that all changes to the configuration should go into the **httpd.conf** file. You will also notice in the **httpd.conf** file that those two files are typically set to **/dev/null**—in other words, they are not used.

The best way to learn more about the configuration files is to read the **httpd.conf** file. The default installation file is heavily commented, explaining each entry, its role, and the parameters you can set.

Common Configuration Changes

The default configuration settings work just fine right out of the box and need no modification. Nevertheless, most site administrators will want to make the alterations described in this section.

Making Nobody Somebody

Apache's default user, nobody, allows Apache to run without root permissions. Of course, since other subsystems will use the nobody login as well, you will want to limit their access to certain files.

Create a new user whose login is clearly intended for a specific group of files, for example, www. To accompany this login, you'll want to create a group called www as well. For the www login:

- Set the shell setting to **/bin/false** so that users cannot log in to the account.

- Set a password to * so that no one can use FTP to access the account.

(Don't worry—these settings on the user account won't keep a process from running as that user.)

Once the www account and group are created, edit the **httpd.conf** file so that the entries for **User** and **Group** are set to www:

```
User www
Group www
```

Don't forget to change the permissions on all the files in the **/usr/local/apache** directory so that they are owned by www and have a group setting of www, as follows:

```
[root@ford /root]# cd /usr/local;chown -R www.www httpd-2.0.43
```

Changing Host Names

At many sites, servers fulfill multiple purposes. An intranet Web server that isn't getting heavy usage, for example, should probably share its usage allowance with another service. In such a situation, the computer name www used in the preceding section wouldn't be a good choice, because it suggests that the machine has only one purpose.

It's better to give a server a neutral name and then establish DNS CNAME entries or multiple host name entries in the **/etc/hosts** file. In other words, you can give the system several names for accessing the server, but it needs to know only about its real name. Consider a server whose host name is dioxin.eng.domain.org that is to be a Web server as well. You might be thinking of giving it the host name alias www.eng.domain.org. However, since dioxin will know itself only as dioxin, users who visit www.eng.domain.org will be confused by seeing in their browsers that the server's real name is dioxin.

Apache provides a way to get around this using the **ServerName** directive. By specifying what you want Apache to return as the host name of the Web server, a system with a name like dioxin can have an alias of www, invisible to users of the site. Here is an example of the **ServerName** directive:

```
ServerName www.eng.domain.org
```

Server Administrator

It's often a good idea, for a couple of reasons, to use an e-mail alias for a Web site's administrator. First, there may be more than one administrator. By using an alias, it's possible for the alias to expand out to a list of e-mail addresses. Second, if the current administrator leaves, you don't want to have to make the rounds of all those Web pages and change the name of the site administrator.

Assuming you have set up the e-mail alias so that www@domain.com represents your Web administrator (see Module 15 for doing this using Postfix and Linux), you need to edit the **ServerAdmin** line in the **httpd.conf** file so that it reads as follows:

```
ServerAdmin www@domain.com
```

NOTE

Obviously, we can't cover everything about the Apache HTTP server in a few short pages. The software's online manual comes with the distribution and will give you the information you need. It's written in HTML, so you can access it in a browser. Simply point to the file:**/usr/local/apache/htdocs/manual/index.html**.

Progress Check

1. How do you change the ownership on the **htdocs** directory to the user www and group www?

2. What is the main configuration file for httpd?

3. What variable in the **httpd.conf** file controls what user the server will run as?

Configuring Virtual Domains

One of the most used features of Apache is its ability to support virtual domains—that is, to allow multiple domains to be hosted from the same IP address. This is accomplished by the HTTP 1.1 protocol, which specifies the desired site in the HTTP header rather than relying on the server to know what site to fetch based on its IP address.

NOTE

Don't forget that it is not merely enough to configure a virtual domain using Apache. You must also get the domain itself from a company that sells domain names, like Register.com. Once you have the domain name, you can either use your registrar's DNS server or you can set up your own DNS server. Either way, you will need to establish the necessary entries so that www.*yourdomain*.com points to your Web server. Of course, if you are just playing around and don't want to set up a site for real, you can simply set up a local DNS server and create fictitious domains and IP addresses, or even just add the necessary entries to the **/etc/hosts** file.

---

1. **chown -R www.www /usr/local/httpd-2.0.43/htdocs**
2. **httpd.conf**
3. The **User** directive controls what user the server runs as.

To set up a new virtual domain, open the **httpd.conf** file in your favorite text editor and scroll toward the end of the file. There you will find a commented-out example of a virtual host entry that looks something like this:

```
#
# VirtualHost example:
# Almost any Apache directive may go into a VirtualHost container.
#
#<VirtualHost ip.address.of.host.some_domain.com>
#   ServerAdmin webmaster@host.some_domain.com
#   DocumentRoot /www/docs/host.some_domain.com
#   ServerName host.some_domain.com
#   ErrorLog logs/host.some_domain.com-error_log
#   CustomLog logs/host.some_domain.com-access_log common
#</VirtualHost>
```

Simply clone this entry and substitute in your own information. For example, for my domain, planetoid.org, the virtual host entry would look like this:

```
#
# Virtual Host Settings for planetoid.org
#


<VirtualHost planetoid.org>
  ServerAdmin linuxadmin@planetoid.org
  DocumentRoot /www/htdocs/planetoid.org
  ServerName planetoid.org
  ErrorLog /www/logs/planetoid.org/error_log
  CustomLog /www/logs/planetoid.org/access_log common
</VirtualHost>
```

Note that you have to do this for each host you want visible. So if I want to have both www.planetoid.org and planetoid.org resolve to the same Web page, I need to set up a second virtual host setting for www.planetoid.org, as well. (Both www.planetoid.org and planetoid.org can have the same configuration information, but they must remain separate virtual host entries.)

Once you have the information in there, simply restart Apache using the **/usr/local/httpd-2.0.43/bin/httpdctl restart** command.

TIP

If you have problems with Virtual Hosts, use the **httpd** binary with the **-S** option. This will show you if you have configured the virtual host directives correctly.

CRITICAL SKILL
14.3 Troubleshoot Apache

The process of changing configurations (or even the initial installation) can sometimes not work as smoothly as you'd like. Thankfully, Apache does an excellent job at reporting in its error log file why it failed.

The error log file is located in your **logs** directory. If you are running a stock Red Hat installation, this is in the **/var/log/httpd** directory. If you installed Apache yourself using the installation method discussed earlier in this module, the logs are in the **/usr/local/httpd-2.0.43/logs** directory. In these directories, you will find two files: **access_log** and **error_log**.

The **access_log** file is simply that—a log of which files have been accessed by people visiting your Web site. It contains information about whether the transfer completed successfully, where the request originated (IP address), how much data was transferred, and what time the transfer occurred. This is a very powerful way of determining the usage of your site.

The **error_log** file contains all of the errors that occur in Apache. Note that not all errors that occur are fatal—some are simply problems with a client connection from which Apache can automatically recover and continue operation. However, if you started Apache but still cannot visit the Web site, then take a look at this log file to see why Apache may not be responding. The easiest way to see the last ten error messages is by using the **tail** command, like so:

```
[root@ford logs]# tail -10 error_log
```

If you need to see more log information than that, simply change the number 10 to the number of lines that you need to see. If that number of lines exceeds the length of your screen, you can pipe the output through **more** so you can see one screen at a time, like so:

```
[root@ford logs]# tail -100 error_log | more
```

This will display the last 100 lines of the error log, one screen at a time. Of course, if you have a spare xterm open, you can run the following to constantly view the error logs:

```
[root@ford logs]# tail -f error_log
```

This command will constantly tail the logs until you terminate the program (CTRL-C).

Module 14 Mastery Check

1. What does an HTTP server do?

2. What port does a Web server typically run on?

3. What is a **VirtualHost** directive?

4. Are you safe from malicious users if you run your Web server on port 81?

5. What directory is used in a user's home directory for public HTML files?

6. Why should you *not* run httpd as the root user?

7. In what situations should you run httpd as a user other than nobody?

8. What command would you issue to restart the httpd server?

9. What is an HTTP response header?

10. What is an HTTP request header?

11. How would you troubleshoot a problem with **VirtualHost**?

12. What is the **DocumentRoot** variable for in the **httpd.conf** file?

13. What is the **ServerRoot** variable for in the **httpd.conf** file?

Module 15

SMTP

The Simple Mail Transfer Protocol (SMTP) is the de facto standard for mail transport across the Internet. Anyone who wants to have a mail server capable of sending and receiving mail across the Internet must be able to support it. Many internal networks have also taken to using SMTP for their private mail services because of its platform independence and availability across all popular operating systems. In this module, we'll first discuss the mechanics of SMTP as a protocol and its relationship to other mail-related protocols, such as POP and IMAP. Then we will go over the Postfix SMTP server, one of the easier and more secure SMTP servers out there.

CRITICAL SKILL
15.1 Understand SMTP

The SMTP protocol defines the method by which mail is sent from one host to another. That's it. It does not define how the mail should be stored. It does not define how the mail server should send the mail readable by the recipient.

SMTP's strength is its simplicity, and that is due to the dynamic nature of networks during the early 1980s. (The SMTP protocol was originally defined in 1982.) People were linking networks together with everything short of bubble gum and glue. SMTP was the first mail standard that was independent of the transport mechanism. This meant people using TCP/IP networks could use the same format to send a message as someone using two cans and a string.

SMTP is also independent of operating systems, which means each system can use its own style of storing mail without worrying about how the sender of a message stores his mail. You can draw parallels to how the phone system works: each phone service provider has its own independent accounting system. However, they all have agreed upon a standard way to link their networks together so that calls can go from one network to another transparently.

Rudimentary SMTP Details

Ever had a "friend" who sent you an e-mail on behalf of some government agency informing you that you owe taxes from the previous year, plus additional penalties? Somehow a message like this ends up in a lot of people's mailboxes around April Fool's Day. We're going to show you how they did it, and what's even more fun, how you can do it yourself. (Not that I would advocate such behavior, of course.)

The purpose of this example is to show how the SMTP protocol sends a message from one host to another. After all, more important than learning how to forge an e-mail is learning how to troubleshoot mail-related problems. So in this example, you are acting as the sending host, and whichever machine you connect to is the receiving host.

The SMTP protocol requires only that a host be able to send straight ASCII text to another host. Typically, this is done by contacting the SMTP port (port 25) on a mail server. You can do this using the Telnet program. For example,

```
[root@ford /root]# telnet mailserver 25
```

where the host *mailserver* is the recipient's mail server. The 25 that follows *mailserver* tells Telnet that you want to communicate with the server's port 25 rather than the normal port 23. (Port 23 is used for remote logins, and port 25 is for the SMTP server.)

The mail server will respond with a greeting message such as this:

```
220 mail ESMTP Sendmail 8.9.3/8.9.3; 26 Aug 1999 23:17:44 -0700 (PDT)
```

You are now communicating directly with the SMTP server.

Although there are many SMTP commands, the four worth noting are

- **HELO**

- **MAIL FROM:**

- **RCPT TO:**

- **DATA**

The **HELO** command is used when a client introduces itself to the server. The parameter to **HELO** is the host name that is originating the connection. Of course, most mail servers take this information with a grain of salt and double-check it themselves. For example:

```
HELO super-duper-strong-coffee.com
```

If you aren't coming from the super-duper-strong-coffee.com domain, many mail servers will respond by telling you that they know your real IP address, but they will not stop the connection from continuing. (Some mail servers include a comment asking why you didn't use a truthful **HELO** statement.)

The **MAIL FROM:** command requires the parameter of the sender's e-mail address. This tells the mail server the e-mail's origin. For example,

```
MAIL FROM: dilbert@domain.com
```

means the message is from dilbert@domain.com.

The **RCPT TO:** command also requires the parameter of an e-mail address. This e-mail address is of the recipient of the e-mail. For example,

```
RCPT TO: pointy-hair-manager@domain.com
```

means the message is destined to pointy-hair-manager@domain.com.

Now that the server knows who the sender and recipient are, it needs to know what message to send. This is done by using the **DATA** command. Once issued, the server will expect the entire message with relevant header information followed by one empty line, a period, and then another empty line. Continuing the example, dilbert@domain.com might want to send the following message to pointy-hair-manager@domain.com:

```
DATA
354 Enter mail, end with "." on a line by itself
From: Dilbert <dilbert@domain.com>
To: Pointy Hair Manager <pointy-hair-manager@domain.com>
Subject: On time and within budget.
Date: Sat, 1 Apr 2000 04:01:00 -0700 (PDT)

Just an fyi, boss. The project is not only on time, but it is within
budget too!

.
250 NAA28719 Message accepted for delivery
```

And that's all there is to it. To close the connection, enter the **QUIT** command.

This is the basic technique used by applications that send mail—except, of course, they usually use C code rather than Telnet, but the actual content sent between the client and server remains the same.

Security Implications

Sendmail, the mail server a majority of Internet sites use, is the same package most Linux distributions use. Like any other server software, its internal structure and design are complex and require a considerable amount of care during development. In recent years, however, the developers of Sendmail have taken a very paranoid approach to their design to help alleviate these issues. The Postfix developers took it one step further and wrote the server from scratch with security in mind. Basically, they ship the package in a very tight security mode and leave it to us to loosen it up as much as we need to for our site. This means the responsibility falls to us of making sure we keep the software properly configured (and thus not vulnerable to attacks).

Some issues to keep in mind when deploying any mail server are

● When an e-mail is sent to the server, what programs will it trigger?

● Are those programs securely designed?

● If they cannot be made secure, how can you limit their damage?

● Under what permissions do those programs run?

In Postfix's case, we need to back up and examine its architecture.

Mail service has three distinct components. The *mail user agent (MUA)* is what the user sees, such as the Eudora, Outlook, and Pine programs. An MUA is responsible only for reading mail and allowing users to compose mail. The *mail transfer agent (MTA)* handles the process of getting the mail from one site to another; Sendmail and Postfix are MTAs. Finally, the *mail delivery agent (MDA)* is what takes the message, once received at a site, and gets it to the appropriate user mailbox.

Many mail systems integrate these components. For example, Microsoft Exchange Server integrates the MTA and MDA functionalities into a single system. (If you consider the Web interface to Exchange Server, it is also an MUA.) Lotus Domino also works in a similar fashion. Postfix, on the other hand, works as an MTA only, passing the task of performing local mail delivery to another external program. This allows each operating system or site configuration to use its own custom tool if necessary (that is, to be able to use a special mailbox store mechanism).

In most straightforward configurations, sites prefer using the Procmail program to perform the actual mail delivery (MDA). This is because of its advanced filtering mechanism as well as its secure design from the ground up. Many older configurations have stayed with their default **/bin/mail** program to perform mail delivery. The security issues in using that particular program vary from operating system to operating system.

CRITICAL SKILL
15.2 Install the Postfix Server

By far the most popular e-mail system on the Internet is Sendmail. Sendmail has been around for many years and has massive volumes of documentation that go along with the software. This module will cover the installation of the Postfix mail server. We chose it for its ease of use, and because it was written from the ground up to be much more secure than Sendmail. Postfix can perform most of the things that the Sendmail program can do—in fact, the typical installation procedure for Postfix is to replace the Sendmail binaries completely. The rest of this section will cover the process of obtaining the source code and installing the software on your Linux server.

Project 15-1 Installing Postfix

This project will cover installing Postfix from source to your Linux system. The steps are easy to follow, and the writers of Postfix did a good job of making Postfix supplant the Sendmail system. The following steps describe how to compile and install Postfix on your system.

Step by Step

1. Download Postfix from http://www.postfix.org/. As of this writing, the current release is postfix-1.1.11.

2. Extract the source code from the gziped tar archive:

    ```
    [root@ford /usr/local/src]# tar -xvzf postfix-1.1.11.tar.gz
    ```

3. Change your current directory to **postfix-1.1.11**:

    ```
    [root@ford /usr/local/src]# cd postfix-1.1.11
    ```

(continued)

4. Type **make** to compile the software:

```
[root@ford /usr/local/src/postfix-1.1.11]# make
```

5. Create the **postfix** user and **postdrop** group. The **postdrop** group must not have any users in the group.

```
[root@ford /usr/local/src/postfix-1.1.11]# useradd postfix
[root@ford /usr/local/src/postfix-1.1.11]# groupadd postdrop
```

6. Back up your current Sendmail binaries:

```
[root@ford /usr/local/src/postfix-1.1.11]# cd /usr/sbin
[root@ford /usr/sbin]# mv sendmail sendmail.orig
[root@ford /usr/sbin]# cd ../bin
[root@ford /usr/bin]# mv mailq mailq.orig
[root@ford /usr/bin]# mv newaliases newaliases.orig
```

7. Stop Sendmail if it is running and flush the mail queue:

```
[root@ford /usr/sbin]# /etc/init.d/sendmail stop
[root@ford /usr/sbin]# sendmail.orig -v -q
```

8. Change back to the Postfix source directory and run **make install**:

```
[root@ford /usr/bin]# cd /usr/local/src/postfix-1.1.11
[root@ford /usr/local/src/postfix-1.1.11]# make install
```

9. Follow the onscreen questions. The defaults noted in brackets [ ] are acceptable; change them to your liking as necessary.

Project Summary

By following the previous steps, you have now compiled and installed the Postfix mail system. The **make install** script will exit and prompt you for any changes that are wrong, such as forgetting to add the **postfix** user. Now that you have installed the Postfix server, you can change directories to **/etc/postfix** and configure the Postfix server.

CRITICAL SKILL
15.3 Configure the Postfix Server

Now that you have the Postfix server ready for use, you need to configure the server through the **/etc/postfix/main.cf** configuration file. It's obvious from its name that this configuration file is the main configuration file for Postfix. The other configuration file of note is the **master.cf** file. This is the process configuration file for Postfix, which allows you to change how Postfix processes are run. This can be useful for setting up Postfix on clients so that it doesn't accept e-mail and forwards to a central mail hub. For more information on doing this, see the documentation at http://www.postfix.org/. Now let's move on to the **main.cf** configuration file.

The main.cf File

The **main.cf** file is too large to list all of its options in this module, but we will cover the most important options that will get your mail server up and running. Thankfully, the configuration file is well documented and explains clearly what each option is used for. The first option you will look at is the **myhostname** parameter.

myhostname

This parameter is used to set the name that Postfix will be receiving e-mail for. Typical examples of mail server host names are mail.wugaa.com or mail.yahoo.com.

```
myhostname = mail.foo.com
```

mydomain

This parameter is the mail domain that you will be servicing, such as homenet.com or yahoo.com.

```
mydomain = foo.com
```

myorigin

All e-mail sent from this e-mail server will look as though it came from this parameter. You can set this to either **$myhostname** or **$mydomain**, like so:

```
myorigin = $mydomain
```

Notice that you can use the value of other parameters in the configuration file by placing a **$** sign in front of the variable name.

mydestination

This parameter lists the domains that the Postfix server will take as its final destination. Typically, this value is set to the host name of the box, the domain name, and can contain other names, as shown here:

```
mydestination = $myhostname, localhost.$mydomain, $mydomain,
mail.$mydomain, www.$mydomain, ftp.$mydomain
```

mail_spool_directory

You can run the Postfix server in two modes of delivery, directly to a user's mailbox or to a central spool directory. The typical way is to store the mail in **/var/spool/mail**. Either way has its pros and cons. The variable will look like this in the configuration file:

```
mail_spool_directory = /var/spool/mail
```

mynetworks

The **mynetworks** variable is an important configuration option. This lets you configure what servers can relay through your Postfix server. You will usually want to allow relaying from local client machines and nothing else. Otherwise, spammers can use your mail server to relay messages. An example value of this variable would be

```
mynetworks = 192.168.1.0/24, 127.0.0.0/8
```

If you define this parameter, it will override the **mynetworks_style** parameter. The **mynetworks_style** parameter allows you to specify any of the keywords **class**, **subnet**, or **host**. These settings tell the server to trust these networks that the server belongs to.

smtpd_banner

This variable allows you to return a custom response when a client connects to your mail server. It is a good idea to change the banner to something that doesn't give away what server you are using. This just adds one more step for hackers to try to find faults in your software.

```
smtpd_banner = $myhostname ESMTP
```

There are many other parameters in the configuration file. You will see them when you set the above options. These other options will allow you to set security levels and debugging levels if you need them. Now we will move on to running the Postfix mail system and maintaining your mail server.

Progress Check

1. What user do you need to add before installing Postfix?

2. What command do you type to install the Postfix system?

CRITICAL SKILL
15.4 Run the Postfix Server

Now that you have installed and configured your Postfix system, you need to get it running. This section will cover the various activities that you need to perform when maintaining the Postfix mail server.

---

1. You need to add the **postfix** user, or whatever user you specify in the install script.
2. Type **make install** to install the Postfix server.

Starting the Server

Starting the Postfix mail server is easy and straightforward. Just pass the **start** option to the **postfix** command:

```
[root@ford /usr/sbin]# postfix start
```

When you make any changes to the configuration files, you need to tell Postfix to reload itself to make the changes take effect. Do this by sending the **reload** command to **postfix**:

```
[root@ford /usr/sbin]# postfix reload
```

Checking the Mail Queue

Occasionally, the mail queues on your system will fill up. This can be caused by network failures or various other failures such as other mail servers. To check the mail queue on your mail server, simply type the following command:

```
[root@ford /root]# mailq
```

This command will display all of the messages that are in the Postfix mail queue. This is the first step in testing and verifying if the mail server is working correctly.

Flushing the Mail Queue

Sometimes after an outage, mail will be queued up and it can take several hours for the messages to be sent. Use the **postfix flush** command to flush out any messages that are shown in the queue by the **mailq** command.

The newaliases Command

The file **/etc/aliases** contains a list of e-mail aliases. This is used to create site-wide e-mail lists and aliases for users. Whenever you make changes to the **/etc/aliases** file, you need to tell Postfix about it by running the **newaliases** command. This command will rebuild the Postfix databases and inform you of how many names have been added.

Making Sure Everything Works

Now that you have installed the Postfix mail server, you should test and test again to make sure that everything is working correctly. The first step in doing this is to use a local mail user agent like **pine** or **mutt** to send e-mail to yourself. If this works, great, you can move on to sending e-mail to a remote site, using the **mailq** command to see when the message gets sent. The final step is to make sure that you can send e-mail to the server from the outside network (that is, from the Internet). If you can receive e-mail from the outside world, your work is done.

Mail Logs

On a Red Hat 7.3 system, by default mail logs go to **/var/log/maillog** as defined by the syslog configuration file. If you need to change this, you can modify the syslog configuration file **/etc/syslog.conf** and edit the following line:

```
mail.*                      /var/log/maillog
```

Most sites run their mail logs this way, so if you are having problems you can search through the **/var/log/maillog** file for any messages.

If Mail Still Won't Work

If mail still won't work, don't worry. SMTP is not usually easy to set up. If you still have problems, step logically through all of the steps and look for errors. The first step is to look at your log messages, which might show that other mail servers are not responding. If everything seems fine there, check your DNS settings. Can the mail server perform name lookups? Can it perform MX lookups? Can other people perform name lookups for your mail server? Ninety percent of system administration is proper troubleshooting. Another source of troubleshooting is to look at what others have done. Check the Postfix Web site at http://www.postfix.org/, or check the newsgroups at http://www.google.com/ for the problems you might be seeing.

✓ *Module 15 Mastery Check*

1. What is an MUA?

2. What is an MTA?

3. What does the Postfix server do?

4. What port does SMTP use to communicate?

5. What directory is used as a default for the Postfix mail server?

6. What two configuration files are used for the Postfix mail server?

7. After changing your **/etc/aliases** file, what command should you use to tell Postfix about it?

8. What command will tell Postfix to reload its configuration file?

9. How do you flush the mail queues?

10. What does the `mailq` command tell you?

11. Why would you want to set up the **smtpd_banner** value so it doesn't return the server version?

12. What is the SMTP **HELO** command used for?

13. What does the **mynetworks** variable do in the **config** file?

14. What is the default spool directory for Postfix?

15. Why should you back up your Sendmail binaries before installing Postfix?

Module 16

Post Office Protocol (POP)

The Post Office Protocol (POP) is a standardized mechanism that workstations of any operating system can use to download mail from a mail server. POP was created as a result of two developments:

- The proliferation on the Internet of non-UNIX PCs lacking the capability to run a fully capable SMTP server such as Sendmail

- The proliferation of workstations connected to the Internet via dial-up facilities that are rarely connected 100% of the time

Under POP, mail servers running an SMTP server can accept messages and store them to a mail spool. Users on any type of workstation with a POP-compliant mail reader can then connect to the POP server (which can read the mail spool written to by the SMTP server) and download their mail. When a user wants to send e-mail, the workstation can contact the local SMTP server and relay outgoing messages to it. See Figure 16-1.

This module discusses the POP Version 3 (POP3) protocol in detail, along with the security implications of supporting it. We then step through the process of downloading, compiling, and installing POP3.

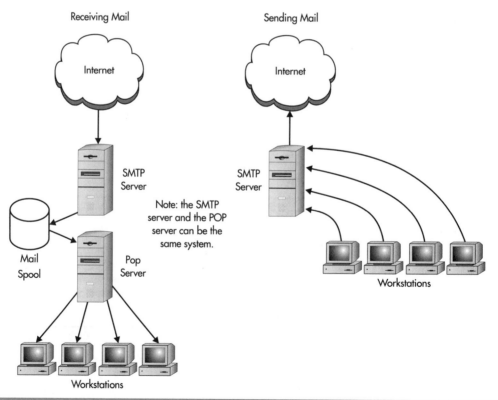

Figure 16-1 Sending and receiving mail with SMTP and POP

CRITICAL SKILL
16.1 Understand the Mechanics of POP

Like the other services we have discussed so far, POP needs a server process to handle requests. The server process listens to these requests on TCP port 110.

Each request to and response from the POP server is in cleartext ASCII, which means it's very easy for you to test the functionality of a POP server using Telnet. (This is especially useful when you have users who claim that the "mail server is broken," although the real problem is that they're unfamiliar with the system.) Like SMTP servers, a POP server can be controlled with a very short list of commands.

To get a look at the most common commands, let's walk through the process of connecting to a POP server, logging in, listing available messages, reading one, and then dropping the connection.

NOTE

We'll use the **telnet** command to read mail only as a means of seeing the actual POP3 commands being sent to the server and the server's responses. In reality, once the server has been set up, you can read your mail with a mail reader such as Eudora or Netscape Communicator or Outlook. Knowing the actual POP3 commands is helpful when you need to track down problems reported by your users. Often, it's easier to use Telnet to check quickly whether the POP server is responding than to try and use a real mail client—especially if you suspect the mail client has a bug!

Reading Mail with Telnet

You begin by **telnet**ing to the POP3 server. From a command prompt, type:

```
[root@ford /root]# telnet pop3server.domain.com 110
```

The POP3 server responds as follows:

```
+OK ready.
```

The server is now waiting for you to give it a command. (Don't worry that you don't see a prompt.) First, you want to log in, and then tell the server your login name via the **USER** command:

```
USER yourlogin
```

Here *yourlogin* is, of course, your login ID. The server responds with:

```
+OK Password required for yourlogin.
```

Now tell the server your password, using the **PASS** command.

CAUTION

The system will echo back your password, so don't do this if you have people looking over your shoulder.

```
PASS yourpassword
```

where ***yourpassword*** is your password. The server responds with:

```
+OK yourlogin has X messages (Y octets)
```

where ***X*** and ***Y*** will be actual numbers. ***X*** represents the number of messages in your mailbox, and ***Y*** represents the number of bytes in your mailbox. You're now logged in and can issue commands to read your mail.

Begin by listing the messages that are waiting, using the **LIST** command. Type:

```
LIST
```

and the server will list all the messages in your mailbox. The first column represents the message number, and the second column represents the site of the message. The response for my mailbox currently looks like this:

```
+OK 5 messages (13040 octets)
1 4246
2 2303
3 2334
4 1599
5 2558
.
```

Now let's try to actually read a message, using the **RETR** command. The only parameter that **RETR** needs is the message number to read. We'll start simply—to read message 1, type:

```
RETR 1
```

The server responds with something like this:

```
Return-Path: <hdc@domain.com>
Received: from localhost (localhost [127.0.0.1])
```

```
            by ford.domain.com (8.9.3/8.9.3) with ESMTP id WAA08271
            for <sshah@localhost>; Wed, 23 Jun 1999 22:32:38 -0700
Received: from domain.com
            by localhost with POP3 (fetchmail-5.0.0)
            for sshah@localhost (single-drop); Wed, 23 Jun 1999 \
              22:32:38 -0700 (PDT)
Received: (from hdc@localhost)
            by deathstar.domain.com (8.9.2/8.8.7) id IAA06752
            for sshah@domain.com; Wed, 23 Jun 1999 08:05:52 -0700 (PDT)
From: "H. D. Core" <hdc@deathstar.domain.com>
Message-Id: <199906231505.06752@deathstar.domain.com>
Subject: by the way
Date: Wed, 23 Jun 1999 08:05:52 -0700 (PDT)
Content-Type: text
Status: RO
Lines: 5

Always remember: It's a great big disco world.

.
```

Normally, mail readers do us the service of parsing out the information and presenting it in a much more readable form than what you see here. But this example gives you an idea of from whom the message is coming, the subject line, and the date.

At this point, you can issue as many **RETR** commands as you'd like to read your messages. Reading a message does not cause it to be deleted. To delete the message, you must explicitly issue a **DELE** command, with a parameter specifying the message number. Now that you've read message 1, you can delete it by typing:

```
DELE 1
```

which gets this response from the server:

```
+OK Message 1 has been deleted.
```

Like the **RETR** command, you can issue the **DELE** command as many times as necessary. The messages aren't actually deleted until you quit the session using the **QUIT** command.

And that's it. Now you know enough about POP3 commands to be able to test servers and, if necessary, to read your mail without a proper mail reader!

Progress Check

1. What port does POP use?

2. What does the acronym POP stand for?

Conflicts Between POP and Other Protocols

IMAP is another protocol that mail readers can use to access mail stored on servers. Though it has properties similar to POP, keep in mind that IMAP is a different protocol and needs its own server daemon to service requests.

NOTE

In the event a user attempts to use both a POP mail reader and an IMAP mail reader, you as the administrator can expect to get a request to restore their mail spool. Because POP and IMAP are independent protocols, their server daemons will work independently, as well. So if both are started at the same time and reading the same mail spool, file corruption is the likely result. When introducing new users to your system, remind them never to use two mail readers at once.

Conflicts like this will happen when people use mail readers such as pine, elm, or mutt, which read the mail spool directly from the disk (typically, through an NFS-mounted spool disk; see Module 18 on the Network File System for additional information). Those readers make copies of the spool file, perform all the changes, and then rewrite the spool file. If another mail reader is used while the process is happening, file corruption can occur. More likely, the user will lose messages or will see old messages reappear.

CRITICAL SKILL
16.2 Learn How to Install Qpopper

It's likely that your distribution of Linux already comes with some version of a POP3 server. Although you'll rarely need to update the POP3 daemon, it is something that you should know how to do. In this section, we'll walk through the process of downloading, compiling, and

---

1. Port 110
2. Post Office Protocol

installing the Qpopper daemon. The UNIX version is free from Qualcomm's Eudora division. The latest version, 4.0.4, is available at ftp://ftp.eudora.com/eudora/servers/unix/popper/.

Installing Qpopper

The latest non-beta version of Qpopper is quite stable and dependable. I've been using this package for several years now and have yet to be able to trace a single problem to the POP daemon itself. User complaints about "the mail server" inevitably have been traced to their mail client or to some network issue. You just can't say that about a lot of software these days!

So let's begin by downloading Qpopper 4.0.4 from ftp://ftp.eudora.com/eudora/servers/ unix/popper/qpopper4.0.4.tar.gz. Remember to download it to a directory large enough to unpack it and compile it. (A good choice is **/usr/local/src**.)

Next, unpack the compressed program. Assuming you've downloaded Qpopper into **/usr/local/src**, use the following command to unpack it:

```
[root@ford src]# tar -xvzf qpopper4.0.4.tar.gz
```

This creates a subdirectory called **qpopper4.0.4**, in which you'll find all the source files and documentation with the program package.

Compiling Qpopper

Before compiling Qpopper, you'll need to configure it. Qpopper comes with a configure script that does much of this for you. All it needs is for you to give it some additional directions, and the rest will take care of itself. If you want to see all of the configuration options, you can run the **configure** command with the **--help** parameter, like so:

```
[root@src qpopper4.0.4]# ./configure --help
```

Table 16-1 lists the options available for use with the **configure** command.

Configuration Option	Description
`--enable-apop=path` `--with-popuid=user`	These two options are used in tandem. The `--enable-apop=path` option enables the APOP service, which is an extension of normal POP3. The APOP extension lets users send their passwords in an encrypted format rather than in cleartext. The **path** parameter specifies the file where the authentication file will reside, typically **/etc/pop.auth**. The **user** parameter specifies the username that will own the file. The bin user is a good choice here.

Table 16-1 `configure` Options for Qpopper

Configuration Option	Description
`--enable-bulletins=path`	*Bulletins* are a handy mechanism for making announcements to all of your users without having to hit all those mailboxes with the same message. Instead, you write a single message, and each user will see it as part of the next mail download. You'll save disk space as well as time, especially if you have many users. The **path** is the directory where new bulletins are posted. Details on bulletins are discussed in "Publishing Bulletins" later in the chapter.
`--enable-servermode`	Server mode is designed to make the Qpopper daemon run more efficiently in heavy-load environments. Consider using this option if you have a large number of active users.
`--enable-specialauth`	This option is required if you are using shadow passwords. (See "Special Authentication" later in this chapter.)

Table 16-2 `configure` Options for Qpopper *(continued)*

Here is an example of a configuration line to enable Authenticated POP, provide support for shadow passwords, and establish the server mode (note, the code is entered on one line; it's shown on two here due to the printing requirements for this book):

```
[root@ford qpopper4.0.4]# configure --enable-apop=/etc/pop.auth
--with-popuid=bin --enable-specialauth --enable-servermode
```

When you run the **configure** script, it will display all the information it finds. Most of this is concerned with library and compiler support issues and is of no interest here.

TIP

In the unlikely event that the **configure** process does error out and you require help, be sure to save and use the information that the script generates.

Once Qpopper is configured, simply run the **make** command to compile the entire program. It should take less than a minute, even on relatively slow systems. The **make** command:

```
[root@ford qpopper4.0.4]# make
```

will leave you with two binary files, **popper** and **popauth**, both in the **popper** subdirectory. The first file is the actual server daemon, and the second is the tool necessary for managing APOP accounts. In addition, you'll have the man pages for **popper** and **popauth**.

Although you have the choice of installing the binaries just about anywhere, it makes the most sense to put them in the **/usr/bin** directory, since it holds many other applications, as well. Here are the commands for copying **popper** and **popauth** into /usr/bin:

```
[root@ford qpopper4.0.4]# cd popper
[root@ford popper]# cp popper /usr/bin
[root@ford popper]# cp popauth /usr/bin
[root@ford popper]# chmod 755 /usr/bin/popper
[root@ford popper]# chmod 4755 /usr/bin/popauth
[root@ford popper]# chown root.root /usr/bin/popper
[root@ford popper]# chown bin.root /usr/bin/popauth
```

NOTE

If you used the **--with-popuid=user** option with the **./configure** statement, make sure the user specified in that option matches the owner of the **/usr/bin/popauth** program. For this installation, I'm assuming you are using the bin user. If you want, you can change bin to your specified user in the **chown bin.root** line shown previously.

Project 16-1   Setting Up Qpopper

The Qpopper service is run through the **inetd** daemon, which was discussed in Module 9. (Red Hat 7 users may remember this as the **xinetd** daemon.) The following project will show how to set up Qpopper on your system.

Step by Step

1. Make sure POP is a service. Edit the **/etc/services** file, and be sure that there exists a service called **pop3** that uses port 110/tcp. The line should look something like this:

```
pop3            110/tcp         pop-3      # POP version 3
```

If it is there, great! You're ready to go. If it is not, be sure to add it and save the **/etc/services** file.

2. Set up Qpopper with **inetd**. If you are using the straight **inetd** daemon, you need to edit the **/etc/inetd.conf** file and be sure that a line that looks like the following exists:

```
pop3    stream  tcp     nowait  root        /usr/bin/popper popper
```

3. Be sure that there are no other lines in the **/etc/inetd.conf** file that begin with **pop3**, or the daemon will be confused. Now send an HUP signal to the daemon, like so:

```
[root@ford /root]# kill -1 -C inetd
```

inetd should now be ready.

(continued)

4. Configure Qpopper with **xinetd**. If an **ipop3** file does not already exist for **xinetd** in the **/etc/xinetd.d** directory, you will need to create one. The file should look like this:

```
# description: The POP3 service allows remote users to access their mail \
#              using an POP3 client such as Netscape Communicator, mutt, \
#              or fetchmail.
service pop3
{
        socket_type             = stream
        wait                    = no
        user                    = root
        server                  = /usr/bin/popper
        log_on_success          += USERID
        log_on_failure          += USERID
}
```

5. Once you have the correct configuration file in place, you need to tell **xinetd** to reread its configuration files by sending it a SIGUSR2 signal.

```
[root@ford /root]# killall -SIGUSR2 xinetd
```

6. Test Qpopper by using the **netstat** command to see if there is a process listening to the POP port, like so:

```
[root@ford /root]# netstat -ant | grep 110
```

One of the output lines should contain a line that looks like this:

```
tcp        0      0 0.0.0.0:110             0.0.0.0:*               LISTEN
```

You can also test this by using the Telnet trick discussed earlier in the module. Simply **telnet** to your own POP server on port 110, and see if you get a response.

Project Summary

You should now be ready to go with the Qpopper server. If anything doesn't work, check the parameters with which you compiled Qpopper. Did you enable any features beyond what was described in this module? Often, trying to add more authentication (such as authentication by using PAM) can lead to difficulty. Are you sure that your version of **inetd** was properly restarted? A typo can mean you sent an HUP or SIGUSR2 signal to the wrong process, and most other processes quietly ignore those signals. Did either **inetd** or **xinetd** have a problem with your config file and fail to start again? (Use the **ps** command to check.) If it had a problem, did you check the system logs (**/var/log/messages**) to see if any messages were written out?

Learn Advanced Qpopper Configurations

In the section "Compiling Qpopper," the table of options available for configuring the protocol includes some advanced parameters such as server mode, special authentication, Authenticated POP, and bulletin support. In this section, we'll examine the processes of setting up these advanced functions, as well as some of the command-line options you can set for Qpopper in **/etc/inetd.conf** or **/etc/xinetd.d/ipop3**.

Server Mode

When a user connects to the Qpopper service, Qpopper makes a backup of the mail spool being read and works with the backup. However, when a user is using a mail client that either deletes all of the mail on the server as soon as it is downloaded or simply leaves all of the mail on the server, making a backup is a waste of system resources.

In server mode, Qpopper doesn't make the backup copy; instead, it feeds the user's requests straight from the original mailbox. This is useful at sites where users tend to accumulate large mail spools. In these situations, using server mode results in faster Qpopper operation and less system overhead.

To turn on server mode, set the option:

```
--enable-servermode
```

when running the **./configure** script.

Special Authentication

Linux supports the use of *shadow password files*. With shadow password files, the normal **/etc/passwd** file is separated into two files: **/etc/passwd** and **/etc/shadow**. In the **/etc/passwd** file are stored the user's login, UID, GID, home directory, and shell, but not the user's encrypted password entry. That information has been moved into the **/etc/shadow** file, which is only readable by the root user (unlike **/etc/passwd**, which is world readable).

Qpopper supports the use of shadow passwords, too. To enable that support, use the following option when running the **./configure** script:

```
--enable-specialauth
```

NOTE

Certainly Qpopper's support for shadow passwords is an advantage, but it does not address the fundamental problem that the POP protocol allows for passwords to be transmitted over the network in cleartext. This, of course, poses a much greater security issue.

Publishing Bulletins

If you need to send a message to all of your users, you can either send the same message to each user or you can use a *bulletin*. Once a bulletin is set up, the system will automatically keep track of whether or not a user has seen it. If a user has not yet seen a bulletin, it will appear as a normal mail message the next time that user checks e-mail. Once the user has downloaded the bulletin, it won't appear ever again, even if the bulletin itself remains available to other users. Slick, isn't it?

To use bulletins, simply use the following line in the **./configure** script:

```
--enable-bulletins=path
```

where **path** is the directory where you intend to place bulletins. A good default location for this storage is **/var/spool/bulletins**.

Creating Bulletins

It's best to name each new bulletin with a filename that alphabetically follows the previous bulletin's filename. A good way to do this is to prefix each filename with a number, like so:

00001-welcome_to_the_system
00002-downtime_on_oct_12
00003-halloween_party_announcement

and so on. The file itself should be structured like a complete e-mail message the way Sendmail would deliver it. For example:

```
From qpop Wed Nov  9 13:31:08 1998
Date: Wed, 9 Nov 1998 13:31:07 -0800 (PST)
From: "Mail Administrator" <helpdesk@domain.com>
Subject: Welcome to the System

Welcome to Domain.Com! We're yet another wild and
exciting Internet company whose stock value will
eventually be used by roller coaster designers all
over the world. If you have any problems with your
computer, send mail to helpdesk@domain.com or call
```

```
extension 411.

Thanks, and welcome to the company.
```

NOTE

In bulletins, be sure to observe the RFC 822 header formats, especially in regard to the date. A lot of mail readers tend to be picky about this element.

Bulletin Directory Maintenance

Whenever a new user signs onto the system, he or she will receive every single bulletin that is in the bulletin directory. Obviously, it doesn't make sense to send the new person an announcement to the office party from last year, so be sure to do periodic housekeeping of the bulletins directory. Orderly naming of bulletin filenames should help you with this task.

Do note, however, that Qpopper will be confused if you reuse a bulletin number. Let's say you erase the second of the three bulletins you have in the system. You erase the second bulletin, but you don't create a new bulletin to take its place in the alphabetical order. Instead, create a new bulletin number. If you're using our suggestion to make bulletin filenames with numbers, you'll want to be sure the next (fourth) bulletin starts with a 00004, even if you erased the second one (00002).

NOTE

Bulletins are a great way to get a message out to all of your users, but this method requires that all of your users read mail using a POP mail reader. Depending on your site, this may not be possible. It's a good idea to verify this before using bulletins for universal announcements.

Securing POP

By default the POP3 protocol sends everything between the client and server in cleartext. If a malicious user is listening in, he can easily read your e-mail. There are two ways to secure your mail using POP: by using APOP or Authenticated POP, or by using SSL. Most modern clients now support SSL and TLSv1, so you shouldn't have too much of a problem with interoperability. Read the user guide that comes with the Qpopper distribution for more information on securing POP.

Module 16 Mastery Check

1. What does the acronym POP stand for?

2. What are bulletins used for?

3. Can you use IMAP and POP at the same time?

4. Are messages downloaded to the client when using POP or do they stay on the server?

5. What command does a POP client send to the server to login the user?

6. What is the difference between SMTP and POP/IMAP?

7. What command does the client send to the server to delete a message from the server?

8. What daemon will run the Qpopper service?

9. Can you reuse bulletin IDs?

10. How does the POP client show the messages that you have in your mailbox?

11. What command does the POP client use to "read" a message from the server?

12. What are some of the common clients that can use POP to access mail?

13. What port does the POP server use?

14. What file contains service to port mappings?

Module 17

The Secure Shell (SSH)

Oone unfortunate side effect of bringing your computer onto a public network (such as the Internet) is that, at one point or another, some folks out there will try to break into your system. Why? Because they stupidly think it's cool to do so. This is obviously not a good thing.

In Module 11, we discussed techniques for securing your Linux system, all of which are designed to limit remote access to your system to the bare essentials. But what if you need to perform system administrative duties from a remote site? Telnet is woefully insecure, because it transmits the entire session (logins, passwords, and all) in cleartext. How can you reap the benefits of a truly multiuser system if you can't securely log in to it?

NOTE

Cleartext means that the data is unencrypted. In any system, when passwords get sent over the line in cleartext, a packet sniffer could determine what a user's password is. This is especially bad if that user is root! Before the Windows NT folks reading this start insisting that their network logins are encrypted by default, let's remember this: after authentication, the PDC returns a token to the NT client for use in lieu of having to reauthenticate every time a user wants to access a network share that's used for the entire life of the login. Thus, if a packet sniffer captures the token, it can be reissued to a thief to gain access to servers. In short, a cracker doesn't even need the password to break in. In the immortal words of Homer J. Simpson, "D'Oh!" Furthermore, it wasn't until Windows 2000 that the ability to log in to a host that is not in your local area network became available. Unfortunately, Win2K only offers this feature through the insecure Telnet protocol.

To tackle the issue of remote login versus password security, a package called Secure Shell (OpenSSH) was developed. (The term "Open" in the title refers to the fact that the source code is open to public inspection, and the resulting binaries can be used in both commercial and noncommercial use.) It allows users to connect to a remote server just as they would using Telnet—except that the session is 100% encrypted. Someone using a packet sniffer merely sees encrypted traffic going by. Should they capture the encrypted traffic, decrypting it could take decades.

In this module, we'll take a brief and general look at the cryptography concept. Then we'll examine the versions of SSH, where to get it, and how to install and configure it.

CRITICAL SKILL
17.1 Understand Public Key Cryptography

Let me begin with a disclaimer: I am not a cryptography expert, and this module is most certainly not the definitive source for cryptography lessons. What you will find here is a general discussion along with some references to good books that approach the topic more thoroughly.

Secure Shell relies on a technology called *public key cryptography*. It works similarly to a safe deposit box at the bank: you need two keys to open the box. In the case of public key cryptography, you need two mathematical keys, a public one and a private one. Your public key can be published on a public Web page, printed on a T-shirt, or posted on a billboard in the busiest part of town. Anyone who asks for it can have a copy. On the other hand, your private key must be protected to the best of your ability. It is this piece of information that makes the data you want to encrypt truly secure. Every public key/private key combination is unique.

The actual process of encrypting data and sending it from one person to the next requires several steps. Let's watch Alice and Bob go through this process one step at a time in Figures 17-1 through 17-5.

Looking at these steps, notice that at no point was the secret key sent over the network. Also note that once the data was encrypted with Bob's public key and Alice's private key, the only pair of keys that could decrypt it were Bob's private key and Alice's public key. Thus, if someone intercepted the data in the middle of the transmission, they wouldn't be able to decrypt the data without the private keys.

To make things even more interesting, SSH regularly changes its private key so that the data stream gets encrypted differently every few minutes. Thus, even if someone happened to figure out the key for a transmission, that miracle would only be valid for a few minutes until the keys changed again.

Key Characteristics

So what exactly *is* a key? Essentially, a key is a very large number that has special mathematical properties. Whether someone can break an encryption scheme depends on their ability to find out what the key is. Thus, the larger the key is, the harder it will be to discover it.

Low-grade encryption has 56 bits. This means there are 2^{56} possible keys. To give you a sense of scale, 2^{32} is equal to 4 billion, 2^{48} is equal to 256 trillion, and 2^{56} is 65,536 trillion. While this seems like a significant number of possibilities, it has been demonstrated that a loose network of PCs dedicated to iterating through every possibility could conceivably break a low-grade encryption code in less than a month. In 1998, the Electronic Frontier Foundation (EFF) published designs for a (then) $250,000 computer capable of cracking 56-bit keys in a few seconds to demonstrate the need for higher-grade encryption. If $250,000 seems like a lot of money to you, think of the potential for credit card fraud if someone successfully used that computer for that purpose!

Figure 17-1 Alice fetches Bob's public key.

Alice   Bob

Bob's public key
+ Alice's private key
+ Data
—————————————
= Encrypted data

Figure 17-2 Alice uses Bob's public key along with her private key to encrypt the data.

Alice   Bob

Encrypted data

Figure 17-3 Alice sends the encrypted data to Bob.

Alice   Bob

Public key

Figure 17-4 Bob fetches Alice's public key.

Alice   Bob

Alice's public key
+ Bob's private key
+ Encrypted data
—————————————
= Decrypted data

Figure 17-5 Bob uses Alice's public key along with his private key to decrypt the data.

NOTE

The EFF published the aforementioned designs in an effort to convince the U.S. government that the laws that limited the export of crypto software were sorely outdated and hurting the United States, since so many companies were being forced to work in other countries. This finally paid off in 2000, when the laws were loosened up enough to allow the export of higher-grade cryptography. (Unfortunately, most of the companies doing cryptography work already exported their engineering to other countries.)

For a key to be sufficiently difficult to break, experts suggest no fewer than 128 bits. Because every extra bit effectively doubles the number of possibilities, 128 bits offers a genuine challenge. And if you want to really make the encryption solid, a key size of 512 bits or higher is recommended. SSH can use up to 1024 bits to encrypt your data.

The tradeoff to using higher-bit encryption is that it requires more math processing power for the computer to churn through and validate a key. This takes time and therefore makes the authentication process a touch slower—but most feel this is a worthy bargain.

NOTE

Though unproven, it is believed that even the infamous National Security Agency (NSA) can't break codes encrypted with keys higher than 1024 bits.

Cryptography References

SSH supports a variety of encryption algorithms. Public-key encryption happens to be the most interesting method of performing encryption from site to site and is arguably the most secure. If you want to learn more about cryptography, here are some good books to look into:

- *PGP* by Simon Garfinkel (O'Reilly and Associates, 1994)

- *Applied Cryptography: Protocols, Algorithms and Source Code in C,* Second Edition, by Bruce Schneier (John Wiley & Sons, 1995)

- *Cryptography and Network Security: Principles and Practice,* Second Edition, by William Stallings (Prentice Hall, 1998)

The *PGP* book is specific to the PGP program, but it also contains a hefty amount of history and an excellent collection of general cryptography tutorials. The *Applied Cryptography* book might be a bit overwhelming to many, especially nonprogrammers, but it very successfully explains how actual cryptographic algorithms work. (This text is considered a bible among cypherheads.) Finally, *Cryptography and Network Security* is heavier on principles than on practice, but it's useful if you're interested in the theoretical aspects of cryptography rather than the code itself.

CRITICAL SKILL
17.2 Understand SSH Versions and Distributions

The first version of SSH that was made available by DataFellows (now F-Secure) restricted free use of SSH to noncommercial activities; commercial activities required that licenses be purchased. But more significant than the cost of the package is the fact that the source code to the package is completely open. This is important to cryptographic software, for it allows peers to examine the source code and make sure there are no holes that may allow hackers to break the security. (In other words, serious cryptographers do not rely on security through obscurity.) Since the U.S. government has relaxed some of its encryption laws, work on the OpenSSH project has increased, and it is a viable alternative to some of the commercial versions of the SSH protocol.

Because the SSH protocol has become an IETF standard, there are also other developers actively working on SSH clients for other operating systems. There are many MS Windows clients, Macintosh clients, and even a Palm client, in addition to the standard UNIX clients. You can find the version of OpenSSH that we will be discussing at http://www.openssh.org/.

OpenSSH and OpenBSD

The OpenSSH project is being spearheaded by the OpenBSD project. OpenBSD is a version of the BSD operating system (another UNIX variant) that strives for the best security of any operating system available. A quick trip to their Web site (http://www.openbsd.org/) shows that they have gone *four years* without a remote exploit in their default installation. Unfortunately, this comes at the expense of not having the most whiz-bang-feature–rich tools available, since they require that anything added to their distribution gets audited for security first. This has made OpenBSD a very popular foundation for firewalls.

The core of the OpenSSH package is considered part of the OpenBSD project, and thus is very simple and specific to the OpenBSD operating system. To make OpenSSH available to other operating systems, a separate group exists to make OpenSSH portable whenever new releases come out. Typically, this only takes a few days from the original release. (For instance, OpenSSH 2.2.0 was released on August 31, 2000. OpenSSH 2.2.0p1, the portable version, was released a mere two days later, on September 2, 2000.)

NOTE

Since we are targeting Linux, we will use the versions suffixed with a "p" indicating that they have been ported.

Alternative Vendors for SSH Clients

Every day, many people work with heterogeneous environments, and it's impossible to ignore all the Windows 95/98/NT and MacOS systems out there. In order to allow these folks to work with a *real* operating system, there must be a mechanism for logging in from remote sites. Because Telnet is not secure, SSH provides an alternative.

Thankfully, F-Secure is not the only organization that makes an SSH client for non-UNIX operating systems. Here is a quick rundown of several SSH clients:

- **PuTTY, for Win32**   http://www.chiark.greenend.org.uk/~sgtatham/putty/
  This is by far the most lightweight SSH implementation. It is one binary with no DLLs, just one executable. Also on this site are tools like **pscp**, which is a Windows command-line version of SCP.

- **NiftySSH, for MacOS 9**   http://www.lysator.liu.se/~jonasw/freeware/niftyssh/
  This is an extension of the NiftyTelnet program that has been available for the Macintosh for quite some time. The SSH extensions work quite nicely and are very stable, even with MacOS 9.

- **OpenSSH, for MacOS X**
  That's right, OpenSSH is part of the MacOS X system. When you open the **terminal** application, you can simply issue the **ssh** command.

- **MindTerm (Multiplatform)**   http://www.mindbright.se/mindterm/
  It supports versions 1 and 2 of the SSH protocol. Written in 100% Java, it works on many UNIX platforms (including Linux) as well as Windows and MacOS. See the Web page for a complete list of tested operating systems.

- **TerraTerm SSH, for Windows**   http://www.zip.com.au/~roca/ttssh.html
  This package is a DLL to the TerraTerm terminal emulator. Both the DLL and main package are free. It supports up to version 1.5 of the SSH protocol. As of this writing, the last time this package was developed was in March of 2001.

- **FreeSSH, for Windows**   http://www.freessh.org/
  This is a site that lists several locations of SSH client and server implementations.

- **SecureCRT, for Windows**   http://www.vandyke.com/products/securecrt/
  This is a commercial implementation of SSH.

The Weakest Link

You've probably heard the saying, "Security is only as strong as your weakest link." This particular saying has a significant meaning in terms of OpenSSH and securing your network: OpenSSH is only as secure as the weakest connection between the user and the server. This means that if a user uses Telnet from host A to host B and then uses **ssh** to host C, the entire connection can be monitored from the link between host A and host B. The fact that the link between host B and C is encrypted becomes irrelevant.

Be sure to explain this to your users when you enable logins via SSH, especially if you're disabling Telnet access altogether. Unfortunately, taking the time to tighten down your security in this manner will be soundly defeated if your users Telnet to a host across the Internet so that they can **ssh** into your server. And more often than not, they won't have the slightest idea of why doing that is a bad idea.

NOTE

When you Telnet across the Internet, you are crossing several network boundaries. Each of those providers has full rights to sniff traffic and gather any information they want. Someone can easily see you reading your e-mail. With SSH, you can rest assured that your connection is secure.

Project 17-1 Downloading, Compiling, and Installing SSH

Although several distributions of Linux are now shipping with OpenSSH, you should know how to download and compile the package yourself in the event you need to upgrade. This project will cover downloading the OpenSSH software and the two components it needs, OpenSSL and zlib. Then you will compile and install the software. If you have a distribution that already has OpenSSH (such as Red Hat 7.X), you can skip this project.

As of this writing, the latest version of OpenSSH is 3.5p1. You can download this from http://www.openssh.com/portable.html. Select the site that is closest to you and download **openssh-3.5p1.tar.gz** to a directory with enough free space. (**/usr/local/src** is a good choice, and we'll use it in this example.)

Once you have downloaded OpenSSH to **/usr/local/src**, unpack it with the **tar** command, like so:

```
[root@ford src]# tar -xvzf openssh-3.5p1.tar.gz
```

This will create a directory called **openssh-3.5p1** inside of **/usr/local/src**.

Along with OpenSSH, you will need OpenSSL 0.9.5a or later. As of this writing, the latest version is OpenSSL-0.9.6g. You can download that from http://www.openssl.org/. Once you have downloaded OpenSSL to **/usr/local/src**, unpack it with the **tar** command, like so:

```
[root@ford src]# tar -xvzf openssl-0.9.6g.tar.gz
```

NOTE

Older zlib, openssl, and openssh packages have been found to have serious security holes in them. If you are running versions older than 1.1.4, 0.9.6.g, and 3.4p1 (respectively), please upgrade your software either from your distribution provider or by compiling it by hand.

Finally, the last package you need is the zlib library, which is used to provide compression and decompression facilities. Most distributions (such as Red Hat) have this already, but if you want the latest version, you need to download it from http://www.gzip.org/zlib/. The latest version as of this writing is 1.1.4. To unpack the package in **/usr/local/src**, use **tar**, like so:

```
[root@ford src]# tar -xvzf zlib-1.1.4.tar.gz
```

Step by Step

1. Begin by going into the **zlib** directory, like so:

```
[root@ford src]# cd zlib-1.1.4
```

2. Then run **configure** and **make**, like so:

```
[root@ford zlib-1.1.4]# ./configure
[root@ford zlib-1.1.4]# make
```

This will result in the zlib library being built.

3. Install the zlib library by running

```
[root@ford zlib-1.1.4]# make install
```

The resulting library will be placed in the **/usr/local/lib** directory.

4. Now you need to compile OpenSSL. Begin by leaving the **zlib** directory and entering the OpenSSL directory, like so:

```
[root@ford zlib-1.1.4]# cd ../openssl-0.9.6g
```

5. Once you are in the OpenSSL directory, all you need to do is run **configure** and **make**. OpenSSL will take care of figuring out the type of system it is on and configure itself to work in an optimal fashion. The exact commands are

```
[root@ford openssl-0.9.6g]# ./config
[root@ford openssl-0.9.6g]# make
```

Note that this step may take a few minutes to complete.

6. Once OpenSSL is done compiling, you can test it by running

```
[root@ford openssl-0.9.6g]# make test
```

(continued)

If all went well, the test should run without event. If there are any problems, OpenSSL will report them to you. If you do get an error, you should remove this copy of OpenSSL, and try the download/unpack/compile procedure again. I have successfully tested this package under several versions of Linux as well as other UNIX and have never had a problem with the compile/test phase.

7. Once you have finished the test, you can install OpenSSL by running

```
[root@ford openssl-0.9.6g]# make install
```

This step will install OpenSSL into the **/usr/local/ssl** directory.

8. You are now ready to compile and install the OpenSSH package. Move into the OpenSSH package directory, like so:

```
[root@ford openssl-0.9.6g]# cd ../openssh-3.1p1
```

As with the other two packages, you need to begin by running the **configure** program. For this package, however, you need to specify some additional parameters. Namely, you need to tell it where the other two packages got installed. You can always run **./configure** with the **--help** option to see all of the parameters, but you'll find that the following **./configure** statement will probably work fine:

```
[root@ford openssh-3.5p1]#./configure --with-ssl-dir=/usr/local/ssl
--with-tcp-wrappers
```

(Note that this is one continuous line and should be entered without pressing ENTER in the middle of it.)

9. Once OpenSSH is configured, simply run **make** and **make install** to put all of the files into the appropriate **/usr/local** directories.

```
[root@ford openssh-3.5p1]# make
[root@ford openssl-3.5p1]# make install
```

Now we can cover the usage of the OpenSSH system.

Project Summary

This project covered downloading, compiling, and installing the OpenSSH system. This involved compiling several other systems, such as OpenSSL and zlib.

Server Startup and Shutdown

If you want users to be able to log in to your system via SSH, you will need to start the server process at boot time. The clean and proper way to do this is to create a startup script (as we discussed in Module 7) for the **/usr/local/sbin/sshd** process to start the Secure Shell server.

However, for the last several years, I've been using SSH and have never once had to shut it down—so here is the "cheat" technique: you can edit the **/etc/rc.d/rc.local** file so that the last instruction in it is as follows:

```
#
# Start the SSH Server Daemon
#
/usr/local/sbin/sshd
```

If for some reason you *do* need to stop the SSH server but not the entire system, you can simply kill the **sshd** process. To find out the server's process number, use the **ps** command:

```
[root@ford /root]# ps -C sshd
  PID TTY          TIME CMD
26847 ?        00:00:00 sshd
```

In this case, the PID for **sshd** is 26847, so to kill this process you'll type

```
[root@ford /root]# kill 26847
```

Of course, you can restart the daemon at any time by simply running

```
[root@ford /root]# /usr/local/sbin/sshd
```

Progress Check

1. What three packages are required to install openssh?

2. What is the name of the SSH server?

Use OpenSSH

OpenSSH comes with several useful programs that we will cover in this section. First, there is the **ssh** client program. Second, there is the Secure Copy (**scp**) program. And lastly, there is the Secure FTP program. The most common application you will probably use is the **ssh** client program.

---

1. openssh, openssl, and zlib

2. **sshd**

The ssh Client

With the **ssh** daemon started, you can simply use the **ssh** client to log in to a machine from remote in the same manner that you would with Telnet. The key difference between **ssh** and Telnet is that **ssh** will not prompt you for your login, but instead will assume that you have the same login across both machines, which is typically the case.

However, if you need to use a different login (for instance, if you are logged in as root on one host and want to **ssh** to another and log in as yourself), all you need to do is provide the **-1** option along with the desired login. For example, if I want to log in to the host ford from arthur, I would type

```
[root@arthur /root]# ssh -l sshah ford
```

Or, I could use the **_username@host_** command format, like so:

```
[root@arthur /root]# ssh sshah@ford
```

and I would be prompted with a password prompt from ford for the user sshah's password. If I just want to log in to the remote host without having to change my login, I can simply run **ssh**, like so:

```
[sshah@ford ~]$ ssh arthur
```

Project 17-2 Creating a Secure Tunnel

This project covers what is typically called the poor man's VPN. Essentially, you can use SSH to create a tunnel from your local system to a remote system. This is a very handy feature when you need to look at an intranet or another system that is not exposed to the outside world on your intranet. For example, you can **ssh** to a file server machine that will set up the port forward to the remote Web server. Figure 17-6 shows what this secure tunnel looks like.

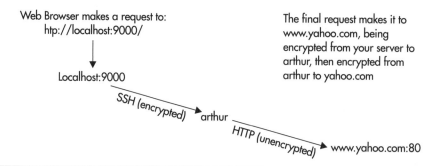

Figure 17-6 A secure tunnel with SSH

Step by Step

1. Log in as the root user using the **su** command (since you will be creating ports on the local system, you need to be root).

2. Once you are root, you will create a tunnel from port 9000 on the local system to port 80 on www.yahoo.com on the remote system.

   ```
   [root@ford #] ssh -L 9000:www.yahoo.com:80 -l sshah arthur
   ```

   The **ssh** client uses the **-L** option to create a port tunnel. The syntax is:

   ```
   -L local_port:destination_host:destination_port bounce_host
   ```

   where *local_port* is the local port you will connect to after the tunnel is set up, *destination_host:destination_port* is the host:port pair where the tunnel will be directed, and *bounce_host* is the host that will perform the forwarding to the end host.

3. When you have successfully logged in to the remote system, use your browser to access the port on the local system and see if the port tunnel is working correctly. For this example, the URL will look like the following: http://localhost:9000/. You should see the home page for Yahoo.

4. To close down the port tunnel session, close all windows that are accessing the tunnel. Then, simply type **exit** at the prompt you used to create the tunnel.

Project Summary

The secure tunnel allows you to secure access to other systems within an intranet or a remote location. It is a great and inexpensive way to create a virtual private network between your host and another host. It is not a full-featured VPN solution since you can't access every host on the remote network, but it gets the job done. In this project, you port-forwarded HTTP traffic. You can tunnel almost any protocol, such as VNC or Telnet. You should note that this is a way for people inside a firewall or proxy to bypass the firewall mechanisms and get to computers in the outside world.

Secure Copy (scp)

Secure Copy (**scp**) is meant as a replacement for the **rcp** command, which allows you to do remote copies from one host to another. The most significant problem with the **rcp** command is that users tend to arrange their remote-access settings to allow far too much access into your system. To help mitigate this, instruct users to use the **scp** command instead. The format of **scp** is identical to **rcp**, so users shouldn't have problems with this transition. For example, if I'm logged in to ford as user sshah and I want to copy the **.tcshrc** file from arthur, I would type

```
[sshah@ford ~]$ scp arthur:.tcshrc .
```

If you want to copy the other way, from the local computer to arthur, you reverse the arguments:

```
[sshah@ford ~]$ scp .tcshrc arthur:.
```

scp will also let you copy to and from machines that you are not even logged in to. For example, if I am on the host ford and want to copy a file from arthur to trillian, I can issue the following command:

```
[sshah@ford ~]$ scp sshah@arthur:.tcshrc sshah@trillian:.tcshrc
```

Of course, you will be asked for your password on both machines.

NOTE
If you are using Windows, you can use the utility **pscp**, available from the same site as PuTTY.

Secure FTP (sftp)

Secure FTP is a subsystem to the **ssh** daemon. You access the Secure FTP server by using the **sftp** command-line tool.

```
[sshah@ford ~]$ sftp sshah@arthur
```

You will then be asked for your password just like when you use the **ssh** client. Once you have been authenticated, you will be given a prompt like the following:

```
sftp> ls
drwxr-x---    7 root     root         4096 May 14 00:18 .
drwxr-xr-x   19 root     root         4096 May 13 23:28 ..
-rw-r--r--    1 root     root           24 Jun 10  2000 .bash_logout
-rw-r--r--    1 root     root         1126 Aug 23  1995 .Xresources
drwx------    4 root     root         4096 Apr 22 21:33 .kde
```

For a listing of all the commands, just type a question mark (**?**):

```
sftp> ?
Available commands:
cd path                          Change remote directory to 'path'
lcd path                         Change local directory to 'path'
chgrp grp path                   Change group of file 'path' to 'grp'
chmod mode path                  Change permissions of file 'path' to 'mode'
chown own path                   Change owner of file 'path' to 'own'
help                             Display this help text
```

```
get remote-path [local-path]    Download file
lls [ls-options [path]]         Display local directory listing
ln oldpath newpath              Symlink remote file
lmkdir path                     Create local directory
lpwd                            Print local working directory
ls [path]                       Display remote directory listing
lumask umask                    Set local umask to 'umask'
mkdir path                      Create remote directory
put local-path [remote-path]    Upload file
pwd                             Display remote working directory
exit                            Quit sftp
quit                            Quit sftp
rename oldpath newpath          Rename remote file
rmdir path                      Remove remote directory
rm path                         Delete remote file
symlink oldpath newpath         Symlink remote file
version                         Show SFTP version
!command                        Execute 'command' in local shell
!                               Escape to local shell
?                               Synonym for help
```

You will notice that the commands look strikingly familiar to the FTP commands in Module 13. This client is very handy if you forget the full name of a file you are looking for.

Files Used by SSH

The configuration files for the SSH client and SSH server typically reside in the directory **/etc/ssh/** on a distribution. If you have installed SSH from source into **/usr/local**, the full path will be **/usr/local/etc/ssh/**. If you want to make any changes to defaults for the SSH client, you need to modify the **ssh_config** file. The **sshd_config** file is for the SSH server.

Within a user's home directory, SSH information is stored in the directory **~username/.ssh/**. The file **known_hosts** is used to hold host key information. This is also used to stop man-in-the-middle attacks. SSH will alert you when the host keys change. If the keys have changed for a valid reason—for instance, if the server was reinstalled—you will need to edit the **known_hosts** file and delete the line with the changed server.

✓ Module 17 Mastery Check

1. What does the **ssh** client do?

2. What is **scp**?

3. What is **sftp**?

4. What file contains configuration information for **sshd**?

5. If a host has been reinstalled, what file in the user's home directory will need to be modified in order to get rid of the man-in-the-middle attack warnings?

6. What is wrong with using the Telnet client?

7. What other operating systems have SSH clients?

8. What binary is the SSH server?

9. How would you make sure that the SSH server is started at boot time?

10. What two methods would you use to shut down the SSH server?

11. What is a secure tunnel?

12. What are some advantages of using a secure tunnel?

13. What are some disadvantages of users running a secure tunnel?

Part IV

Intranet Services

Module 18

Network File System (NFS)

Network File System (NFS) is the UNIX way of sharing files and applications across the network. The NFS concept is somewhat similar to that of Windows NT's disk sharing in that it allows you to attach to a disk and work with it as if it were a local drive—a very handy tool for sharing files or a large disk with coworkers. (Often, it's handy for both.)

Aside from their similar roles, there are some important differences between NFS and NT shares that require different approaches to their management. The tools that you use to control network drives are (of course) different, as well. In this module, we discuss those differences; however, the primary focus of the module is to show you how to deploy NFS under the Linux environment.

CRITICAL SKILL
18.1 Understand the Mechanics of NFS

Module 8 covered the process of mounting and unmounting file systems. The same idea applies to NFS, except each mount request is qualified with the server from which the disk share is coming. Of course, the server must be configured to allow the requested partition to be shared with a client.

Let's look at an example. Making an NFS mount request for **/export/home** from the server **nox**, so that the share appears locally as the **/home** directory, is done as follows:

```
[root@ford /root]# mount nox:/export/home /home
```

Assuming that the command was run from the host named **ford**, all of the users on **ford** would be able to view the contents of **/home** as if it were just another directory. Linux would take care of making all of the network requests to the server.

Remote procedure calls (RPCs) are responsible for handling the requests between the client and server. RPC technology provides a standard mechanism for any RPC client to contact the server and find out to which service the calls should be directed. Thus, whenever a service wants to make itself available on a server, it needs to register itself with the RPC service manager, *portmapper*. Portmapper takes care of telling the client where the actual service is located on the server.

Mount and Access a Partition

Several steps are involved in a client's making a request to mount a server's partition:

1. The client contacts the server's portmapper to find out which network port is assigned as the NFS mount service.

2. The client contacts the mount service and requests to mount a partition. The mount service checks to see if the client has permission to mount the requested partition. (Permission for a client to mount a partition is based on the **/etc/exports** file.) If the client does have permission, the mount service returns an affirmative.

3. The client contacts the portmapper again, this time to find out on which port the NFS server is located. (Typically, this is port 2049.)

4. Whenever the client wants to make a request to the NFS server (for example, to read a directory), an RPC is sent to the NFS server.

5. When the client is done, it updates its own mount tables but doesn't inform the server.

NOTE

Notification to the server is unnecessary, because the server doesn't keep track of all clients that have mounted its file systems. Because the server doesn't maintain state information about clients and the clients don't maintain state information about the server, clients and servers can't tell the difference between a crashed system and a really slow system. Thus, if an NFS server is rebooted, all clients will automatically continue their operations with the server as soon as the server is back online.

Security Considerations for NFS

Unfortunately, NFS is not a very secure method for sharing disks. The steps necessary to make NFS more secure are no different from those for securing any other system. The only catch is that you must be able to trust the users on the client system, especially the root user. If you're the root user on both the client and server, there is a little less to worry about. The important thing in this case is to make sure non-root users don't become root—which is something you should be doing anyway!

If you are in a situation where you cannot fully trust the person with whom you need to share a disk, it will be worth your time and effort to seek alternative methods of sharing resources (such as read-only sharing of the disk).

As always, stay up to date on the latest security bulletins coming from the Computer Emergency Response Team (http://www.cert.org/), and keep up with all the patches from your distribution vendor.

Versions of NFS

NFS is not a static protocol. Standards committees have helped NFS evolve to take advantage of new technologies as well as changes in usage patterns. Today, the standards are up to

18

Network File System (NFS)

version 3.0, with 4.0 in the works. Linux supports both versions 2 and 3 of the NFS protocol; for performance reasons you should run version 3.0.

Most other operating systems supporting NFS probably have an NFS version 2.0 mode, which allows you to use Linux servers. Some of these systems (including IRIX) require that you explicitly specify the NFS mount option (**vers=2**) for servers that only allow NFS 2.0. Refer to the appropriate vendor's documentation for details.

Enable NFS

As of this writing, all distributions of Linux come with the NFS server installed, usually with NFS already enabled. If you aren't sure about your system, use the **ksysv** tool. It will show NFS as started in runlevels 3 and 5.

If you aren't sure if NFS is running, you can check by running **rpcinfo**, as follows:

```
[root@ford /root]# rpcinfo -p
```

If NFS is running on your system, you'll see something like the following:

```
program vers proto   port
 100000   2   tcp    111   rpcbind
 100000   2   udp    111   rpcbind
 100011   1   udp    976   rquotad
 100011   2   udp    976   rquotad
 100005   1   udp    988   mountd
 100005   1   tcp    990   mountd
 100003   2   udp   2049   nfs
```

If NFS isn't running on your system, the entries for **nfs** and **mountd** will be missing. To start NFS without having to reboot, enter this command:

```
[root@ford /root]# /etc/rc.d/init.d/nfs start
```

To stop NFS without having to shut down, enter this command:

```
[root@ford /root]# /etc/rc.d/init.d/nfs stop
```

If you have NFS enabled through **ksysv**, NFS will automatically start up every time you boot the system.

The Components of NFS

NFS under Linux is made up of five parts:

- **rpc.statd**   This daemon handles the file-locking issues between the client and the server.

- **rpc.quotad**   As its name suggests, **rpc.quotad** supplies the interface between NFS and the quota manager. Users will be held to the same restrictions regardless of whether they're working with their data through NFS.

- **rpc.mountd**   When a request to mount a partition is made, the **rpc.mountd** daemon takes care of verifying that the client has enough permission to make the request. This permission is stored in the **/etc/exports** file. (The upcoming "The /etc/exports Configuration File" section tells you more about the **/etc/exports** file.)

- **rpc.nfsd**   The main component to the NFS system. This process actually takes care of handling NFS requests.

- **rpc.lockd**   The **rpc.statd** daemon uses this daemon to handle lock recovery on crashed systems.

CRITICAL SKILL
18.3 Configure the NFS Server

Setting up an NFS server is a two-step process. The first step is to create the **/etc/exports** file. This file defines which parts of your server's disk get shared with the rest of your network and the rules by which they get shared. (For example, is a client allowed to only read a partition? Are they allowed to write to a partition?) The second step is to start the NFS server processes that read the **/etc/exports** file and follow the specifications.

The /etc/exports Configuration File

NFS servers have only one configuration file: **/etc/exports**. This file lists the partitions that are sharable, the hosts they can be shared with, and with what permissions. Here is the format of each entry in the **/etc/exports** file:

```
/dir/to/export      client1(permissions) client2(permissions) \
                    client3(permissions) client4(permissions)
```

- **/dir/to/export** is the directory you want to share with other users, for example, **/export/home**.

- **client1, client2**, and so forth are the host names of the NFS clients.

- **permissions** are the corresponding permissions for each client.

Table 18-1 describes the valid permissions for each client.

Permission Option	Meaning
`secure`	The port number from which the client requests a mount must be lower than 1024. This permission is on by default.
`ro`	Allows read-only access to the partition.
`noaccess`	The client will be denied access to all directories below **/dir/to/mount**. This allows you to export the directory **/dir** to the client, and then to specify **/dir/to** as inaccessible without taking away access to something like **/dir/from**.
`no_root_squash`	A simple security measure causes the server to ignore, by default, requests made by the root user on an NFS mounted partition. If you want to disable this and allow the root user on the client host to access the NFS mounted directory, you need to export that directory with this permission.
`squash_uids=uid-list`	When an NFS request is made, it includes the UID of the user making the request. This allows the NFS server to enforce permissions, as well. Use this option when you want to restrict certain UIDs from accessing a particular shared partition. The variable `uid-list` is a comma-separated list of UIDs you want to deny. Ranges are acceptable, as well—for example: `squash_uids=5, 10-15,20,23`.
`squash_gids=gid-list`	This works just like `squash_uids`, except it applies to GIDs rather than UIDs.
`rw`	Normal read/write access.

Table 18-1 NFS Export Options

TIP

A handy way of keeping UIDs in sync is by using NIS. See Module 19 for details.

Following is an example of a complete NFS **/etc/exports** file:

```
#
# /etc/exports for nfsserver.domain.com
#
/export/home          denon(rw) technics(rw) vestax(rw) \
                      unixadmin(rw,no_root_squash)
/export/usr/local     denon(rw,no_root_squash) \
                      technics(rw,no_root_squash) \
```

Tell the NFS Server Process About /etc/exports

Once you have an **/etc/exports** file written up, use the **exportfs** command to tell the NFS server processes to reread the configuration information. The parameters for **exportfs** are as follows:

exportfs Command Option	Description
-a	Export all entries in the **/etc/exports** file.
-r	Re-export all entries in the **/etc/exports** file.
-u client:/dir/to/mount	Unexport the directory **/dir/to/mount** to the host **client**.
-o options	Options specified here are the same as described in Table 18-1 for client permissions. These options will apply only to the file system specified on the **exportfs** command line, not to those in **/etc/exports**.
-v	Be verbose.

Following are examples of **exportfs** command lines.

- To export all file systems:

```
[root@ford /root]# exportfs -a
```

- To export the directory **/export/stuff** to the host **taos** with the **read/write** and **no_root_squash** permissions:

```
[root@ford /root]# exportfs -o rw,no_root_squash taos:/export/stuff
```

NOTE

In most instances, you will simply want to use **exportfs -r**.

The showmount Command

When configuring NFS, it is helpful to use the **showmount** command to see if everything is working correctly. After you have configured your **/etc/exports** file and exported all of your file systems using **exportfs**, you can run **showmount -e** to see a listing of exported file systems:

```
[root@ford ~]# showmount -e
Export list for ford:
/export/home (everyone)
```

Ask the Expert

Q: Is NFS a secure protocol?

A: No, NFS is not a secure protocol and there are many known exploits to compromise NFS.

Q: Is it a good thing to allow other people to have root access in your network when using NFS?

A: Generally, this is a bad idea. If a person has root access and you are sharing home directories via NFS, that user can mount the NFS share and then **su** to the user he wants to be and get access to that person's home directory. Setting **root_squash** will help, but as soon as they **su** to the user the only chance you have of detecting this is to check the **syslog** messages on the machine that the person used to **su**.

The **-e** option tells **showmount** to list exported directories. If you simply run the **showmount** command with no options, it will list clients connected to the server. By using the **showmount** command, you can quickly determine if you have configured **nfsd** correctly. You can also run this command on clients by passing the server host name as the last argument:

```
[root@trillian ~]# showmount -e ford
Export list for ford:
/export/home (everyone)
```

Common Problems

When exporting file systems, you may find that the server appears to be refusing the client access, even though the client is listed in the **/etc/exports** file. Typically, this happens because the server takes the IP address of the client connecting to it and resolves that address to the fully qualified domain name (FQDN), and the host name listed in the **/etc/exports** file isn't qualified. (For example, the server thinks the client host name is **denon.domain.com**, but the **/etc/exports** file lists just **denon**.)

Another common problem is that the server's perception of the host name/IP pairing is not correct. This can occur because of an error in the **/etc/hosts** file or in the DNS tables. You'll need to verify that the pairing is correct.

CRITICAL SKILL

18.4 Configure the NFS Client

NFS clients are remarkably easy to configure under Linux, because they don't require any new or additional software to be loaded. The only requirement is that the kernel be compiled to support NFS. All of the distributions come with this feature enabled by default. Aside from the kernel, the only other change is to the options in the **mount** command.

The mount Command

The **mount** command was originally discussed in Module 8. Note two changes for NFS partition mounting: the specification of the NFS server name, and the options specified after the **-o** on the **mount** command line.

Following is an example of a **mount** command line:

```
[root@ford /root]# mount -o rw,bg,intr,soft denon:/export/home /home
```

These **mount** options can also be used in the **/etc/fstab** file. This same entry in the **/etc/fstab** file would look like this:

```
denon:/export/home     /home      nfs      rw,bg,intr,soft 0 0
```

In the previous examples, **denon** is the NFS server name. The **-o** options are listed in Table 18-2.

mount -o **Command Option**	Description
bg	Background mount. Should the mount initially fail (for instance, if the server is down), the mount process will send itself to background processing and continue trying to execute until it is successful. This is useful for file systems mounted at boot time, because it keeps the system from hanging at the **mount** command if the server is down.
intr	Specifies an interruptible mount. If a process is pending I/O on a mounted partition, this option allows the process to be interrupted and the I/O call to be dropped. For more information, see "The Importance of the intr Option," later in this section.
soft	Enables a soft mount for this partition, allowing the client to time out the connection after a number of retries (specified with the **retrans=r** option). For more information, see "Soft vs. Hard Mounts," later in this section.

Table 18-2 mount Options for NFS

mount -o **Command Option**	**Description**
retrans=r	The *r* value specifies the maximum number of connection retries for a soft-mounted system. For more information, see "Soft vs. Hard Mounts," later in this section.
rsize=x	Sets the read block size to *x* bytes; the default is 1024 bytes. Increasing this to 8192 bytes often improves performance.
wsize=x	Sets the write block size to *x* bytes; the default is 1024 bytes. Increasing this to 8192 bytes often improves performance.

Table 18-2 mount Options for NFS *(continued)*

NOTE

Remember that NFS servers can also be, at the same time, NFS clients.

Soft vs. Hard Mounts

By default, NFS operations are *hard*, which means they continue their attempts to contact the server indefinitely. This arrangement is not always beneficial, however. It causes a problem if an emergency shutdown of all systems is performed. If the servers happen to get shut down before the clients, the clients' shutdowns will stall while they wait for the servers to come back up. Enabling a *soft* mount allows the client to time out the connection after a number of retries (specified with the **retrans=r** option).

There is one exception to the preferred arrangement of having a soft mount with a **retrans=r** value specified: don't use this arrangement when you have data that must be committed to disk no matter what, and you don't want to return control to the application until the data has been committed. (NFS-mounted mail directories are typically mounted this way.)

Cross-Mounting Disks

Cross-mounting is the process of having server A NFS mounting server B's disks, and server B NFS mounting server A's disks. While this may appear innocuous at first, there is a subtle danger in doing this. If both servers crash, and if both servers require mounting the other's disk in order to boot correctly, you've got a chicken and egg problem. Server A won't boot until server B is done booting, but server B won't boot because server A isn't done booting.

To get around this problem, make sure you don't get yourself into a situation where this happens. All of your servers should be able to completely boot without needing to mount anyone else's disks for anything. However, this doesn't mean you can't cross-mount at all. There are legitimate reasons for needing to cross-mount, such as needing to make home directories available across all servers.

In these situations, make sure you set your **/etc/fstab** entries to use the **bg** mount option. By doing so, you will allow each server to background the **mount** process for any failed mounts, thus giving all of the servers a chance to completely boot and then properly make their NFS mountable partitions available.

The Importance of the intr Option

When a process makes a system call, the kernel takes over the action. During the time that the kernel is handling the system call, the process has no control over itself. In the event of a kernel access error, the process must continue to wait until the kernel request returns; the process can't give up and quit. In normal cases, the kernel's control isn't a problem, because typically, kernel requests get resolved very quickly. When there's an error, however, it can be quite a nuisance. Because of this, NFS has an option to mount partitions with the interruptible flag (the **intr** option), which allows a process that is waiting on an NFS request to give up and move on.

In general, unless you have reason not to use the **intr** option, it is usually a good idea to do so.

NOTE Keep those UIDs in sync! Every NFS client request to an NFS server includes the UID of the user making the request. This UID is used by the server to verify that the user has permissions to access the requested file. However, in order for NFS permission-checking to work correctly, the UIDs of the users must be synchronized between the client and server. Having the same username on both systems is not enough. (You can compare this to keeping SIDs synchronized under Windows NT.)

Performance Tuning

The default block size that gets transmitted with NFS is 1K. This is handy, since it fits nicely into one packet and, should any packets get dropped, NFS has to retransmit very few packets. The downside to this is that it doesn't take advantage of the fact that most networking stacks are fast enough to keep up with segmenting larger blocks of data for transport, and that most networks are reliable enough that it is extremely rare to lose a block of data.

Given these factors, it is often better to optimize for the case of a fast networking stack and a reliable network, since that's what you're going to have 99% of the time. The easiest way to do this with NFS is to use the **wsize** (write size) and **rsize** (read size) options. A good size to use is 8K. This is especially good if you have network cards that support jumbo frames (such as those based around the Alteon Tigon II chipset).

An example entry with **wsize** and **rsize** is as follows:

```
denon:/export/home  /home  nfs    rw,bg,intr,soft,wsize=8192,rsize=8192 0 0
```

CRITICAL SKILL

18.5 Learn Common Uses for NFS Partitions

NFS is the standard file sharing system under Linux or UNIX. You can use NFS to share a central **/usr/local/** directory, home directories, and mail spools to your entire network. Now that we know what we can do with NFS, let's walk through setting up the clients and servers for NFS.

Project 18-1 Client and Server NFS Configuration

In this project, we will walk through the setup and configuration of the **nfsd** server. Once that is accomplished we will cover how to set up an NFS client and make sure that the directories get mounted when the system boots.

Step by Step

1. On the server, edit the **/etc/exports** configuration file. In this project you will share **/usr/local** and **/home**. You will export **/usr/local** as read-only and **/home** as read/write, only to the client **trillian**.

   ```
   #
   /usr/local      trillian(ro,root_squash)
   /home           trillian(rw)
   ```

2. First you need to check if the portmapper is turned on. The easiest way is to run the **rpcinfo -p** command. If the portmapper is turned off, simply **cd** into **/etc/init.d** and run:

   ```
   [root@ford /etc/init.d]#./portmap start
   ```

3. Now you can start the **nfsd** and **mountd** daemons using the **nfs rc** script:

   ```
   [root@ford /etc/init.d]#./nfs start
   ```

4. Typically the **nfs** script will let you know if it started or failed to start the servers. To check if your exports are configured correctly, run the **showmount** command:

   ```
   [root@ford /etc/init.d]#showmount -e
   ```

5. If you don't see the file systems that you put into **/etc/exports**, check **/var/log/messages** for any output that **nfsd** or **mountd** might have made. If you need to make changes to **/etc/exports**, run **/etc/init.d/nfs reload** or **exportfs -r** when you are done and finally run a **showmount -e** to make sure that the changes took effect.

6. Now that you have the server configured, it is time to set up the client. First, see if the **rpc** mechanism is working between the client and the server. You will again use the **showmount**

command to verify that the client can see the shares. If the client cannot, you might have a network problem or a permissions problem to the server.

7. Once you have verified that you can view shares from the client, it is time to see if you can successfully mount a file system. Use the **mount** command as follows:

```
[root@trillian /root]# mount -o rw,bg,intr,soft ford:/home /home
[root@trillian /root]# mount -o ro,bg,intr,soft ford:/usr/local /usr/local
```

8. If these commands succeed, you can add them into the **/etc/fstab** file so they will get mounted upon reboot:

```
ford:/home      /home      nfs    rw,bg,intr,soft 0 0
ford:/usr/local    /usr/local    nfs    ro,bg,intr,soft 0 0
```

Project Summary

You have now learned to configure both an NFS server and client. The process involves editing the **/etc/exports** configuration file, then starting **portmap**, **nfsd**, and **mountd**. The key to making NFS work is to verify that your configuration file works. Using **showmount** and local log files will guide you in finding any problems. The client configuration is fairly simple—you just need to vary the format of the **mount** command to tell it that the file system is on a remote server.

CRITICAL SKILL
18.6 Troubleshoot NFS

Like any major service, NFS has mechanisms to help it cope with error conditions. In this section, I'll discuss some common error cases and how NFS handles them.

Stale File Handles

If a file or directory is in use by one process when another process removes the file or directory, the first process gets an error message from the server. Typically, this error is "Stale NFS File handle."

Most often, stale file handles occur when you're using a system in the X Window System environment and you have two terminal windows open. For instance, the first terminal window is in a particular directory (say, **/home/user/mydir**), and that directory gets removed from the second terminal window. The next time you press ENTER in the first terminal window, you'll see the error message.

To fix this problem, simply change your directory to one that you know exists without using relative directories (for example, **cd /tmp**).

Permission Denied

You're likely to see the "Permission denied" message if you're logged in as root and are trying to access a file that is NFS mounted. Typically, this means that the server on which the file system is mounted is not acknowledging root's permissions. (Usually, this occurs for security reasons.)

The quick way around this problem is to become the user who owns the file you're trying to control. For example, if you're root and you're trying to access a file owned by the user **hdc**, use the **su** command to become **hdc**:

```
[root@ford /root]# su - hdc
```

When you're done working with the file, you can exit out of **hdc**'s shell and return to root.

Note that this workaround assumes that **hdc** exists as a user on the system and has the same UID on both the client and the server.

Module 18 Mastery Check

1. What is NFS?

2. What does the **mountd** program do?

3. What file tells NFS the directories that need to be shared?

4. Why would you want to run with the **no_root_squash** option?

5. How do you tell **nfsd** to reread its configuration file?

6. Would you want to share **/usr/local** as read-only? Why or why wouldn't you want to do this?

7. What is needed for a Linux client to be able to connect to an NFS share?

8. What is the difference between a hard and soft mount?

9. What command can be used to show services using the RPC mechanism?

10. What service is used to tell the client what port to connect to?

11. Do UIDs have to be the same when accessing an NFS share?

12. Should NFS servers be configured to mount other NFS shares?

13. What is the **mount** command to mount the file system **/export/home** residing on **trillian** to the local file system **/home?**

14. Does NFS maintain state between the client and the server?

15. Name some security risks involved with using NFS.

Module 19

Network Information Service (NIS)

The Network Information Service (NIS) makes possible to share the data of critical files across the local area network. Typically, files such as **/etc/passwd** and **/etc/group**, which ideally would remain uniform across all hosts, are shared via NIS. In this way, every network machine that has a corresponding NIS client can read the data contained in these shared files and use the network versions of these files as extensions to the local versions. However, NIS is not limited to sharing just those two files. Any tabular file where at least one column has a unique value throughout the file can be shared via NIS. You'll find many such files to exist in your system, including the Sendmail aliases file, the Automounter files, and even the **/etc/services** file.

The main benefit achieved from using NIS is that you can maintain a central copy of the data, and whenever that data is updated, it automatically propagates to all of the network users. To your users, features of NIS give the appearance of a more uniform system—no matter what host they may be working on, all of their tools and files are always there.

If you're coming from a Windows NT background, you might think of NIS as a substantially more versatile Primary Domain Controller (PDC). In fact, NIS is actually much more in line with Windows 2000 directory services than PDCs.

In this module, we'll explore NIS, how it works, and how it can benefit you. I will then explain how to set up the client and server portions of the NIS configuration. Finally, we'll discuss some of the tools related to NIS.

CRITICAL SKILL
19.1 Learn the Basics of NIS

The Network Information Service is really just a simple database that clients can query. It contains a series of independent tables. Each table originated as a straight text file, such as **/etc/passwd**, which is tabular in nature and has at least one column that is unique for every row (a database of key/pair values). NIS keeps track of these tables by name and allows querying to happen in one of two ways:

● Listing the entire table

● Pulling a specific entry based on a search for a given key

Once the databases are established on the server, clients can query the server for database entries. Typically this happens when a client is configured to look to the NIS *map* when an entry cannot be found in the client's local database. A host may have a simple file containing only those entries needed for the system to work in single-user mode (when there is no network connectivity)—for example, the **/etc/passwd** file. When a program makes a request to look up user password information, the client checks its local **passwd** file and sees that the user doesn't exist there; the client then makes a request to the NIS server to look for a corresponding entry in the passwd table. If the NIS does have an entry, it is returned to the client and then to the program that requested the information in the first place. The program itself is unaware that NIS was used. The same is true if the NIS map returns an answer that the user password entry does not exist. The program would be passed the information without its knowing how much activity had happened in between.

This of course applies to all the files that you tell NIS to share. Other popular shared files include **/etc/group** and **/etc/hosts**.

NOTE

Although it is technically correct to refer to NIS's tables as a database, they are more typically called maps. (In this context, you are mapping keys to values.) Using the **/etc/passwd** file as an example, you map a user's login name (which you know is always unique) to the rest of the password entry.

The NIS Servers

NIS can have only one authoritative server where the original data files are kept (this is somewhat similar to DNS). This authoritative server is called the *master* NIS server. If your organization is large enough, you may need to distribute the load across more than one machine. This can be done by setting up one or more *secondary* (*slave*) NIS servers. In addition to helping distribute the load, secondary servers also provide a mechanism to better handle server failures. The secondary NIS server can continue answering queries even while the master or other secondary servers are down.

NOTE

A server can be both a server and a client at the same time.

Secondary NIS servers receive updates whenever the primary NIS server is updated, so that the masters and slaves remain in sync. The process of keeping the secondary servers in sync with the primary is called a *server push*. As part of its update scripts, the NIS master also pushes a copy of the map files to the secondary server. Upon receiving these files, the secondary servers update their databases, as well. The NIS master does not consider itself completely up to date until the secondary servers are up to date, as well.

NOTE

A server pull mechanism also exists for NIS. However, this solution is typically reserved for more complex configurations, such as when you have hundreds of slave servers. In a smaller network, this should not be an issue.

Domains

Primary NIS servers establish *domains* that are similar to the domains of a PDC. A significant difference is that the NIS domain does not require the NIS server administrator to explicitly allow a client to join. (Bear in mind that the NIS model assumes that all clients are members of the same administrative domain and are thus managed by the same system administrators.) Furthermore, the NIS server only sends out data; it does not perform authentication. The process of authenticating users is left to each individual host; NIS merely provides a centralized list of users.

TIP

Since NIS domains must be given names, it's a good practice (though not mandatory) to use names that are different from your DNS domain names. You'll have a much easier time discussing your network domains with fellow administrators when everyone knows which is which.

<table>
<tr><td>CRITICAL SKILL</td></tr>
<tr><td>19.2</td></tr>
</table>

Configure the Master NIS Server

Linux distributions typically come with NIS already compiled and installed. All that is left for you to do is enable the service (if it isn't enabled already). To do so, you use the **ksysv** tool, and make sure **ypserv** is part of the startup process in runlevels 3 and 5.

Once NIS is enabled, you'll need to configure it. There are four steps to doing this:

1. Establish the domain name.

2. Start the **ypserv** daemon to start NIS.

3. Edit the makefile.

4. Run **ypinit** to create the databases.

Establishing the Domain Name

Setting the NIS domain name is done with the **domainname** command. Let's say you're setting up a domain called orbnet.domain.com; you can tell the system the name of the NIS domain like this:

```
[root@ford /root]# domainname orbnet.domain.com
```

Of course, to have this established every time you reboot, you need to place the **domainname** command in an **rc** script.

● If you are using Red Hat, you can edit the **/etc/sysconfig/network** script and add this line:

```
NIS_DOMAIN=orbnet.domain.com
```

● Non–Red Hat folk can edit the **/etc/rc.d/init.d/ypserv** script. Do a search for the line containing **domainname**, and if you can't find one, add one anywhere after the first line. The line should read like so:

```
domainname orbnet.domain.com
```

You should also replace **orbnet.domain.com** with your own NIS domain name. Setting the domain name should occur before the NIS servers start.

Starting NIS

The **ypserv** daemon is responsible for handling NIS requests. If you are installing NIS on a live server, most likely you will not want to reboot the server to complete the installation. Instead, you can simply run the **init** script yourself, like so:

```
[root@ford /root]# /etc/rc.d/init.d/ypserv start
```

If you need to stop the NIS server at any time, you can do so with the following command:

```
[root@ford /root]# /etc/rc.d/init.d/ypserv stop
```

Progress Check

1. What is an NIS domain name?

2. What is the daemon responsible for handling NIS requests?

1. An NIS domain name is the domain in which you want to query NIS databases.
2. **ypserv**

Editing the Makefile

You've seen the use of the **make** command to compile programs in many other modules. The **make** tool doesn't do the compilation, however—it simply keeps track of what files need to be compiled and then invokes the necessary program to perform the compilation. The file that actually contains the instructions for **make** is called a *makefile*.

Putting this concept to work on NIS is very straightforward. In this case, there's a series of straight text files that need to be converted into database format. You want a tool that will reconvert any files that have been changed—you can see how **make** fits the bill!

Changing over to the **/var/yp** directory, you see a file called **Makefile** (yes, all one word). This file lists the files that get shared via NIS, as well as some additional parameters for how they get shared and how much of each one gets shared. Open the makefile with your favorite editor, and you can see all the configurable options. Let's step through the makefile options that apply to Linux.

Designating Slave Servers: NOPUSH

If you plan to have NIS slave servers, you'll need to tell the master NIS server to push the resulting maps to the slave servers. Change the NOPUSH variable to false if you want slave servers.

NOTE

If you don't need slave servers now but think you will need them later, you can change this option when you do add the servers.

```
# If we have only one server, we don't have to push the maps to the
# slave servers (NOPUSH=true). If you have slave servers, change this
# to "NOPUSH=false" and put all hostnames of your slave servers in
# the file /var/yp/ypservers.
NOPUSH=true
```

Remember to list the hostnames of your slave servers in the **/var/yp/ypservers** file. And for each hostname you list there, be sure to list a corresponding entry in the **/etc/hosts** file.

Designating Filenames

The following makefile segment shows the files that are preconfigured to be shared via NIS. Just because they are listed here, however, does not mean they are automatically shared. This listing simply establishes filenames for later use in the makefile.

Most of the entries start with:

```
$(YPPWDDIR)
```

which is a variable that is set up right before this section in the makefile. The default value for this variable is /etc, which means any occurrence of **$(YPPWDDIR)** will be replaced with /etc when the makefile is run. Thus, GROUP will become equal to /etc/group, PASSWD will become /etc/passwd, and so forth. The variable **$(YPSRCDIR)**, as well, is set to /etc.

```
# These are the files from which the NIS databases are built. You
# may edit these to taste in the event that you wish to keep your NIS
# source files separate from your NIS server's actual configuration
# files.
#
GROUP       = $(YPPWDDIR)/group
PASSWD      = $(YPPWDDIR)/passwd
SHADOW      = $(YPPWDDIR)/shadow
GSHADOW     = $(YPPWDDIR)/gshadow
ADJUNCT     = $(YPPWDDIR)/passwd.adjunct
#ALIASES    = $(YPSRCDIR)/aliases      # could be in /etc or/etc/mail
ALIASES     = /etc/aliases
ETHERS      = $(YPSRCDIR)/ethers       # ethernet addresses (for rarpd)
BOOTPARAMS  = $(YPSRCDIR)/bootparams # for booting Sun boxes
                                     # (bootparamd)
HOSTS       = $(YPSRCDIR)/hosts
```

What Gets Shared: The all Entry

In the following makefile entry, all of the maps listed after **all:** are the maps that get shared:

```
all:  passwd group hosts rpc services netid protocols netgrp mail \
      #shadow publickey # networks ethers bootparams amd.home \
      #auto.master auto.home passwd.adjunct
```

Notice that the line continuation character, the backslash (\ ), is used to ensure that the **make** program knows to treat the entire entry as one line, even though it is really three lines. In addition, note that the second line begins with a pound sign (#), which means the rest of the line is commented out.

Based on this format, you can see that the maps configured to be shared are **passwd**, **group**, **hosts**, **rpc**, **services**, **netid**, **protocols**, **netgrp**, and **mail**. These entries correspond to the filenames listed in the preceding section of the makefile. Of course, not all sites want these entries shared, or they want some additional maps shared (such as the **automounter** files, **auto.master** and **auto.home**). To change any of the maps you want shared, alter the line so that the maps you *don't* want shared are listed after a # symbol.

Using ypinit

Once you have the makefile ready, you need to initialize the YP (NIS) server using the **ypinit** command.

NOTE

Remember that you must already have the domain name set before you run the **ypinit** command. This is done with the **domainname** utility as shown in "Establishing the Domain Name" earlier in this module.

```
[root@ford /root]# /usr/lib/yp/ypinit -m
```

Here, the **-m** option tells **ypinit** to set the system up as a master NIS server. Assuming you are running this on a system named ford.domain.com, you would see the system respond as follows:

```
At this point, we have to construct a list of the hosts that
will run NIS servers. ford.domain.com is in the list of NIS
server hosts. Please continue to add the names for the other
hosts, one per line. When you are done with the list, type
a <control-D>.
        next host to add:  ford.domain.com
        next host to add:
```

Continue entering the name of all the secondary NIS servers. Press CTRL-D when you have added all necessary servers. These entries will be placed in the **/var/yp/ypservers** file for you; if needed, you can change them by editing the file later.

Once you are done, **ypinit** will run the **make** program automatically for you, to build the maps and push them to any secondary servers you have indicated.

Makefile Errors

If you made a mistake in the makefile, you may get an error when **ypinit** runs the **make** program. Don't worry if you see this error:

```
gmake[1]: *** No rule to make target '/etc/shadow', needed by 'passwd.byname'.
Stop.
```

This means you have specified a file to share that doesn't exist (in this error message, the file is **/etc/shadow**). You can either create the file or go back and edit the makefile so that the file is not shared. (See the previous section "What Gets Shared: The all Entry.")

Another common error message is:

```
failed to send 'clear' to local ypserv: RPC: Program not registered
Updating passwd.byuid...
failed to send 'clear' to local ypserv: RPC: Program not registered
gmake[1]: *** No rule to make target '/etc/gshadow', needed by
'group.byname'.
```

```
Stop.
gmake[1]: Leaving directory '/var/yp/orbnet.planetoid.org'
```

There are actually two error messages here. You can ignore the first one, which indicates that the NIS server hasn't been started yet. The second error message is the same one described in the preceding paragraph. Once you've fixed it, type the following command to rebuild the maps, as described in the next section:

```
[root@ford /root]# cd /var/yp;make
```

Updating NIS Maps

If you have updated the files configured to be shared by NIS with the rest of your network, you need to rebuild the map files. (For example, you may have added a user to the **/etc/passwd** file.) To rebuild the maps, use the following **make** command:

```
[root@ford /root]# cd /var/yp;make
```

Project 19-1   Setting Up the NIS Server

This project will quickly cover the steps needed to make an NIS server.

Step by Step

1. Set the NIS domain name of the system with the **domainname** command.

2. Make any changes to the **Makefile** file in **/var/yp/** that reflect your NIS needs.

3. Initialize the server with the **/usr/sbin/ypinit -m** command. This will build the NIS maps.

4. If you need to make changes to the NIS maps, make sure that you run **make** in **/var/yp** after you have made any changes.

5. Start the NIS server by doing the following:

```
[root@ford /root]# /etc/init.d/ypserv start
```

Project Summary

If everything went smoothly, you should have a working NIS server on your hands. To verify that everything is working correctly, you need to configure an NIS client to run some queries against the server.

CRITICAL SKILL
19.3 Configure an NIS Client

Thankfully, NIS clients are much easier to configure than NIS servers! To set up an NIS client, you need to do the following:

1. Edit the **/etc/yp.conf** file.

2. Set up the startup script.

3. Edit the **/etc/nsswitch.conf** file.

Editing the /etc/yp.conf File

The **/etc/yp.conf** file contains the information necessary for the client-side daemon, **ypbind**, to start up and find the NIS server. You need to make a decision regarding how the client is going to find the server, by either using a broadcast or by specifying the hostname of the server.

The broadcast technique is appropriate when you need to move a client around to various subnets, and you don't want to have to reconfigure the client so long as an NIS server exists in the same subnet. The downside to this technique, of course, is that you must make sure that there is an NIS server in every subnet.

NOTE

When you use the broadcast method, you must have an NIS server in every subnet because broadcasts do not span multiple subnets. If you are uncertain whether a particular NIS server is in the same subnet, you can find out by pinging the broadcast address. If the NIS server is one of the hosts that responds, then you know for sure that the broadcast method will work.

The other technique for client-to-server contact is specifying the hostname of the server. This method works well when you need to subnet your network, but you don't need an NIS server in every subnet. This allows a client to move anywhere inside your network and still be able to find the NIS server. However, if you need to change a client so that it points to another NIS server (to balance the network load), you'll need to change that yourself.

● **Broadcast method**   If you choose the broadcast technique, edit the **/etc/yp.conf** file so that it reads as follows:

```
domain mydomainname broadcast
```

where **mydomainname** is the name of your NIS domain. Remember that if you need failover support, you will need to have two NIS servers in every subnet in order for broadcast to find the second server.

- **Server hostname method** If you want to specify the name of the NIS server directly, edit the **/etc/yp.conf** file so that it reads as follows:

```
domain mydomainname server servername
```

where **mydomainname** is the name of your NIS domain, and **servername** is the name of the NIS server to which you want this client to refer.

NOTE

Remember that you also have to have an entry for **servername** in the **/etc/hosts** file. At the time NIS is started, you may not yet have access to DNS, and you most certainly don't have access to the NIS hosts table yet! For this reason, the client must be able to do the hostname-to-IP resolution without the aid of any other services.

Setting Up the Startup Script

The NIS client runs a daemon called **ypbind** in order to communicate with the server. Typically, this is started in the **/etc/rc.d/init.d/ypbind** startup script. Check your startup scripts with the **ksysv** program and verify that **ypbind** is started at runlevel 3 and 5.

- To start the daemon without having to reboot, use this command:

```
[root@ford /root]# /etc/rc.d/init.d/ypbind start
```

- If you need to stop the daemon first, type:

```
[root@ford /root]# /etc/rc.d/init.d/ypbind stop
```

Editing the /etc/nsswitch.conf File

The **/etc/nsswitch.conf** file is responsible for telling the system the order in which to search for information. The format of the file is as follows:

```
filename:    servicename
```

where **filename** is the name of the file that needs to be referenced, and **servicename** is the name of the service to use to find the file. Multiple services can be listed, separated by spaces. Here are the valid services:

`files`	Use the actual file on the host itself.
`yp`	Use NIS to perform the lookup.
`nis`	Use NIS to perform the lookup (`nis` is alias for `yp`).
`dns`	Use DNS for the lookup (applies only to hosts).

[NOTFOUND =return]	Stop searching.
nis+	Use NIS+. (Due to the experimental status of the NIS+ implementation under Linux at this writing, avoid using this option.)

Here is an example entry in the /etc/nsswitch.conf file:

```
passwd:     files nis
```

This setting means search requests for password entries will first be done in the /etc/passwd file. If the requested entry isn't found there, NIS will then be checked.

The /etc/passwd file should already exist and contain most of the information needed. You may need to adjust the order in which certain *servicename*s are listed in the file. (If you installed a DNS server as discussed in Module 12, you have already adjusted this file appropriately.)

Testing Your NIS Client Configuration

After the /etc/yp.conf and /etc/nsswitch.conf files are established, and the **ypbind** client daemon is all set up, you should be able to use the **ypcat** command to dump a map from the NIS server to your screen. To do this, type the following command:

```
[root@ford /root]# ypcat passwd
```

This dumps the **passwd** map to your screen—that is, of course, *if* you are sharing your **passwd** map via NIS. If you aren't, pick a map that you *are* sharing and use the **ypcat** command with that filename.

If you don't see the map dumped out, you need to double-check your client and server configurations and try again.

Progress Check

1. How do you re-create the NIS databases when you have made changes?

2. What does the /etc/nsswitch.conf file do?

---

1. **cd /var/yp;make**

2. The **/etc/nsswitch.conf** file tells the system what service (NIS, files, DNS) to use when trying to get information about users and hostnames.

CRITICAL SKILL
19.4 Set Up a Secondary NIS Server

As your site grows, you'll undoubtedly find that there is a need to distribute the NIS service load to multiple hosts. NIS supports this through the use of secondary NIS servers. These servers require no additional maintenance once they are configured, because the master NIS server sends them updates whenever you rebuild the maps (with the **yp;make** command, as described in "Editing the Makefile" earlier in this module).

There are three steps to setting up a secondary NIS server:

1. Set the domain name.

2. Set up the NIS master to push to the slave.

3. Run **ypinit** to initialize the slave server.

Setting the Domain Name

Like configuring a master NIS server, you establish the NIS domain name before starting up the actual initialization process for a secondary server:

```
[root@ford /root]# domainname mydomainname
```

where **mydomainname** is the NIS domain name for your site.

NOTE

Be sure to set the domain name by hand before you continue with the **ypinit** step of the installation.

Setting Up the NIS Master to Push to Slaves

If you haven't already configured the master NIS server that will push to the slave NIS servers, you should do so now. This requires two tasks: first, edit the **/var/yp/ypservers** file so that it lists all the secondary NIS servers to which the master server will push maps. For example, if you want the master server to push maps to the hosts **technics** and **denon**, you'll edit **/var/yp/ypservers** so that it looks like this:

```
technics
denon
```

Second, you'll need to make sure the makefile has the line **NOPUSH=false**. See the earlier section "Configure the Master NIS Server" for more details.

Running ypinit

With these setup steps accomplished, you're ready to run the **ypinit** command to initialize the secondary server. Type the following command:

```
[root@ford /root]# /usr/lib/yp/ypinit -s master
```

where the **-s** option tells **ypinit** to configure the system as a slave server, and *master* is the name of the NIS master server.

The output of this command will complain about **ypxfrd** not running—you can ignore this. What the secondary server is trying to do is pull the maps from the master server down, using the **ypxfrd** daemon. This won't work, because you didn't configure the master NIS server to accept requests to pull maps down via **ypxferd**. Rather, you configured the master server to push maps to the secondaries whenever the master has an update. The server process at this point must be started by hand. It's the same process as for the primary server: **ypserv**. To get it started, run this command:

```
[root@ford /root]# /etc/rc.d/init.d/ypserv start
```

NOTE

Be sure to have the server process start as part of the boot process. You can use the **ksysv** program to do this. The **ypserv** program should start in runlevels 3 and 5.

To test the secondary server, go back to the master server and try to do a server-side push. Do this by running the **make** program again, as follows:

```
[root@ford /root]# cd /var/yp;make all
```

This should force all of the maps to be rebuilt and pushed to the secondary servers. The output will look something like this:

```
Updating passwd.byname....
Pushed passwd.byname map.
Updating passwd.byuid...
Pushed passwd.byuid map.
Updating hosts.byname...
Pushed hosts.byname...
[etc...]
```

The **[etc...]** on the last line means the listing will go on for all the maps that you are sharing.

CRITICAL SKILL
19.5 Use NIS Tools

To help you work with NIS, a handful of tools have been written to let you extract information from the database via the command line:

- **ypcat**

- **ypwhich**

- **ypmatch**

- **yppasswd**

The first tool, **ypcat**, dumps the contents of an NIS map. This is useful for scripts that need to pull information out of NIS: **ypcat** can pull the entire map down, and then **grep** can be used to find a specific entry. The **ypcat** command is also useful for simple testing of services, as demonstrated earlier in this module.

The **ypwhich** command returns the name of the NIS server that is answering your requests. This is also a good diagnosis tool if NIS doesn't appear to be working as expected. For example, let's say you've made a change in the master NIS tables, but your change can't be seen by a specific client. You can use **ypwhich** to see to which server the client is bound. If it's bound to a secondary server, it might be that the secondary server is not listed in the primary server's **/var/yp/ypservers** file.

An example of **ypwhich** usage is as follows:

```
[root@ford /root]# ypwhich
```

The **ypmatch** command is a close relative of **ypcat**. Rather than pulling an entire map down, however, you supply a key value to **ypmatch** and only the entry corresponding to that key is pulled down. Using the **passwd** map as an example, you can pull down the entry to **sshah** with this simple command:

```
[root@ford /root]# ypmatch sshah passwd
```

The **yppasswd** command is the NIS version of the standard Linux **passwd** command. The difference between the two is that the **yppasswd** command allows the user to set their password on the NIS server. The behavior is otherwise identical to **passwd**. In fact, many sites rename the standard **passwd** command to something like **passwd.local** and then create a symlink from **passwd** to **yppasswd**.

19.6 Use NIS in System Configuration Files

One of the most popular uses of NIS is the sharing of the **/etc/passwd** file so that everyone can log in to all hosts on the network by making a single modification to the master **/etc/passwd** map. Some distributions of Linux automatically support this feature once they see NIS running. Others still require explicit settings in **/etc/passwd** so that the login program knows to check NIS as well as the base password file.

NOTE

Whether a system automatically uses NIS for logins depends on which C library the system uses. The newer glibc-based distributions (such as Red Hat and Caldera) automatically use NIS, whereas libc5-based versions (such as Debian) do not. Not all distributions have settled on one library or another, and the subject is a hot topic of debate. With libc5 development stopped, however, it's inevitable that all distributions will use glibc.

Let's assume that you need to add the special tokens to your **/etc/passwd** file to allow logins from users listed in the NIS **passwd** file.

Here is the basic setting you should add to your client's **/etc/passwd** file to allow host login for all users listed in the NIS **passwd** list:

```
+:*:::::
```

NOTE

glibc-based systems do not need this addition to the **/etc/passwd** file, but having it there will not confuse glibc or otherwise make it behave badly.

And here is the setting if you want to deny everyone from logging in to that host except for those listed explicitly in the **/etc/passwd** file:

```
+:::::::/bin/false
```

This overrides all the user's shell settings so that when login to the client is attempted, the login program tries to run **/bin/false** as the user's login program. Since **/bin/false** doesn't work as a shell, the user is immediately booted out of the system.

To allow a few explicitly listed users into the system while still denying everyone else, use these commands:

```
+username
+username2
+username3
+::::::/bin/false
```

This allows only **username**, **username2**, and **username3**, specifically, to log in to the system.

✓ Module 19 Mastery Check

1. What service does NIS provide?

2. What command will show the NIS password file?

3. How do you tell which NIS server a client has bound to?

4. How does an end user change his password using NIS?

5. Can you think of anything wrong with allowing anyone to read your NIS password database?

6. What does the **ypinit** command do?

7. Where is the Makefile for **yp** stored?

8. What file needs to be modified on the client to make it authenticate using NIS?

9. Why would you want to make the NIS password UIDs start at 500 instead of zero?

10. How do you set the NIS domain name?

11. What is the name of the NIS server?

12. What startup script will allow you to start and stop the NIS server?

13. What must you watch out for if you tell the client to broadcast for an NIS server?

14. How would you find the user **sshah** in the NIS password database from a client?

15. Can you store information other than system information, such as a phone book, using NIS?

Module 20

Samba

CRITICAL SKILLS

S amba is a powerful tool for allowing UNIX-based systems (such as Linux) to interoperate with Windows-based systems. Samba does this by understanding the Microsoft networking protocol, CIFS (Common Internet File System), which used to be known as *SMB* (Session Message Block). From a system administrator's point of view, this means being able to deploy a UNIX-based server without having to install NFS, LP, and some kind of UNIX-compatible authentication support on all the Windows clients in the network. Instead, the clients can use their native tongue to talk to the server—which means fewer hassles for you and seamless integration for your users. No wonder Samba is so popular!

This module covers the procedure for downloading, compiling, and installing Samba. Thankfully, Samba's default configuration requires little modification, so we'll concentrate on how to perform customary tasks with Samba and how to avoid some common pitfalls. In terms of administration, you'll get a short course on using Samba's Web Administration Tool (SWAT), and on the **smbclient** command-line utility. We'll end by documenting the process of using encrypted passwords.

No matter what task you've chosen for Samba to handle, be sure to take the time to read the program's documentation, especially since it now comes with a complete book! It is well written, complete, and thorough. For the short afternoon it takes to get through most of it, you'll gain a substantial amount of knowledge.

NOTE

Samba has actually been ported to a significant number of platforms—almost any variant of UNIX you can imagine and even several non-UNIX environments. In this discussion, we are of course most interested in Samba/Linux, but keep in mind that Samba can be deployed on your other UNIX systems as well.

CRITICAL SKILL
20.1 # Understand the Mechanics of CIFS

To fully understand the Linux/Samba/Windows relationship, you need to understand the relationships of both operating systems to their files, printers, users, and networks. To better see how these relationships compare, let's examine some of the fundamental issues of working with both Linux and Windows in the same environment.

NOTE

For a thorough coverage of the Samba system, you can view the book *Using Samba*, available for free from http://www.ora.com/catalog/samba/chapter/boot/index.html and from the SWAT homepage.

Usernames and Passwords

The UNIX login/password mechanism is radically different from the Windows PDC (Primary Domain Controller) model and the Windows 2000 Active Directory model. Thus it's important for the system administrator to maintain consistency in the logins and passwords across both systems. Users need to access both systems without having to worry about reauthentication or cached passwords that don't match a particular server.

You have several management options for handling username and password issues:

- **The Linux Password Authentication Module (PAM)** Allows you to authenticate users against a PDC. This means you still have two user lists—one local and one on the PDC—but your users need only keep track of their passwords on the Windows system.

- **Samba as a PDC** Allows you to keep all your logins and passwords on the Linux system, while all your Windows boxes authenticate with Samba. (Unfortunately, support for this still appears to be a bit unreliable.)

- **Custom solution using Perl** Allows you to use your own custom script. For sites with a well-established system for maintaining logins and passwords, it isn't unreasonable to come up with a custom script. This would be done using WinPerl and the Perl modules that allow changes to the Security Access Manager (SAM) to update the PDC's password list. A Perl script on the Linux side can communicate with the WinPerl script to keep accounts synchronized.

In the worst-case situation, you can always maintain the two systems by hand (which some early sysadmins did indeed have to do!), but this method is error prone and not much fun to manage.

Encrypted Passwords

Starting with Windows NT 4/Service Pack 3, Windows 98, and Windows 95 OSR2, Windows uses encrypted passwords when communicating with the PDC and any server requiring authentication (including Linux and Samba). The encryption algorithm used by Windows is different from UNIX's, however, and therefore is not compatible.

Here are your choices for handling this conflict:

- Edit the Registry on Windows clients to disable use of encrypted passwords. The Registry entries that need to be changed are listed in the **docs** directory in the Samba package.

- Configure Samba to use Windows-style encrypted passwords.

The first solution has the benefit of not pushing you over to a more complex password scheme. On the other hand, you have to apply the Registry fix on all your clients. The second option, of course, has the opposite effect: For a little more complexity on the server side, you don't have to modify any of your clients.

The process of setting up Windows-style encrypted passwords is discussed in "Understand CIFS Encrypted Passwords" later in this module.

The Differences Between smbd and nmbd

The code of the Samba server is actually composed of two daemons: **smbd** and **nmbd**. The **smbd** daemon handles the actual sharing of file systems and printer services for clients. It starts by binding to port 139 and then listens for requests. Every time a client authenticates itself, **smbd** makes a copy of itself; the original goes back to listening to port 139 for new requests, and the copy handles the connection for the client. This new copy also changes its effective user ID from root to the authenticated user. (For example, if the user sshah authenticated against **smbd**, the new copy would run with the permissions of sshah, not the permissions of root.) The copy stays in memory as long as there is a connection from the client.

The **nmbd** daemon is responsible for handling NetBIOS name server requests. It begins by binding itself to port 137; unlike **smbd**, however, **nmbd** does not create a new instance of itself to handle every query. In addition to name server requests, **nmbd** also handles requests from master browsers, domain browsers, and WINS servers.

Both daemons must be started for Samba to work properly.

NOTE

With the release of Windows 2000, Microsoft moved to a pure DNS naming convention as part of its support for Active Directory in an attempt to make name services more consistent between the Network Neighborhood and the hostnames that are published in DNS. In theory, you shouldn't need **nmbd** anymore, but the reality is that you will. Especially if you intend to allow non–Windows 2000 hosts on your network to access your Samba shares. Unfortunately, it will be many years before we see the complete demise of the horror known as NetBIOS.

Compiling and Installing Samba

Samba comes installed on most Linux distributions. Nevertheless, like all the other services we've discussed in this book, you should be able to compile the software yourself in the event you want to upgrade the package to a new release. Since its inception, Samba has had users across many different UNIX platforms and so has been designed to handle various versions of UNIX (including Linux). There is rarely a problem during the compilation process.

As of this writing, the latest version of Samba is 2.2.5.

NOTE

If you are running Red Hat Linux 7, you should already have Samba installed. To check, look for the **/usr/sbin/smbd** file. If it is there, you are ready to go. If it isn't, you can either install it via RPM from the CD-ROM or you can download and compile. For more information about installing via RPM, see Module 4, as well as the following section to find out about the differences between where a compiled version places files and where RPM places files. If you are running an older version of Red Hat or if your distribution did not come with Samba 2.2.5, you should consider uninstalling the existing package and upgrading. If you choose to remain with the version you currently have, remember that not all of the features that we discuss in this module will be available (although most should be).

Begin by downloading the Samba source code from http://www.samba.org/ into the directory where you want to compile it. For this example, we'll assume this directory is **/usr/local/src**.

1. Unpack Samba using the **tar** command:

   ```
   [root@ford src]# tar -xvzf samba-2.2.5.tar.gz
   ```

2. Step 1 creates a subdirectory called **samba-2.2.5** for the source code. Change to that directory.

TIP

Using your favorite text editor, start by reading the file titled **Manifest**. This explains all the files that came with Samba and gives you the location of the Samba documentation. While this isn't immediately crucial, it will help you in the long run.

3. Within the **samba-2.2.5** directory, there will be another subdirectory called **source**. Change to that directory like so:

   ```
   [root@ford samba-2.2.5]# cd source
   ```

4. Before you run **./configure**, evaluate the options that you want to configure for your Samba installation. The options available are as follows:

   - **--with-smbmount**   To include support for the **smbmount** command. (This feature is currently Linux-specific. Future Samba versions will include a general-purpose **mount** tool that will work across multiple operating systems.) The **smbmount** command allows you to attach shares off of NT servers (or other Samba servers) in a similar way that you can mount NFS partitions.

   - **--with-pam**   If your distribution of Linux comes with PAM (as does Red Hat), enable this feature so that Samba can take advantage of the options available through the Password Authentication Module.

5. Run the **./configure** command with the options you've chosen for your Samba installation. For example, to support both the **smbmount** and PAM features, you would enter this command:

```
[root@ford source]# ./configure --with-smbmount --with-pam
```

6. Run **make** like so:

```
[root@ford source]# make
```

7. Run **make install** like so:

```
[root@ford source]# make install
```

8. Samba is now installed in the **/usr/local/samba** directory.

9. Now copy the default configuration file into the **/usr/local/samba/lib** directory. Assuming you unpacked Samba into the **/usr/local/src** directory, the default configuration file will be **/usr/local/src/samba-2.2.5/examples directory**. To copy the correct file, enter these commands:

```
[root@ford man]# cd /usr/local/src/samba-2.2.5/examples
[root@ford examples]# cp smb.conf.default /usr/local/samba/lib/smb.conf
```

10. The default permissions on the Samba directories allow only the root user to access them. You will need to allow other users to access the files, except for the **private** directory. To do this, issue these commands:

```
[root@ford examples]# cd /usr/local/samba
[root@ford samba]# chmod -R 755 bin lib man var
```

NOTE

The **/usr/local/samba/bin** directory is typically not found in the search path for shells. You can either add it there or you can simply copy the binaries from **/usr/local/samba/bin** to **/usr/local/bin** (assuming, of course, that **/usr/local/bin** is in your path).

Red Hat 7 and RPM Installations

If you choose to use the version of Samba that comes preinstalled with Red Hat 7 or that gets installed via RPM, you will need to be aware of the locations of files. Because this book does not focus solely on Red Hat 7, we use the directory locations that are from the compiled version. Simply map those filenames to the Red Hat–isms, and you should be fine. Under Red Hat 7 simply issue the following commands to list the files and their locations associated with the RPM:

```
[root@ford /root]# rpm -q -l samba-common
[root@ford /root]# rpm -q -l samba-client
[root@ford /root]# rpm -q -l samba-server
```

These commands will tell you where all of the files that came with the system are located.

20.2 Administer Samba

This section describes some of the issues of administering Samba. You'll see how to start and stop Samba, how to do common administrative tasks with SWAT, and how to use **smbclient**. Finally, we'll examine the process of using encrypted passwords.

Starting and Stopping Samba

Most distributions of Linux have scripts that will start and stop Samba without your needing to pay much attention. If you're using the Samba installation that came with your Linux distribution, you shouldn't need to change the scripts. They take care of startup at boot time and stopping at shutdown. If you are using Red Hat 7, you can use the **/etc/rc.d/init.d/smb** script to start and stop the services. For example, to explicitly start the service using this script, you would run:

```
[root@ford /root]# /etc/rc.d/init.d/smb start
```

And to stop the service using this script, you would run:

```
[root@ford /root]# /etc/rc.d/init.d/smb stop
```

Make sure you have the appropriate symlinks pointing to this script in the **/etc/rc3.d** and **/etc/rc5.d** directories so that Samba starts up automatically at boot time. See Module 7 for details on checking for this and setting up the symlinks if you don't have them already.

NOTE

If you don't have scripts to automatically start Samba, it's a good idea to take the time to write them. See Module 7 for details on writing and placing the scripts.

Starting Samba takes just two steps. First, start the **smbd** process. Although you can set many parameters on the command line, it's often better to set them in the configuration file (**smb.conf**). If you're using SWAT, it will maintain that file for you. The only command-line parameter you're likely to have is the **-D** option to tell Samba to run as a daemon:

```
[root@ford samba]# /usr/local/samba/bin/smbd -D
```

Next, start the **nmbd** process. Like **smbd**, many parameters can be set through the command line, but you'll probably find it easier to maintain if you keep configuration changes in the **smb.conf** file. The only command-line parameter you're likely to have is the **-D** option to tell **nmbd** to run as a daemon.

```
[root@ford samba]# /usr/local/samba/bin/nmbd -D
```

NOTE

You should start both **smbd** and **nmbd** as the root user.

Stopping Samba is little trickier than starting it up. Use the **ps** command to list all of the Samba processes. From this list, find the instance of **smbd** that is owned by root, and kill this process. This will also kill all of the other Samba connections.

NOTE

If you make a change to the configuration of Samba, you'll need to stop and then restart Samba in order for those changes to take effect. It's the client's responsibility to reestablish the connection. This is part of the SMB protocol, and not a limitation of Samba.

Progress Check

1. What does CIFS stand for?

2. How do you list all of the files that were installed with the Samba-client RPM package?

---

1. Common Internet File System
2. **rpm -q -l samba-client**

CRITICAL SKILL
20.3 Use SWAT

Prior to version 2.0 of Samba, the official way to configure it was by editing the **smb.conf** file. Though verbose in nature and easy to understand, this file was rather large and cumbersome. It also meant that setting up shares under NT was still easier than setting up shares with Samba. Many individuals developed graphical frontends to the editing process. Many of these tools are still being maintained and enhanced—you can read more about them by visiting Samba's Web site at http://www.samba.org/. As of version 2.0, however, Samba ships with SWAT, the Samba Web Administration Tool.

Using SWAT is remarkably easy. All configuration is done via a Web browser. SWAT then takes the information from the browser and builds an **smb.conf** file. For those who are used to editing configuration files, this may be a bit annoying because SWAT doesn't preserve comments in the configuration file itself. Therefore, server configuration documentation must remain external to Samba rather than embedded in the configuration file in the form of comments.

NOTE

If you prefer maintaining comments in your configuration file, or if you need to write some of your own tools to automate certain administration chores, you should not use SWAT. Herein lies the beauty of text-based configuration files. You have a choice— you don't have to use the GUI if you don't want to, and since the file format is public, anyone can write their own administration tool if they want to.

Project 20-1 Setting Up SWAT

SWAT is the Samba Web Administration Tool with which you can manage Samba through a browser interface. It's an excellent alternative to editing the Samba configuration files by hand, but don't let it make you believe that the configuration files are complex!

What makes SWAT a little different from other browser-based administration tools is that SWAT does not rely on a Web server (like Apache). Instead, SWAT performs all the needed Web server functions without implementing a full Web server. This is mostly accomplished by running through the **inetd** daemon.

Step by Step

1. Set the permissions on **/usr/local/samba/swat** to be world readable:

```
[root@ford samba]# chmod -R 755 /usr/local/samba/swat
```

2. Edit the **/etc/services** file so that it includes the following line:

```
swat    901/tcp
```

(continued)

3. If you are using **xinetd** (Red Hat 7), make sure the **/etc/xinetd.d/swat** file looks like this:

```
# description: SWAT is the Samba Web Admin Tool. Use swat \
#              to configure your Samba server. To use SWAT, \
#              connect to port 901 with your favorite web browser.
service swat
{
        port    = 901
        socket_type     = stream
        wait    = no
        only_from = 127.0.0.1
        user    = root
        server  = /usr/local/samba/bin/swat
        log_on_failure  += USERID
}
```

4. Remember that if you are using the RPM install of Samba, the **server=** line should be set to **/usr/sbin/swat**.

5. If you are using **xinetd**, send a SIGUSR1 signal to the **xinetd** process with this command:

```
[root@ford src]# killall -SIGUSR1 xinetd
```

Project Summary

Simply point Netscape Navigator to your Samba server at port 901 to get a login prompt for entering SWAT. Note that if you are using **xinetd**, this configuration only allows you to connect to SWAT from the same machine on which you are running Samba. This was done for the purpose of security, since you don't want to allow random people to be able to probe your machine remotely. But not to worry—it is most likely that you got Netscape Navigator installed with your installation. Simply run Netscape on the server itself and go to http://localhost:901/.

CAUTION

Logging in as root through SWAT causes the root password to be sent from the Web browser to the Samba server. Therefore, avoid doing administration tasks across an untrusted network. Preferably, run Navigator on the server itself, or set up an SSH tunnel between the client host and the Samba server host.

Using SWAT from Other Hosts

If you used **inetd**, you can use SWAT from any other host as long as it has TCP/IP connectivity and a Web browser. Simply point your browser to your server's port 901. For example, if your server name is arthur, you can visit http://arthur:901/ and get to the SWAT tool. However, with this configuration, it is possible for other people to get to your SWAT install as well. If this means that untrustworthy people can poke at your system, this is *not good*. What you should do is use TCPWrappers in your **inetd.conf** file (read the man pages for **tcpd**, **hosts.allow**, and **hosts.deny** for more information) so that you can specify which hosts can access that port and which cannot.

   If you used **xinetd**, you already have TCPWrappers functionality built into the configuration file. Take a look at Module 9 for more information on how to limit which hosts can connect to your server.

The SWAT Menus

When you connect to SWAT and log in as root, you'll see the main menu shown in Figure 20-1. From here, you can find almost all the documentation you'll need for Samba's configuration

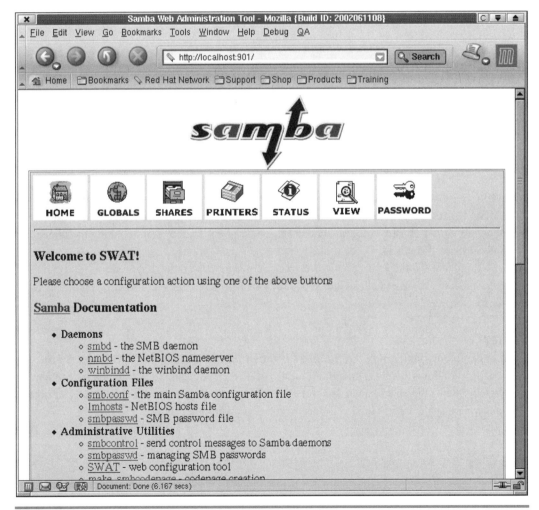

Figure 20-1 The SWAT home page

files, daemons, and related programs. None of the links point to external Web sites, so you can read them at your leisure without connecting to the Net.

At the top of the window are buttons for the following menu choices:

- **Home**   The main menu page

- **Globals**   Configuration options that affect all operational aspects of Samba

- **Shares**   For setting up disk shares and their respective options

- **Printers**   For setting up printers to be accessible to NT clients

- **Status**   The status of the **smbd** and **nmbd** processes, including a list of all clients connected to these processes and what they are doing (the same information that's listed in the **smbstatus** command-line program)

- **View**   The resulting **smb.conf** file

- **Password**   Password settings

Globals

The globals page lists all settings that affect all aspects of Samba's operation. These settings are divided into five groups: base, security, logging, browse, and WINS. To the left of each option is a link to the relevant documentation of the setting and its values.

Shares

Under Windows NT, setting up a *share* means creating a new folder, right-clicking it, and allowing it to be shared. Additional controls can be established by right-clicking the folder and selecting Properties.

Using SWAT, these same actions are accomplished by creating a new share. You can then select the share and click Choose Share. This brings up all the configurable parameters for the share.

Printers

Samba automatically makes all printers listed in the **/etc/printcap** file available for use via SMB to Windows clients. Through this series of menus, you can modify Samba's treatment of these printers or even add additional printers. The one thing you cannot do here is add printers to the main system; see Module 21 for information on adding printers.

Status

The Status page shows the current status of the **smbd** and **nmbd** daemons. This information includes what clients are connected and their actions. The page automatically updates every 30 seconds by default, but you can change this rate if you like (it's an option on the page itself). Along with status information, you can turn Samba on and off or ask it to reload its configuration file. This is necessary if you make any changes to the configuration.

View

As you change your Samba configuration, SWAT keeps track of the changes and figures out what information it needs to put into the **smb.conf** file. Open the View page, and you can see the file SWAT is putting together for you.

Password

Use the Password page if you intend to support encrypted passwords. You'll want to give your users a way to modify their own passwords without having to log in to the Linux server. This page allows users to do just that.

NOTE

It's almost always a good idea to disallow access to your servers for everyone except support personnel. This reduces the chances of mistakes being made that could affect the performance or stability of your server.

Project 20-2 Creating a Share

Creating shares with SWAT is a straightforward procedure. In this project, you will create a share called MYSHARE to share to the network.

NOTE

Samba uses a special share name of **homes** to share user home directories. See the Samba documentation on how to set this up.

Step by Step

1. Click the Shares button on the main SWAT window.

2. In the text box next to the Create Share button, enter the name of the share you want to create and click Create Share. For instance, to create a share called MYSHARE, the screen will look like Figure 20-2.

(continued)

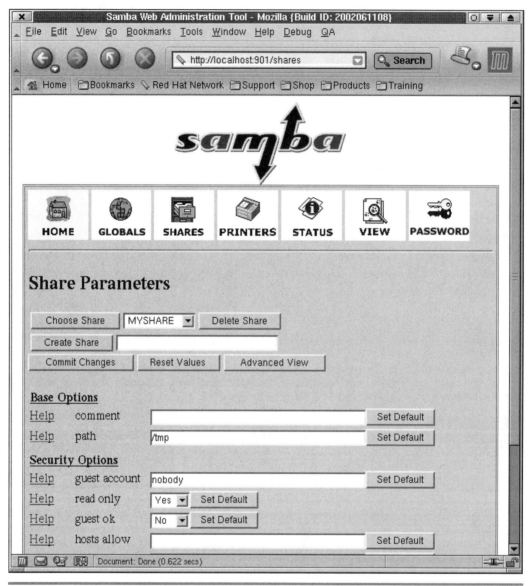

Figure 20-2 Editing MYSHARE

3. Change the settings for your share. You may want to customize the share's comment (which will show up in Windows Explorer), the directory where all the contents of the share should reside, and various security and browse options.

4. Once you've entered all the information, click the Commit Changes button near the top of the screen.

5. To make the changes appear to any systems that browse your server, restart the **smbd** daemon by going into the Status menu and clicking the Restart Smbd button.

Project Summary

And that's it. You should now be able to see this share from Windows clients browsing the network. Creating shares is pretty simple through the SWAT interface. You can also create special shares like **[homes]** that will export all of your home directories. The default options for a share are usually enough; if you need to configure more you can click on the Advanced View button to get access to *all* of the configuration options for a share.

CRITICAL SKILL
20.4 Use smbclient

The **smbclient** program is a command-line tool that allows your Linux system to act as a Windows client. You can use this utility to connect to other Samba servers or even to real Windows NT/2000 servers. **smbclient** is a very flexible program and can be used to browse other servers, send and retrieve files from them, or even print to them. As you can imagine, this is also a great debugging tool since you can quickly and easily check whether a new Samba installation works correctly without having to find a Windows client to test it.

In this section, we'll show you how to do basic browsing, remote file access, and remote printer access with **smbclient**. However, remember that **smbclient** is a very flexible program, limited only by your imagination.

Browsing a Server

With so many graphical interfaces around, we've come to equate browsing with "point and click." But when your intention is to simply find out what a server has to offer, it's not enough of a reason in itself to support an entire GUI.

Using **smbclient** with the **-L** option allows you to view the offerings of an NT or Samba server without having to use a GUI. Here's the format of the command:

```
[root@ford root]# smbclient -L hostname
```

where **hostname** is the name of the server. For example, if you want to see what the host ford has to offer, type:

```
[root@ford root]# smbclient -L ford
```

This will return information that looks something like the following:

```
Added interface ip=192.168.1.1 bcast=192.168.1.255 nmask=255.255.255.0
Password:
Domain=[MYGROUP] OS=[UNIX] Server=[Samba 2.2.5]

        Sharename       Type        Comment
        ---------       ----        -------
        MYSHARE         Disk
        IPC$            IPC         IPC Service (Samba Server)
        lp              Printer

        Server                      Comment
        ---------                   -------
        FORD                        Samba Server

        Workgroup                   Master
        ---------                   -------
        MYGROUP
```

NOTE

Depending on server configuration, you might get prompted for a password. If the server allows guest browsing, you can simply press ENTER at the **password:** prompt and see the browse list. Otherwise, you'll need to enter your password.

Remote File Access

The **smbclient** utility allows you to access files on an NT or Samba server with a command-line hybrid DOS/FTP client interface. For its most straightforward usage, you'll simply run the following:

```
[sshah@ford ~]$ /usr/local/samba/bin/smbclient //server/share
```

where **server** is the server name and **share** is the share name to which you want to connect. By default, Samba automatically sets up all users' home directories as shares. (For instance, the user sshah can access his home directory on the server ford by going to **//ford/sshah**.)

Once it's connected, you'll be able to browse directories using the **cd**, **dir**, and **ls** commands. You can also use **get**, **put**, **mget**, and **mput** to transfer files back and forth. The online help explains all of the commands in detail. Simply type **help** at the prompt to see what is available.

Following are some command-line parameters you may need to use with **smbclient** to connect to a server:

- **-I** *destIP*   The destination IP address to which you want to connect

- **-U** *username*   The user you want to connect as, instead of the user you are logged in as

- **-W** *name*   Sets the workgroup name to *name*

- **-D** *directory*   Starts from *directory*

NOTE

smbclient has a **tar** mode, as well. You'll find it is easier to access this mode from the **smbtar** command, since **smbtar** provides an interface much more consistent with regular **tar**. The man page for **smbtar** will tell you more about it.

Progress Check

1. How do you browse a server using **smbclient**?

2. Do you have to restart the **smbd** daemon after you make changes to the configuration file?

Remote Printer Access

So the head of marketing got a brand-new color laser printer, but your request for a wrist brace to help with your carpal tunnel was turned down. It's only fair that you get to use the printer, right?

If that printer is sitting on an NT server that doesn't have **lpd** configured, but it does share the printer via SMB so other Windows workstations can print to it, you're in luck. You can use **smbclient** to submit print jobs to other NT or Samba servers just as a Windows client would.

To connect to a printer on a server using **smbclient**, use the **-P** parameter and specify the service name for the printer, as shown here:

```
[root@ford root]# smbclient //ford/lp -P
```

---

1. **smbclient -L** *servername*

2. Yes, by using the SWAT interface or **/etc/init.d/smb** restart.

This connects you to the service as a printer. You can then issue the **print** command along with a local filename. For example, if you have a file called **blecker** in the directory from which you run **smbclient**, you can issue this command to print the contents of the file **blecker**:

```
smb:> print blecker
```

Possible uses for this remote printer access feature include setting up special filters in **/etc/printcap** files so that all files printed to a particular printer are automatically redirected to a Windows printer on the network. (For more information, see Module 21.)

CRITICAL SKILL
20.5 Use smbmount

If your kernel is configured to support the SMB file system (as are most kernels that come with Linux distributions), you can actually mount an NT or Samba share onto your system in much the same way you would mount an NFS partition. This is very handy for accessing a large disk on a remote server without having to shuffle individual files across the network.

To use **smbmount**, simply run this command:

```
[root@ford /mnt]# smbmount //ford/sshah /mnt/sshah
```

where **//ford/sshah** is the share being mounted, and **/mnt/sshah** is the directory to which it is being mounted. To unmount this directory, run **umount**:

```
[root@ford /mnt]# umount /mnt/sshah
```

CRITICAL SKILL
20.6 Understand CIFS Encrypted Passwords

Because Windows uses a password-hashing algorithm different from Linux's, Samba needs to maintain its own password file in order to support encrypted password support. The quick way to get a list of existing users in the **/etc/passwd** file for whom to implement encrypted password support is to use the **mksmbpasswd.sh** script that comes with Samba. You can find it in the script directory of the source tree (**/usr/local/src/samba-2.2.5/source/script/mksmbpasswd.sh**) or, if you have the Red Hat 7 RPM installed, in the **/usr/bin** directory (**/usr/bin/mksmbpasswd.sh**). If you have it in the source tree directory, copy it to the Samba **/usr/local/samba/bin** directory, like so (although note that *it should be on one line*; it's two lines here, due to printing constraints for the book):

```
[root@ford /root]# cp /usr/local/src/samba-2.2.5/source/script/mksmbpasswd.sh/
usr/local/samba/bin
```

NOTE

These features require that the **/usr/local/samba/private** directory already exist. If it does not exist, create it using the **mkdir** command. Be sure that the directory has the permissions set to 0700 and is owned by root.

mksmbpasswd.sh's usage is as follows:

```
[root@ford /root]# cd /usr/local/samba/private
[root@ford private]# ../bin/addtosmbpass < /etc/passwd > smbpasswd
[root@ford private]# chmod 500 .; chmod 600 smbpasswd
```

NOTE

If you are using NIS, you will want to use **ypcat** passwd to get the password list from the NIS server and store that to a file. Then, instead of using **/etc/passwd**, use the file containing the results from **ypcat** passwd.

The foregoing command will create the **smbpasswd** list with the appropriate file permissions. Unfortunately, because UNIX passwords cannot be reversed to generate a cleartext password that can then be rehashed to work under Samba, the **smbpasswd** file's list of users does not contain valid passwords. That needs to be set by the user using the **smbpasswd** command or via SWAT's interface.

Allowing NULL Passwords

If you need to allow users to have no passwords (which is a bad idea), you can do so by using the **smbpasswd** program with the **-n** option, like so:

```
[root@ford /root]# smbpasswd -n username
```

where **username** is the name of the user whose password you want to set to empty.

In addition to using **smbpasswd**, you can do this via the SWAT program.

Changing Passwords with smbpasswd

Users who prefer the command line over the Web interface can use the **smbpasswd** command to change their Samba password (note that this is different from the **smbpasswd** file, which is in the **/usr/local/samba/private** directory). This program works just like the regular **passwd** program, except this program does not update the **/etc/passwd** or NIS **passwd** files. Because **smbpasswd** uses the standard protocol for communicating with the server regarding password changes, you can also use this to change your password on a remote Windows machine.

CRITICAL SKILL
20.7 Troubleshoot Samba

There are four typical solutions to connectivity problems with Samba.

- **Restart Samba.** This may be necessary because either Samba has entered an undefined state or (more likely) you've made changes to the configuration but forgot to restart Samba so that the changes take effect.

- **Make sure the configuration options are correct.** Errors in the **smb.conf** file are typically in directory names, usernames, network numbers, and hostnames. A common mistake is when a new client is added to a group that has special access to the server, but Samba isn't told the name of the new client being added.

- **Monitor encrypted passwords.** These may be mismatched—the server is configured to use them and the clients aren't—or (more likely) the clients are using encrypted passwords and Samba hasn't been configured to use them. If you're under the gun to get a client working, you may just want to disable client-side encryption using the **regedit** scripts that come with Samba's source code (see the **docs** subdirectory).

- **Monitor-cached passwords.** Windows often caches passwords in files that end in **pwl**. Not only is this a security risk (the **pwl** files are poorly encrypted), but if your password has changed on the server, Windows may continue feeding the cached password instead of prompting you for a new one. Simply remove the **pwl** files to force Windows to prompt you for a password.

Module 20 Mastery Check

1. What port does the **smbd** daemon bind to?

2. What port does the **nmbd** daemon bind to?

3. Is the password encryption the same for Linux and Windows?

4. How do you change a Samba password for a user?

5. What is the name of the Samba configuration file?

6. What port does SWAT run on?

7. Is it a good idea to allow other networks to access port 901 on your Samba servers?

8. What two daemons are associated with the Samba system?

9. What command-line tool is used to allow a Linux client to act like a Windows client?

10. How would you "browse" the server **ford** with **smbclient**?

Module 21

Printing

Printing under Linux and UNIX typically has not been a straightforward process. With the advent of the CUPS printing system, Linux printing is much easier to configure and use. Previously, the only printers typically supported were Postscript printers from Hewlett-Packard and other manufacturers. As Linux has become a viable desktop workstation, a better printing solution was needed, and the solution is the Common UNIX Printing System (CUPS). This module will cover the installation of the CUPS system along with the administrative tasks involved in maintaining your printing environment.

CRITICAL SKILL
21.1 Understand the CUPS System

CUPS is gaining widespread acceptance in Linux and the UNIX community as a whole. Even the new version of Apple's OS X 10.2 Jaguar supports CUPS. What this means is that you have a ubiquitous printing environment no matter what operating system you are using. Along with the standard UNIX printing protocol of LPR, CUPS supports Samba printing and the new Internet Printing Protocol. Using the concept of print *classes*, the CUPS system will print a document to a group of printers for use in high-volume printing environments. It can act as a central print spooler, or just supply the printing method for your local printer.

CRITICAL SKILL
21.2 Install CUPS

The CUPS software was developed by Easy Software Products and is available at http://www .easysw.com/. There are two methods of installation, through your Linux distribution or by compiling from source. The first method is highly recommended as the distributions typically have all of the popular printer support built into CUPS. With compiling by hand, you have to get drivers for your printers yourself.

Distributions

If you have a Linux distribution such as Mandrake or Red Hat, CUPS should be available as an RPM or a package. This is the recommended method for using CUPS. The distribution vendor has done the hard work to make sure that CUPS works well with their system. If you are unfortunate enough to have a Linux distribution that doesn't have CUPS, you can compile the package from source code.

Once you have installed the CUPS software, you need to turn on the CUPS daemon. In Red Hat, you would do the following:

```
[root@ford /]# /etc/init.d/cups start
```

This will start the CUPS printing system and allow you to connect to the Web interface and add printers.

Compiling from Source

If you have to compile CUPS from source, follow the directions that come with the software package. I have found it is much easier to just install the RPM for CUPS than it is to compile and install by hand. The source code for CUPS can be found at http://www.cups.org/. Installation instructions are bundled with the software. You will also want to look at the Foomatic package located at http://www.linuxprinting.org; they provide numerous printer drivers for various printing systems including CUPS.

CRITICAL SKILL
21.3

Add Printers

The first step after you have finished compiling or have turned on the CUPS system is to log in to the Web interface. The Web interface is available through port 631. In your Web browser, you just have to enter **http://localhost:631**. By default, you must be logged in to the same server that you are trying to administer. The interesting thing to note is that 631 is the same port that CUPS uses for accepting print jobs. When you connect to the Web page, you will see a page similar to Figure 21-1.

NOTE

If you want to administer printers from other locations than the server that you are working on, you need to modify the **cupsd.conf** file to allow other hosts to connect. The **cupsd.conf** file typically resides in the directory **/etc/cups/**.

Local Printers and Remote Printers

You have a couple of options when adding a printer. If you have a home system with Linux or you are setting up a print server, that machine will connect to the printer over the printer cable or USB. The other option is to print to the printer over the network. CUPS allows you to print over the network via three main options: HP JetDirect, LPD/LPR printer, and the Internet Printing Protocol. If your office is flooded with HP printers that are network enabled, you can choose the HP option (you can also print via LPR to an HP printer over the network). In the UNIX environment, the second choice is typical. So keep in mind that you don't have to just print to the locally attached printer. The CUPS menus describe how to add these printers that aren't attached directly to your server.

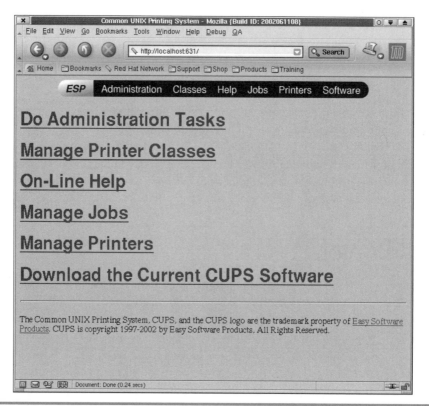

Figure 21-1 The CUPS administration page

Project 21-1 Adding a Printer

This project will walk you through setting up a printer through the CUPS Web interface. You can also add a printer through the command-line interface, but the Web interface is plain and simple to use.

Step by Step

1. Connect to the CUPS Interface on http://localhost:631, assuming that you are on the local computer.

2. Click the Printers button.

3. Click the Add Printer button.

4. Fill in the information for that printer, such as its name, location, and description.

5. Set the device of the printer. If it is a USB printer, typically the device will be **/dev/usb/lp0**. If you have a printer connected directly to the computer via a printer cable, the device will be **/dev/lp0**.

6. Select the model driver for your printer.

7. When you are done, click the Printers button again.

8. Select Print Test Page to test your printing configuration.

Project Summary

Adding a printer with the CUPS Web interface is very easy (and the CUPS Web interface can be used by any browser). If you are feeling adventurous, you can browse the CUPS documentation to see how to add printers through the command line. Figure 21-2 shows the printer configuration page after you have successfully added your printer.

Project
21-1

Adding a Printer

CRITICAL SKILL
21.4 Manage Print Jobs

When a client machine prints, the job gets sent to the print server and is spooled. Spooling is simply the act of putting a print job into the print queue. This is also known as a print job. The job typically has a couple of states that it can be in. One is *in progress*. The other is *paused*, where the administrator has paused printing. The printer being out of paper can also be a

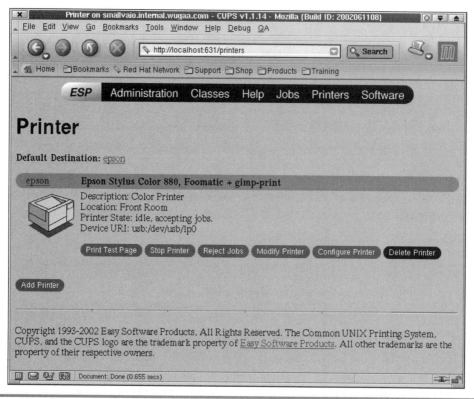

Figure 21-2 Printer configuration

reason for a job being paused. When something goes awry with the printer, print jobs can queue up and create a problem when the printer comes back up.

Listing Print Jobs

As an administrator, you need to periodically check the print queues to make sure that everything is going smoothly. The Jobs button on the Web interface will bring up a screen similar to Figure 21-3. As you can see, you have three options to choose from if there are jobs in the queue. If not, you will only see a button called Show Completed Jobs. You have the option of either holding the job (pausing it) or canceling the job altogether.

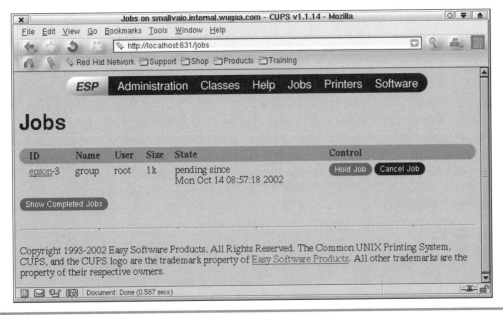

Figure 21-3 Listing print jobs

Progress Check

1. What does the acronym CUPS stand for?

2. What port does CUPS use for its Web interface?

CRITICAL SKILL
21.5 Use Client Side Printing Tools

Now that we've covered the aspects of installing CUPS and administering the system, it is time to cover how to do the actual printing with the Linux system. CUPS is designed to replace the

---

1. Common UNIX Printing System
2. CUPS uses port 631 by default.

current de facto printing system on Linux. This is typically the **lp** system. Any time a user wants to print, they use the **lpr** command. The following sections will cover the user's view of printing.

lpr

lpr is the command the user uses to print documents. Most Postscript and text documents can be printed by directly using the **lpr** command. If you are using Abiword or StarOffice, you will have to set up those applications to print to the correct device.

```
[root@ford /root]# lpr foo.txt
```

NOTE

On Red Hat 7.3, the **lpr** command is linked to the print spooler that you are using. When I tried setting up printing, I couldn't figure out why the page wasn't printing. Finally, when I did an **ls -l** on the **/usr/bin/lpr** command, I noticed that it was linked to the standard **lpr** command, not **lpr.cups**. You will need to link the **lp** commands to the correct CUPS programs. See Module 6 for information on how to link files.

This will print the document **foo.txt** to the default printer, which is usually the first one you install.

```
[root@ford /root]# lpr -Pepson foo.txt
```

This command prints the document **foo.txt** to the printer named Epson. Once you have entered this command, the printer should start printing fairly quickly unless you are printing a large file. To see the status of your print job, use the **lpq** command.

lpq

After you have submitted the job, you can view what is on the print spooler by using the **lpq** command. If you've just printed a job and notice that it doesn't come out of the printer, use the **lpq** command to display the current list of jobs that are spooled on the printer. Typically, you'll see a bunch of jobs in the queue, and upon further investigation you'll discover the printer is out of paper. If you need to unspool the print job from the printer, you can use the **lprm** command discussed in the next section.

lprm

When you've suddenly realized that you didn't mean to print the document you just typed **lpr** for, you might have a chance to delete it before it gets printed. To do this, use the **lprm** command. This will unspool the print job from the printer.

```
[root@ford /root]# lprm -Pepson foo.txt
```

If you are the root user, you can purge all print jobs from the printer by issuing the **lprm** command as follows:

```
[root@ford /root]# lprm -Pepson -
```

With these three commands you have all you need to print out your documents. You will find that other applications also use the **lpr** system. Since the CUPS print commands take the same arguments as the **lp** commands, you shouldn't have too many problems printing from any Linux application.

✓

Module 21 Mastery Check

1. What command does the user use to print documents?

2. What command is used to view the print jobs for a printer?

3. What does the **lprm** command do?

4. What is known as a "class" of printers?

5. What port do you connect to to administer the CUPS system?

6. What does the following command do?

   ```
   [root@ford /root]# lprm -Pepson -
   ```

7. How do you tell the **lp** tools to use a printer other than the default?

8. How do you start the CUPS printing system on a Red Hat derived system?

9. Why would you want to pause printing on a printer?

10. What port does the CUPS version of **lpr** send jobs to?

Module 22

DHCP

405

Configuring IP addresses for a handful of servers is a fairly simple task. However, manually configuring IP addresses for an entire department, building, or enterprise of heterogeneous systems can be daunting.

The Linux DHCP (Dynamic Host Configuration Protocol) client and server can assist with these tasks. The client machine is configured to obtain its IP address from the network. When the DHCP client software is started, it broadcasts a request onto the network for an IP address. If all goes well, a DHCP server on the network will respond, issuing an address and other necessary information to complete the client's network configuration.

Such dynamic addressing is also useful for configuring mobile or temporary machines. Folks who travel from office to office can plug their machines into the local network and obtain an appropriate address for their location.

In this module, we'll cover the process of configuring a DHCP server and client. This includes compiling and installing the necessary software and then walking through the process of writing a configuration file for it. At the end of the module, we'll step through a complete sample configuration.

TIP

DHCP is a standard. Thus, any operating system that can communicate with other DHCP servers and clients can work with the Linux DHCP tools. One common solution that includes using the Linux DHCP server component is in office environments where there are a large number of Windows-based clients. The Windows systems can be configured to use DHCP and contact the Linux server to get their IP address. This reduces the need for yet another Windows NT server and the associated licensing costs surrounding it.

The Roots of DHCP

Long before the fad of network computers (NCs), and back when disk storage space was at a premium cost, network workstation manufacturers built machines with no local hard drives, mounting them from a shared server instead. These "diskless" machines would boot using a protocol known as BOOTP (Boot Protocol), obtaining their addresses from a server. The Dynamic Host Configuration Protocol (DHCP) was originally derived from the BOOTP protocol. In fact, much of the DHCP protocol was taken directly from BOOTP.

Understand the Mechanics of DHCP

When a client is configured to obtain its address from the network, it asks for an address in the form of a DHCP request. A DHCP server listens for client requests. Once a request is received, it checks its local database, and it issues an appropriate response. The response always includes the address and can include name servers, a network mask, and a default gateway. The client accepts the response from the server and configures its local settings accordingly.

The DHCP server maintains a list of addresses it can issue. Each address is issued with an associated *lease*, which dictates how long a client is allowed to use the address before it must contact the server to renew the address. When the lease expires, the client is not allowed to use the address.

The implementation of the Linux DHCP server includes several key features common to many DHCP server implementations. The server can be configured to issue any free address from a pool of addresses or to issue a specific address to a specific machine. In addition to serving DHCP requests, the Linux DHCP server also serves BOOTP requests.

CRITICAL SKILL
22.2 Use the DHCP Server

dhcpd, the DHCP server, is responsible for serving IP addresses and other relevant information upon client request. Since the DHCP protocol is broadcast-based, a server will have to be present on each subnet for which DHCP service is to be provided.

Downloading, Compiling, and Installing a DHCP Server

The ISC DHCP server is the de facto implementation for UNIX machines. This version is released with many Linux distributions. If you don't find it in a distribution, the sources for the ISC DHCP server can be obtained from the ISC site at http://www.isc.org/. As of this writing, the most current version of the server is 3.0p1.

Once the package is downloaded, unpack the software as follows. For this example, assume the source directory is **/usr/local/src**:

```
[root@delirium src]#  tar -xfvz dhcp-latest.tar.gz
```

Enter the directory and configure the package with the **configure** command:

```
[root@delirium dhcp-3.0p11]#  ./configure
```

To compile and install, issue the **make; make install** commands:

```
[root@delirium dhcp-3.0p11]#  make; make install
```

Progress Check

1. What is DHCP used for?

2. Where can you download the source for DHCP? What other popular software is located here?

1. To dynamically configure an IP address for a host.
2. http://www.isc.org/. You can also find the DNS name server **bind**.

Configuring the DHCP Server

The default primary configuration file of the ISC DHCP server is **/etc/dhcpd.conf**. The configuration file encapsulates two ideas:

● A set of declarations to describe the networks, hosts, or groups attached to the system and possibly the range of addresses that can be issued to each respective entity. Multiple declarations can be used to describe multiple groups of clients. Declarations can also be nested in one another when multiple concepts are needed to describe a set of clients or hosts.

● A set of parameters that describe the behavior of the server and configure appropriate responses. Parameters can be global or local to a set of declarations.

NOTE

Since every site has a unique network with unique addresses, it is necessary that every site be set up with its own configuration file. If this is the first time you are dealing with DHCP, you might want to start with the sample configuration file presented toward the end of this module and modify it to match your network's characteristics.

Like most configuration files in UNIX, the file is ASCII text and can be modified using your favorite text editor. The general structure of the configuration file is as follows:

```
Global parameters;
Declaration1
    [parameters related to declaration1]
    [nested sub declaration]

Declaration2
    [parameters related to declaration2]
    [nested sub declaration]
```

As this outline indicates, a declaration block groups a set of clients. Different parameters can be applied to each block of the declaration.

Declarations

You may want to group different clients for several reasons, such as organizational requirements, network layout, and administrative domains. To assist with grouping these clients, we introduce the following declarations.

group   Individually listing parameters and declarations for each host again and again can make the configuration file difficult to manage. The **group** declaration allows you to apply a set of parameters and declarations to a list of clients, shared networks, or subnets. The syntax for the **group** declaration is as follows:

```
group label
    [parameters]
    [subdeclarations]
```

where *label* is a user-defined name for identifying the group. The ***parameters*** block contains a list of parameters that are applied to the group. The ***subdeclarations*** are used in the event that a further level of granularity is needed to describe any additional clients that may be a member of the current declaration.

Ignore the ***parameters*** block for now. We will go into further detail about it in the upcoming "Parameters" section.

host   A **host** declaration is used to apply a set of parameters and declarations to a particular host in addition to the parameters specified for the group. This is commonly used for fixed address booting or for BOOTP clients. The syntax for a **host** declaration is as follows:

```
host label
    [parameters]
    [subdeclarations]
```

The *label* is the user-defined name for the host group. The ***parameters*** and ***subdeclarations*** are as described in the **group** declaration.

shared-network   A **shared-network** declaration groups a set of addresses of members of the same physical network. This allows parameters and declarations to be grouped for administrative purposes. The syntax is

```
shared-network label
    [parameters]
    [subdeclarations]
```

The *label* is the user-defined name for the shared network. The ***parameters*** and ***subdeclarations*** are as described in the previous declaration.

subnet   The **subnet** declaration is used to apply a set of parameters and/or declarations to a set of addresses that match the description of this declaration. The syntax is as follows:

```
subnet subnet-number netmask netmask
    [parameters]
    [subdeclarations]
```

The **subnet-number** is the network that you want to declare as being the source of IP addresses for giving to individual hosts. The **netmask** is the netmask (see Module 23 for more details on netmasks) for the subnet. The **parameters** and **subdeclarations** are as described in the previous declaration.

range   For dynamic booting, the **range** declaration specifies the range of addresses that are valid to issue to clients. The syntax is as follows:

```
range [dynamic-bootp] starting-address [ending-address] ;
```

The **dynamic-bootp** keyword is used to alert the server that the following range of addresses is for the BOOTP protocol. The **starting-address** and optional **ending-address** fields are the actual addresses of the start and end blocks of IP addresses. The blocks are assumed to be consecutive and in the same subnet of addresses.

Parameters

We introduced this concept briefly earlier in the module. Turning on these parameters will alter the behavior of the server for the relevant group of clients.

always-reply-rfc1048   This parameter's syntax is as follows:

```
always-reply-rfc1048;
```

This is used primarily for BOOTP clients. There are BOOTP clients that require the response from the server to be fully BOOTP RFC–compliant. Turning on this parameter ensures that this requirement is met.

authoritative   This parameter's syntax is as follows:

```
authoritative;
not authoritative;
```

The **authoritative** parameter is used to tag a particular network as "authoritative." By default, the server will assume that it's authoritative. When a network segment is "not authoritative," the server will send a DHCPNAK back to a client. The client will presumably retry its request at that time.

default-lease-time   This parameter's syntax is as follows:

```
default-lease-time seconds;
```

The value of **seconds** is the lease time allocated to the issued IP address if the client did not request any duration.

dynamic-bootp-lease-cutoff
This parameter's syntax is as follows:

```
dynamic-bootp-lease-cutoff date;
```

BOOTP clients are not aware of the lease concept. By default, the DHCP server assigns an IP address that never expires. There are certain situations where it may be useful to have the server stop issuing addresses for a set of BOOTP clients. In those cases, this parameter is used.

The *date* is specified in the form *W YYYY/MM/DD HH:MM:SS*, where *W* is the day of the week in cron format (0=Sunday, 6=Saturday), *YYYY* is the year, *MM* is the month (01=January, 12=December), *DD* is the date in two-digit format, *HH* is the two-digit hour in 24-hour format (0=midnight, 23=11P.M.), MM is the two-digit representation of minutes; and *SS* is a two-digit representation of the seconds.

dynamic-bootp-lease-length
This parameter's syntax is as follows:

```
dynamic-bootp-lease-length seconds;
```

Although the BOOTP clients don't have a mechanism for expiring the addresses they receive, it's sometimes safe to have the server assume that they aren't using the address anymore, thus freeing it for further use. This is useful if the BOOTP application is known to be short in duration. If so, the server can set the number of *seconds* accordingly and expire it after that time has past.

CAUTION
Use caution with this option, as it may introduce problems if it issues an address before another host has stopped using it.

filename
This parameter's syntax is as follows:

```
filename filename;
```

In some applications, the DHCP client may need to know the name of a file to use to boot. This is often combined with **next-server** to retrieve a remote file for installation configuration or diskless booting.

fixed-address
This parameter's syntax is as follows:

```
fixed-address address [, address ·];
```

This parameter appears only under the **host** declaration. It specifies the set of addresses assignable to the client.

get-lease-hostname This parameter's syntax is as follows:

```
get-lease-hostname [true | false];
```

If set to **true**, the server will resolve all addresses in the declaration scope and use that for the **hostname** option.

hardware This parameter's syntax is as follows:

```
hardware [ethernet|token-ring] hardware-address;
```

In order for the server to identify a specific host, the **hardware** parameter must be used. The **hardware-address** (sometimes referred to as the MAC address) is the physical address of the interface, typically a set of hexadecimal octets delimited by colons. This parameter is used for fixed-address DHCP clients and is required for BOOTP clients.

max-lease-time This parameter's syntax is as follows:

```
max-lease-time seconds;
```

A client has the option to request the duration of the lease. The request is granted as long as the lease time doesn't exceed the number of seconds specified by this option. Otherwise, it's granted a lease to the maximum of the number of seconds specified here.

next-server This parameter's syntax is as follows:

```
next-server server-name;
```

When booting from the network, a client can be given a filename (specified by the filename parameter) and a server from which to obtain booting information. This server is specified with the **next-server** parameter.

server-identifier This parameter's syntax is as follows:

```
server-identifier hostname;
```

Part of the DHCP response is the address for the server. On multihomed systems, the DHCP server issues the address of the first interface. Unfortunately, this interface may not be reachable by all clients of a server or declaration scope. In those rare instances, this parameter can be used to send the IP of the proper interface that the client should communicate to the server.

server-name   This parameter's syntax is as follows:

```
server-name name;
```

where **name** is the host name of the server that is being booted by a remote booting client. This parameter is used for remote clients or network install applications.

use-host-decl-names   This parameter's syntax is as follows:

```
use-host-decl-names [true|false];
```

This parameter is used in the same scope of other host declarations. It will add the **host-name** option to the **host** declaration, using the host name in the declaration for the option **host**.

use-lease-addr-for-default-route   This parameter's syntax is as follows:

```
use-lease-addr-for-default-route [true|false];
```

Some network configurations use a technique known as *ProxyARP* so that a host can keep track of other hosts that are outside its subnet. If your network is configured to support ProxyARP, you'll want to configure your client to use itself as a default route. This will force it to use *ARP* (the Address Resolution Protocol) to find all remote (off the subnet) addresses.

CAUTION

The **use-lease-addr-for-default-route** command should be used with caution. Not every client can be configured to use its own interface as a default route.

Options

Currently, the DHCP server supports more than 60 options. The general syntax of an option is as follows:

```
option option-name [modifiers]
```

Table 22-1 summarizes the most commonly used DHCP options.

Option	Description
broadcast-address	An address on the client's subnet specified as the broadcast address
domain-name	The domain name the client should use as the local domain name when performing host lookups
domain-name-servers	The list of DNS servers for the client to use to resolve host names
host-name	The string used to identify the name of the client
nis-domain	The NIS domain name (see Module 19)
nis-servers	A list of the available NIS servers to bind to
routers	A list of routers the client is to use in order of preference
subnet-mask	The netmask the client is to use

Table 22-1 Common DHCP Options

Progress Check

1. What does the **routers** declaration do for a client?

2. How do you specify the broadcast address for the client?

A Sample dhcpd.conf File

The following is an example of a simple DHCP configuration file:

```
subnet 192.168.1.0 netmask 255.255.255.0 {
        # Options
        option routers 192.168.1.1;
        option subnet-mask 255.255.255.0;

        option domain-name "uidzero.com";
        option domain-name-servers delirium.uidzero.com;

        # Parameters
        default-lease-time 21600;
```

1. This specifies the default route for the client, so it can communicate outside of its local network.
2. Use the **broadcast** declaration to specify the broadcast address.

```
max-lease-time 43200;

# Declarations
range dynamic-bootp 192.168.1.25 192.168.1.49;

# Nested declarations
host vertigo
      hardware ethernet 00:80:c6:f6:72:00;
      fixed-address 192.168.1.50;
}
```

In this example, a single subnet is defined. The DHCP clients are instructed to use 192.168.1.1 as their default route and 255.255.255.0 as their subnet mask. DNS information is passed to the clients; they will use uidzero.com as their domain name and delirium.uidzero.com as their DNS server. A lease time of 21600 seconds is set, but if the clients request a longer lease, they may be granted a lease that can last as long as 43200 seconds. The range of IP addresses issued starts at 192.168.1.25 and can go as high as 192.168.1.49. The machine with a MAC address of 00:80:c6:f6:72:00 will always get assigned the IP address 192.168.1.50.

General Runtime Behavior

Once started, the daemon patiently waits for a client request to arrive prior to performing any processing. When a request is processed and an address is issued, it keeps track of the address in a file called **dhcpd.leases**. In the event of a server failure, the contents of this file are used to keep track of the addresses that have been issued to specific clients.

CRITICAL SKILL
22.3 Configure the DHCP Client Daemon

dhcpd, the client daemon included with many popular Linux distributions, is the software component used to talk to a DHCP server described in the previous sections. If invoked, it will attempt to obtain an address from an available DHCP server and then configure its networking configuration accordingly.

Downloading, Compiling, and Installing a DHCP Client

In the event that the **dhcpd** software is not already part of your Linux distribution, it can be obtained, compiled, and installed manually. The Linux DHCP client included with many Linux distributions can be found at http://www.phystech.com/download/. As of this writing, the most current version of the software is 1.3.22-pl1.

This package follows the standard GNU software package model, so you can follow the steps in Module 4 to compile the software.

Configuring the DHCP Client

The client is typically run from the startup files, but it can also be run by hand. It's typically started prior to other network services, since other network services aren't started if the DHCP client daemon can't obtain an address. Refer to Module 7 for more details on creating a startup script.

On the other hand, the client can be invoked at the command line after startup. The client daemon can be started without additional options. If successful, the client will make a copy of itself in background mode and quit. Older versions print out the assigned address. Here is how to start the client from the command line:

```
[root@delirium root]# dhcpcd
```

Optionally, the client daemon can be started with additional flags that slightly modify the behavior of the software. The full syntax of the command is shown here:

```
dhcpcd [-dkrDHR] [-t timeout] [-c filename] [-h hostname]
[-i vendorClassID] [-I clientID] [-l leasetime] [interface]
```

The options are described in detail in Table 22-2.

Option	Description
-c filename	The client daemon will execute the specified filename after obtaining and configuring its networking. This is useful if there are services that need to be started only after the network has been configured. Typically, most network services can be started without the network being present and should behave properly when the network becomes configured.
-d	This flag turns on debug mode. In debug mode, **dhcpcd** will provide verbose output to **syslog**.
-D	If invoked with this option, **dhcpcd** will set the local machine's domain name to that specified by the server. The client does not do this by default.
-i vendorClassID	Provides additional information for the DHCP server. The vendor class is a string that can be used to help the server classify the client into a particular group. By default, **dhcpcd** sends system name, system release, and machine type as a string.

Table 22-2 Common DHCP Client Configuration Options

Option	Description
`-I clientID`	Instead of sending the Ethernet address, you can force the client to send another identifier string. Most servers use the Ethernet address as an identifier, but there are exceptions.
`-h hostname`	Includes the specified host name in the DHCP messages sent by **dhcpcd**. There are DHCP servers that can be configured to accept DHCP messages from a set list of clients.
`-H`	Forces **dhcpcd** to set the host name to that specified by the server. The client does not do this by default.
`-k`	Terminates the currently running **dhcpcd** client daemon.
`-l leasetime`	The requested number of seconds the client wants the DHCP lease. Of course, the server can reject this value and issue a lease time less than the requested value.
`-r`	If invoked with this option, **dhcpcd** will act like a BOOTP client. This is for the rare case when there is only a BOOTP client available, or for testing.
`-R`	By default, **dhcpcd** will replace the **/etc/resolv.conf** file so that DNS resolution will be configured with the parameters returned by the server. There are situations in which you do not want this to happen. Specifying this option will prevent it.
`-t timeout`	The timeout is the number of seconds **dhcpcd** will try to obtain an address.
`interface`	Specifies an interface to have **dhcpcd** configure. If nothing is specified, **dhcpcd** will configure the first Ethernet interface (**eth0**).

Table 22-2 Common DHCP Client Configuration Options *(continued)*

Project 22-1 DHCP Client Configuration

Once you have the DHCP client daemon, you need to get it working with your system. Using Red Hat Linux, it is fairly simple to make an interface use DHCP. This project will go over the step-by-step method to get your client up and running on the network using DHCP.

Step by Step

1. Edit the file **/etc/sysconfig/network-scripts/ifcfg-eth0** and make it look like the following configuration:

```
DEVICE=eth0
BOOTPROTO=dhcp
ONBOOT=yes
```

(continued)

2. Restart the network system by using the **/etc/init.d/network rc** script:

```
[root@delirium  root]# /etc/init.d/network restart
```

3. Run **ifconfig etho** to verify that DHCP actually worked and you have an IP address.

4. Perform some basic network connectivity tests to see if your network connection works.

Project Summary

This project quickly goes through the steps of configuring your client for use with DHCP. The thing to remember is to verify that the changes actually took effect. A lot of the time administrators will configure this and then walk away assuming that it works. Always check to see if the configuration changes that you just made work. For more information on configuring your network devices, see Module 23.

Module 22 Mastery Check

1. What does the acronym DHCP stand for?

2. In what situations would you not want to configure a client to get its address from DHCP?

3. In what situations would you want to configure a client to get its address from DHCP?

4. Where is the configuration file for **dhcpd** stored?

5. What file stores information on which DHCP leases have been given out?

6. Can **dhcpd** be configured to give out the same IP address for a given hardware address?

7. What does the **range** option in the configuration file do?

8. How would you specify the default gateway to give to clients in the **dhcpd** configuration file?

9. Why would you want to keep your lease times high?

10. What does the **next-server** option in the **dhcpd** configuration file do?

11. What would you have to change in your network configuration to make Linux use DHCP to get an address?

12. Is it a good idea to give out static IP addresses that are in a DHCP range?

13. What is another name for the hardware address?

14. Does the Linux **dhcpd** server work with other operating systems?

Module 23

Network Configuration

K nowing how to configure your network services by hand can be terribly important for several reasons. First and foremost is that when things are breaking and you can't start your favorite GUI, being able to handle network configuration from the command line is crucial. Another reason is remote administration: you may not be able to run a graphical configuration tool from a remote site. Issues such as firewalls and network latency will probably restrict your remote administration to command line only. Finally, it's always nice to be able to perform network configuration through scripts, and command-line tools are best suited for scriptability.

In this module, we will tackle the two tools necessary for performing command-line administration of your network interface: **ifconfig** and **route**.

Modules and Network Interfaces

Network devices under Linux break the tradition of accessing all devices through the file metaphor. Not until the network driver initializes the card and registers itself with the kernel does there exist a mechanism for anyone to access the card. Typically, Ethernet devices register themselves as being eth$X$, where X is the device number. The first Ethernet device is eth0, the second is eth1, and so on.

Depending on how your kernel was compiled, the device drivers for your network interface cards may have been compiled as a module. For most distributions, this is the default mechanism for shipping since it makes it much easier to probe for hardware.

If the driver is configured as a module, and you have autoloading modules set up, you will need to tell the kernel the mapping between device names and the module to load in the **/etc/modules.conf** file. For example, if your eth0 device is a 3Com 3C905 Ethernet card, you would add the following line to your **/etc/modules.conf** file:

```
alias eth0 3c59x
```

where 3c59x is the name of the device driver.

You will need to set this up for every network card you have. For example, if you have a network card based on the DEC Tulip chipset and an SMC-1211 (based on the RealTek 8139 chipset, a popular chipset among cheap 100BaseT cards) in the same machine, you would need to make sure your **/etc/modules.conf** file includes the lines:

```
alias eth0 tulip
alias eth1 rtl8139
```

where tulip refers to the NIC with the DEC Tulip chip on it, and rtl8139 refers to the SMC 1211 card.

NOTE

These alias commands will not be the only entries in the **/etc/modules.conf** file.

CRITICAL SKILL
 # Configure Network Interfaces

The **ifconfig** program is responsible for setting up your network interface cards (NICs). All of its operations can be performed through command-line options, and in its native format, it has no menus or graphical interface.

Many tools have been written to wrap around **ifconfig**'s command-line interface to provide menu-driven or graphical interfaces, many of which are shipped with distributions of Linux. For example, Caldera users can configure their network interface through COAS, and Red Hat users can use the **netconfig** program. The KDE and GNOME desktops also provide some form of network configuration. The **linuxconf** program can also be found on most Linux distributions.

As an administrator, you should at least know how to configure the network interface by hand; knowing how is invaluable. For that reason, this section will cover the use of the **ifconfig** command-line tool.

Simple Usage

In its simplest usage, all you need to do is provide the name of the interface being configured and the IP address. The **ifconfig** program will deduce the rest of the information based on the IP address. Thus, you could enter:

```
[root@ford /root]# ifconfig eth0 192.168.1.42
```

to set the eth0 device to the IP address 192.168.1.42. Because 192.168.1.42 is a class C address, the calculated netmask will be 255.255.255.0, and the broadcast address will be 192.168.1.255.

If the IP address you are setting is a class A or class B address that is subnetted differently, you will need to explicitly set the broadcast and netmask address on the command line, like so:

```
[root@ford /root]# ifconfig dev ip netmask nmask broadcast bcast
```

where **dev** is the network device you are configuring, **ip** is the IP address you are setting it to, **nmask** is the netmask, and **bcast** is the broadcast address. For example, the following will set the eth0 device to the IP address 1.1.1.1 with a netmask of 255.255.255.0 and a broadcast address of 1.1.1.255:

```
[root@ford /root]# ifconfig eth0 1.1.1.1 netmask 255.255.255.0 broadcast 1.1.1.255
```

TIP

You can list all of the active devices by running **ifconfig** with no parameters. You can list all devices, regardless of whether they are active, by running **ifconfig -a**.

Setting Up NICs at Boot Time

Unfortunately, each distribution has taken to automating their setup process for network cards a little differently. As Red Hat Linux is so popular, we'll cover it separately in the next section. For other distributions, you need to handle this procedure in one of two ways:

- Use the administrator tool that comes with that distribution to add network card support. This is probably the easiest and most reliable method. Caldera Linux, for example, uses the COAS tool.

- Find the startup script that is responsible for configuring network cards. (Using the **grep** tool to find which script runs **ifconfig** works well.) At the end of the script, add the necessary **ifconfig** statements. Another place to add **ifconfig** statements is in the **rc.local** script—not as pretty, but it works equally well.

Setting Up NICs Under Red Hat Linux

Red Hat Linux has a system setup that makes it easy to configure network cards at boot time. It is done through the creation of files in the **/etc/sysconfig/network-scripts** directory that are read at boot time. All of the graphical tools under Linux create these files for you, but for the power-user inside of you just dying to edit the files by hand, the following is what you need to know.

For each network interface, there is an **ifcfg** file in **/etc/sysconfig/network-scripts**. This filename is suffixed by the name of the device, thus **ifcfg-eth0** is for the eth0 device, **ifcfg-eth1** is for the eth1 device, and so on.

The format of each of these files is as follows:

```
DEVICE="eth0"
IPADDR="192.168.1.1"
NETMASK="255.255.255.0"
NETWORK=192.168.1.0
BROADCAST=192.168.1.255
ONBOOT="yes"
BOOTPROTO="static"
```

NOTE

Sometimes if you are running other protocols like IPX you might see variables that start with IPX. If you don't have to run IPX (which is typical), you can safely remove the lines that have IPX in them.

These fields determine the IP configuration information for the eth0 device. Note how each of these values corresponds to the parameters in **ifconfig**. To change the configuration information for this device, simply change the information in the **ifcfg** file and run:

```
[root@ford /root]# cd /etc/sysconfig/network-scripts
[root@ford network-scripts]# ./ifdown ifcfg-eth0
[root@ford network-scripts]# ./ifup ifcfg-eth0
```

If you need to configure a second network interface card, copy the **ifcfg-eth0** file to **ifcfg-eth1** and change the information in **ifcfg-eth1** to reflect the second network card's information. Once there, Red Hat will automatically configure it during the next boot. If you need to activate the card immediately, run:

```
[root@ford /root]# cd /etc/sysconfig/network-scripts
[root@ford network-scripts]# ./ifup ifcfg-eth1
```

Additional Parameters

The format of the **ifconfig** command is as follows:

```
[root@ford /root]# ifconfig device address options
```

where **device** is the name of the Ethernet device (for instance, eth0), **address** is the IP address you wish to apply to the device, and **options** are one of the following:

Option	Description
Up	Enables the device. This option is implicit.
Down	Disables the device.
Arp	Enables this device to answer **arp** requests (default).
-arp	Disables this device from answering **arp** requests.
Mtu value	Sets the maximum transmission unit (MTU) of the device to **value**. Under Ethernet, this defaults to 1500. (See the following Tip regarding certain Gigabit Ethernet cards.)
netmask address	Sets the netmask to this interface to **address**. If a value is not supplied, **ifconfig** calculates the netmask based on the class of the IP address. A class A address gets a netmask of 255.0.0.0, class B gets 255.255.0.0, and class C gets 255.255.255.0.
broadcast address	Sets the broadcast address to this interface to **address**. If a value is not supplied, **ifconfig** calculates the broadcast address based on the class of the IP address in a similar manner to netmask.
pointtopoint address	Sets up a point-to-point connection (PPP) where the remote address is **address**.

TIP

Many Gigabit Ethernet cards now support jumbo Ethernet frames. A jumbo frame is 9000 bytes in length, which (conveniently) holds one complete NFS packet. This allows file servers to perform better, since they have to spend less time fragmenting packets to fit into 1500-byte Ethernet frames. Of course, your network infrastructure as a whole must support this in order to benefit. If you have a network card and appropriate network hardware to set up jumbo frames, it is very much worth looking into how to toggle those features on. If your Gigabit Ethernet card supports it, you can set the frame size to 9000 bytes by changing the MTU setting when configured with `ifconfig` (for example, `ifconfig eth0 192.168.1.1 mtu=9000`).

Progress Check

1. What does `ifconfig` do?

2. What does an alias do in the **/etc/modules.conf** file?

23.2 Use Routes

If your host is connected to a network with multiple subnets, you need a *router* or *gateway*. This device, which sits between networks, redirects packets toward their actual destination. (Typically, most hosts don't know the correct path to a destination; they only know the destination itself.)

In the case where a host doesn't even have the first clue about where to send a packet, it uses its *default route*. This path points to a router, which ideally does have an idea of where the packet should go, or at least knows of another router that can make smarter decisions.

NOTE

On Red Hat systems, the default route is typically stored as the variable GATEWAY in the file **/etc/sysconfig/network**.

---

1. `ifconfig` allows you to configure the network interface.
2. Aliases in the **/etc/modules.conf** file tell the system what module to load for that device or alias.

Ask the Expert

Q: What is a hub?

A: A hub is a pretty dumb device. All it knows how to do is receive traffic on one port and broadcast to all other ports. So if a machine needs to talk to another on the same hub, *all* machines on the network will be able to see the traffic going across the hub.

Q: What is a switch?

A: A switch is a device that "learns" what devices are plugged into it. So if you have a four-port switch and four machines plugged into it, the switch will use the MAC address to determine where to send packets. If the machine plugged into port 1 wants to talk to port 4, the switch will smartly transmit the data between ports 1 and 4. Ports 2 and 3 will not see any of the conversation between machines 1 and 4 (unless configured to do so via *port mirroring*). In the olden days, a switch was called a bridge, so if you hear someone call it that you will know that it is just a switch.

Q: What is a router or gateway?

A: A router or gateway is a device that interconnects networks. These networks typically involve media changes as well. So a router might have 32 10/100 Ethernet ports and a T1 line to an ISP, or a T3 line to your other office down the street. The router knows how to get packets from one location to the other via static and dynamic routes.

A typical Linux host knows of three routes: the first is the loopback route, which simply points toward the loopback device. The second is the route to the local area network so that packets destined to hosts within the same LAN are sent directly to them. Finally, the third route is the default route. This route is used for packets that need to leave the local area network to communicate with other networks.

If you set up your network configuration at install time, this setting is most likely already taken care of for you, so you don't need to change it. However, this doesn't mean you can't.

NOTE

There are actually instances where you will need to change your routes by hand. Typically, this is necessary when multiple network cards are installed into the same host where each NIC is connected to a different network. You should know how to add a route so that packets can be sent to the appropriate network based on the destination address.

Simple Usage

The typical **route** command is structured as follows:

```
[root@ford /root]# route cmd type addy netmask mask gw gway dev dn
```

The parameters are as follows:

Parameter	Description
Cmd	Either **add** or **del** depending on whether you are adding or deleting a routing. If you are deleting a route, the only other parameter you need is **addy**.
Type	Either **-net** or **-host** depending on whether **addy** represents a network address or a router address.
Addy	The destination network to which you want to offer a route.
netmask *mask*	Sets the netmask of the **addy** address to *mask*.
gw *gway*	Sets the router address for **addy** to *gway*. Typically used for the default route.
dev *dn*	Sends all packets destined to **addy** through the network device *dn* as set by **ifconfig**.

Here's how to set the default route on a sample host, which has a single Ethernet device and a router of 192.168.1.1:

```
[root@ford /root]# route add -net default gw 192.168.1.1 dev eth0
```

This command line sets up a system so that all packets destined to 192.168.1.42 are sent through the first PPP device:

```
[root@ford /root]# route add -host 192.168.1.42 netmask 255.255.255.255 dev ppp0
```

Here's how to delete the route destined to 192.168.1.42:

```
[root@ford /root]# route del 192.168.1.42
```

NOTE

If you are using a gateway, you need to make sure a route exists to the gateway before you reference it for another route. For example, if your default route uses the gateway at 192.168.1.1, you need to be sure you have a route to get to the 192.168.1.0 network first.

Progress Check

1. What is a route?

2. What is a gateway or router?

Displaying Routes

There are two ways you can display your route table: the **route** command and **netstat**.

Route

Using **route** is the easiest way to display your route table—simply run **route** without any parameters. Here is a complete run, along with the output:

```
[root@ford /root]# route
Kernel IP routing table
Destination     Gateway      Genmask          Flags Metric Ref Use Iface
10.10.2.0       *            255.255.255.0    UH    0      0   0   eth1
192.168.1.0     *            255.255.255.0    U     0      0   0   eth0
127.0.0.0       *            255.0.0.0        U     0      0   0   lo
default         firewall     0.0.0.0          UG    0      0   0   eth1
```

You see two networks. The first is the 192.168.1.0 network, which is accessible via the first Ethernet device, eth0. The second is the 10.10.2.0 network, which is connected via the second Ethernet device, eth1. The default route is 10.10.2.4; however, because the IP address resolves to the host name firewall in DNS, **route** prints its host name instead of the IP address.

---

1. A route is a path that a packet will take to get to the endpoint destination.

2. A gateway or router is a device that interconnects networks.

We have already discussed the destination, gateway, netmask (referred to as **genmask** in this table), and **Iface** (interface, set by the **dev** option on **route**). The other entries in the table have the following meanings:

Entry	Description
Flags	A summary of connection status, where each letter has a significance: **U** The connection is up. **H** The destination is a host. **G** The destination is a gateway.
Metric	The cost of a route, usually measured in hops. This is meant for systems that have multiple paths to get to the same destination, but one path is preferred over the other. A path with a lower metric is typically preferred. The Linux kernel doesn't use this information, but certain advanced routing protocols do.
Ref	The number of references to this route. This is not used in the Linux kernel. It is here because the route tool itself is cross-platform. Thus it prints this value, since other operating systems do use it.
Use	The number of successful route cache lookups. To see this value, use the **-F** option when invoking **route**.

Note that **route** displayed the host names to any IP addresses it could look up and resolve. While this is nice to read, it presents a problem when there are network difficulties, and DNS or NIS servers become unavailable. The **route** command will hang on, trying to resolve host names and waiting to see if the servers come back and resolve them. This wait will go on for several minutes until the request times out.

To get around this, use the **-n** option with **route** so that the same information is shown, but **route** will make no attempt to perform host name resolution on the IP addresses.

netstat

Normally, the **netstat** program is used to display the status of all of the network connections on a host. However, with the **-r** option, it can also display the kernel routing table. You should note that most other UNIX-based operating systems require that you use this method of viewing routes.

Here is an example invocation of **netstat -r** and its corresponding output:

```
[root@trillian /root]# netstat -r
Kernel IP routing table
Destination     Gateway       Genmask        Flags MSS Window irtt Iface
192.168.1.0     0.0.0.0       255.255.255.0  U     0   0      0    eth0
127.0.0.0       0.0.0.0       255.0.0.0      U     0   0      0    lo
default         192.168.1.1   0.0.0.0        UG    0   0      0    eth0
```

In this example, you see a simple configuration. The host has a single network interface card, is connected to the 192.168.1.0 network, and has a default gateway set to 192.168.1.1.

Like the **route** command, **netstat** can also take the **-n** parameter so that it does not perform host name resolution.

Project 23-1   Performing Network Setup

This project is going to walk you through the setup of your Linux network by hand. First you will get all of the device information set up and working. Then you will configure the networking devices using **ifconfig** and set up the necessary routes using **route**. Finally, you will modify your startup scripts to make sure that the information is loaded the next time the system boots.

The following project will assume that you are using the RealTek 8139 NIC and you have two interfaces in your system. You are going to connect the Linux box to two networks, 192.168.1.0/24 on eth0 and 172.16.1.0/24 on eth1. This network is displayed in Figure 23-1.

Step by Step

1. Determine what network interface card you have. This can be done by looking at the card and trying to determine the model number of the card. Typically, 3Com cards have this information on the circuit board. If you cannot get any information that way, you can use the **dmesg** command to see if the kernel detected the device.

2. Once you know the device driver you need, make sure that the appropriate modules are set up in the **/etc/ modules.conf** file. In this case, you'll add the following lines:

```
alias eth0 rlt8139
alias eth1 rlt8139
```

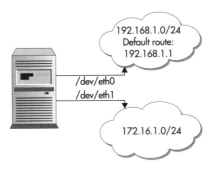

Figure 23-1 Project 23-1 Network Topology

(continued)

3. Set up the **/dev/eth0** interface:

```
[root@ford /root]# ifconfig eth0 192.168.1.2 netmask 255.255.255.0
```

4. Set up the **/dev/eth1** interface:

```
[root@ford /root]# ifconfig eth1 172.16.1.2 netmask 255.255.255.0
```

NOTE

In step 3, you could have omitted the **netmask** argument since 192.168.1.X is considered a class C network by default. In step 4, you must specify the netmask as a class C since 172.16.X.X is considered a class B network by default.

5. Now you need to set the routes up. By default, you will prefer the 192.168.1.1 router. You'll add a static route for the 172.16.1.0/24 network.

```
[root@ford /root]# route add default gw 192.168.1.1
[root@ford /root]# route add -net 172.16.1.0 netmask 255.255.255.0 dev eth1
```

6. Now use the common network testing tools to see if the network is set up correctly; **ping** and **traceroute** should work well. **netstat** can be used to make sure that your route tables are correct.

7. Now that you have verified the configuration works, you need to make the changes permanent by modifying the appropriate configuration scripts. The file **ifcfg-eth0** in **/etc/sysconfig/network-scripts** should look like the following:

```
DEVICE="eth0"
IPADDR="192.168.1.1"
NETMASK="255.255.255.0"
NETWORK=192.168.1.0
BROADCAST=192.168.1.255
ONBOOT="yes"
BOOTPROTO="static"
```

8. The file **ifcfg-eth1** should look like the following:

```
DEVICE="eth1"
IPADDR="172.16.1.1"
NETMASK="255.255.255.0"
NETWORK=172.16.1.0
BROADCAST=172.16.1.255
ONBOOT="yes"
BOOTPROTO="static"
```

NOTE

If you want to disable a device, just change the variable **ONBOOT** to "no".

9. Now add the route commands to either **/etc/rc.local** or your own startup script so that the routes are set up correctly.

Project Summary

This project walked you through the setup of the device driver, the configuration of network interfaces using **ifconfig**, and setting up routes using the **route** command. You also learned how to make such changes permanent by adding them to either the configuration files or the **rc** startup scripts.

✓ Module 23 Mastery Check

1. What does the **ifconfig** command do?

2. What does the **route** command do?

3. What configuration files would you put IP information in?

4. If you need to add more than the default route, what file would you put those commands in?

5. What file stores information about kernel modules?

6. What is the effect of the following line in **/etc/modules.conf**?

```
alias eth0 rtl8139
```

7. What command can you use to see if the kernel has detected your NIC?

8. What is a gateway?

9. What network class does 172.16.1.1 usually belong to?

A Class A

B Class B

C Class D

D Class C

10. What network class does 192.168.1.1 usually belong to?

   A Class A

   B Class B

   C Class D

   D Class C

11. Does a Linux box send a packet to the default gateway if the packet is destined for the local network?

12. What is the name of the third Ethernet device?

13. Knowing what you know about shells, how would you remotely restart the networking subsystem? (Remember, as soon as you shut down the network, you kick yourself out of the system.)

Part V

Appendixes

Appendix A

Mastery Check Answers

Module 1: Technical Summary of Linux Distributions and Windows 2000

1. A Linux distribution is a collection of developer tools, editors, GUIs, networking tools, and the GNU/Linux OS.

2. The kernel is the core of the operating system. It provides scheduling and memory management, and it provides the interface to the hardware via system calls.

3. Flat db (/etc/passwd), NIS, and LDAP

4. You don't need the regedit/regedt32 editor to edit the binary registry. You can easily edit configuration files with your favorite editor. You can easily automate the configuration of boxes with flat text files.

5. You have a centralized location for any configuration of the system. You have a standard configuration format and standard ways of editing the registry.

6. No, typically the user never really knows that a network share is mounted. To the user, the share seems to be part of the Linux filesystem hierarchy, by design.

7. Since the X Window System runs as a user process, it cannot easily bring down the system if there are any problems with the video driver. If there is a memory access error, Linux will take care of the process and continue. If the X Window System had a memory access error in the kernel, the results would be much more catastrophic.

8. GNU's Not Unix

9. GNU Public License

10. Some benefits of releasing code under the GPL include that the programmer is not liable for any damages caused by their software and that it can become a possible global development effort.

Module 2: Installing Linux in a Server Configuration

1. Workstation, server, custom, or you can choose to upgrade your system.

2. Off of the Red Hat CD-ROM, the file is **/images/boot.img**.

3. **rawrite.exe**

4. No, you are just adding regular users to the system.

5. **/etc/password** and possibly (recommended) **/etc/shadow**

6. NIS, LDAP, Kerberos

7. XFree86

8. Yes, it could save you some heartache if your computer runs into trouble.

9. The Swap file system is used for the virtual memory of the Linux system.

10. **/home** is usually where users' home directories are stored.

11. **/dev/hdc**

12. Four, two drives per chain.

13. Usually, it is twice the physical memory of the computer. Of course, if you have a gigabyte of memory, you probably only need between 500MB and 1G of swap space.

14. If Linux is the main operating system, you can install GRUB on the MBR.

Module 3: GNOME and KDE

1. KDE is the K Desktop Environment, a desktop manager that makes using Linux fairly easy.

2. GNOME is the GNU Network Object Model Environment, another desktop manager that is similar to KDE but has its own pros and cons.

3. The X Window System is the windowing environment for Linux. Desktop managers and window managers interact with the X Window System to provide the user interface.

4. The X Window System is a user process, so it can't cause the system to crash since it doesn't run alongside the kernel like Windows does.

5. The X Window System is a bit slower since it isn't tied directly into the operating system. The X Window System is a beast to write code for, yet with the KDE and GNOME environments it is becoming a little easier.

6. The **.xinitrc** file tells **startx** what commands to run when you start your X server.

7. Simply add the command **startkde**.

8. Simply add the command **gnome-session**.

9. The **startx** command starts the X Window System.

10. http://www.kde.org/

11. http://www.gnome.org/, http://www.ximian.com/

Module 4: Installing Software

1. A **gz** file is a file that has been compressed with the **gzip** program.

2. The **tar** command allows you to create archives of files and directories and extract them again.

3. First read the **README** file, then type **./configure**, then **make**, and then **make install**.

4. Typically, the file named **Makefile** in the current directory tells **make** what to do.

5. `rpm -ivh hello-1.3.i386.rpm`

6. `rpm -qa`

7. `rpm -Va`

8. **README** and **INSTALL**.

9. Troubleshooting can become an artform for a system admin. In this situation, you want to see if the software works for the **root** user. If so, then you might have a permissions problem. If the software doesn't work for the **root** user, you should then go back and take a look at any log files, **README** files, and **INSTALL** files. You might have missed an important step.

10. Use the **su** command.

11. Advantages to using the RPM tool include ease of use, ease of maintenance, and a centralized repository of installed software.

12. Disadvantages to using the RPM tool include that the package might not have been compiled on the same hardware as your system, and the fact that you might want the software installed in **/usr/local** and the rpm is not relocatable.

13. The **make** program iterates through the file **Makefile** in the current directory and typically compiles software as defined in the makefile.

14. The **make clean** command typically cleans out any object files, temporary files, and binaries that are created as the result of compiling the software.

15. You would issue the **make install** command.

Module 5: Managing Users

1. The **/etc/password** file contains information about a user.

2. The **/etc/shadow** contains the user password and other information that shouldn't be accessible to anyone but root.

3. The system always uses your UID to identify you. When you do an `ls -l` in a directory, the `ls` program is translating any UIDs to logins so they are more user friendly.

4. If that program has a buffer overflow problem, a user can possibly get the SetUID user's permission level. So if there is a bug in a program that runs SetUID as root, you could have a root exploit. Staying current with software updates will usually keep you out of trouble.

5. *Login Name* : *Encrypted Password*: *UID*: *GID*: *GECOS*: *Home Directory*: *Shell*

6. The GECOS entry is typically used to store the user's full name. Some people store other information such as office number in the GECOS field.

7. Put an * character in their password.

8. Group names and users associated with that group are stored in this file.

9. *group_name*: *encrypted_password*:*group_id*:*comma_separated_members*

10. That user will typically get dropped into the / directory when they log in.

11. **/etc/shells**

12. Startup scripts are used to set parameters, variables, and paths when logging in to the system.

Module 6: The Command Line

1. **vi** is a text editor that comes with virtually any UNIX system.

2. **pine** is a mail user agent that allows you to read your e-mail.

3. The **su** command is used to switch to a different user.

4. You use the **kill** command.

5. `ps -auxww`

6. The user will have full permissions; group and other will have read permissions to the file.

7. Add read and execute permissions to the **owner** and **group** attributes; set the **others** attribute to read and execute.

8. If you just want to change the ability to execute a file or directory, the symbolic form will keep the current permissions and change only the attribute you specify, so you don't destroy the original permissions of the file.

9. Section 5 of the man pages.

10. The **printenv** program will print out all of the currently defined environment variables.

11. Job control allows you to run multiple processes in the same shell, and you can stop/start/pause those processes.

12. This choice is yours, stick to one and learn it well!

13. The `tar` command allows you to create and extract archives, similar to the zip utility found on Windows.

14. The `cat` command simply displays a file's contents.

Module 7: Booting and Shutting Down

1. LILO is the Linux Loader. It is the boot loader for Linux.

2. GRUB is the Grand Unified Bootloader, a newer and better way to boot Linux as well as other operating systems.

3. LILO is a two-stage boot loader.

4. A three-stage boot loader is a boot loader that first loads the second stage program into memory. This second stage program allows you to select a kernel to load from the file system. The third and final stage loads the kernel into memory and begins execution of the OS.

5. Usually, a three-stage boot loader is better. It allows you more flexibility and safety—for example, you don't have to write the boot block to the MBR every time you make a change with GRUB. Using LILO, you have to write to the MBR every time a change happens.

6. /etc/rc5.d/

7. The scripts in the **rc** directories all start with either an S or a K, followed by a two-digit number ranging from 00 to 99. When starting a runlevel, all of the S scripts are run in order. When exiting a level, all of the K scripts are run to shutdown the process.

8. Rename the script to something like **CSXX_foo** in the directory **/etc/rc3.d/**.

9. Yes; remember, each runlevel's S scripts get run.

10. Runlevel 6 is the runlevel that causes the system to reboot.

11. With LILO, just type the image name plus the `single` keyword after it. GRUB has a menu-oriented way to boot into single-user mode.

12. Single-user mode is when the operating system only allows the root user onto the system. This is good for performing maintenance when you don't want users on the system.

13. The configuration file for **init** is **/etc/inittab/**.

14. Edit the **/etc/inittab** file and change the option `initdefault` to 5.

Module 8: File Systems

1. The partition code for the native Linux file system is 83.

2. The partition code for the swap file system is 82.

3. **/etc/fstab**

4. **fsck** does a file system consistency check to make sure all the i-nodes and superblocks are correct—that is, it makes sure there is no file corruption.

5. Supply the **-f** option to **fsck** to force a file system check.

6. The **mount** command allows you to attach file systems to the Linux file system hierarchy.

7. A superblock is a block of data on the file system that is the catalog of all the i-nodes on the partition.

8. The main difference is that ext3 is a journaling file system.

9. This command makes a file system on partition 3 of the slave IDE hard drive on the first IDE chain of the system.

10. **tunefs -j /dev/device_name**

11. **mkswap /dev/device_name**

12. An i-node is a block of information that contains information on that file, such as ownership, permissions, and pointers to the actual data of the file.

13. A journaling file system is a file system that logs every write that occurs on the file system. In the case of system failure, this system merely has to "replay the logs" and everything is up and running.

Module 9: Core System Services

1. **init**

2. The **/etc/inittab** file tells the **init** program what to do at each runlevel.

3. Change the line that says **id:5:initdefault:** to **id:3:initdefault:**.

4. You can use either **reboot** or **init 6**.

5. **init** is the parent of all processes on the system. When you kill **init**, you throw the OS into a state of chaos, typically ending in a reboot or a crash. Some systems won't even let you kill the **init** process.

6. Send it the HUP signal via the **killall** command: **killall -HUP xinetd**.

7. **inetd** and **xinetd** have to **fork()** and **exec()** a process off each time a connection comes to the server. Forking and execing a process takes time and resources. If you run the server in daemon mode, you bypass this problem.

8. The **cron** program allows users to run periodic programs.

9. Run the **crontab** program and add the following line:

```
*/5 * * * * /root/scripts/foo.sh
```

10. **crontab -e**

11. **/etc/crontab**

12. **syslog** is the UNIX logging server.

13. **/etc/syslog.conf**

14. This would be useful if you have one system that acts as a logging server. It has no other network access so the only thing it is used for is to log access. If an admin wants to see activity, he would log in through the console.

15. No, since **syslog** uses UDP (an unreliable network protocol), **syslog** messages could be dropped in high load situations.

Module 10: Compiling the Linux Kernel

1. This would be a beta kernel since the patch level is an odd number, 5 in this case.

2. http://www.kernel.org/

3. **/usr/src**

4. **uname -r**

5. **make xconfig**

6. **make dep;make bzImage;make modules**

7. Typically, it is in **/usr/src/linux/arch/i386/boot**.

8. Yes, you need to add a configuration line for the new kernel in order for GRUB/lilo to boot the new kernel.

9. A loadable module is a kernel module that can be loaded or unloaded from the kernel depending on the need for it to be loaded. If a device is not in use, the kernel will unload the module and free the resource that it was using.

10. **cat /proc/pci**

11. **make modules_install**

Module 11: Securing an Individual Server

1. `netstat -antu`

2. For the most part, if you are not using it, you should shut the service off. If there is no need to run Telnet, don't. If you shut the service off, you don't have to worry about any vulnerabilities.

3. Set the **enable** option to **yes** in the service's configuration file.

4. The syslog service will log most activity on your computer. In fact, most hackers typically will try to wipe out these files the first chance they get, via a script. If you have an automated process to parse through your log files and do some analysis, it can warn you about any mysterious actions.

5. SATAN is the System Administrators Tool for Analyzing Networks. It probes systems for known holes.

6. It will be completely obvious if something is going on when you notice a 128KB stream coming from your Linux server going to the outside world for a day or so. This could indicate someone trying to attack another site—that is, if you don't run any services on your computer (file sharing, HTTP, and so on).

7. Yes, as soon as you have physical access to the computer, the system is vulnerable. With a boot floppy disk, I can instantly get to anything on the system. There are also other ways to get at the data; one way would be to yank the hard drive out and make a copy.

8. TripWire will inform you when a file has changed.

9. `rpm --verify`

Module 12: DNS

1. The format of the **/etc/resolv.conf** file is as follows:

```
search domainname
nameserver IP-address
```

where **domainname** is the default domain name to search, and **IP-address** is the IP address of your DNS server.

2. The **/etc/nsswitch.conf** file tells the system which name service to query information from.

3. A PTR record maps an IP address to a host name.

4. An A record maps a host name to an IP address.

5. The resolver is the client-side utility that will perform DNS queries.

6. BIND can be obtained from the ISC Web site at http://www.isc.org/.

7. **/etc/named.conf** is the main configuration file for BIND.

8. An NS record is the name server record used to find name servers for a domain.

9. The SOA is the start of authority. It tells BIND domain-level configuration options, such as how long the TTLs are and other information.

10. MX records are the mail exchangers. These records are used by the SMTP protocol to send e-mail.

11. A caching name server is exactly what it sounds like. The server simply caches any responses that it knows about. Almost all DNS servers are caching for performance reasons.

12. There are two ways to tell **named** to reload its configuration file. First, you can send **named** a HUP signal. Second, you can use the **ndc reload** command.

13. The **whois** tool will tell you the owner of a domain.

14. Simple testing can be performed with the **ping** command. If that doesn't work, you can use the **dig** and **nslookup** tools to do more investigating.

15. The in-addr.arpa domain is the reverse lookup top-level server for mapping IPs to names.

Module 13: FTP

1. The configuration file is typically **/usr/local/etc/proftpd.conf**.

2. The **get** command downloads the file from the remote FTP server to the local client.

3. To download multiple files, use the **mget** FTP command.

4. If you transfer **.tgz** files in ASCII mode, you will get file corruption since some binary values don't map into ASCII.

5. Use the **lcd** command.

6. This is a security feature. If there is an exploit in the server and it is running as nobody, the chances of a total compromise of your system is lowered.

7. Using the **<Limit WRITE> DenyAll </Limit>** directive will disallow writes.

8. By globally setting **<Limit LOGIN> DenyAll</Limit>** you will disallow regular users.

9. The standard FTP ports are 20 and 21 (run: **grep ftp /etc/services**).

10. The **bind** option tells **xinetd** what IP address to listen on.

11. The **ftpcount** utility will tell you how many users are logged in.

12. The **ftpwho** utility will show all of the current users logged in.

13. The **welcome.msg** file displays information about the FTP server.

Module 14: Setting Up Your Web Server Using Apache

1. The HTTP server provides Web content by using the HTTP protocol.

2. Port 80

3. The **VirtualHost** directive allows you to configure the Apache server to accept requests based off of different host names.

4. No. People can simply scan your server for open ports and see that 81 is open.

5. **~/public_html**

6. If any exploits exist in the Web server, it will allow the malicious attacker to gain full access to the system.

7. Some situations require that you run as a user with higher privileges than the nobody user.

8. **httpdctl restart**

9. Response headers are what the server sends back to the client.

10. Request headers are what the client sends the server when making a request.

11. Run the command **httpd -S** to show the current **VirtualHost** configuration.

12. The **DocumentRoot** directive tells the server where the directory is that contains the content for the Web site.

13. The **ServerRoot** directive tells the Apache server where to find files associated with the running of the httpd server.

Module 15: SMTP

1. An MUA is a mail user agent. Examples include pine, mutt, Outlook, and Netscape mail.

2. An MTA is a mail transfer agent. This is the server that transfers e-mail messages from one server to another.

3. The Postfix mail server is an MTA. It delivers e-mail to other systems on the network and locally, if specified.

4. 25

5. **/etc/postfix**

6. **main.cf** and **master.cf**

7. **/usr/bin/newaliases**

8. **/usr/bin/postfix reload**

9. **/usr/bin/postfix flush**

10. The **mailq** command displays a list of e-mail messages that are in the mail queue and why they are there.

11. That way, hackers will have a harder time figuring out what kind of mail server and version you are using. If they instantly know that you are running postfix-0.1.1, they can look for scripts to break in using known vulnerabilities.

12. This command is used so that the client can introduce itself with the server.

13. The **mynetworks** variable lets you allow only clients from the IP addresses you specify.

14. The default is **/var/spool/postfix**.

15. In some cases, you might need to keep running Sendmail to flush out the Sendmail queues. It is also handy to have Sendmail around in case you need to revert back.

Module 16: Post Office Protocol (POP)

1. Post Office Protocol

2. They are used to post messages to users who check their mail through POP.

3. Generally, it is a bad idea for a user to use both, as they can conflict with each other.

4. Some clients automatically download the mail to the local machine. You must unset the option to delete mail when reading from the server.

5. The client sends **USER** *loginname*.

6. SMTP is a mail transfer protocol; it handles sending messages to other mail servers. POP and IMAP, on the other hand, are protocols for retrieving mail from the server.

7. It sends a **DELE** *messagenumber*.

8. **xinetd** or **inetd**

9. No, Qpopper will get confused.

10. The POP client will use the **LIST** command.

11. Via the **RETR** *messagenumber* command.

12. Notable Windows clients are Eudora, Outlook Express, and Outlook. On the Linux side of things, you have pine, mutt, fetchmail, and mozilla.

13. 110

14. **/etc/services**

Module 17: The Secure Shell (SSH)

1. The **ssh** client allows you to create an encrypted connection to another server or workstation.

2. **scp** is a way of copying files from one computer to another via an encrypted connection.

3. **sftp** is another way of copying files using the **ssh** daemon. It acts like an FTP server.

4. **/etc/ssh/sshd_config** is the typical location for **sshd**. If you installed SSH in **/usr/local**, then it will most likely be located in **/usr/local/etc/ssh/**.

5. The file ~/.ssh/known_hosts contains the list of hosts and keys for each host. To get rid of man-in-the-middle warnings, you need to delete the line for the appropriate server.

6. The Telnet protocol sends passwords in the clear. You have no guarantees that the network you are using doesn't have sniffers. When you use Telnet, such sniffers can instantly get your password.

7. Almost all the variants of UNIX can use the SSH protocol. There is no reason not to use it!

8. The SSH server binary is **/usr/local/sbin/sshd**.

9. To make sure the **sshd** daemon is started at boot time, you need to add it to your startup scripts, either in **rc.local** or in the **rc3.d** directory.

10. Either use the **kill** command or send a **stop** argument to your **sshd** startup script.

11. A secure tunnel is a link between two computers that has been secured by some encryption algorithm.

12. You have a nice secure channel for transmitting data. You can use ports other than the SSH ports for doing work.

13. The one side effect is that users can bypass firewalls by using allowed ports to connect to an outside computer.

Module 18: Network File System (NFS)

1. NFS is the UNIX way of sharing file systems on the network.

2. The **mountd** program makes sure that a mount request coming from a client has permission to actually mount the exported file system.

3. **/etc/exports**

4. The only time you would want to enable **no_root_squash** is if you need to have clients access the exported file system as root. Normally, you do want to squash root access to the NFS share.

5. **killall -HUP rpc.nfsd**

6. If you allow write access to an exported **/usr/local** file system, a hacker could feasibly install a rogue binary in **/usr/local/bin** and grab passwords or get root on the system.

7. The Linux client simply needs NFS support compiled into the kernel. This is usually the case.

8. A *hard* mount tells the NFS client to block if the NFS server crashes. This can be very disruptive but necessary. To get by this problem, you can mount a share as *soft;* the NFS client will not block, so you can do other things on the system.

9. `rpcinfo -p`

10. Portmapper

11. Yes, otherwise you will not have a consistent file system and you will have permission problems.

12. You don't usually want an NFS server to mount other NFS shares. If you can't get around this, you need to know what dependencies exist in order to properly get the system up and running with these cross-mounts.

13. `mount -t nfs trillian:/export/home/home`

14. No, NFS is a stateless protocol.

15. NFS doesn't check the identity of the client machine, thus any user with root access could possibly get access to home directories. Also, everything with NFS is sent in clear text so someone could possibly "sniff" the network and read the files.

Module 19: Network Information Service (NIS)

1. NIS provides a network database that clients can query from, typically account information.

2. `ypcat passwd`

3. `ypwhich`

4. `yppasswd`

5. If anyone can access your NIS password database, they can get the encrypted passwords and try to crack the passwords.

6. `ypinit` initializes an NIS server as master or slave.

7. **/var/yp/Makefile**

8. **/etc/nsswitch.conf**

9. You don't want to expose root and other system accounts via NIS; this is a security risk.

10. Through the **domainname** command.

11. **ypserv**

12. /etc/init.d/ypserv

13. You have to make sure there is an NIS server on every subnet since broadcasts shouldn't propagate through subnets.

14. **ypmatch sshah passwd**

15. Yes, nothing stops you from making an NIS accessible phone book.

Module 20: Samba

1. Port 139

2. Port 137

3. No

4. You use the **smbpasswd** command.

5. **smb.conf**

6. 901

7. It is not a good idea to allow other people to attach to port 901 since they could possibly break into the SWAT interface.

8. **nmbd** and **smbd**

9. **smbclient**

10. **smbclient -L ford**

Module 21: Printing

1. A user uses the **lpr** command to print documents.

2. **lpq -P** *printer* **name**

3. The **lprm** command removes a print job from a printer.

4. CUPS uses a concept of classes to group printers together for distributing printing loads.

5. Port 613

6. This command removes all print jobs from the printer.

7. Supply the **-P** *printer* **name** arguments

8. **/etc/init.d/cups start**

9. This comes in handy when you need to perform maintenance on the printer, such as adding more paper or changing the toner cartridge.

10. Port 631

Module 22: DHCP

1. Dynamic Host Configuration Protocol

2. You typically would not want servers to be configured off of DHCP.

3. Any clients that are mobile are good for using DHCP. Also, when installing hundreds of computers, it is helpful to let them get their IP addresses from DHCP.

4. **/etc/dhcpd.conf**

5. **dhcpd.leases**

6. Yes, by using the **hardware ethernet** and **fixed-address** parameters.

7. This option specifies the range of IP addresses to give out.

8. By the **option routers** declaration.

9. If you keep lease times really low, clients will constantly be requesting IP addresses and you could have collisions of IP address.

10. This option tells the client to contact the server for booting information.

11. You would need to make the configuration file **/etc/sysconfig/network-scripts/ifcfg-eth0** look like the following:

```
DEVICE=eth0
BOOTPROTO=dhcp
ONBOOT=yes
```

12. No, you can have an IP address conflict and a lot of headaches!

13. Another name for a hardware address is a MAC address.

14. Yes, Windows, UNIX, Linux, and even OS X will work with **dhcpd** since DHCP is a standard.

Module 23: Network Configuration

1. The **ifconfig** command allows you to configure a network interface on the system.

2. The **route** command tells the Linux system what interface to send a packet on if the destination of that packet matches the route.

3. **/etc/sysconfig/network-scripts/ifcfg-*dev***, where *dev* is the device you want to configure.

4. You would put **route** commands in either **/etc/rc.local** or another startup script.

5. **/etc/modules.conf**.

6. The module **rtl8139** will get loaded for the first Ethernet device.

7. Either **ifconfig** or **dmesg**.

8. A gateway is a device that interconnects networks and makes smart forwarding decisions.

9. B.

10. B.

11. No, the default route is only used when the local box doesn't know what to do with the packet; for example, if the destination for the packet is on another network.

12. **/dev/eth2**

13. The following command is a useful trick:

```
(/etc/init.d/network stop;/etc/init.d/network start)
```

Putting the commands in parentheses causes the shell to fork another process to run the commands. This works because a forked process still runs when you are kicked out of the box.

Appendix B

Programming Languages that Accompany Linux

This appendix highlights some of the programming languages that typically accompany the GNU/Linux system. If you are looking to learn a new programming language, I would recommend Python. This is a very well-designed programming language, and it isn't too hard to get really good at it. You will find that a typical Linux system uses all of the languages below and many more to keep the system running. Most of the Linux core is written in C, all of the startup scripts are written in bash, and automation tasks are typically done with Expect. System maintenance scripts are typically written with Perl or Python. You have your choice of which language you would like to learn, and since you're running Linux you have only one investment to make: time.

Python

Red Hat Linux uses Python for its install program, called **anaconda**. Python is a scripting language much like Perl, but it provides a much cleaner syntax and its learning curve is fairly short. It is a full-featured, high-level programming language that allows for object-oriented design. It is quickly becoming a popular choice. For more information on the Python programming language, check out http://www.python.org/.

Perl

Perl is the system administrators' programming language of choice. Perl is a very good language for parsing text and is also popular among Web developers. While its syntax can get really nasty, it is a very powerful language, and if you are good you can write a lot of one-line scripts that would take 100 lines of C code to do. For more information on Perl, see the Perl Web site at http://www.perl.com/.

The C/C++ Programming Suite

Red Hat Linux comes with GCC, which stands for the Gnu Compiler Collection. GCC provides a complete C and C++ programming suite. This includes the compilers (**gcc/g++**), preprocessors (**cpp**), and debugger (**gdb/xxgdb**). The compilers come with a complete set of header files and libraries, including an implementation of the STL library. Migrating code from other C compilers to **gcc** is reasonably straightforward. Migrating other code from C++ compilers to **g++** is not quite as clean, mostly due to continuing disagreements over the C++ standards. The official C++ standard was established at the end of 1998, so hopefully we will see an easier transition path soon.

Linux's fully integrated development environment that works with the C and C++ compilers is the K Develop Environment (http://www.kdevelop.org/), which has a striking resemblance to Microsoft's Visual Studio. The entire environment is available under the GNU Public License and supports KDE/Qt, Gnome, and plain C/C++ projects.

Java

While the GCC tools will compile Java code, the Java compiler from Sun Microsystems still rules the day in my book. Java is a purely object-oriented language that resembles C++ but doesn't have some of the hassles, such as pointers. If you are concerned with speed, C/C++ might be a better choice since Java uses a virtual machine to execute code. Java was really popular with easy to construct GUIs with the swing toolkit; now with J2EE it is a standard for Web services with BEA and IBM application servers. JBOSS is an open source J2EE application server that is very popular. For more information on the Java programming language, see http://www.javasoft.com/.

Expect

An extension of TCL, Expect is a scripting language geared toward automating other applications, such as Telnet and FTP. It essentially allows you to have the script send certain inputs to the application upon seeing certain outputs. If you're used to some of the scripting tools that come with terminal emulation packages like ProComm or Telix, you should feel right at home with Expect. And because it has the full power of TCL behind it, you can perform some very interesting feats, given a little creativity. You must have TCL installed to use Expect.

TCL

TCL is a fairly popular scripting language that is easy to learn. If you want to learn Expect, I recommend looking into TCL first since it is the foundation for Expect. For more information on TCL and TCK, see http://www.tcltk.com/.

Tk

The Tk Widget Set is a series of widgets that make it even easier to write GUIs that work in the UNIX, Windows, and Macintosh environments. The designer's goal is to provide an environment where writing GUIs takes only a little longer than writing text-based applications. You must have TCL installed to use Tk.

awk

awk is a scripting language similar to Perl, but it's not nearly as feature rich. Most folks who use awk generally use it in conjunction with shell script since it provides a quick and easy way to perform complex filtering that typically requires multiple lines in Perl. However, for more complex solutions, Perl is usually a better choice.

Appendix C

Getting the Usual Done

The focus of this book is taking care of systems administration duties under Linux. While that's all fun and nice, it doesn't address the recent trend of companies trying to make Linux more friendly to the desktop and their goal of removing the need for anyone to have to reboot their systems to start Microsoft Windows. It is possible to live in a Windows world using Linux as your desktop operating system. The purpose of this appendix is to introduce some of the tools that allow you to do so. While it is a far cry from an exhaustive list, it is nonetheless a good start.

StarOffice

StarOffice is a complete MS Office-like suite of tools that includes a word processor, spreadsheet, presentation maker, calendar, e-mail, HTML authoring tool, and browser. Folks who are familiar with MS Office should find it a very easy transition, especially with its support for importing and exporting MS Office documents.

While free for educational use, version 6.0 of StarOffice is retailing for about $75 (you can buy online from Sun's Web site or find it in your local computer store). If you would like a free version, you can look at http://www.openoffice.org/, which is the core that StarOffice is built upon. This is the same thing that Netscape does with Mozilla, though of course you don't pay for Netscape.

Stability-wise, StarOffice is a relatively solid package. The first draft of this book was written in it, using a template developed in Word 7.0.

ApplixWare

The ApplixWare suite is another competitor to the MS Office series, as well as to StarOffice. It isn't quite as heavy as StarOffice in terms of memory or disk consumption, and as a result, it tends to respond much faster. This speed comes at the expense of features, but if you need an Office-like package that isn't overly complex, you may find this is a great tool to work with.

You can find out more about ApplixWare at http://www.applix.com/.

Corel WordPerfect

For those who remember when WordPerfect was king (I still have WordPerfect 5.1), there is WordPerfect for Linux. It looks quite impressive. You can find out more about it and the Corel Linux Distribution at http://www.corel.com/.

Web Browsers

Netscape has offered its browser for Linux for a very long time. (Remember mcom.com?) As far as Web browsers go, Netscape's is a complete package that supports e-mail, netnews, and browsing. And because the Windows version of Netscape is derived from the same source code, you will find the two versions identical feature-for-feature and menu-for-menu.

Red Hat Linux and Caldera Linux both ship with Netscape preinstalled. If you want to get the latest information on Netscape, check out http://www.netscape.com/. There you will also find information on the latest plug-ins available for Linux, including Macromedia's Flash module.

The Netscape browser is based on Mozilla, the open source browser. If you want cutting edge features or are tired of Netscape, you can download Mozilla from http://www .mozilla .org/. Mozilla has just recently achieved version 1.0 status after many years of hard work.

The Opera browser is another addition to the Web browser market. The most significant difference between Opera and the other offerings is that it is not free. Once the 30-day trial period is over, you must pay for the browser to continue using it. However, those who have paid for it claim it is worth the price. Opera was designed with efficient memory utilization in mind and thus, unlike all of the other browsers available, offers a very small memory footprint. Because Opera is small, it also tends to be faster than the others.

The Konquerer browser is the KDE group's contribution. Based on the Mozilla engine, its goal is to provide tight integration between the Web and the desktop, similar to what Internet Explorer does for Windows. This browser is free and available from http://www.kde.org/.

Painting/Image Manipulation Tools

Five great tools exist for painting and image manipulation. On the painting front is kpaint, which bears a striking resemblance to the Windows Paint tool. You can also use xpaint, which is slightly more flexible, but which uses a different (and still intuitive) interface.

On the image viewing/manipulation front are Electric Eyes (ee) and xv. The first is a simple viewer that has started to ship with Red Hat Linux as a replacement to xv because of licensing restrictions on xv. The xv tool is still available on the Internet and is quite a bit more powerful and flexible than Electric Eyes. However, commercial usage requires that you buy a license.

The GNU Image Manipulation Program (GIMP) is a full-featured package aimed at being the Photoshop for Linux. It offers many filters and tools for manipulating photo-realistic images.

If you are looking for a commercial graphic manipulation program, you can check out Corel's Web site for their Corel Draw graphic suite for Linux.

Finance Tools

Spreadsheets are, of course, every finance person's dream tool, and both StarOffice and ApplixWare come with a spreadsheet that is capable of reading and writing Excel files. Also KDE has kspread and GNOME comes with gnumeric. Both are capable spreadsheet programs able to read Microsoft Excel spreadsheets. Beyond these two packages, there are several noteworthy tools: BB Stock Tool from Falkor Technologies is a comprehensive stock tracking and analysis tool that is available for Linux, Windows, Solaris, and Irix. You can see more about it at http://www.falkor.com/.

For home finances, there is GnuCash. It isn't yet quite where Quicken is, but it does offer basic functionality, and for those of us who don't need the advanced features of Quicken, it is a welcome simplification. The GnuCash Web site is at http://www.gnucash.org/.

Desktop Tools

Korganizer is a personal information manager that allows you to easily store calendar and scheduling information, contacts, and other miscellaneous things you would stash in your Palm or use Outlook for. What makes korganizer especially nice is that it uses the vCalendar file format, which is a standard supported by all of the big name PIM tools, such as Lotus Notes, Netscape, Outlook, and Palm. This makes exchanging your information very straightforward. You can get more information about korganizer at http://people.redhat .com/pbrown/korganizer/.

E-mail Clients

The most popular graphical e-mail-based client under UNIX is Netscape Communicator's package. Besides the fact that it is already there with Netscape and is free, the feature set is quite nice. It comes with a spell checker, good folder management, and a generally pleasant interface. Communicator comes preinstalled with many distributions of Linux, but you can always see the latest version at http://www.netscape.com/.

Folks used to Eudora or similar mail clients will probably be more at home with kmail. It offers a fully graphical interface while maintaining compatibility with the mail folder files from text-based mail clients, such as Pine, Mutt, or Elm.

The folks at Ximian have an awesome mail reader called Evolution. It looks like Microsoft Outlook with its calendar, notes, and to-do list, and allows you to read e-mail. They also have a connector that sells for about $50 that allows you to connect to an Exchange mail server. Well worth the price if you don't want to run Windows to check your e-mail.

Audio Tools

What desktop is complete without a nifty tool to play music with? For those interested in MP3s, XMMS makes a tool that is comparable to WinAmp. You can find out more about XMMS at http://www.xmms.org/.

If your favorite Web site/radio station uses Real Audio, you can download the Linux version of Real Player at http://www.real.com/.

A nice CD player (for real CDs) is kscd, which comes with the KDE environment.

Real-Time Chat

Two notable entries in the real-time chat arena have Linux clients. Yahoo offers a Linux client for their chat technology, which you can download at http://www.yahoo.com/. If you are already familiar with Yahoo, you won't find any differences between the various Yahoo clients, since they are all the same program written in a platform-independent language.

For the ICQ folks, take a look at GnomeICQ at http://gnomeicu.gdev.net/. It is a complete ICQ client that is compatible with existing ICQ specifications.

Suggested Web Sites

The amount of new software that comes out for Linux grows daily. Especially with the recent development of KDE and GNOME, many programmers have taken an interest in graphical-based development of user tools.

If you're looking for new software, here's a handful of active sites that you can visit to find out about the latest goings-on:

- **http://www.linuxapps.com/**   A complete guide to new Linux applications that are in various stages of development. The site is very neatly organized, which makes finding the tool you need quite easy.

- **http://www.freshmeat.net/**   Freshmeat is a great mixture of applications and small tools. As a system administrator, you'll find plenty of reasons to visit this site to see what new and exciting developments have come about to make your life a little easier.

- **http://apps.kde.com/**   Here's the Web site of KDE applications. You'll find the latest applications developed to take advantage of the KDE environment.

- **http://www.linuxjournal.com/**   Although this is really a magazine's Web site, the editors and writers do a great job of profiling a lot of software, both commercial and noncommercial. The articles themselves are nice, too.

- **http://www.linuxsoftware.org/**   Here's another well-organized site containing pointers to applications and tools for all sorts of interests and needs.

- **http://www.linuxberg.com/**   Linuxberg offers a slightly different way of organizing a collection of software. Specifically, they break down their software into user interface categories at the highest level, which is great when the application you are looking for must work within certain criteria. (For example, the application must be command-line driven, and so on.) This site is also known as www.tucows.com.

- **http://www.rpmfind.net/**   This site is a comprehensive collection of packages that are available for quick install in the RPM format. It's not as pretty as some of the other sites, but it's well worth a look.

Index

S